Catholic Theological Ethics

Ancient Questions, Contemporary Responses

Michael G. Lawler and Todd A. Salzman

University Press of America,® Inc.
Lanham • Boulder • New York • Toronto • Plymouth, UK

Copyright © 2016 by University Press of America,® Inc.
4501 Forbes Boulevard, Suite 200, Lanham, Maryland 20706
UPA Acquisitions Department (301) 459-3366

Unit A, Whitacre Mews, 26-34 Stannary Street,
London SE11 4AB, United Kingdom

Library of Congress Control Number: 2015952131
ISBN: 978-0-7618-6687-9 (pbk : alk. paper)—ISBN: 978-0-7618-6688-6 (electronic)

♾️™ The paper used in this publication meets the minimum requirements of American
National Standard for Information Sciences Permanence of Paper for Printed Library
Materials, ANSI/NISO Z39.48-1992.

This book is dedicated to our various children,
Ian, Aaron, Emily, Michael, Anya, and David,
from whom we have learned much about contemporary human reality

Contents

v

Prologue

In 1965, as the Second Vatican Council rushed to its conclusion, it turned its attention to the training of priests. It prescribed the teaching of philosophy "in such a way as to lead students gradually to a solid and consistent knowledge of man [anthropology], the world [cosmology], and God [theology]." "Special care," it insisted, "should be given to the perfecting of moral theology."[1] In this book, we seek to give special care to moral theology or Catholic ethics by offering a critique of some of the magisterium's absolute proscriptive moral norms and the ethical methods used to justify those norms, and suggesting proposals for its entry into the contemporary world. When Pope John XXIII announced the Council in 1959 and convoked it in 1962, there was already a growing disconnect in Catholic ethics between the Church's absolute proscriptive moral norms and the lived experience of the Catholic faithful. This disconnect was particularly noticeable in the area of the Church's sexual ethics, and that particular disconnect was widened by the publication of Pope Paul VI's encyclical *Humanae vitae* in which, against the advice of the Commission he had confirmed to study the question, he reaffirmed the Church's teaching proscribing any form of artificial contraception. The well-known Catholic sociologist, Andrew Greeley, described the encyclical as "the great disaster of post-conciliar Catholicism,"[2] and always argued that its teaching was the reason why so many Catholics were leaving the Church.

This book is a collection of essays with two connected themes. The dominant theme is Catholic moral theology, the sub theme is Catholic sexual ethics and the theologians who practice them. There is a broad division of moral or ethical theologians in the contemporary Catholic tradition. "Traditionalist" is the general label given to moral theologians who support and defend absolute Church norms prohibiting certain types of acts such as premarital sex, artificial birth control, artificial reproductive technologies, masturbation, and homosexual acts. The Traditionalist school is contrasted with the "Revisionist" school. "Revisionist" is the general label given to moral theologians who question many of these absolute ethical norms, not *qua ethical* but *qua absolute*, and propose alternatives. These two groups disagree on many specific ethical norms because they disagree, more fundamentally, on the methodology and anthropology that either supports these norms or questions their legitimacy and credibility. We are generally listed in the theological Revisionist school. We have a different method from Traditionalists and we deal with our method in Chapter One. We have a different relationship with the teaching Church than Traditionalists and we deal with that in Chapter Two. We have a different approach to human sexuality, which we deal with in Chapter Three, and sexual ethics which we deal with in Chapters Six, Seven, Eight, Nine, and Ten. We emphasize different sources for our ethical theory and we deal with two of those sources, experience and science in Chapters Four and Five.

The special care the Second Vatican Council demanded for the perfecting of moral theology had already begun while the Council was in session, led by the German Redemptorist priest, Bernard Häring. His book, *The Law of Christ*,[3] insisted, contrary to the prevailing pre-conciliar moral theology, that the Christian life was not primarily a matter of, first, knowing in detail what actions were sinful and, then, avoiding them. It was, rather, a matter of love, or charity, as we shall see in our discussion of virtue in Chapter Seven, of coming to know and appreciate the steadfast love of God for women and men, especially as personified in Jesus, and of practically living that love in everyday lives. The gospel Jesus gives us innumerable examples of that practical love and instructs us to "go and do likewise" (Luke 10:37). His great commandment is better known than obeyed: "love your neighbor as yourself" to which he immediately adds "there is no other commandment greater" (Mark 12:31; see also Lev 19:18). The Apostle Paul adds his own judgment to that of Jesus: "The whole law is fulfilled in one word, 'You shall love your neighbor as yourself'" (Gal 5:14; see Rom 13:8–10). He has no hesitation in making the judgment that "faith, hope, love abide, these three; but the greatest of these is love" (1 Cor 13:13). Häring's approach had a great influence in developing post-conciliar Catholic moral theology and ethics from a focus on acts, both moral and immoral, to a focus on the personal love between women and men in general and between lovers in particular. In post-conciliar Catholic ethics, the focus is not on the *act* of lying or contraception, for instance, but on the personal *actors* and what the act *means* relationally and contextually for them.

Traditional Catholic sexual morality is marital morality. In 1976, the Congregation for the Doctrine of the Faith asserted that, to be moral, "any human genital act whatsoever may be placed only within the context of marriage."[4] Earlier, in 1968, Pope Paul VI asserted that in marriage "each and every marriage act [sexual intercourse] must remain open to the transmission of life."[5] In traditional Catholic sexual morality, therefore, every moral sexual act takes place only within marriage, and in marriage each and every act of sexual intercourse must be open to procreation. Michel Foucault's comment accurately describes the traditional Catholic situation. "The conjugal family took custody of [sexuality] and absorbed it into the serious function of reproduction." Sexual intercourse is exclusively for marriage and procreation. In the Catholic tradition every intentional genital act outside of marriage is morally and seriously sinful.[6]

Traditional Catholic morality focused on *acts*, sometimes called ontological acts and always physical acts: stroking, kissing, intercourse. *Gaudium et spes*, which Joseph Selling lauds as "a manifesto for contemporary moral theology,"[7] advances a *personal* model of human sexuality, expressing the marital relationship as "an intimate partnership of life and love."[8] Contemporary Catholic moral theologians have followed this theological lead and put in the forefront of their analysis not the acts performed but the relational meaning of the acts for the persons performing them. This is our approach in this book.

Louis Janssens points out that the official commentary on *Gaudium et spes* applies this personalist criterion not only to human sexuality but also to all human activity, so that "human activity must be judged insofar as it refers to the human person integrally and adequately considered."[9] To answer the question of what precisely is the human person integrally and adequately considered, Janssens advances eight dimensions of the human person that must be considered to determine the moral nature of any act, including any sexual act. The human person is: (1) a rational subject, (2) in corporeality, (3) in relation to the material world, (4) in relation to others, (5) in relation to social groups, (6) in relation to God, (7) a developmental historical being, and (8) fundamentally equal to all other human beings and yet uniquely original.[10] Janssens opts for the term *dimension* rather than the term *definition* of the human person to insinuate that our understanding of these dimensions may evolve and develop as human understanding evolves and develops in history. Intentions and acts that facilitate the flourishing of persons integrally and adequately considered as described above are morally acceptable; intentions and acts that frustrate that flourishing are morally unacceptable.

What is clear in the move to personalism in both *Gaudium et spes* and Janssens' elaboration of it is that a static and absolutist sexual anthropology like that of the Catholic Church is no longer adequate, because human persons integrally and adequately considered are grounded in and shaped by the changing historical, existential lived reality of social human experience and relationships. This personalist context must be the point of departure for any adequate sexual anthropology and for morally evaluating human sexual actions. It is the point of departure for every analysis throughout this book.

The logical implication for sexual ethics of this shift to a more personalist, relation-centered approach is that, while the Church could and should teach norms guiding sexual relationships, those norms, given the historical and existential context of human relationships, cannot always be posited as absolutes. This assertion may be exemplified by reference to the question of birth control, which we do not deal with in this book.[11] The Church's only approved method of birth regulation, natural family planning, presumes a fundamental equality and mutual respect between the spouses within the marital relationship so that they can regulate their births. The reality is, however, that the majority of cultures throughout the world are patriarchal cultures in which the husband is the unchallenged authority in the household and in the marital relationship, and the fundamental equality required to peacefully practice natural family planning is absent. In this existential and social context, it may be oppressive for the Church to prescribe an approach to regulating births that is so countercultural and may create an undue marital burden, especially for wives. In a personalist sexual anthropology, morality cannot be and is not a one-size-fits-all approach as it was and still is in the traditional act-centered morality grounded in a presumed universal human nature and the biological laws of reproduction. The complex natures of both the human person integrally and adequately considered and human sexuality do not permit such a universal, abstract, absolutist, and juridical approach.

Bernard Lonergan introduced the important notion of *conversion* in his groundbreaking *Insight*, and developed it further in his *Method in Theology*.[12] Conversion, a process that involves "a radical about-face in which one repudiates characteristic features of one's previous horizon,"[13] may be threefold. Intellectual conversion abandons "the myth that fully human knowing is to be conceived on an analogy with seeing, and replaces it with the affirmation of a self that knows because it understands correctly." Moral conversion is "a shift in the criterion of one's choices from satisfaction to values." Religious conversion is simply "falling in love with God."[14] Lonergan's initial analysis of conversion took place within the analysis of the human knower in general, and re-occurred within the analysis of the theologian-knower in particular. Theological conversion, it is important to note, is not an about-face in what the theologian *says* but "a fundamental and momentous change in what the theologian *is*."[15] Conversion changes what the theologian is; it is radical development of personal foundations and perspectives. It is clear that from different foundations and perspectives converted and unconverted theologians will interpret the Catholic tradition in different ways and will draw radically different conclusions from it. We will deal with this phenomenon in Chapter Two. For the moment we note that different conclusions, which we will draw throughout this book, do not warrant the further conclusion that one theologian is Catholic and the other is not.

The conversion we explore in this book is primarily intellectual, theological conversion, with implications, of course, for both moral and religious conversion. In examining the Catholic ethical and sexual tradition in this book, we note a conversion in the tradition that is highlighted in the disconnect between many of the Church's absolute sexual norms and the methodological and anthropological developments explicitly recognized and endorsed in the tradition, especially since the Second Vatican Council. This conversion is marked by anthropological developments that invite a reconsideration of moral norms and their justification. The methodological developments include a fundamental shift from a classicist worldview to a historically conscious worldview. The classicist worldview asserts that reality is static, necessary, fixed, and universal. The method utilized, the anthropology formulated, and the norms taught in this worldview are timeless, universal, and immutable, and the acts condemned by these norms are condemned in every circumstance. The historically conscious worldview fundamentally challenges this view of reality. In the historically conscious worldview, reality is dynamic, evolving, changing, and particular. The method utilized, the anthropology formulated, and the norms taught in this worldview are contingent, particular, and changeable, and the acts condemned by these norms are morally evaluated in terms of evolving human knowledge and understanding.

The conversion from a classicist to a historically conscious worldview is reflected in the Church's endorsement, in Pius XII's encyclical *Divino afflante spiritu* and the Second Vatican Council's *Dei verbum*, of the historical-critical method for interpreting scripture. This method requires that scriptural texts be read in "the literary forms" of the writer's "time and culture."[16] Though this method is clearly established and marks an explicit shift in the Catholic tradition in how sacred scripture is to be read, interpreted, and applied to moral issues, the Church's magisterial teaching continues to prooftext scripture to justify absolute moral norms condemning certain sexual acts. This approach to scripture reflects the classicist exegetical method of the nineteenth century manuals rather than the historically conscious method of the post-conciliar tradition.

The *Catechism of the Catholic Church*, for instance, references Genesis 19:1–29, the story of Sodom, as a scriptural foundation for the absolute prohibition of all homosexual acts.[17] Most biblical scholars, however, relying on the historical-critical method the Church endorses, assert that the central meaning of this text is about hospitality and homosexual rape and has no relevance to the contemporary discussion of gay and lesbian couples in committed, stable, just, and loving relationships. Though the Church espouses the historical-critical method for interpreting scripture and advocates dialogue with the sciences in the formulation of its teaching,[18] it fails to fully consider and then integrate the normative implications of these methodological developments into its teaching, especially its teaching on the (im)morality of many sexual acts. It continues to cite particular passages to condemn sexual acts, even when its own endorsed method indicates that these passages are peripheral, if not irrelevant, to the acts it is condemning. Scholars frequently admit to being surprised that neither the Old nor New Testament provides a systematic code of sexual ethics or even an approach to sexual ethics.[19] Neither historical consciousness nor the historical-critical method supports this classicist approach to justifying norms.

A similar disconnect exists between sexual anthropological developments in the Catholic tradition and the formulation and justification of absolute sexual norms. *Gaudium et spes* marks a radical evolution in Catholic sexual teaching and, by implication, the sexual anthropology reflected in that teaching, by eliminating the language of the hierarchy of the ends of marriage. Prior to the Second Vatican Council, procreation was advanced as the primary end of marriage and union between spouses was advanced as its secondary end. In *Gaudium et spes*, hierarchical language for the two ends of marriage is rejected and "the nature of the human person and his acts"[20] is posited as the foundational principle for harmonizing the ends of marriage. This marked a fundamental shift and development in Catholic sexual teaching and anthropology, but there is little evidence that the Church's Magisterium has fully incorporated this shift into its sexual anthropology or into its formulation and justification of sexual norms. As we will demonstrate throughout this book, the emphasis in that teaching continues to be on the "nature" of the act rather than on the meaning of the act for the human person.

This book has two objectives, one explicit and one implicit. The explicit objective is to explore the normative implications for both general and sexual ethics of the methodological and anthropological developments in Catholic tradition. The implicit objective is to stimulate dialogue in the Church about ethics, particularly sexual ethics, a dialogue that must necessarily include all in the communion-Church, laity, theologians, and hierarchy.[21] Pope John Paul II teaches that dialogue is rooted in the nature and dignity of the human person. It "is an indispensable step along the path towards *human self-realization*, the self-realization of *each individual* and of *every human community*."[22] We agree that every dialogue involves the subjectivity of each person in the dialogue. Each must, therefore, attend carefully to the data emerging in the dialogue, must marshal the data as fully as possible, come to understand it, formulate that understanding in mutually understandable concepts, and eventually pass judgment on the truth or falsity of his or her understanding. It is only after this rational judgment is passed that any true knowledge is achieved in the dialogue. After the passing of judgment, there is the final step of considering possible courses of action, evaluating them, making a decision about which course of action to follow, and then translating that decision into action. In all of this, the participants in the dialogue must be equal partners, with none being privileged over any others, for it is only on the basis of this equality that any individual in the dialogue may reach intellectual and, perhaps, also moral conversion.

We are wide open to dialogue in this book. We have to be, given the theological positions we embrace in it and in our theological lives. We are like two men at a third-story window getting only a restricted third-story perspective on the landscape outside the window, and we have to be open to the complementation of perspectives provided by women and men at sixth-, ninth-, and twenty-first-story windows. In theological parlance, therefore, we situate this book in the category of *quaestio disputata*, the disputed question, so beloved of the medieval Scholastics. The Scholastic Master had three tasks: *lectio* or commentary on the Bible; *disputatio* or teaching by objection and response to a theme; *praedicatio* or proclamation of the theological word.[23] Peter Cantor speaks for all of them when he argues that "it is after the *lectio* of scripture and after the examination of the doubtful points thanks to the *disputatio, and not before*, that we must preach."[24] It is important for the reader to be aware that this book seeks to be *lectio*, accurate interpretation of biblical and doctrinal texts, and *disputatio*, elucidation of themes by objection and response, before it is *praedicatio*, pastoral proclamation of the theological word.

We freely confess that it is not for theologians alone to formulate the theological or moral doctrine and practice of their Church. That task is for the whole communion-Church. The task of the theologian in the Church is a different and critical one. In the words of the Congregation for the Doctrine of the Faith's International Theological Commission, it is the task of "interpreting the documents of the past and present Magisterium, of putting them in the context of the whole of revealed truth, and of finding a better understanding of them by the use of hermeneutics."[25] The theologian "is charged with developing the tradition beyond its current state so that it can meet new questions, needs, and circumstances."[26] It is that difficult and frequently dangerous theologian's task of "maintaining the balance between 'immobilism' and 'eccentricity,'"[27] we seek to fulfill, positively and not destructively, in this book. Since we believe that genuine and respectful dialogue about sexual morality, and indeed about all that is involved in the life of Christian discipleship, is sorely needed to clarify Christian truth today, we intend this book to be part of a genuine dialogue.

Our dialogue partners in the book, as you will discover as you proceed, are the Traditionalist theologians who argue from different starting points, employ different methods, and reach different conclusions about Catholic morality than we do. Our intent is neither to prove ourselves right or them wrong. Convinced of the central role that love, desire, and fertility play in a human life, and therefore also in a life of Christian discipleship, we seek only to suggest an anthropology that might lead to the enhancement of human relationships, including sexual relationships, and flourishing.[28] What we suggest is to be read as submitted to the experience, attention, intelligence, reasonableness, and response of our fellow believers in the communion-Church. Since we do not dare suggest, in a pilgrim Church,[29] that the Spirit of God has breathed the final word about either the communion-Church or the anthropology of its members, we invite our dialogue partners to be as critical in their reading as we are in our writing. Both our critiques and theirs, however, should be such that they are not destructive of the communion instituted by Christ and constituted by the Spirit of Christ who, as the Spirit of God, is also the Spirit of "righteousness and peace and joy" (Rom 14:17).

NOTES

1. *Optatum totius*, n. 15.
2. See George Weigel, "Remembering Andrew Greeley," *First Things* (July 3, 2013), http://www.firstthings.com/web-exclusives/2013/07/remembering-andrew-greeley.
3. Bernard Häring, *The Law of Christ: Moral Theology for Priests and Laity* (Paris: Mercier, 1963).
4. CDF, *Persona humana*, n. 7.
5. Paul VI, *Humanae vitae*, n. 11.
6. Michel Foucault, *History of Sexuality*, vol. 1 (New York: Pantheon Books, 1978), 3.
7. Joseph. A. Selling, "*Gaudium et spes*: A Manifesto for Contemporary Moral Theology," in *Vatican II and its Legacy*, ed. M. Lamberigts and L. Kenis (Leuven: Leuven University Press, 2002), 145–62.
8. *Gaudium et spes*, n. 48.
9. Louis Janssens, "Artificial Insemination: Ethical Considerations," *Louvain Studies* 8, no. 1 (1980): 4.
10. Ibid., 5–13.
11. Those who are interested in the question of birth control might wish to consult our book *Sexual Ethics: A Theological Introduction* (Georgetown: Georgetown University Press, 2012), 95–122.
12. Bernard J. F. Lonergan, *Insight: A Study of Human Understanding* (London: Longman's 1958), 431–87; and *Method in Theology* (New York; Herder, 1972), 237–44 and 270–71.
13. Robert M. Doran, *Theology and the Dialectics of History* (Toronto: University of Toronto Press, 1990), 35.
14. Ibid., 36.
15. Lonergan, *Method in Theology*, 270, emphasis added.
16. Pius XII, *Divino afflante spiritu*, Acta Apostolicae Sedis 35 (1943): 297–325; *Dei verbum*, n. 12.
17. *Catechism of the Catholic Church*, n. 2357.
18. *Gaudium et spes*, n. 62.
19. Lisa Sowle Cahill, *Women and Sexuality* (New York: Paulist, 1992), 33; Raymond F. Collins, *Sexual Ethics and the New Testament* (New York: Crossroad, 2000).
20. *Gaudium et spes*, n. 51.
21. For the notion of Church as communion, see Michael G. Lawler and Thomas J. Shanahan, *Church: A Spirited Communion* (Collegeville, MN: Liturgical Press, 1995).
22. John Paul II, *Ut unum sint*, n. 28; emphasis added.
23. See Jean-Pierre Torell, *St. Thomas Aquinas*, vol. 1 (Washington, DC: Catholic University of America Press, 1996), 54–74.

24. Peter Cantor, *Verbum abreviatum*, 1, *Patrologia Latina* 205, 25; emphasis added.

25. International Theological Commission, *Theses on the Relationship between the Ecclesiastical Magisterium and Theology* (Washington, DC: USCC, 1977), 6.

26. Johann Sebastian Drey, *Brief Introduction to the Study of Theology with Reference to the Scientific Standpoint of the Catholic System*, trans. with an Introduction by Michael J. Himes (Notre Dame: University of Notre Dame Press, 1944), xxv.

27. Ibid., xxvi.

28. For a recent exemplar of this approach, see Julie Hanlon Rubio, "Beyond the Liberal/Conservative Divide on Contraception," *Horizons* 32, no. 2 (2005): 270–94.

29. See *Lumen gentium*, n. 48.

Chapter One

Method and Catholic Theological Ethics in the 21ˢᵗ Century

James Keenan recently addressed the issue of ethical method and highlighted its fundamental importance for Catholic theological ethics in the 21ˢᵗ century.[1] We agree with that judgment and add the importance of making one's ethical method transparent. Recently also, the International Theological Commission published a document, "Theology Today" (hereafter, ThT) that recognizes a "plurality of theologies" [2] and specifies a plurality of perspectives, principles, and methodological criteria, for doing theology.[3] There is also a consistent call from the academic community of Catholic ethicists for an ongoing "faithful reconstruction"[4] of moral theology and its transformation into a holistic "theological ethics."[5] All this suggests a need for reflection on the method of such a reconstructed and transformed ethics. Method is a foundational variable dividing Catholic ethicists and different methods are at the root of many anthropological and normative differences between them. It is imperative, then, to investigate Catholic ethical method, and we investigate it in this essay with two specific purposes: first, to elucidate our own method and, second, to issue an invitation to Catholic ethicists to dialogue. Such dialogue, we believe, is mandated by the present divisions among them, by the need to clarify different and legitimate Catholic ethical methods, and above all by faithfulness to the Christian injunction not to "quench the Spirit" (1 Thess 5:19).

Bernard Lonergan defines method as "a normative pattern of recurrent and related operations yielding cumulative and progressive results."[6] Operations are such things as gathering evidence, understanding, marshaling, and weighing evidence, making judgments and evaluating their truth, and deciding to act. To construct a normative pattern, ethical method must account for both epistemic claims about how we know ethical truth and normative claims

1

about the content of that truth. We begin with a definition: *Catholic ethical method is a theological method that proposes both an epistemology for reaching ethical truth and a normative pattern for reaching a definition of human dignity and formulating and justifying norms for its attainment.*

In this essay, we address two issues. First, we explore and address the charge of moral relativism leveled implicitly and explicitly by the magisterium against Catholic ethicists whose ethical method leads to different normative conclusions than that of the magisterium. We propose Lonergan's perspectivism as an epistemological tool that accounts for a plurality of Catholic ethical methods while maintaining an objectivist metaethic. Second, we explore virtue ethics, virtue epistemology, and a Christian stance that contribute to a reconstructed Catholic ethical method for the construction of a theological anthropology that defines human dignity and leads to the formulation and justification of ethical norms that facilitate, and do not frustrate, its attainment.

RELATIVISM OR PERSPECTIVISM?

On his March 2012 *ad limina* visit to the Vatican, Bishop John Quinn of Winona commented on the growing concern among young people with "the prison of relativism."[7] Cardinal Joseph Ratzinger, in his homily at the opening of the 2005 conclave, spoke of the "dictatorship of relativism" which "does not recognize anything as definitive and whose ultimate standard consists solely of one's own ego and desires." [8] In this essay, we are specifically concerned with moral relativism, which denies the existence of universal, objective, valid-for-all-circumstances ethical truth. Such truth is necessary, the magisterium argues, as the foundation for absolute norms which assert that certain acts, contraceptive and homosexual acts, for example, are intrinsically evil and can never be morally justified regardless of motive, context, or circumstance. Concern about relativism is undoubtedly warranted in the twenty-first century, but the magisterium fails to discern the difference between *relativism*, which rejects all objective ethical truth, and *perspectivism*, which acknowledges that there is objective ethical truth, albeit partial. It also fails to discern legitimate theological pluralism, which ThT advances as an essential criterion of Catholic theology. We consider relativism and perspectivism in turn in more detail.

The Magisterium on Relativism

In modern times, moral relativism has been the subject of much magisterial concern. Pius XII condemned "situation ethics" which, he believed, is a form of relativism that denies universal ethical truth.[9] Paul VI warned of moral relativism that claims that "some things are permitted which the Church had previously declared intrinsically evil," and that this vision "clearly endangers the Church's entire doctrinal heritage."[10] In his *Veritatis splendor*, John Paul II warned of the dangers of relativism which detaches human freedom from any objective or universal foundation and proposes certain methods "for discovering the moral norm" which reject absolute and immutable norms and precepts taught by the magisterium. Some Catholic ethicists complain that in *Veritatis splendor* John Paul falsely accused them of "canonizing relativism."[11] In both a 1993 speech to the presidents of the Asian Bishops' conferences[12] and a 1996 speech to the presidents of the doctrinal commissions of the Bishops' conferences of Latin America,[13] Cardinal Ratzinger warned of the dangers of a relativism that denies the existence of objective truth, calling it "the gravest problem of our time."[14] This concern with relativism and its impact, especially in the area of morality, has continued to be a central concern of his pontificate as Benedict XVI.

These and other magisterial statements not only fail to distinguish between relativism and legitimate theological disagreement on objectivist claims to ethical truth but also mistakenly conflate such legitimate disagreement and relativism. Philosophical ethics can aid in distinguishing between the two.

Metaethical Relativism

The Second Vatican Council's document, *The Decree on Priestly Formation,*[15] and more recently ThT,[16] highlight the essential importance of philosophy for doing theology. Philosophical ethical theory distinguishes three levels of ethical discourse, namely, moral judgments, normative ethics, and metaethics.[17] These distinctions shed light on understanding claims that a particular moral position is an expression of relativism. As persons endowed with reason and the ability to choose, humans regularly make moral judgments on the basis of what they believe is right, obligatory, or good. This is the realm of daily moral decision-making. These daily moral decisions serve as the source for both normative ethics and meta-ethics. It is the obligation of all rational human beings to make moral judgments in light of what they think is right or wrong. It is the task of theological ethicists to critically reflect upon, analyze, and develop these moral judgments into a comprehensive, systematic, rational ethical theory. The synopsis and synthesis of daily moral judgments into an ethical theory is the area of normative ethics and metaethics. Normative ethics formulates and justifies norms, rules, or laws that prescribe right actions and good motives and proscribe wrong actions and bad motives. Metaethics, which literally means above or beyond ethics, is the foundation of all normative ethics and daily morality. It asks two foundational questions. First, do moral terms like *good* and *right* have any meaning; second, if they do have meaning, how is that meaning justified?

Modern metaethical inquiry emerged in the early part of the twentieth century with G.E. Moore's seminal work, *Principia Ethica*,[18] and since then various metaethical theories on the meaning of moral terms have been developed. Nihilism claims that moral facts, moral truths, and moral knowledge do not exist and that, therefore, ethics is a meaningless discipline.[19] Emotivism asserts that moral terms are defined by individual emotions and desires; for emotivism, there is no objective or universal truth since emotions are relative to each individual.[20] Relativism claims there are no universal truths; moral terms and moral truth are defined either socially or individually. Social or cultural relativism claims that moral judgments are nothing more than descriptions of customs or practices of a society or culture.[21] Individual relativism or subjectivism claims that moral judgments are nothing more than judgments about one's personal emotions or feelings.[22] This latter is the type of relativism castigated in Ratzinger's claim that relativism's "ultimate goal consists solely of one's own ego and desires." Both social and individual relativism deny that the good can be defined universally and, therefore, they assert that there is no objective basis on which to justify claims to universal truth and absolute norms or intrinsically immoral acts.

Objectivist metaethical theories claim both that moral terms do have meaning and that their meaning can be justified.[23] In Catholic theological ethics, the moral terms *good* and *right* are defined in relation to *human dignity*, *human fulfillment*, *human flourishing*, or some cognate formulation. What is good or right facilitates human dignity and flourishing; what is evil or wrong frustrates human dignity and flourishing. Virtually every Catholic theological ethicist espouses an objectivist metaethics and defines the good or right on the basis of what facilitates human dignity. There are, however, among them a variety of theological anthropologies and understandings of human dignity, and this variety explains the different formulations and justifications of norms facilitating or frustrating human dignity. Sometimes these formulations and justifications are at variance with magisterial formulations and justifications.

For example, whereas the magisterium teaches that artificial contraception within a marital relationship frustrates human dignity and is, therefore, intrinsically immoral, social scientific data clearly show that the vast majority of Catholic couples approve of artificial contraception and, by implication, do not accept either that it frustrates human dignity or that it is intrinsically immoral.[24] Reflecting on the reasoned and conscientious experience of these married Catholic couples, we could formulate an alternative moral norm to the magisterium's as follows. Whether or not artificial contraception facilitates or frustrates human dignity depends on the reasons for choosing or not choosing it and on how it impacts one's relationships with oneself, one's spouse, and one's God. The difference between the magisterium's formulation and justification of a moral norm that facilitates human dignity and alternative formulations and justifications may or may not indicate metaethical relativism, but whether they do or not can be determined only by careful, case by case analysis of the reasons for their formulation and justification.

If there is difference of opinion about specific norms that facilitate or frustrate human dignity, this does not *eo ipso* indicate a relativistic metaethical theory. To prove relativism it is not sufficient simply to demonstrate that basic moral judgments or norms are different. One also needs to demonstrate that these moral judgments or norms "would still be different even if they were fully enlightened, conceptually clear, shared the same factual beliefs, and were taking the same point of view."[25] Such a standard is high and, for this reason, Frankena believes metaethical relativism has not been proven. The fact that people disagree with the magisterium on basic moral judgments or norms, such as the absolute norm forbidding contraception, in and of itself proves nothing. It may be that people deny the existence of universals, in which case they are certainly relativists. It may also be that they have a different objective definition of human dignity and the norms that facilitate or frustrate it, in which case they would be not relativists but objectivists.

Objectivism does not *per se* eliminate difference in either definitions of human dignity or in the formulation and justification of norms that facilitate its attainment, as the magisterium's documented evolution in its own moral teachings related to slavery, usury, religious freedom, and torture well illustrate.[26] These are clear examples of the magisterium's evolution of its understanding of human dignity, commonly assisted by the scholarly contributions of theologians and accompanied by a corresponding evolution in the formulation and justification of norms. Catholic ethicists can espouse and defend metaethical objectivism and still disagree on the objective definition of human dignity and the norms that facilitate or frustrate it. What accounts for this variability is the second question of metaethics, namely, the epistemic justification of the definition of ethical terms. Bernard Lonergan proposes *perspectivism* as a theory that justifies truth claims and contrasts it with relativism.

Perspectivism vs Relativism

Lonergan's theory of perspectivism, different definitions derive from different perspectives, adequately accounts for the different definitions of human dignity and the norms that facilitate or frustrate it, and addresses magisterial charges of relativism aimed at those who disagree with some of its absolute norms. Writing on the nature of historical knowledge, Lonergan notes the following: "Where relativism has lost hope about the attainment of truth, perspectivism stresses the complexity of what the historian is writing about and, as well, the specific difference of historical from mathematical, scientific and philosophic knowledge." [27] Relativism concludes to the falsity of a judgment; perspectivism concludes to its *partial* truth.

Lonergan offers three factors that give rise to perspectivism in human knowledge, including moral knowledge. First, human knowers are finite, the information available to them at any given time is as yet incomplete, and they cannot attend to or master all the data available to them. Second, the knowers are selective, given their different socializations, personal experiences, and ranges of data offered to them. Third, knowers are individually different, and we can expect them to have different interpretations of the data available to them. The theologian-knower trained in the philosophy of Plato, Augustine for instance, will attend to different data, achieve different understanding, make different judgments, and act on different decisions from the theologian-knower trained in the philosophy of Aristotle, Aquinas for instance. Augustine and Aquinas produce different theologies, both of which are necessarily partial and incomplete explanations of a very complex theological reality. They are like two viewers at fourth-story and thirteenth-story windows of the Empire State Building; each gets a different, but no less partial, view of all that lies outside the window. We could expect that if they ascended to a higher level they would get a fuller, but still partial, view again.

Every human judgment of truth, including every judgment of ethical truth, is a limited judgment and decision based on limited data and understanding. "So far from resting on knowledge of the universe, [a judgment] is to the effect that, no matter what the rest of the universe may prove to be, at least *this* is so."[28] It is precisely the necessarily limited nature of human sensations, understandings, judgments, and knowledge that leads to perspectivism, not as to a source of falsity but as to a source of partial truth. Though he said it on the basis of God's incomprehensibility, Augustine's restating of earlier Greek theologians, cited in ThT, is *à propos* and accurate here: "*Si comprehendis non est Deus*, if you have understood, what you have understood is not God."[29] Aquinas agrees: "Now we cannot know what God is, but only what God is not; we must, therefore, consider the ways in which God does not exist rather than the ways in which God does exist."[30]

No single objectivist definition of human dignity comprehensively captures the full truth of human dignity. Perspectivism, however, accounts for the plurality of partial truths embedded in various definitions. It is a theory of knowledge that presents human persons as they exist, that selects those dimensions of the human person that are deemed most important for defining human dignity, that interprets and prioritizes those dimensions if and when they conflict, and that formulates and justifies norms that facilitate, and do not frustrate, the attainment of human dignity. The only way for humans to achieve knowledge that is universal is via perspectives that are particular.[31] It is focus on different particular perspectives that leads to different and partially true definitions of human dignity and the formulation of different norms that facilitate or frustrate it.

In summary, there is broad metaethical agreement within Catholic theological ethics. First, it accepts some version of metaethical objectivism; there *are* objective definitions of human dignity. Second, it defines the ethical terms *good* and *right* in relation to some objective definition of human dignity or some cognate formulation. Third, given different perspectives, it can and sometimes does disagree on both the specific definition of human dignity and the formulation and justification of norms that facilitate or frustrate its attainment. Fourth, Lonergan's theory of perspectivism, which recognizes the inherent limitations of human knowledge, helps to account for the different definitions of human dignity and the different formulations and justifications of norms that facilitate or frustrate it. Fifth, the variability that arises from perspectivism is an essential part of an objectivism that recognizes universals; the good is *objectively* defined as human dignity. Different objective definitions of human dignity are not *eo ipso* a form of relativism that denies universals.

"Theology Today: Perspectives, Principles, and Criteria"

ThT illustrates Lonergan's insight into and perspectivist method of reaching moral truth and its justification. The method can account for the difference in objectivist definitions of the *good* defined as human dignity and the difference in the norms that facilitate or frustrate it. We consider each in turn.

The word *perspectives* in ThT's subtitle highlights the reality of a "plurality of theologies" in Catholic theology which are "undoubtedly necessary and justified."[32] ThT distinguishes between the "legitimate pluralism of theology" as a rational enterprise, which "can be evaluated in relation to a common universal truth,"[33] and relativism, which does not recognize a common universal truth. It cautions, with the long tradition of Catholic theology, that theology cannot know the fullness of divine truth. The plurality "results primarily from the abundance of divine [theological] truth itself, which human beings can only ever grasp under its specific aspects and never as a whole, and moreover never definitively, but always, as it were, with new eyes."[34] Searching for unity among the plurality of theologies, ThT formulates the following criterion to guide this search. Catholic theology "attempts to integrate a plurality of enquiries and methods into the unified project of the *intellectus fidei*, and insists on the unity of truth and therefore on the fundamental unity of theology itself. Catholic theology recognizes the proper methods of other sciences and critically utilizes them in its own research. It does not isolate itself from critique and welcomes scientific dialogue."[35] In the case of Catholic theological ethics, however, this criterion leaves unanswered the question: what truly constitutes the unity of ethical truth? Is it a truth reflected in a univocal definition of human dignity and corresponding univocal norms that facilitate its attainment? Or is it a more perspectival account of truth reflected in plural definitions of human dignity that recognize and embrace the difference in fourth-story, thirteenth-story, and twenty-first story accounts of human dignity and the difference in the formulation and justification of norms that facilitate its attainment.

ThT and Catholic tradition itself give some indication of the answers to these questions. ThT's Chapter 2, part 4, entitled "Responsible adherence to the ecclesiastical Magisterium," discusses, first, the nature and authority of the various levels of the magisterium and magisterial teaching and, then, the proper relationship between the magisterium, theologians, and theologies. This section ends with a call for responsible adherence to the magisterium, but it also recognizes the importance of dialogue between theologians and the magisterium and the "chronic collisions or contrasts" that can threaten this relationship.[36] That is part of the inevitable tension in relationships "wherever there is genuine life."[37] And "while 'dissent' towards the magisterium has no place in Catholic theology, investigation and questioning is justified and even necessary if theology is to fulfill its task."[38] One must distinguish between dissent from the magisterium as an authoritative teaching body and dissent from what the magisterium teaches. Catholic tradition justifies the latter, never the former.

The young Ratzinger underscores the need for the investigation and questioning of what is taught. "Not everything that exists in the Church must for that reason be also a legitimate tradition; in other words, not every tradition that arises in the Church is a true celebration of the mystery of Christ. There is a distorting, as well as a legitimate tradition... [and] ...consequently tradition must not be considered only affirmatively but also critically."[39] Thanks to changing socio-historical perspectives, there has been a major evolution in the Catholic tradition of the definition of human dignity and this evolution has been reflected in Catholic moral norms about what facilitates or frustrates attaining human dignity. At one time, the tradition approved slavery; then it condemned it as violating human dignity. It condemned the taking of interest on loans and then approved it. It approved torture and then condemned it. It condemned religious freedom and then approved it as an inviolable human right. These developments in Catholic moral teaching are intrinsically linked to the evolution in methods and theologies, guided by evolving historical, cultural, and spiritual perspectives. The definition of human dignity is part of that development as is the corresponding formulation and justification of norms that facilitate its attainment.

All contemporary Catholics can agree that the good and the right are defined in terms of human dignity, but human dignity itself is subject to plural Catholic objectivist definitions guided by theological perspectives, principles, and criteria that recognize the understanding of human dignity as an evolving reality. Formulating and justifying norms that facilitate or frustrate the attainment of human dignity must be done as a communion-church through the dialogue of charity recommended by John Paul II,[40] recognizing that there will be partial truths and disagreements on specific definitions of human dignity and the particular norms that facilitate or frustrate its attainment. These disagreements, however, we repeat again, are not to be automatically labeled as relativism; rather they reflect a perspectival objectivism. Such perspectival objectivism is well within the parameters of both ThT's "plurality of theologies" and a pilgrim church in search of practical ethical truth.

SOURCES FOR A RECONSTRUCTED ETHICAL METHOD

The second part of this essay explores the sources involved in the reconstruction of an ethical method that promotes the search for practical ethical truth. First, we explain the shift towards virtue, which is a Copernican-style revolution in Catholic ethical method. This shift is evident in virtue ethics and virtue epistemology. Second, we present a Christian vision or stance that serves as a hermeneutical lens for the selection, interpretation, prioritization, and integration of the sources of moral knowledge.[41]

Virtue Ethics and Epistemology

The call for renewal in moral theology at the Second Vatican Council emphasized bringing "forth fruit in charity for the life of the world."[42] This emphasis on charity reflects earlier Catholic theological efforts to reform the manual method for doing moral theology.[43] Though the Second Vatican Council did not issue a specific call for a shift to virtue ethics from the legalistic and reductionist approach of the manuals, contemporary Catholic ethicists have been investigating and developing such a shift in the method and the application of virtue ethics.

Virtue Ethics

Normative Catholic method for the formulation and justification of norms initially focused on two methodological approaches, deontology and teleology. Deontology emphasizes rules, obligations, and duties; teleology emphasizes the consequences of actions and the maximizing of their good or value.[44] The Council's call for a focus on charity and the renewed attention to virtue ethics in philosophical ethics, especially through the work of Alasdair MacIntyre,[45] have been an impetus for transforming Catholic ethical method from an ethics of law or consequences to an ethics of virtue. Virtue ethics gives precedence, not to the actions of agents but to their personal character formed in their moral communities and learned through the imitation of respected role models in those communities. We share with MacIntyre the judgment that neither deontology nor teleology offers an adequately comprehensive ethical method, indeed that, because of them, "We have – very largely if not entirely – lost our comprehension, both theoretical and practical, of morality."[46] We join with him and the many other modern ethicists who advance virtue ethics as a normative ethics more promising to the moral life than deontology or teleology.[47]

With the shift from deontology and teleology to virtue ethics comes also a fundamental methodological shift in what John Greco labels the "direction of analysis,"[48] which is a Copernican-style methodological shift. Traditional approaches to ethics understand the normative properties of an action in terms of the normative properties of the act involved, for example, its intrinsic meaning or consequences. The direction of analysis is from acts to persons. We judge an act to be right or wrong based on law or consequences, and morally evaluate the person's character as virtuous or vicious based on the acts chosen. A virtue approach to ethics understands the normative properties of acts in terms of the normative properties of persons. The direction of analysis is from personal character to personal acts. In other words, "virtue theories make rightness…follow from an action's…source in a virtue, rather than the other way around."[49] This methodological shift prioritizes persons over acts, virtues over rules and consequences, the subject over the object.

A number of Catholic ethicists have returned to the virtue theories of Aristotle and Aquinas and combined their visions of virtue with modern philosophical and theological developments and insights to methodologically construct a virtue ethic.[50] Aristotle defined virtue as "a state of character concerned with choice, lying in a mean."[51] Aquinas stands in Aristotle's tradition but rephrases Aristotle's definition. A virtue for him is a habit[52] or disposition ordered to an act.[53] As character states or habits, virtues explain not only why a person acts this way on this particular occasion but also why the person can be relied on to act this way always or, given human frailty, at least most of the time. Virtues also involve a judgment of truth and a choice of action. They involve *phronesis* or practical wisdom, which is the ability to reason correctly about practical decisions. Without *phronesis*, Aristotle argues, no virtue is possible.[54] For Aquinas, the virtue that corresponds to *phronesis* is *prudentia* or prudence, which is, therefore, cardinal. Without prudence, he argues, no other virtue is possible. Virtue ethics is informed by interdisciplinary research between theology and secular disciplines of knowledge to construct a comprehensive virtue theory. In terms of application, virtue ethics are used to explore sexual,[55] ecological,[56] genetic,[57] legal,[58] and professional[59] ethical issues.

Virtue Epistemology

Central to a theory of virtue is the notion that virtues are not only preconditions for human flourishing but also constituents of that flourishing. "A virtue is a character trait that human beings, given their physical and psychological nature, need to flourish (or to do and fare well)."[60] The person with the virtue of justice will *be* a just person who will, therefore, *act* justly. Moral virtues are bases of excellent human being and functioning, and so too "epistemic virtues are bases of excellent epistemic [being] and functioning."[61] The moral virtues facilitate the attainment of human dignity; the epistemic or intellectual virtues facilitate the attainment of true knowledge to define human dignity and to formulate and justify norms that facilitate its attainment. "Moral responsibility for what we do is often...dependent on epistemic responsibility for what we believe."[62] The shift towards virtue in ethical method has parallels with a shift towards virtue in epistemology and, combined with Lonergan's perspectivism, can ground a virtuous perspectivist epistemology to account for pluralism in ethical methods and pluralism in both definitions of human dignity and the formulation and justification of norms that facilitate its attainment. To explain virtuous perspectivism, we define virtue epistemology and its methodological shift, the types and interrelationships of epistemic virtues, virtue epistemology's parallels with Lonergan's perspectivist epistemology, and illustrate the application of virtue ethics and virtue epistemology with a specific example.

Virtue epistemology is a relatively new movement in philosophy that has developed over the last thirty years. While the discipline includes diverse schools and methods, they all adhere to four basic commitments. First, virtue epistemology is a normative discipline. Second, rational persons and communities are the foundational source of epistemic value and the foundational focus of epistemic evaluation.[63] Third, Greco's "shift in the direction of analysis" evident in virtue ethics is applied to virtue epistemology, and this shift distinguishes it from traditional epistemological methods. "Non-virtue theories try to analyze virtuous character in terms of justified belief, defining the former in terms of dispositions to achieve the latter." Greco proposes a directional reversal, "defining justified belief in terms of virtuous character. Virtuous character is then defined in terms of successful and stable dispositions to form belief."[64] "Justified beliefs," Christopher Hookway explains, "are those that issue from responsible inquiries of virtuous inquirers. It is a mistake to put it the other way round: epistemic virtues are those habits and dispositions that lead us to have justified beliefs. The primary focus is on how we order activities directed at answering questions and assessing methods of answering questions; it is not upon the epistemic status of beliefs." [65] Fourth, epistemic virtues are prioritized in the search for justified belief and knowledge.

Epistemic or Intellectual Virtues

An epistemic or intellectual virtue is "an innate ability or acquired habit that allows one to reliably achieve some intellectual good, such as truth in a relevant matter."[66] Epistemic virtues include "faculty-virtues" such as imagination, perception, memory, intuition, introspection, and "character virtues" such as reliability, responsibility, conscientiousness, perceptiveness, carefulness, and open-mindedness. Faculty-virtues are indispensable to account for knowledge from the past. Character virtues are indispensable to account for ongoing intellectual achievements and developments such as understanding and wisdom, which presuppose past knowledge, but which also build upon and transcend it. The development, exercise, and prioritization of the intellectual virtues in the theological ethicist and their impact on the marshalling of the evidence—the selection, interpretation, prioritization, and integration of the sources of moral knowledge and additional methodological considerations—accounts for the epistemological justification of a theological anthropology that defines human dignity and for the formulation and justification of norms that facilitate its attainment.

Interrelationship between Epistemic and Ethical Virtues

Virtue epistemologists agree on the directional shift in epistemology and the centrality of intellectual virtues in the process of attaining knowledge. They disagree on the interrelationship between virtue epistemology and virtue ethics, on whether or not and how epistemic appraisal is related to ethical appraisal, on whether or not and how the epistemic *ought* relates to the ethical *ought*. Lorraine Code agrees with Greco's and Ernest Sosa's directional shift in epistemology that emphasizes the cognitive activities of a person in community guided by the social practices of investigation. She criticizes Sosa, however, for not integrating the insights from ethical virtue theory with virtue epistemology. Specifically, Code believes that epistemology should emphasize virtues that relate to human agency in the process of attaining and justifying knowledge. To that end, she proposes as a virtue epistemology theory *responsibilism*, which posits the agent's epistemic responsibility as the primary intellectual virtue in virtue epistemology. Responsibility emphasizes both the knower as active agent and the agent's choice as essential elements in the pursuit and justification of knowledge. All other intellectual virtues emanate from this central virtue.[67] It is on the basis of responsibility that we can ensure accountability and impute praise or blame to the person for epistemic claims.

James Montmarquet agrees with Code that ethical virtue theory and virtue epistemology should be more closely aligned. Whereas Code, however, focuses on *responsibility* as the foundational intellectual virtue for epistemic claims Montmarquet focuses on *conscientiousness*, which he defines as an

appropriate desire for truth.[68] He specifies conscientiousness in three categories of regulative virtues. The virtue of *impartiality* includes openness to an
other's ideas, willingness to dialogue to exchange ideas and learn from an
other, suspense of personal bias towards an other's ideas, and recognition of
one's own fallibility. The virtue of *intellectual sobriety* disposes the sober-
minded inquirer, "out of sheer love of truth, discovery, and the excitement of
new and unfamiliar ideas, to embrace what is not really warranted, even
relative to the limits of his own evidence." The virtue of *intellectual courage*
includes "the willingness to conceive and examine alternatives to popularly
held beliefs, perseverance in the face of opposition from others (until one is
convinced one is mistaken), and the determination required to see such a
project through to completion."[69] The different virtues of responsibility and
conscientiousness account for different selection, interpretation, prioritization and integration of the sources of moral knowledge in defining human
dignity and formulating and justifying norms for its attainment. They also
emphasize the need to enter into dialogue with, and justify these claims to,
others and the courage to revise, if necessary, one's perspective based on this
process.

Reliabilism vs Responsibilism

An emphasis on the responsibility and conscientiousness of the knower-
agent, we suggest, is necessary in virtue epistemology, but it is not sufficient.
One can be very responsible and conscientious in intellectual activity and
still be incorrect in one's knowledge claims. While all virtue epistemologists
accept the change in the direction of analysis, defining justified belief and
knowledge in reference to their source in the virtues, they disagree on how to
define virtuous character. For Greco, who represents the "reliabilist" school,
virtuous character is "defined in terms of successful and stable dispositions
to form belief" and a consequential focus on "reliable success in producing
true belief."[70] For Hookway, who represents the "responsibilist" school, a
virtuous character decentralizes "questions of the epistemic status of beliefs
in favor of questions of agency and inquiry."[71] The reliabilist school focuses
on getting knowledge right; the responsibilist school focuses on the agent's
motives in seeking right and justified knowledge.

The reliabilist/responsibilist debate, we suggest, ought not to be construed
as an either/or but as a both/and debate. Guy Axtell argues that there is a
shared assumption in virtue epistemology of a "dual component" account of
the justification of true knowledge that reflects a complementarity between
reliabilism and responsibilism. Such an account "integrates constraints on an
agent's faculty reliability with constraints on the agent's responsibility in
gathering and processing evidence."[72] Linda Zagzebski's "dual component"
account of the justification of true knowledge balances the *motivation* of the

knower with *success* and objective reliability in achieving true knowledge. The intellectual virtues have "a characteristic motivation to produce a certain desired end and reliable success in bringing about that end."[73] In Sosa's virtue perspectivism a proposition is reflectively known by a person "only if *both* he is rationally justified in believing it *and* is in a position to know…whether it is true."[74] Greco's "mixed theory" account of justification is that "an adequate account of knowledge ought to contain both a responsibility condition and a reliability condition. Moreover, a virtue account can explain how the two are tied together. In cases of knowledge, objective reliability is grounded in epistemically responsible action."[75] A dual component virtue epistemology, which we espouse, seeks an integration and balance between reliabilist and responsibilist accounts of justified belief and knowledge.

Virtuous Perspective

The emphasis in virtue ethics on the agent rather than on the agent's actions is replicated in virtue epistemology's holistic emphasis on the knowing subject rather than on the subject's separate Scholastic faculties of intellect and will. This emphasis on the knowing subject and the subject's virtues, the directional shift in analysis, and the complementarity proposed by Sosa, Zagzebski and Greco between the subjective motivation of the knowing subject and the subject's success in achieving true knowledge all closely parallel perspectivism. According to Lonergan, human knowing is not simply "taking a look" at reality. It is endlessly discursive; it cycles and recycles through various levels of cognitive operations until knowledge and truth are reached in the judgment, deliberated on, and a decision is made for action according to the truth achieved in the judgment. It begins with attention and cycles on through perception, imagination (sometimes as memory), insight, conceptualization, deliberation and weighing of evidence, and culminates in the judgment of truth.[76] It is in the judgment of truth and only in the judgment of truth that genuine human knowledge and truth are achieved.

Perception is critical in the process of coming to know. Perception, Lonergan argues, is a function of a subject's relationship to an object, the subject's active patterning of the object in the phenomenal world. The phenomenal object does not simply impress itself upon rational subjects, as it impresses itself upon non-rational animals, nor do rational subjects simply construct or project it. Rather, the appearances of the phenomenal world are shaped by the subjects' attention, interests, loves of varying intensity, immediate and ultimate goals, emotional interactions, and in general the character lens through which they view the object.[77] According to virtue epistemology, that character lens is shaped by both the intellectual and character virtues. The phenomenal world persons encounter and attend to is not a world of naked sense data that is "out, there, now, real,"[78] but a world shaped by their subjective interpretations called perceptions. Perception is an exercise of a person's practical reason leading to choice. What we "see" is a function of who we are, and who we are, according to virtue epistemology, is fashioned by the intellectual and character virtues we adopt, define, and prioritize. Both virtue epistemology and perspectivism emphasize that this adoption, definition, and prioritization is influenced, in turn, by social context and historical narrative.

Who we are as knowing subjects is discerned, in particular, by responding to two of Lonergan's factors for knowing. First, human knowers are selective, given their past socialization, personal experience, range of data offered to them and, we add, given the intellectual and character virtues they adopt, prioritize, and excel in. Second, knowers are individually different and, given all the variables just enumerated, we can expect them to make different selection of data and exercise different intellectual and character virtues.

Code articulates similar factors for knowing in her virtue epistemology. Traditional epistemology underestimates the impact of contextual and social dimensions of the knowing subject. It does so because it begins with the object, not the subject. Beginning with the knowing subject, as virtue epistemology and perspectivism do, requires that we give greater attention to those dimensions that shape, first, the subject and, then as a consequence, the knowledge claims of the subject. Drawing from MacIntyre, Code argues that we understand the knowing subject and the subject's virtues through lived narrative.[79] Lived narrative is the context for adopting, prioritizing, and excelling in virtue. Integrating a virtuous perspective into ethical method recognizes the essential engagement of the theological ethicist, his or her perspective or stance, in the discipline. Klaus Demmer argues that theological ethics "inevitably contains a biographical element that reflects the personality of theologians and their particular life story."[80] This life-story is particularly evident in the habits of virtues, moral and intellectual, that shape the perception of the theological ethicist and his or her selection, interpretation, prioritization, and integration of the sources of moral knowledge. This personal narrative provides an adequate context for evaluating epistemic claims and highlights the richness and complexity of criteria for evaluating such claims.

Rooting epistemology in the knowing subject's character and virtues revealed through the subject's narrative history highlights the complexity of formulating and applying criteria for epistemic evaluation. All knowledge claims are made in a particular historical, social, and cultural context, all of which help to fashion the knowing subject's narrative and knowledge claims. In traditional epistemologies, the historical, social, and cultural dimensions of knowledge and their impact on the knowing subject's narrative history are largely ignored. Virtue epistemology and perspectivism acknowledge these variables and attempt to integrate them more fully into epistemological theory. Their integration marks a fundamental transition from classicism, where knowledge is a static, permanent achievement to historical consciousness, where knowledge is a dynamic, ongoing process. This distinction is as valid for epistemology as it is for Christian ethics or any other discipline.

In the Christian tradition ethics is never learned or done in isolation, but always in community. So too, virtue is never learned or practiced in isolation but always in community. Jennifer Herdt comments that "contemporary revivers of virtue ethics...have enthusiastically embraced the notion that habituation in virtue takes place within the context of a community and its practices."[81] Since community is essential to the individual's perceiving, understanding, judging, deciding, and acting, an ongoing challenge for virtue ethics and virtue epistemology is to discern the particularity of the plural perceptions of community and how these plural perceptions impact the definition of human dignity and the formulation and justification of norms that facilitate its attainment. In the Christian community, believers learn a Christian perspective or stance and that stance, we assert, fundamentally shapes the virtuous perspective of Christian theological ethicists.

Christian Stance

Charles Curran argues that perspective or stance "is drawn from the visual experience and expresses the way we look at something that puts everything else into focus."[82] A foundational question to be asked of Christian ethical method, then, is what perspective or stance guides the Christian ethicist in her perception of reality. Metaethical objectivism justifies the claim that the good can be defined and, in the Christian tradition, it is defined as human dignity or a similar cognate; perspectivism, virtue ethics, and virtue epistemology explain the epistemological foundations to justify that definition. Faith in the living Christ provides the vision, stance, or hermeneutical lens to formulate that definition and to formulate and justify norms that facilitate attaining human dignity. Drawing from what he calls the "fivefold Christian mysteries," Curran formulates a Christian stance that serves as a paradigm and point of departure for Christian ethical method.[83] "Curran's stance demonstrates the significance of 'postethical' levels of moral discourse or, in other words, of background beliefs and loyalties that provide a larger framework of justification and orientation for ethics without being a sufficient condition for determining particular moral action."[84] Curran proposes that the following mysteries are inherent in a Christian stance: creation, sin, incarnation, redemption, and resurrection destiny.[85]

The mystery of creation nurtures the belief that God has created the universe and everything in the universe, including human being and sexuality, and that God's creation is fundamentally good. Through rational reflection on the universe and God's creation, humans have the capacity to discern ethical truth. Sin is a demonstrable reality of human existence, and it came into creation through human actions contrary to God's plan of creation. Though the mystery of sin does not destroy the basic goodness of God's creation, it does deform it. It impacts human reason, the ability to discern the meaning of human existence, the call to holiness, and the recognition of and respect for human dignity. The mystery of incarnation asserts that Jesus is fully human and fully divine and "supports and strengthens the fundamental goodness of everything human." It eliminates the possibility of any dualism between body and soul or spirit and flesh. If sin deforms the human image of God in creation, the mystery of redemption, "the successful struggle of Jesus against the power of sin and evil," restores that image. "Resurrection destiny" or "the fullness of the reign of God" and the triumph of Jesus over evil, sin, and death, exist in the tension between the "already" and "not yet." Christian ethics must "live with an eschatological tension between the present time of redemption and the unrealized future of resurrection destiny."[86]

For Curran, stance "serves as an interpretive tool in understanding the basic mysteries of Christian life."[87] For Philip Keane, stance "is a creative, integrating, imaginative grasp of the meaning of life."[88] A Christian ethicist's stance, the selection, interpretation, prioritization, and integration of these and other mysteries, shape her perspective and guide the process of formulating a definition of human dignity and the norms that facilitate its attainment. Often times, an ethicist's stance is implied rather than stated in her writings. Drawing attention to stance, however, is crucial to Christian ethical method. It may shift the focus from the formulation and justification of specific norms for the moral life, which is often polarizing and not necessarily conducive to dialogue among Christian ethicists, to perspectives on creation, sin, incarnation, redemption, and resurrection destiny and how those mysteries shape a stance, provide common ground for constructive and charitable dialogue, and build community. Vatican II's and ThT's calls for constructing interdisciplinary theological methods could foster such dialogue and community building.

Virtuous Perspective: Chastity

We illustrate the interrelationship between a virtuous perspective and a Christian stance by asking which virtue is central for defining human dignity in sexual ethics. In Christian tradition, chastity is that central virtue. The *Catechism of the Catholic Church* provides a succinct definition: chastity is "the successful integration of sexuality within the person and thus the inner unity of [the hu]man in his [and her] bodily and spiritual being. Sexuality, in which [the hu]man's belonging to the bodily and biological world is expressed, becomes personal and truly human when it is integrated into the relationship of one person to another in the complete and lifelong mutual gift of *a man and a woman.*"[89]

Chastity: A Traditional Stance

The *Catechism's* definition of chastity, closely informed by other magisterial teachings, suggests a stance on the selection, interpretation, prioritization, and integration of four Christian mysteries, creation, incarnation, redemption, and sin, and asserts two claims, one anthropological and the other normative. Anthropologically, the mystery of creation recognizes the fundamental goodness of God's creation in general and of human sexuality in specific. Normatively, according to the phrase we have underscored in the *Catechism's* definition of chastity, human sexuality can be realized morally only in a permanent relationship between a man and a woman. Elsewhere, creation's design for human sexuality is referred to as ontological or sexual complementarity between a man and a woman whereby a man and a woman, though fundamentally equal and complete in themselves,[90] are incomplete as a couple.[91] Sexual complementarity completes the couple in marriage by bringing the male and female, physiological and psychological elements together in a unified whole. Creation is designed to complete man and woman as a couple in complete and lifelong mutual self-gift. The mystery of the incarnation affirms the "inner unity" of body and soul, mind and spirit in human sexuality; there is no dualism. The mystery of redemption recognizes the possibility of the successful integration "into the relationship of one person to another in the complete and lifelong mutual gift of a man and a woman."

Original sin, however, has damaged the fundamental goodness of creation, including human persons and their sexuality. The Christian tradition has always been suspicious of sexuality and has regarded human sexuality in general as "objectively disordered" as a consequence of original sin,[92] but this morally suspicious view of human sexuality is gradually being corrected in the tradition. Heterosexual orientation is objectively ordered; marital sexuality is fully affirmed as good; and heterosexual marital reproductive sexual acts are morally good. Creation, incarnation, and redemption fully affirm the goodness of heterosexual, marital sexuality and the virtue of chastity, as defined in the *Catechism*, specifies how this good is to be realized. Original sin, however, continues to damage the goodness of human sexuality in both the ontological and moral orders. Homosexual orientation is one instance of this ontological damage and is an "objective disorder." Mark Jordan makes an important association between original sin and homosexual orientation that is evident in a subtle revision, approved by the Vatican, to the United States Bishops' *Always Our Children.*[93]

> In the original letter, sexual orientation is described as a 'fundamental dimen-
> sion' of human beings; in the revised version, it is a 'deep-seated dimen-
> sion'…. 'Fundamental' might suggest that sexual orientation is part of one's
> being as a divine creation, while 'deep-seated' only implies that sexual orien-
> tation is stubborn. Humanity is fundamental; Original Sin is deep-seated.
> Homosexuality is more like Original Sin than like humanity.[94]

According to the CDF, a homosexual orientation "is a more or less strong
tendency ordered toward an intrinsic moral evil;"[95] if acted upon, this orientation leads to intrinsic evil in the moral order.

The *Catechism's* definition of chastity and its suggested selection, interpretation, and integration of the Christian mysteries contain an anthropological claim and a normative claim. The anthropological claim is that creation
justifies only heterosexual orientation and heterosexual mutual self-gift as
objectively ordered and natural and prescribes that mutual self-gift can be
realized only in sexual complementarity between a man and a woman in
marriage. The mystery of sin justifies homosexual orientation and homosexual mutual self-gift as "objectively disordered" and unnatural. The normative
claim is that only reproductive sexual acts, or at least sexual acts of a repro-
ductive-kind,[96] within a heterosexual marriage can be moral; all non-reproductive sexual acts, heterosexual, homosexual, or bisexual, are immoral.

Chastity: An Alternative Catholic Stance

An alternative Catholic stance agrees with the *Catechism's* suggested selection of four Christian mysteries to define chastity. Further, it accepts the
Catechism's definition on the authentic integration of a person's sexuality
into human relationship and the practical living out of that relationship in
fidelity and commitment to another person. This alternative stance, however,
discards the final clause that limits this integration to heterosexual relationships and extends it to homosexual and bisexual relationships. Discarding
and extending the final clause are contingent on the relationship of the mystery of sin to sexual orientation and have implications also for the mysteries
of creation and redemption.

Relying on secular disciplines of knowledge, some Catholic ethicists disagree with the traditional stance on the mystery of sin that justifies the claim
that homosexual orientation is "objectively disordered." Credible science
finds that homosexual orientation is a not-infrequent reality in creation. Peer-
reviewed scientific literature has documented that human sexual practice has
been incredibly varied across time and cultures[97] and has identified same-sex
practice in over 300 species of vertebrates as a natural component of the
social system.[98] Based on such studies, James Allison challenges the claim
that a homosexual orientation is objectively disordered. "There is no longer
any reputable scientific evidence of any sort: psychological, biological, ge-

netic, medical, neurological – to back up the claim."[99] In fact, there is substantial scientific evidence to the contrary. In addition, it is accepted in contemporary scientific and theological literature, including the *Catechism*[100] and other magisterial documents,[101] that people do not choose their sexual orientation. Sexual orientation, "the sustained erotic attraction to members of one's own gender, the opposite gender, or both – homosexual, heterosexual, or bisexual respectively,"[102] is given and not chosen. It is a result of a mix of genetic, psychological, and social "loading."[103] Such evidence leads evolutionary biologist Joan Roughgarden to assert the following: "To the extent that information about nature can inform theological discourse on human and biological diversity, the message for full and proper inclusion of gay, lesbian, and transgender persons is clear and unequivocal."[104]

On the basis of the evidence of the contemporary sciences, some Catholic ethicists argue, the mystery of sin does not justify the claim that homosexual orientation is objectively disordered in the ontological order. This theological claim, according to the CDF, is contingent on whether or not homosexual acts are intrinsically immoral: "Although the particular inclination of the homosexual person is not a sin, it is a more or less strong tendency ordered toward an intrinsic moral evil; *and thus* the inclination itself must be seen as an objective disorder." [105] The central reason why homosexual orientation is labeled as objectively disordered is because it has a "strong tendency ordered toward an intrinsic moral evil." If it can be established that homosexual acts are not intrinsically evil, then the understanding of the mystery of sin that justifies the claim that homosexual orientation is objectively disordered must be reconsidered.

Scientific and theological arguments have much to tell us about the morality of homosexual acts between homosexual couples. Regarding the judgment that homosexual acts are intrinsically disordered and therefore violate chastity and frustrate human dignity, credible social-scientific studies indicate that this is not the case. Lawrence Kurdek, who has carried out extensive social-scientific research on gay and lesbian couples, reports that they experience similar levels of relationship satisfaction to heterosexual couples.[106] A growing body of peer-reviewed social-scientific data demonstrates that committed, stable, and justly loving gay and lesbian unions are as personally complementary and fulfilling as heterosexual ones. Gay and lesbian acts of making just love are as unitive as heterosexual acts of making just love. An equally impressive body of social-scientific data shows that, contrary to magisterial claims with no supporting evidence, partnered gays and lesbians raise children to be every bit as healthily developed and heterosexual as the children of heterosexuals.[107]

Some Catholic ethicists reject the magisterium's normative claim that homosexual acts are intrinsically disordered, but disagree on how to describe these acts. Richard McCormick, for instance, labels homosexual acts as premorally evil. Such acts are "premoral evils in that their sheer presence does not *necessarily* make the total act or relation of which they are a part 'morally evil or sinful.'"[108] For McCormick, such acts can be considered premorally evil because "homogenital acts always depart from the ideal or the normative."[109] Other Catholic ethicists reject this judgment because of its implicit anthropological and normative implications. These disagreements must be sorted out to substantiate our claims to redefine the mysteries and the implications these redefinitions have for the virtue of chastity.

The claim that homogenital acts depart from the ideal or normative can only be made if there is a definition of the normative, and that normative is established based on a heterosexist anthropological norm. According to this anthropology, heterosexual orientation is the norm and anything that departs from this norm is "objectively disordered." [110] There is tension in McCormick's thought here. On the one hand, he resists labeling homosexual orientation an objective disorder. On the other hand, by labeling homosexual acts premorally evil, he implies not only that these acts are non-normative but also that there is something normative in the human person that makes such acts non-normative. Exploration of this tension will provide us with an essential anthropological and normative insight that warrants a revision of the traditional definition of the mystery of sin in relation to homosexual orientation.

McCormick presents and critiques the CDF's 1975 Declaration *Persona Humana*, regarding human sexuality, homosexual orientation, and its moral correlation with homosexual acts. Regarding human sexuality, the CDF states the following:

> The human person, present-day scientists maintain, is so profoundly affected by sexuality that it must be considered one of the principal formative influences of a man or woman. In fact, sex is the source of the biological, psychological and spiritual characteristics which make a person male or female and which thus considerably influence each individual's progress towards maturity and membership of society. [111]

McCormick notes the problematic between claiming, on the one hand, that one's sexuality as reflected in one's sexual orientation is "one of the principal formative influences in the person" and, on the other hand, that in the case of persons with a homosexual orientation this principal influence is disordered. Such a statement means, quite simply, "that the person is disordered."[112] McCormick responds to this by claiming that the CDF has drawn too close an association between the immorality of homosexual acts and the objective disorder of homosexual orientation, such that the orientation itself becomes morally decisive. In effect, McCormick is resisting the CDF's moral method of moving from an established definition of homosexual acts as intrinsically evil to an anthropological claim that homosexual orientation is disordered. The latter claim has moral implications from the former for, so runs the argument, while a homosexual inclination is not a sin, it is a more or less strong tendency ordered toward an intrinsic evil. McCormick resists this move to draw a moral correlation between homosexual acts and homosexual persons, and asks "what is achieved by designating homosexual orientation as a 'disorder'"?[113]

We believe there is a similar correlation in McCormick's own thought, not between homosexual acts as *intrinsically* evil and homosexual orientation but between homosexual acts as *premorally* evil and homosexual orientation. We pose the following question: what is achieved by designating homosexual acts as premoral evils? Does this label not insinuate a negative judgment on homosexual orientation, aligning it with a definition of the mystery of sin that justifies the claim that homosexual orientation is an objective disorder similar to that advanced by the CDF? After all is said and done, is not a "premoral evil," precisely as "evil," a "disordered" value? It seems to us that one could draw a similar conclusion on the disorderedness of the person's orientation from McCormick's statement that homosexual acts are a premoral disvalue and from the CDF's statement that homosexual acts are "intrinsically disordered."[114] Both take their stance on the unproven anthropological perception and claim that heterosexual orientation is the norm of sexual morality for humans and that homosexual orientation, therefore, must be objectively disordered. We believe that labeling heterosexual acts as normative, and acts that depart from this ideal as premorally evil, does not give the human sexual person adequately considered due consideration. The interrelationship between a premoral value or disvalue and sexual anthropology requires further consideration.

By claiming that heterosexual acts are normative, one has already made a judgment about sexual anthropology and implicitly affirmed the magisterium's position that heterosexual orientation is, in the words of Jordan, a "fundamental" normative dimension of humanity as a "divine creation" and that a homosexual orientation is "deep-seated" and "stubborn," "more like Original Sin than like humanity." Any sexual expression that deviates from that norm is, therefore, by definition, at least premorally evil. McCormick and other ethicists, however, leave room for the possibility that some homosexual acts, while they may be premorally evil, are not morally evil and may, indeed, be morally good. McCormick's resistance to labeling sexual orientation disordered, and his further assertion that some homosexual acts can be morally good,[115] would seem to imply that homosexual acts are not premoral evils. What may be at the root of this dilemma, and a way out of it, is how we define sexual orientation in relation to sexual anthropology and determine premoral disvalue in light of this anthropology.

Homosexual acts, whether judged intrinsically or premorally evil, are being measured against an already defined sexual anthropology that posits *heterosexual* orientation and acts, rather than simply *sexual* orientation and acts, as normative for human beings. This is a classicist and deductive approach to anthropology, and it betrays fundamental methodological commitments. It is classicist, because it accepts heterosexual orientation as the absolute and unchanging anthropological norm. While this may be true statistically, as the magisterium realizes,[116] there are people with a permanent homosexual orientation who do not choose that orientation; for them, a homosexual orientation *is* normative. It is deductive, because it accepts that heterosexual orientation is normative and deduces from that principle that all homosexual activity is morally or premorally evil. Catholic ethicists who oppose this stance typically utilize an historically conscious and inductive method, which looks at human beings in their particularity and draws out anthropological generalizations that reflect this particularity.

From an historically conscious worldview, defining anthropology is a necessarily ongoing venture,[117] and the definition of what constitutes a premoral value or disvalue must be in dialogue with anthropology. As an anthropology evolves, the definition of what constitutes a premoral value and disvalue will also evolve. Historical consciousness recognizes the givenness of sexual orientation and the need to incorporate it as an essential component of sexual anthropology. It further recognizes that heterosexual and homosexual orientations, as integral parts of the "biological, psychological and spiritual characteristics which make a person male or female,"[118] are normative for heterosexual or homosexual human beings respectively. An ethical method that assesses sexual behavior must be founded on that anthropological insight, and formulate its values and norms for assessing sexual persons and sexual acts in light of that insight. Christian stance, in turn, which selects, interprets, prioritizes, and integrates Christian mysteries as a hermeneutical lens to view reality, must allow those mysteries to be informed by an accurate anthropology.

If the scientific data and our revision of certain Catholic theological arguments are correct, then homosexual acts are not intrinsically evil and, when holistically complementary, just, and loving,[119] can be morally good. If homosexual acts are not intrinsically evil the CDF's central reason for labeling a homosexual orientation objectively disordered is eliminated. The interpretation of the mystery of sin and its implications for the other mysteries and their relevance for the virtue of chastity and their anthropological and normative implications for the sexual person must be revised in light of that correction. The mystery of sin does not justify the claim that homosexual and bisexual orientations are "objectively disordered" and unnatural; they are more like humanity as created than like original sin. The mystery of creation justifies that heterosexual, homosexual, and bisexual orientations, and heterosexual, homosexual, and bisexual mutual self-gifts, are objectively ordered for heterosexual, homosexual, and bisexual persons respectively. It further justifies that holistic complementarity, i.e., *an integrated orientation, personal, and biological complementarity,* can be realized between a man and a woman, a man and a man, and a woman and a woman, depending on the person's sexual orientation. The mystery of incarnation affirms the "inner unity" of body and soul, mind and spirit in human sexuality; there is no dualism. The mystery of redemption justifies that the integration into the relationship of one person to another can occur in the complete and lifelong mutual self-gift of a man and a woman, a man and a man, and a woman and a woman.

To define the normative, then, we propose the following definition of a premoral value and disvalue with regard to homosexual and heterosexual sexual acts. Sexual activity that is consonant with one's sexual orientation and that strives for sexual integrity in light of one's orientation is a premoral value; sexual activity that is not consonant with one's sexual orientation and that does not strive for sexual integrity in light of one's orientation is a premoral disvalue. While this definition may seem to reflect the moral plane, rather than the premoral plane, it does not. Until all the variables of the human person adequately considered are assessed, one cannot make a *moral* judgment on whether or not a particular sexual activity *actually* integrates the sexual person and his or her human relationships and is, therefore, morally right, or *actually* disintegrates the person and his or her relationships and is, therefore, morally wrong. This revised definition provides a hermeneutical lens to justify both a definition of human dignity that includes sexual orientation as an objective, intrinsic dimension of the sexual person and a definition of chastity, allied to the virtues of justice and love, as "the successful integration of [heterosexual, homosexual, or bisexual orientation] within the person and thus the inner unity of [the hu]man in his [and her] bodily and spiritual being."

CONCLUSION

There are differences in Catholic definitions of chastity because there is a foundational difference in Christian stance toward the interpretation and integration of the Christian mysteries that lead to different definitions of human dignity and the norms that facilitate or frustrate its attainment. For some, human sexual dignity rests only in heterosexuality and only reproductive-type sexual acts within marriage facilitate human dignity. For others, human sexual dignity rests in heterosexuality, homosexuality, and bisexuality, and both reproductive-type and non-reproductive type *holistically complementary, just, and loving* sexual acts facilitate human dignity. The different definitions of chastity, human dignity, and acts that facilitate or frustrate human dignity reflect virtuous Christian perspectives from different stories of the philosophical-theological Empire State Building and account for the variability in how the evidence is marshaled and construed into a comprehensive and comprehensible normative pattern or method. Different theological methods produce different theological syntheses, and in theological ethics they produce different moral norms for moral practice. We consider the practicalities of this situation in the next chapter.

QUESTIONS FOR REFLECTION

1. What do you understand by the term "method"? What operations are involved in a theological, ethical method?
2. What do you understand by the term "relativism" and by the term "perspectivism"? What is the essential difference between the two realities?
3. What do you understand by the terms "metaethics," "normative ethics," and "ethical actions." What are the functions in ethics of each of these three realities? What is their relationship one to the other?
4. What do you understand by the terms "teleology," "deontology," and "virtue ethics"? How do the three function in ethics? What is the "direction of analysis" in each of them? Which seems to you most helpful to a person wishing to lead an ethical life?
5. Is there, do you think, a specific *Christian* stance in ethics. If there is, what, in your opinion, is it? Why do you make this specific judgment? In your opinion how does stance influence an approach to the virtue of chastity?

NOTES

An earlier version of this essay appeared in *Theological Studies* 74, no. 4 (2013): 903–33. It is reprinted here with permission.

1. James F. Keenan, S.J., "Note: Vatican II and Theological Ethics," *Theological Studies* 74, no. 1 (2013): 162–90.

2. International Theological Commission, "Theology Today: Perspectives, Principles and Criteria," *Origins* 41, no. 40 (March 15, 2012): n. 5.

3. This pluralism extends to the application of principles and is reflected in the USCCBs' document *The Challenge of Peace*: "the pastoral letter makes specific applications, observations and recommendations which allow for diversity of opinion on the part of those who assess the factual data of a situation (sic) differently" (Washington, DC: USCCB, 1983), i.

4. Bryan Massingale, "Beyond Revisionism: A Younger Moralist Looks at Charles E. Curran," in *A Call to Fidelity: On the Moral Theology of Charles E. Curran*, ed. James J. Walter, Timothy O'Connell, and Thomas A. Shannon (Washington, DC: Georgetown University Press, 2002), 267.

5. Norbert Rigali, S.J., "On Presuppositions of Theological Ethics," *Horizons* 38, no. 2 (2011): 211–12.

6. Bernard J. F. Lonergan, S.J., *Method in Theology* (Toronto: University of Toronto Press, repr. 2003), 4.

7. Benjamin Mann, "Bishop sees new generation seeking truth, rejecting relativism," *Catholic News Agency*, March 13, 2012, http://www.catholicnewsagency.com/news/bishop-sees-new-generation-seeking-truth-rejecting-relativism/.

8. Joseph Ratzinger, "Cappella Papale Mass 'Pro Eligendo Romano Pontifice' Homily of His Eminence Card. Joseph Ratzinger of the College of Cardinals," April 18, 2005, http://www.vatican.va/gpII/documents/homily-pro-eligendo-pontifice_20050418_en.html.

9. See Pius XII, "Allocution to the Federation mondiale des jeunesses feminines Catholiques [Word Federation of Catholic Female Youth]," *Acta Apostolicae Sedis* (hereafter, *AAS*) 34 (January 18, 1952): 413–19; "Radio Message about the Christian Conscience," *AAS* 34 (March 23, 1952): 270–78; and "Instruction of the Holy Office, February 2, 1956," in *Enchiridion*, ed. H. Heinrich Denzinger and Adolf Schönmetzer (Rome: Herder, 33rd ed., 1965), n. 3918.

10. Paul VI, "'Address' to Members of the Congregation of the Most Holy Redeemer," *AAS* 59 (1967): 962.

11. Maura Anne Ryan, "'Then Who Can Be Saved?': Ethics and Ecclesiology in *Veritatis splendor*," in *Veritatis splendor: American Responses*, ed. Michael E. Allsopp and John J. O'Keefe (Kansas City, MO: Sheed and Ward, 1995), 11.

12. Cardinal Joseph Ratzinger, "Christ, Faith and the Challenge of Cultures" (March 2–5, 1993), http://www.ewtn.com/library/CURIA/RATZHONG.HTM.

13. Cardinal Joseph Ratzinger, "Relativism: The Central Problem for the Faith Today" (May, 1996), http://www.ewtn.com/library/CURIA/RATZRELA.HTM.

14. Ratzinger, "Christ, Faith and the Challenge of Cultures."

15. *Optatam totius*, n. 15.

16. "Theology Today," nn. 64–66.

17. See Henry J. McCloskey, *Meta-Ethics and Normative Ethics* (The Hague: Martinus Nijhoff, 1969), 7; and John D. Arras, Bonnie Steinbock and Alex John London, "Moral Reasoning in the Medical Context," in *Ethical Issues in Modern Medicine*, ed. John D. Arras and Bonnie Steinbock (London: Mayfield, 1999, 5th ed.), 1–40.

18. George E. Moore, *Principia Ethica* (Cambridge: Cambridge University Press, 1903, repr. 1968).

19. Gilbert Harman, *The Nature of Morality: An Introduction to Ethics* (New York: Oxford University Press, 1977), 11.

20. For a discussion of emotivism, see Charles L. Stevenson, *Ethics and Language* (Yale, 1944).

21. Robert Veatch, "Does Ethics Have an Empirical Basis," *Hastings Center Studies* 1 (1973): 52–53. See also, David F. Kelly, *Contemporary Catholic Health Care Ethics* (Washington, DC: Georgetown University Press, 2004), ch. 9.

22. Veatch, "Does Ethics," 55.

23. William K. Frankena, *Ethics* (Englewood Cliffs, NJ: Prentice Hall, 1973, 2nd ed.), 97–102. Veatch distinguishes between four types of absolutist theories, Supernatural, Rationalist, Intuitionist, and Empirical. Catholic natural law is considered an empirical absolutist theory. See Kelly, *Contemporary Catholic*, 81–85.

24. Studies in the U.S. indicate 75–85% of American Catholics, who consider themselves good Catholics, approve a form of contraception forbidden by the Church (see William V. D'Antonio, *et al.*, *Laity American and Catholic: Transforming the Church* (Kansas City: Sheed and Ward, 1996), 131; James D. Davidson, *et al.*, *The Search for Common Ground: What Unites and Divides Catholic Americans* (Huntington, IN: Our Sunday Visitor, 1997), 131. For a similar situation in England, see Michael Hornsby-Smith, *Roman Catholicism in England: Customary Catholicism and Transformation of Religious Authority* (Cambridge: Cambridge University Press, 1991), 177. A 2010 survey of English Catholics reveals that "just 4 per cent of Catholics believe the use of artificial contraception is wrong" (Christopher Lamb, "Few Now View Contraception as Immoral," *The Tablet* [September 18, 2010]: 45).

25. Frankena, *Ethics*, 110.

26. See John T. Noonan, "Development in Moral Doctrine," *Theological Studies* 54, no. 4 (1993): 674–75; and Bernard Hoose, *Received Wisdom?: Reviewing the Role of Tradition in Christian Ethics* (London: Geoffrey Chapman, 1994).

27. Lonergan, *Method in Theology*, 217.

28. Bernard J.F. Lonergan, *Insight: A Study of Human Understanding* (London: Longmans, 1957), 344, emphasis added. See also *Method in Theology*, 217–19.

29. *Sermo* 52, 16, in *Patrologiae Cursus Completus: Series Latina*, ed. J. P. Migne, 221 vols. (Paris: Gamier, 1844-1904) (hereafter, *PL*) 38, 360; and "Theology Today," n. 97. For a detailed analysis, see Victor White, *God the Unknown* (New York: Harper, 1956) and William Hill, *Knowing the Unknown God* (New York: Philosophical Library, 1971).

30. Thomas Aquinas, *Summa Theologiae* (hereafter *ST*), *1, 3*, preface.

31. Massingale, "Beyond Revisionism," 258.

32. "Theology Today," n. 77.

33. Ibid., n. 78.

34. Ibid., n. 77.

35. Ibid., n. 75.

36. Ibid., n. 42.

37. Ibid.

38. Ibid., n. 41.

39. Joseph Ratzinger, "The Transmission of Divine Revelation," in *Commentary on the Documents of Vatican II*, vol. 3, ed. Herbert Vorgrimler (New York: Herder and Herder, 1969), 185.

40. *Ut unum sint*, n. 17.

41. The four established sources of moral knowledge, scripture, tradition, secular disciplines of knowledge, and experience, are often referred to as the Wesleyan Quadrilateral. Due to space limitations in this essay we do not explore the sources and their selection, interpretation, prioritization, and integration to define human dignity and formulate and justify norms that facilitate attaining human dignity; this will be done in a subsequent essay. For scholars who have explored these sources in relation to method, see Lisa Sowle Cahill, *Between the Sexes: Foundations for a Christian Ethics of Sexuality* (Cincinnati, OH: Fortress Press, 1985), 4–7; Charles E. Curran, *The Catholic Moral Tradition Today: A Synthesis* (Washington, DC: Georgetown University Press, 1999), 47–55; Margaret A. Farley, *Just Love: A Framework for Christian Sexual Ethics* (New York: Continuum, 2006), 182–96; James T. Bretzke, S.J., *A Morally Complex World: Engaging Contemporary Moral Theology* (Collegeville, MN: Liturgical Press, 2004), 9–41; and Todd A. Salzman, *What are They Saying about Roman Catholic Ethical Method?* (Mahwah, NJ: Paulist Press, 2003).

42. *Optatam totius*, n. 16.

43. See Gerard Gilleman, *The Primacy of Charity in Moral Theology* (Westminster, MD: Newman Press, 1959).

44. See Todd A. Salzman, *Deontology and Teleology: An Investigation of the Normative Debate in Roman Catholic Moral Theology* (Leuven, Belgium: Peeters Press, 1995).

45. Alasdair MacIntyre, *After Virtue,* 2ⁿᵈ edition (Notre Dame: University of Notre Dame, 1984).

46. MacIntyre, *After Virtue*, 2. See also G. E. M. Anscombe, "Modern Moral Philosophy," *Philosophy* 33 (1958): 1–19; Philippa Foot, "Moral Beliefs," *Proceedings of the Aristotelian Society* 59 (1958-9): 83–104.

47. In addition to Foot and MacIntyre, whom most judge to be the preeminent modern virtue theorists, other important theorists in the field of virtue ethics will be introduced as the essay unfolds.

48. John Greco, "Virtue Epistemology," *Stanford Encyclopedia of Philosophy* (July 9, 1999), http://plato.stanford.edu/entries/epistemology-virtue/.

49. Guy Axtell, *Knowledge, Belief, and Character: Readings in Virtue Epistemology* (Lanham, MD: Rowman and Littlefield, 2000), xiii.

50. See, for example: James F. Keenan, S.J., *Virtues for Ordinary Christians* (Lanham, MD: Sheed and Ward, 1996); and "Proposing Cardinal Virtues," *Theological Studies* 56, no. 4 (1995): 709–29; Jennifer A. Herdt, *Putting on Virtue: The Legacy of the Splendid Vices* (Chicago: University of Chicago, 2008); Paul J. Wadell, *Happiness and the Christian Moral Life: An Introduction to Christian Ethics,* 2ⁿᵈ ed. (Rowman & Littlefield, 2012); Simon G. Harak, S.J., *Virtuous Passions: The Formation of Virtuous Character* (Mahwah, NJ: Paulist, 1993);

William C. Mattison III, *Introducing Moral Theology: True Happiness and the Virtues* (Grand Rapids: Brazos, 2008); Todd A. Salzman and Michael G. Lawler, "Virtue Ethics: Natural and Christian," *Theological Studies* 74/2 (2013): 442–73.

51. Aristotle, *Nicomachean Ethics*, trans. David Ross (Oxford: Oxford University Press, 2009) II, 6, 1106b.

52. *ST, 1–2,* 49, 1.

53. Ibid., 49, 3.

54. See Hursthouse, *On Virtue Ethics*, 12.

55. See Martin Rhonheimer, *Natural Law and Practical Reason: A Thomist View of Moral Autonomy*, trans. G. Malsbary (New York: Fordham University Press, 2000); John Grabowski, *Sex and Virtue: An Introduction to Sexual Ethics* (Washington, DC: Catholic University of America Press, 2003); Farley, *Just Love*; Todd A. Salzman and Michael G. Lawler, *The Sexual Person: Toward a Renewed Catholic Anthropology* (Washington, DC: Georgetown University, 2008); and *Sexual Ethics: A Theological Introduction* (Washington, DC: Georgetown University, 2012).

56. Louke van Wensveen, "Virtues, Feminism, and Ecology," in *Virtue: Readings in Moral Theology No. 16*, ed. Charles E. Curran and Lisa A. Fullam (Mahwah, NJ: 2011), 137–56.

57. Celia Deane-Drummond, *Genetics and Christian Ethics* (New York: Cambridge University Press, 2006).

58. Lawrence B. Solum, "Virtue Jurisprudence: A Virtue-Centered Theory of Judging," *Metaphilosophy* 34, no. 1/2 (2003): 178–213.

59. William F. May, "Virtues in Professional Life," in *Virtue: Readings in Moral Theology*, 95–116.

60. Rosalind Hursthouse, "Applying Virtue Ethics," in *Virtues and Reason: Philippa Foot and Moral Theory*, ed. Rosalind Hursthouse, Gavin Lawrence, and Warren Quinn (Oxford: Clarendon, 1995), 68.

61. Robert C. Roberts and W. Jay Wood, *Intellectual Virtues: An Essay in Regulative Epistemology* (Oxford: Oxford University Press, 2007), 7.

62. James A. Montmarquet, *Epistemic Virtue and Doxastic Responsibility* (Lanham, MD: Rowman and Littlefield, 1993), vii.

63. John Greco, *Virtue Epistemology: Contemporary Readings* (Boston: MIT, 2012).

64. John Greco, "Agent Reliabilism," in *Philosophical Perspectives* 13 (1999): 290.

65. Christopher Hookway, "Cognitive Virtues and Epistemic Evaluations," *International Journal of Philosophical Studies* 2, no. 2 (1994): 211, 225.

66. John Greco, "Virtue Epistemology."

67. See Lorraine Code, *Epistemic Responsibility* (Hanover, NH: University Press of New England, 1987).

68. Montmarquet, *Epistemic Virtue*, 23.

69. Ibid.

70. Guy Axtell, Alvin Goldman, Ernest Sosa, and Hilary Kornblith, *Knowledge, Belief, and Character* (Lanham, MD: Rowman and Littlefield, 2000), xiv.

71. Ibid., xiii–xiv.

72. Ibid., 188.

73. Linda Zagzebski, *Virtues of the Mind: An Inquiry into the Nature of Virtue and the Ethical Foundations of Knowledge* (Cambridge: Cambridge University Press, 1996), 134.

74. Ernest Sosa, *Knowledge in Perspective: Selected Essays in Epistemology* (New York: Cambridge University Press, 1991; repr. 1995), 28.

75. Greco, "Virtue Epistemology."

76. Lonergan, *Insight*, 273–74.

77. Ibid., 190.

78. Ibid., 251; see also Lonergan, *Method*, 263.

79. Code, *Epistemic Responsibility*, 222.

80. Klaus Demmer, *Shaping the Moral Life: An Approach to Moral Theology* (Washington, DC: Georgetown University Press, 2000), 1.

81. Herdt, *Putting on Virtue*, 350.

82. Curran, *The Catholic Moral Tradition Today*, 30.

83. Curran, *Moral Theology: A Continuing Journey* (Notre Dame: University of Notre Dame Press, 1982), 38–44; *The Catholic Moral Tradition Today*, 30.

84. James M. Gustafson, "Charles Curran: Ecumenical Moral Theologian Par Excellence," in *A Call to Fidelity*, 225–26.

85. Other scholars (James M. Gustafson, *Christ and the Moral Life* [New York: Harper and Row, 1968], 242–48; James T. Bretzke, *A Morally Complex World*, 33–35) have proposed Christ as the foundational stance for Christian ethics. While Christ is the *norma normans non normata*, proposing him as foundational stance begs the question of Christology. We concur with Curran that, given the complexity of Christological questions and the danger of a narrow Christology (*The Catholic Moral Tradition Today*, 31–32) and further, given that the mysteries which Curran cites are directly related to questions of Christology, these mysteries may adequately account for a Christian stance.

86. Curran, *The Catholic Moral Tradition Today*, 33–34.

87. Curran, *Moral Theology*, 43.

88. Philip S. Keane, *Christian Ethics and Imagination* (New York: Paulist Press, 1984), 65.

89. *Catechism of the Catholic Church*, n. 2337. We have corrected the *Catechism's* language to be gender inclusive. The gender exclusive language of the *Catechism* and most magisterial documents is a revealing indicator of stance.

90. John Paul II, "Authentic Concept of Conjugal Love," *Origins* 28, no. 37 (March 4, 1999): 655.

91. John Paul II, "Letter to Women," *Origins* 25, no. 9 (July 27, 1995): 141.

92. Mark Jordan, *The Silence of Sodom: Homosexuality in Modern Catholicism* (Chicago: University of Chicago Press, 2000), 34.

93. USCCB, "Always Our Children: A Pastoral Message to Parents of Homosexual Children and Suggestions for Pastoral Ministers" (1997), http://www.usccb.org/issues-and-action/human-life-and-dignity/homosexuality/always-our-children.cfm.

94. Jordan, *The Silence of Sodom*, 47.

95. CDF, "Letter to the Bishops of the Catholic Church on the Pastoral Care of Homosexual Persons," *Origins* 16, no. 22 (November 13, 1986): 379, n. 3.

96. See John Finnis, "Law, Morality, and Sexual Orientation," *Notre Dame Law Review* 69, no. 5 (1994): 1067.

97. Michel Foucault, *The History of Sexuality*, trans. Robert Hurley, 3 volumes (New York: Vintage Books, 1988–90).

98. See Bruce Bagemihl, *Biological Exuberance: Animal Homosexuality and Natural Diversity* (New York: St. Martin's Press, 1999).

99. James Allison, "The Fulcrum of Discovery Or How the 'Gay Thing' is Good News for the Catholic Church," unpublished essay, 8.

100. *Catechism*, n. 2358.

101. USCCB, *Always Our Children*, n. 5.

102. Richard C. Pillard and J. Michael Bailey, "A Biological Perspective on Sexual Orientation," *Clinical Sexuality* 18, no. 1 (1995): 1.

103. This terminology articulates our position that homosexual orientation is neither exclusively genetic nor exclusively social in origin. See John E. Perito, *Contemporary Catholic Sexuality: What is Taught and What is Practiced* (New York: Crossroad, 2003), 96.

104. Joan Roughgarden, "Evolutionary Biology and Sexual Diversity," in *God, Science, Sex, and Gender: An Interdisciplinary Approach to Christian Ethics*, ed. Patricia Beattie Jung and Aana Marie Vigen, with John Anderson (Chicago: University of Illinois Press, 2010), 103.

105. CDF, "Letter to the Bishops of the Catholic Church," 379, n. 3, emphasis added.

106. Lawrence A. Kurdek, "What Do We Know about Gay and Lesbian Couples?" *Current Directions in Psychological Science* 14, no. 5 (2005): 251–54; "Differences between Partners from Heterosexual, Gay, and Lesbian Cohabiting Couples," *Journal of Marriage and Family* 68, no. 2 (2006): 509–28; "Lesbian and Gay Couples," in *Lesbian, Gay and Bisexual Identities over the Lifespan*, ed. Anthony R. D'Augelli and Charlotte J. Patterson (New York: Oxford University, 1995), 243–61; "Are Gay and Lesbian Cohabiting Couples *Really* Different From Heterosexual Married Couples?" *Journal of Marriage and Family* 66, no. 4 (2004): 880–900. See also, Ritch C. Savin-Williams and Kristin G. Esterberg, "Lesbian, Gay, and Bisexual

Families," in *Handbook of Family Diversity*, ed. David H. Demo, Katherine R. Allen, and Mark A. Fine (New York: Oxford University, 2000), 207–12; and Philip Blumstein and Pepper Schwartz, *American Couples: Money, Work, Sex* (New York: Morrow, 1983).

107. See Salzman and Lawler, *Sexual Ethics*, 173–75.

108. Richard A. McCormick, S.J., *Notes on Moral Theology, 1981 Through 1984* (Lanham, MD: University Press of America, 1984), 11, citing Lisa Sowle Cahill, "Moral Methodology: A Case Study," in *A Challenge to Love: Gay and Lesbian Catholics in the Church*, ed. Robert Nugent (New York: Crossroad, 1983), 91, emphasis added.

109. Richard A. McCormick, S.J., *Critical Calling: Reflections on Moral Dilemmas since Vatican II* (Washington, DC: Georgetown University Press, 1999), 312.

110. CDF, "Vatican List of Catechism Changes," *Origins* 27, no. 15 (September 25, 1997): 257.

111. CDF, *Persona humana*, n. 1.

112. McCormick, *Critical Calling*, 310.

113. Ibid., 311.

114. CDF, *Persona humana*, n. 8.

115. McCormick, *Critical Calling*, 309.

116. CDF, *Persona humana*, n. 8; USCCB, "Always Our Children," n. 6.

117. See McCormick, "Human Significance and Christian Significance," in *Norm and Context in Christian Ethics*, ed. Gene H. Outka and Paul Ramsey (New York: Charles Scribner's Sons, 1968), 233–61; *Notes on Moral Theology: 1981 through 1984*, 181–82.

118. CDF, *Persona humana*, n. 1.

119. For a full explanation of these criteria for sexual morality, see Todd A. Salzman and Michael G. Lawler, "*Quaestio Disputata*. Catholic Sexual Ethics: Complementarity and the Truly Human," *Theological Studies* 67, no. 3 (2006): 625–52; *The Sexual Person*, 156–61; *Sexual Ethics*, 60–86.

Chapter Two

Theologians and the Magisterium

A Proposal for a Complementarity of Charisms through Dialogue

In the opening chapter we analyzed theological method and noted that different methods will yield different theological syntheses. In this chapter, we consider both the sometimes different theological syntheses of the Catholic Magisterium and Catholic theologians and the different theological methods that produce them. Some thirty years ago, Archbishop Joseph Bernardin wrote on the nature of the relationship between the magisterium and theologians. Bernardin's recommendation was that two extremes are to be avoided. On the one hand, there cannot be any imperialism in which the magisterium[1] co-opts theological scholarship as a mere mouthpiece and instrument for defending and propagating its teachings. On the other hand, there cannot be "secessionism," any divorce between the magisterium and theologians that would grant the latter absolute autonomy and freedom from accountability. Instead, Bernardin proposes that in defining the relationship between magisterium and theologians "it is essential to keep before us a reasonably clear and unambiguous notion of complementarity, particularly complementarity in the work of arriving at magisterial teaching."[2] He made no attempt, however, either to specify that notion of complementarity or to explain how it would be exercised.

This paper argues in three cumulative sections that charisms, gifts of the Holy Spirit to believers, provide a traditional means of formulating a model of complementarity for theologians and the magisterium. First, we present a brief overview of charisms in the Christian tradition. Second, we explore both the charism of teaching as it is exercised by theologians and the magisterium and the relationship between the two. Third, relying on the model of "dialogue of charity," outlined in Pope John Paul II's *Ut unum sint*[3] and echoing Paul VI's *Ecclesiam suam*,[4] we propose a dialogical complementarity of charisms. Such complementarity of magisterium and theologians necessarily raises the issue of authority and how it is exercised by the magisterium. This will be an underlying theme throughout this essay. While the topic is directly about *internal* dialogue within the Catholic tradition, it is relevant also to dialogue *external* to that tradition, and that for three reasons. First, theological development in the teaching function within the Catholic Church, although it is based on specifically Catholic principles, will have ecumenical implications.[5] Second, not only is the question of the exercise of authority a divisive issue for Catholics but it is also often a stumbling block for ecumenical relations. Finally, John Paul II's "dialogue of charity," we propose, may also facilitate a complementarity of charisms between theologians and the magisterium.

CHARISMS

In this section, we intend not so much an extensive analysis of the history of charisms as a highlighting of points related to the tripolar relationship that recurs throughout this essay, namely, the relationship between bishops, theologians, and the entire body of the faithful. Rene Laurentin defines charisms as "free gifts of the Spirit intended for the building up of the church, the Body of Christ."[6] In 1 Corinthians, Paul writes that spiritual gifts are given to each member of the Body of Christ "for the common good" (1 Cor. 12:7), and lists a number of charisms (1 Cor 12:8–11; 28–30). These and other texts have led many to conclude that ministry in Paul's churches was charismatic. The letters to Timothy give a different account of ministry and the charisms associated with it. Ministry became more institutionalized and dominated by officeholders in the church called *presbyteroi* and *episkopoi*, and charisms become more identified with those officeholders. John Haughey summarizes this change: "the Corinthians' ministry of charismata seems to have been superseded by one exercised largely by the presbyters and bishops. And the legitimacy of their ministry is not due to their charisms but to their being in a continuum with the apostles. The real bearers of the Spirit to the church are now the officeholders."[7] This development marks the beginnings of a very significant shift in the perception of ecclesiastical ministry and the charisms associated with it, and this shift created tensions throughout Christian history between charismatics and ecclesiastical officeholders who will seek to control their charisms.

This tension was not much in evidence at the Council of Trent which seemed to understand the complementary charisms of the *inquisitio* of theologians and the *auctoritas* of bishops,[8] but it became very much in evidence in the period after Trent when there was a radical shift in the role and function of the theologian in relation to the magisterium. The era in which theologians were consultants for, and collaborators with, bishops was largely replaced with an era in which theologians were asked to explain church doctrines and to engage in apologetics. The term "the magisterium" came to describe hierarchical officeholders and their teaching function. "Rather than serving the truth, the official church became the organ of the truth which was its possession,"[9] and ecclesiology from the Reformation onwards "was concerned almost exclusively with the institutional factors in the church."[10] These institutional factors concentrated on the juridical power of hierarchical officeholders, *magisterium cathedrae pastoralis*, to the detriment of the scholarly authority of theologians, *magisterium cathedrae magistralis*.[11] Pius XII's statement regarding theologians in *Humani generis*, which explains the task of the theologian as demonstrating the truth of what the magisterium teaches through Scripture and tradition,[12] sums up this development and is a far cry from the charism exercised by theologians in the middle ages.

The tension between the charisms of hierarchical officeholders and the charisms of theologians and the entire body of the faithful continued in and after the Second Vatican Council. "The terms 'charisma' and 'charismatic' occur in fourteen passages of the Second Vatican Council,"[13] but the inclusion of references to charisms in the Council documents was not without tension. *Lumen gentium* juxtaposes two kinds of gifts, hierarchical and charismatic,[14] although it later eases the tension between the two, describing charisms as special gifts that the Spirit of God distributes among *the faithful of every rank*, making them "fit and ready to undertake the various tasks or offices advantageous for the renewal and upbuilding of the church."[15] The Council affirmed charism as "a grace-given capacity and willingness for some kind of service that contributes to the renewal and upbuilding of the church, "[16] but it struggled with the tension between the charisms gifted to all the faithful in the church and the charisms gifted only to hierarchical officeholders. This struggle has been evident ever since in the ongoing tension between the teaching charisms of theologians and the magisterium.

THEOLOGIANS, MAGISTERIUM, AND THEIR INTERRELATIONSHIP

Avery Dulles notes that the church has two kinds of teachers: "a class of official teachers whose task is to establish the official doctrine of the church and a class of theologians whose function is to investigate the questions concerning faith in a scholarly way."[17] Though these two classes are intrinsically linked, they are "irreducibly distinct." Both classes are gifted with the charism to teach, the hierarchical magisterium specifically with the charism to teach authoritatively. This formal authority, however, must be qualified. "The office must be used in order to acquire the knowledge, understanding and discretion needed to express the Christian message in a pastorally effective way."[18] In this sense, it is dependent upon scholarly technicians or theologians. Official functionaries within the church have the responsibility to examine and make judgments regarding the exercise of particular charisms within the church, especially those that pertain to teaching, but "they must not suppress them when they are genuine."[19]

Instruction

Any judgment of whether or not the charism of the theologian is specific and genuine is dependent on how one defines the charisms of theologians and the magisterium, and the relationship between the two. The Congregation for the Doctrine of the Faith's *Instruction on the Ecclesial Vocation of the Theologian*[20] attempts to do just that. It begins by emphasizing that theology is "important for the church in every age," especially "in times of great spiritual and cultural changes," as a means to "a deeper 'understanding of the realities and the words handed on'" in revelation and tradition. Theology, however, also experiences "moments of crisis and tension,"[21] and these moments seem to be of overarching concern for the *Instruction* in Parts II-IV. An extended exegesis of the *Instruction*, which has already been done elsewhere,[22] is not necessary to our purpose here. We summarize and critically analyze the *Instruction* only as it throws light on the possibilities and limits of our ecclesial tripolar grouping.

Part II: "The Vocation of the Theologian"

The *Instruction* does not refer to theologians' "proper charisms"[23] until Part IV, when it discusses dissent. Through reason, guided by prayer, the theologian "is to pursue in a particular way an ever deeper understanding of the Word of God found in the inspired Scriptures and handed on by the living Tradition of the church,"[24] and theology leads people to the truth attained in faith "so that the faith might be communicated."[25] This approach seems to identify theology with catechesis, and we will have to return to this below. Theology has developed into a "true and proper science."[26] As such, it draws upon philosophy, human sciences, and historical disciplines to understand the meaning of revelation and to communicate it accurately and responsibly, offering the People of God teaching "which in no way does harm to the doctrine of faith." While theology enjoys freedom of inquiry with its proper methods, and may even include "new proposals" for understanding the faith, the truth of these proposals must be discerned through time, patience and "fraternal dialogue."[27] The magisterium alone is responsible for judging whether or not a theological proposal coincides with the truth of revelation.

Part III: "The Magisterium of the Church's Pastors"

Although Part III briefly discusses the infallibility of the People of God, the emphasis falls clearly on the charism of the infallibility of the pastors. Drawing support from the section on "The Infallibility of the Universal Church" in *Mysterium Ecclesiae*, Part III begins by citing the gift of the Holy Spirit, bestowed upon the whole church, "a participation in [God's] own infallibility."[28] It then goes on to cite a classic text from *Lumen gentium*, "The body of the faithful as a whole...cannot err in matters of belief."[29] *Mysterium ecclesiae* interprets this text strictly: "But by divine institution it is the exclusive task of these pastors alone, that is with the authority of Christ shared in different ways; so that the faithful, who may not simply listen to them as experts in Catholic doctrine, must accept their teaching given in Christ's name, with an assent that is proportionate to the authority that they possess and that they mean to exercise."[30] *Mysterium ecclesiae* cites *Lumen gentium*, n. 5, in support of this passage, but in this passage of *Lumen gentium*, the focus is on Jesus' founding of the church and outpouring of the Spirit upon the church; there is no reference to the authority of the church's pastors. *Mysterium ecclesiae* and, by implication, the *Instruction*, narrowly define the charism of the infallibility of the church to the church's pastors, and an emphasis on this hierarchical charism is a central concern throughout the *Instruction*.[31]

This charism of magisterial authority is extended to two realms. First, it extends to doctrine on faith and morals, either "contained in revelation" or, "even if not contained among the truths of faith, are nonetheless intimately connected with them."[32] These latter truths comprise the so-called secondary object of infallibility. Second, the *Instruction* extends the divine assistance in this charism, though not the charism *per se*, to "magisterial decisions in matters of discipline," which "call for the adherence of the faithful."[33] Part III ends by calling upon the theologian "to be faithful to his role in service to the truth"[34] and to collaborate with the magisterium.

Part IV: "The Magisterium and Theology"

Part IV is divided into two sections: "Collaborative Relations" and "The Problem of Dissent." Though the goal of the magisterium and theology is the same, "preserving the People of God in truth which sets free," each has different gifts and functions. The gifts of theology are explained in terms of a "reciprocal relationship" between itself and the magisterium. The magisterium "authentically teaches the doctrine of the Apostles. And, benefiting from the work of theologians, it refutes objections to and distortions of the faith and promotes, with the authority received from Jesus Christ, new and deeper comprehension, clarification, and application of revealed doctrine."

For its part, "theology strives to clarify the teaching of Revelation with regard to reason and gives it finally an organic and systematic form."[35]

The *Instruction* advances a two-fold rule when tensions arise between theologians and the magisterium. "When there is a question of the communion of faith, the principle of the 'unity of truth' (*unitas veritatis*) applies. When it is a question of differences which do not jeopardize this communion, the 'unity of charity' (*unitas caritatis*) should be safeguarded."[36] In cases where theologians' scholarly findings present difficulties that may challenge church unity on doctrinal teaching, a different tone is taken.

The section on the problem of dissent begins by noting the danger dissent can cause to the church community. A central cause of dissent is said to be "philosophical liberalism" which has a "tendency to regard a judgment as having all the more validity to the extent that it proceeds from the individual relying upon his own powers." This philosophy leads to a freedom of thought that "comes to oppose the authority of tradition, which is considered a servitude." This freedom of thought is contrasted with the "legitimate demand for freedom" accepted by the church in its teaching that "nobody is to be forced to embrace the faith against his will."[37] The contrast between legitimate freedom of conscience manifested in the choice to pursue what one believes to be a religious truth and illegitimate freedom of conscience manifested in dissent from noninfallible teaching allows the *Instruction* to make a distinction between punitive action against a theologian's "intellectual position" but not against "the person of the theologian." On the basis of this distinction, it can claim that, "while procedures might be improved" for a "thorough investigation" of a theologian whose position has departed "from the doctrine of faith," a canonical mission can be removed without any "violation of human rights."[38] The distinction itself seems to us to be a straw man.

It is only in the section on dissent that the *Instruction* discusses the "proper charisms" of theologians. "As for theologians, by virtue of their own proper charisms, they have the responsibility of participating in the building up of Christ's Body in unity and truth. Their contribution is needed more than ever, for evangelization on a world scale requires the efforts of the whole People of God."[39] There is no specification of the theologian's charisms. Rather, the *Instruction* specifies that if theologians "encounter difficulties due to the character of their research, they should seek their solution in trustful dialogue with the pastors, in the spirit of truth and charity which is that of the communion of the church." Other than "established procedures," which "might be improved," to allow the theologian "to clear up possible misunderstandings of his thought,"[40] there is very little explanation of the nature of this "trustful dialogue." The *Instruction* proposes fraternal and trustful dialogue in charity, but the present reality, unfortunately for the magisterium, theologians, and the entire body of the faithful, is a fundamental mistrust between the magisterium and the majority of theologians who challenge both how it exercises its charism of infallibility and its extension of that charism to truths that do not meet the defined criteria for possible infallibility as defined by the First Vatican Council.[41] A critique of the *Instruction* will illustrate the nature of the mistrust.

Instruction: A Critique

"The Vocation of the Theologian"

To begin with, it is curious that the *Instruction* does not associate any "proper charism" with theologians until it addresses dissent. Though it never lists or specifies the nature of the theologian's charisms, the *Instruction* does note that "their contribution is needed more than ever" and identifies this contribution with the need for evangelization.[42] Reference is made to *Christifideles laici*, 32–35, which details the charism of the faithful: to "earnestly cooperate in presenting the Word of God, especially *by means of catechetical instruction*."[43] In these paragraphs, the focus is on the lay faithful, evangelization, and catechesis and closely reflects a description of theology in the *Instruction*. "Theology therefore offers its contribution so that the faith might be communicated."[44]

What the *Instruction* includes in the theologian's charism, emphasis on catechesis, and excludes, reference to anything other than catechesis, is revealing. It is easy to conclude that the *Instruction* identifies the theologian's charism with catechesis. Yves Congar agrees that the charism of *didaskalos*-teacher in the primitive church was more like catechesis than scientific theology, but he also points out that the theological schools that developed and flourished in the second and third centuries and thereafter moved away from focusing strictly on catechesis to speculative thought on the nature of the faith and salvation. Tension developed between the doctors' speculation and apostolic statements traced to apostolic succession.[45] Defining the charism of the theologian in terms of catechesis and locating this definition in the section on dissent appears to send a message: to avoid conflicts with the magisterium that may lead to investigation and censure, the theologian should focus his or her efforts on explaining and defending magisterial positions. There is, however, we suggest, an important distinction between catechesis and theology that should always be maintained.

"Catechesis is an *education in the faith*…which includes especially the teaching of Christian doctrine imparted…in an organic and systematic way, with a view to initiating the hearers into the fullness of Christian life."[46] Though theology may include catechesis, it is also more than catechesis. Theology uses scholarly principles and methods not only to communicate truths of the faith but also to explore the understanding of and new ways of articulating those truths. Theologians have a mediating function between the magisterium and the entire body of the faithful. Francis Sullivan explains that this two-directional mediation is "from the faith, culture and questionings of the people toward the magisterium; and from the pronouncements of the magisterium back to the people."[47] The first mediation comes before magisterial pronouncements; it requires theologians to do preparatory work to get a sense of the questions, issues, and concerns of the faithful. The magisterium relies upon this theological work to address any concerns in its pronouncements. The second mediation comes after magisterial pronouncements; it requires theologians to interpret and explain those pronouncements for the faithful in terms that are culturally, intellectually, and developmentally appropriate. The *Instruction*'s emphasis is clearly on the second mediation and is highlighted in its treatment of the canonical mission or *mandatum* whereby "the theologian is officially charged with the task of presenting and illustrating the doctrine of the faith in its integrity and with full accuracy."[48] Such a charge is clearly part of the theologian's vocation, but it does not exhaust that vocation.

The first mediation, which is virtually absent from the *Instruction*, is also part of the theologian's vocation. As the magisterium relies more heavily on "safe" theologians for consultation, those "who hold a single theology"[49] and function as methodological and theological apologists for the magisterium, other theological voices are silenced or ignored and the two-directional mediation is short-circuited. Theologians considered "unsafe," those whose scholarly-grounded positions differ from the magisterium's, are discounted in the consultative process.

A contemporary example of this preferential option for "safe" theologians is John Paul II's encyclical *Veritatis splendor*. Evidence suggests that Chapter Two in the encyclical was composed largely by the Pro-Rector of the Catholic University of Lublin, Andrzej Szostek, whose doctoral dissertation examined and critiqued a "new wave" of Catholic moral theologians who are lumped together as "proportionalists," and who were the targets of criticism in Chapter Two.[50] One of the examiners of that dissertation was Karol Wojtyla, soon to become Pope John Paul II. Richard McCormick detects also in Chapter Two the ideas of John Finnis, an advocate of New Natural Law Theory, who was at the time a member of the International Theological Commission. Comparison of the encyclical with some of Finnis' writings show clear parallels between the two.[51] There is no evidence that any proportionalist was consulted for the encyclical.

Including the ideas of only "safe" theologians and excluding the ideas of "unsafe" theologians cuts like a two-edged sword. One edge permits the claim that the pronouncement has been made with theological consultation and the agreement of theologians; the other edge provokes a theological response from those who have not been consulted, and sometimes their response is critical, which then permits their labeling as "dissenters." Determining whether or not a pronouncement communicates the faith of the People of God is settled in advance by safe theologians, leaving those excluded from the consultative process with no other option but critique post-factum.

This situation serves well no segment of our tripolar ecclesial relationship, neither magisterium, nor theologians, nor the entire body of the faithful. For the magisterium, it creates polarization between itself and the other two segments considered unsafe, the faithful who disagree with doctrinal pronouncements and theologians who articulate this disagreement and/or formulate arguments that challenge these pronouncements. Their reflections are necessarily limited to either affirming or critiquing magisterial pronouncements arrived at without broad consultation, which makes it appear that dissent among theologians and faithful is no longer "limited and occasional" but rampant. [52] In fact, however, many theologians are forced into the overly-simplistic, and inaccurate, classification of dissenters because they have been deprived of a consultative voice that might temper both the formulation of pronouncements and subsequent criticism of them. Basing magisterial pronouncements on the arguments of only those who hold a single Roman theology oversimplifies the complexity of a doctrinal reality that would be better clarified by open scholarly, theological debate. This oversimplification may result in pronouncements that rely more upon ideology than compelling theological evidence and argumentation that has resulted from open and honest debates and consultation with the faithful. Such an approach damages both the credibility of the magisterium and the faithful's real understanding of complex Christian truth.

Polarization permeates the theological community as well. By consulting with safe theologians, the magisterium implicitly endorses one school of theology over another and provides a sort of sanction for that school's work. This results in debates being settled by a claim of authority rather than by rational argumentation, and this further results in the perpetuation of a vicious cycle among theologians. The magisterium issues pronouncements that rely upon safe theologians; those safe theologians, buoyed by these pronouncements, cite them in the scholarly literature to justify their position and to attack theologians who disagree with them; this inevitably, and incorrectly, leads to the labeling of these latter theologians as "dissenters," which leads to their further exclusion from official consultation. Narrowly defining the mediation of theologians as one of explaining and defending magisterial pronouncements forces "unsafe" theologians to serve not as consultants for, but critics of, magisterial pronouncements.

The lack of broad theological consultation can be damaging also to the entire body of the faithful who detect a tension between the magisterium and a large majority of theologians. These tensions are frequently aired by both magisterium and theologians in the media, and they often escalate into outright hostility. In this hostile climate of charge and counter-charge, complex issues are never accurately or fairly presented, serving neither side well and leading to suspicion, distrust, and cynicism among the faithful. Many lay theologians, who are contextually well placed to articulate lay issues and concerns, are not consulted, and so magisterial pronouncements can appear detached from the lived reality of the lay faithful. This has been noticeably true, for instance, on sexual and women's issues.

There is another consideration. Not only has the theologian's role of mediation been narrowly defined, so that many have no option but to serve, not as consultants for, but as critics of magisterial pronouncements, but also the demographics of theologians and the nature of the theological enterprise have evolved. Up until the Second Vatican Council, almost all theologians were clerics who taught primarily in seminaries; since the Council, theology has become largely a lay profession exercised predominantly in Catholic and non-Catholic colleges and universities.[53] This changed demographic has introduced voices into the theological conversation, especially women's and third world voices, which have never before been heard in the conversation. These new voices challenge the traditional, male, hierarchical, Eurocentric voices that have historically dominated the Catholic tradition and demand that the magisterium take seriously the fullness of that tradition[54] and Pope John Paul II's commitment to human experience as an essential component of theological reflection.[55] The experiences of lay faithful and lay theologians, especially lay and "underside"[56] women, reflect a Spirit-wind that requires communal, dialogical discernment to decide whether it blows to confirm or to challenge magisterial pronouncements.

The discipline of theology has evolved as well. Norbert Rigali notes that, in the past, professional theological discourse took place in two contexts: "professor-to-students" and "theologian-to-other-theologian." One of the most important changes effected by the Second Vatican Council was the empowerment of the laity to become more active in the church and, with this increased activity, theology now has a third context, that of "an open public forum in the church." Given their easy Internet access to magisterial documents and popular theological magazines, laity are becoming ever more theologically educated, and theologians are now "directly in dialogue with the laity in teaching and writing."[57] Rigali's point is well made. The community of Catholic theologians "has primary responsibility for meeting contemporary educated Catholics' need for 'faith seeking understanding,' and the individual theologian must accept his or her share of that collective responsibility as the need and opportunity occur."[58]

The context for Rigali's reflections is the CDF's action against Roger Haight and his book, *Jesus, Symbol of God*,[59] and the Catholic Theological Society of America's response to this action.[60] Rigali underscores in both actions the failure to extend to the educated church the discussions between theologians and between theologians and the magisterium. Both the magisterium's response to Haight and the CTSA's response to the magisterium fail "to address adequately the problem of how the contemporary church should respond to controversial theological claims about fundamental Christian beliefs."[61] Given an educated laity and the theologian's responsibility to be in dialogue with and to educate that laity, the theological process must be extended to doing theology "in the open forum of today's church."[62]

This open forum will provide for the lay faithful, who share through baptism Christ's charisms of priest, prophet, and king,[63] their right to be active in a teaching-learning church.[64] We agree with Paul Lakeland's judgment that "the single biggest need in the process of creating an adult [and more dialogical] church is to allow a genuine voice for the entire body of the faithful."[65] Such an adult and dialogical church, we believe, is demanded by the Pauline extension of charisms beyond offices to individual believers for the upbuilding of the church, and is supported by a central claim of the Second Vatican Council: "the body of the faithful as a whole, anointed as they are by the Holy One...cannot err in matters of belief."[66]

The collective responsibility of theologians as teachers of the whole church has profound implications for them and their relationship with the magisterium. For their part, theologians must be prudent in their presentation of controversial theological issues to Catholic lay people. For its part, the magisterium must be patient in allowing open debate on controversial topics among theologians and slow to intervene prematurely to close such debates. That patience also requires dialogue between the magisterium and theologians, without threat of disciplinary or punitive action. The tone of the *Instruction* neither evinces nor encourages such patience. We must look elsewhere for a model of dialogue grounded in the "unity of charity."[67]

The Magisterium of the Church's Pastors

If the charism of theologians has been too narrowly defined in the *Instruction*, the charism of the church's pastors has been too broadly defined. It notes that Christ bestowed on the pastors "the charism of infallibility in matters of faith and morals,"[68] and that bestowal is in no way being called into question in this chapter. What is being called into question are the tasks associated with that charism, the structures of governance in which it is exercised, the material to which it is extended, noninfallible teachings, and the claim of "divine assistance" in matters of disciplining theologians. We consider each of these points in turn.

The Task of the Charism of Infallibility

The task associated with the charism of infallibility is described as "authentically interpreting Revelation."[69] While this task might describe how the magisterium has been exercised in recent history, there is a serious question that challenges the full magisterial realization of this task. Sullivan points out that "authoritatively interpreting the Word of God, both in Scripture and Tradition," is problematic, for the exegesis of scripture and the documents of tradition is dependent upon a theological expertise that "few bishops are qualified for."[70] The late Cardinal Bernardin confirms this judgment.[71] If bishops are not qualified to do this scholarly work then they must consult with theologians who are qualified. As noted above, however, consultation is narrowly exercised in many magisterial pronouncements and is often limited to one school of theology, that school which uncritically supports the magisterial position. In addition, bishops who would consult with a broader contingent of voices may be criticized or ignored by Roman curial officials due to Roman centralization.[72] This centralization severely hampers bishops in the consultative process, limits the possibility of dialogue, and raises the issue of wise governance in the church.

Bishops and Structures of Government

Nicholas Lash comments insightfully on the current situation in the church. "The subordination of *education* to *governance* is at the very heart of the crisis of contemporary Catholicism."[73] Authority in the church has collapsed into governance without proper preparation, and the teaching that results from this collapse is "proclamation construed as command." Yves Congar, arguably the leading Catholic ecclesiologist of the twentieth century, points out that obedience to church authorities is called for when the church is conceived as a monarchy and dialogue and consensus are called for when it is conceived as a communion. "It is certain," he adds, "that this second conception was the one that prevailed effectively during the first thousand years of Christianity, whereas the other one dominated in the West between the eleventh-century reformation and Vatican II."[74] Today the magisterium seeks to command without having to "explain, prove, convince, appeal to human intelligence,"[75] and this has created both a crisis in credibility for church authority and a strain for the possibility of dialogue between the magisterium, theologians, and the entire body of the faithful.[76] What developments have taken place in the church to create this crisis of governance?

During Pope John Paul II's pontificate there was increasing Roman centralization, prioritizing the voice of the Roman Curia over the voices of local bishops and bishops' conferences.[77] With Roman centralization the magisterium has jeopardized one of its primary functions, "setting forth of truths which are especially relevant to the current situation;" such a setting forth of relevant truths is dependent upon accurately listening to, assessing, and responding to the needs of the local churches. Besides, doctrinal criteria for choosing bishops has come to hinge on a few litmus-test issues which carry disproportionate weight and ignore many of the pastoral needs of the local churches.[78] This narrowing of the pool of candidates for the episcopacy on the basis of restricted theological viewpoints has also negatively affected dialogue between bishops and theologians. Roman centralization, doctrinal litmus tests for appointing bishops, and continued exclusion of many theologians from the conversation will hamper the magisterium in realizing what it claims as one of its primary functions and further damage its credibility.

Charism of Infallibility and Non-Infallible Teaching

The *Instruction* seems to have difficulty finding a balance in the extension of the charism of infallibility to noninfallible teaching. While recognizing the legitimacy of theological inquiry, it is suspicious of theological pluralism. When it comes to noninfallible teaching, it takes an authoritarian posture and calls for submission and obedience. One detects in this approach Congar's monarchical church and creeping infallibilism. When new ideas are presented, all too frequently "discussion of new questions among theologians is cut off prematurely by doctrinal statements which are treated as definitive teaching."[79]

Discipline and Divine Assistance

Finally, the *Instruction* claims for the magisterium "divine assistance" in matters of discipline and asserts that the claim of a "violation of human rights" in such matters "is out of place."[80] A statement from the Catholic Theological Society of America accuses the CDF of failing "to honor fundamental human rights" when investigating theologians, and the *Instruction* formulates a response to this accusation on two counts. First, it distinguishes between the theologian and his or her "intellectual positions." Persons have rights, intellectual positions do not; to judge and censure an intellectual position does not involve an issue of human rights. Theologians who have undergone a magisterial investigation, however, testify to not only censure of their intellectual positions but also personal violations of justice, charity, due process, and human rights. The CDF seems to recognize this by proceeding to justify itself with a second response. It notes that there is a hierarchy of rights in which the individual's rights appear to be subordinate to the rights of the ecclesial community and the common good.[81] However, arguing for a hierarchy of rights does not mean that one can sacrifice the rights of one person in order to guarantee the rights of another, even if that other is the magisterium, and even if "truth" might be at stake. Pope John Paul II says as much in *Ut Unum Sint*. One cannot defend an exercise of the charism of authority that assaults basic human rights. A morally evil means never justifies an end, even when that end serves the magisterium's agenda.

UT UNUM SINT: COMPLEMENTARITY AND DIALOGUE

There appears to be a fundamental inconsistency in the magisterium's approach to dialogue depending on whether the dialogue partner is internal or external to the Catholic community. Internally, the *Instruction* juxtaposes the "unity of truth" with the "unity of charity" and is willing to sacrifice the latter where differences between theologians and the magisterium may jeopardize communion. Externally, the magisterium is open to dialogue in charity with those who are not within the Catholic community as they seek truth together. It was Pope John Paul II who, emphasizing the Council's commitment to ecumenism, introduced the concept of a "dialogue of charity."[82] This same dialogue of charity could be a starting point also *ad intra*, to facilitate a complementarity of charisms between theologians and magisterium. The model of dialogue rhetorically described in John Paul II's *Ut unum sint*, which provides an extensive discussion of the parameters for fruitful dialogue grounded in charity, could facilitate both objectives.

John Paul II presents a personalist approach to dialogue "rooted in the nature of the person and his dignity." Dialogue, he insists, is "an outright necessity, one of the church's priorities;"[83] it is "not simply an exchange of ideas [but] an exchange of gifts."[84] Open dialogue facilitates the exchange of charismata and, indeed, could itself be considered a charism, which should be exercised with all due respect, justice, and charity. The dialogue of charity includes also reciprocity. "It is necessary to pass from antagonism and conflict to a situation where each party recognizes the other as a *partner*. When undertaking dialogue, *each side must presuppose in the other a desire for reconciliation*, for *unity in truth*. For this to happen, any display of mutual opposition must disappear. Only thus will dialogue help to overcome division and lead us closer to unity."[85] The dialogue of charity, in the words of *Gaudium et spes*, requires us first of all to create in the church itself

> mutual esteem, reverence, and harmony, and to acknowledge all legitimate diversity; in this way, all who constitute the one People of God will be able to engage in ever more fruitful dialogue, whether they are pastors or other members of the faithful…Let there be unity in what is necessary, freedom in what is doubtful, and charity in everything.[86]

If human experience is a source for moral theology, as we argue in Chapter Four and as is universally agreed, and the theological experience in the Church is of plural theologies, then dialogue between those who theologically differ is a key toward mutual understanding, unity, and peace. Moral theologian, Jack Mahoney, judges that "it is from this dialectic, for the Church as for all believers, between belief and experience that there results what theology has come to term the development of doctrine."[87]

The commitment in ecumenical discussion to the dialogue of charity, grounded in the dignity of the human person and seeking to foster mutual understanding, reconciliation, and unity, is different from the juridical and authoritarian approach to dialogue presented in the *Instruction*. Given *Ut unum sint*'s reliance upon Vatican II's *Decree on Ecumenism* and *Declaration on Religious Freedom*, especially in its treatment of the nature and guidelines for dialogue, it is curious that these guidelines are not included in the *Instruction*. The human rights of theologians who are said to dissent from magisterial pronouncements are not protected by the religious freedom and the tolerance for the freedom of conscience eulogized in *Dignitatis humanae*.[88] It is ironic that the magisterium would emphasize dialogue in charity and even extend a hand of reconciliation to our separated brothers and sisters[89] but deny it to its own sons and daughters living out their vocations as Catholic theologians.[90] Instead of defending human dignity and human rights through dialogue in charity, the *Instruction* takes a defensive position vis-à-vis accusations that magisterial judgments against individual theologians might violate human rights, and it presents an implicit justification for sacrificing human rights in favor of "the ecclesial community and her common good."[91]

A COMPLEMENTARITY OF CHARISMS: NEW DIRECTIONS

If Bernardin's "unambiguous notion of complementarity in the work of arriving at magisterial teaching"[92] is ever to be realized, the model of dialogue of charity outlined in *Ut unum sint* must be allied to a development in the understanding of the respective charisms of the magisterium and theologians. Complementarity intends that certain, different realities belong together and produce together a reality that neither produces alone. The complementarity of the charisms of theologians and magisterium, as already noted, is intended to build up the church by preserving "the People of God in truth which sets free...."[93] We conclude with a treatment of those complementary charisms.

First, few theologians challenge the charism of magisterial infallibility; many challenge the extension of that charism to noninfallible magisterial teaching. To consistently refer to the charism of magisterial infallibility in reference to noninfallible teaching is misplaced. Even John Paul II notes that the fact that the dogmatic development which culminated in the solemn definition of the First Vatican Council has stressed the magisterium's charism of infallibility and clarified the conditions of its exercise "must not lead to the magisterium's being considered only from this standpoint."[94] This is a particularly trenchant warning in the case of noninfallible teaching. We grant a presumption of truth for noninfallible teaching, but the reality remains that such teaching may be, and historically has been, judged to be in error and reformed.[95]

In light of this fact, we propose that the phrase "the charism of infallibility" be eliminated from all discussions of noninfallible teaching and be replaced with the term, "the charism of learner-teacher,"[96] and that charism be seen as available to the whole communion-church, bishops, theologians, and the entire body of the faithful alike. A Scholastic rule exemplifies our meaning here. The Scholastic master had three tasks: *lectio*, or commentary on the Bible; *disputatio*, or teaching by objection and response; *praedicatio*, or communication of the theological word. "It is [only] after the *lectio* of scripture and after the examination of the doubtful points thanks to the *disputatio*, *and not before*, that we must preach."[97] Learning, which should always precede teaching, must involve a broad consultative process embracing bishops, theologians, and the entire body of the faithful living out their faith in a particular socio-historical context. We repeat that John Paul II's *Ut unum sint* offers a useful model of dialogue in charity for such a consultative process, though we regret that dialogue of charity has been evidenced more in words than in deeds in recent dealings between magisterium and theologians.

Second, the charism of teaching, as it relates to bishops, needs clarification. The "Working Paper for the Tenth Ordinary Assembly of the Synod of Bishops" notes that "the episcopal charism of teaching is uniquely the responsibility of each bishop" and it goes on to identify this charism as "proclaiming and living the word of God."[98] This statement is contained under the section entitled "Committed to Catechesis." The distinction made above between catechesis and theology applies here. John Henry Cardinal Newman highlighted the importance of the interaction between the prophetical, sacerdotal, and regal offices in the church, prioritizing the prophetic office over the others to correct their potential excesses. Within the prophetical office, he distinguished between preaching and teaching, ascribing preaching to the apostolic office and teaching to the *schola theologorum*.[99] Given Sullivan's assertion, which is undoubtedly true, that many contemporary lay theologians "are more competent to have an informed opinion on a theological question than are many bishops,"[100] it is perhaps wise that the Working Paper chose to identify the teaching of bishops with catechesis. We make that statement, however, without prejudice to what we asserted above, namely, that the charism of learner-teacher extends to every segment of our tripolar ecclesial relationship, magisterium, theologians, and the entire body of the faithful.

Third, the church should be careful not to identify charisms *exclusively* with offices. Charisms are gifts from the Spirit of God to persons who are to use them for the upbuilding of the community; they are not given as a result of office or for personal glory.[101] The history of the church makes it abundantly clear that the charisms often associated with the episcopal office do not guarantee a wise and pastoral rule or the ability to teach. The abuse of power by bishops in the recent sexual abuse scandal, [102] the centralization of church power in Rome and the Roman Curia, the doctrinal, non-pastoral litmus tests for the appointment of bishops, all suggest that the process for selecting bishops and structures of governance need reconsideration. [103]

We are not suggesting that the Spirit of Truth cannot give charisms to persons in offices, even *because* they are in offices, for that Spirit may and does give her gifts as she wills. We are suggesting, rather, that there must be an empirical, experiential means of verifying the charisms of bishops in the church independently from the office they hold, as there must also be a means of verifying the charisms of theologians and of the entire body of the faithful. The importance of such verification is suggested by the theological fact that the recipients of the Spirit's charisms have the duty, and, therefore, the right, to use them for the upbuilding of the church.

The charism of theologians also needs clarification and development. We can glean some insight into this charism by describing the theologian's role. In the nineteenth century, Michael Himes notes, Johann Sebastian Drey was one of the first Catholic theologians to recognize that shifts and developments in notions of doctrine, liturgy, and the institution itself "entailed a shift in the theologian's role." [104] The theologian could no longer be the uncritical defender of what had been previously taught and done. Through training, ability, and leisure to study, Himes further notes, theologians are "charged with trying to discern what ought to be taught and done in new circumstances." [105] The shift in the theologian's role implies a corresponding shift in her or his charisms. The implicit identification of the charism of theology with catechesis is incomplete. It ignores the evolving nature of theology as a scientific discipline and its task of exploring new questions with methods appropriate to that exploration. Theologians are called to serve the church through the charism of prayerful, scientific exploration and investigation. While such a charism should be exercised with prudence and caution, it is essential that it be exercised, in service of the church in its pursuit of a deeper understanding and more perfect formulation of doctrine.

The changing demographics of laity, clergy, and theologians within the church, to which we have already called attention, makes it even more critical to verify charisms so that they can be exercised without undue restraint by those who are discerned to be gifted with them. First, a more educated laity requires that the charism of teaching be discerned and perhaps redefined by theologians and the magisterium in dialogue. That charism demands a balance between presenting ideas that address the contextual needs, concerns, and questions of the faithful and not causing scandal. Second, as clerical vocations continue to decline and lay people continue to be more active in the church, governance in the church should reflect these changes. The principle of subsidiarity or participatory justice in leadership and church governance demands the discernment of the charism of leadership in both educated laity and theologians. The exclusion of the full spectrum of theological voices from the table of governance and decision making risks silencing voices that need to be heard.

Third, related to the principle of subsidiarity is the process of consultation by the magisterium *before* making magisterial pronouncements. This consultation should embrace all theologians, those whom Rome considers "safe" and "unsafe," those who may agree or disagree with magisterial positions on specific issues. Fourth, the changing demographics of theologians also demands discernment. Theologians today are primarily lay women and men, from first and third world countries, from multiple socio-ethnic backgrounds, of homosexual and heterosexual orientation, married and single, with and without children, who bring a variety of experiences, relationships, and reflections to the theological discipline. As theologians are plural, so too are their theological positions. The magisterium must learn to appreciate this diversity and to seriously consider its contributions as a manifestation of the Holy Spirit at work in the world, not as a threat to be controlled and silenced.

Although the introduction of ideas that challenge magisterial teaching may cause tension, it is an essential way for a pilgrim church to move towards the full possession of truth. The believer's journey toward an understanding of the infinite God is, as Karl Rahner used to say, an asymptotic journey into the Holy Mystery.[106] Journeys always surprise the traveler with the unexpected, but confronting the unexpected in the company of the gracious Spirit who leads into all truth ought not to be a fearful experience for a faithful church. Magisterium, theologians, and the entire body of the faithful might do well to ponder Joan Chittister's oyster parable and what she calls the ministry or charism of irritation. "During the spawning season…when the sand invades the oyster, the oyster emits a gel to protect itself from the sand…. The more sand that comes in, the more gel is excreted. So at the end of the process…you have a pearl, [and] the oyster is more valuable."[107] If it is through irritation by sand that real pearls are created, so too it is through irritation by faithful criticism, from whatever source, that theological and doctrinal pearls are created.

Finally, the pursuit of truth and the personalist model of dialogue developed in *Ut unum sint* must inform the charism of both theologians and bishops:

> Truth is to be sought after in a manner proper to the dignity of the human person and his social nature. The inquiry is to be free, carried on with the aid of teaching or instruction, communication, and dialogue. In the course of these, people explain to one another the truth they have discovered, or think they have discovered, in order thus to assist one another in the quest for truth. Moreover, as the truth is discovered, it is by a personal assent that individuals are to adhere to it.[108]

This truly personalist, as distinct from authoritarian, model of dialogue facilitates the sharing and mutual enhancement of charisms and could itself be considered a charism, which must be exercised with due respect, justice, and charity.

CONCLUSION

We conclude with a statement from the International Theological Commission.

> The exercise of their tasks by the magisterium and by theologians often gives rise to a certain tension. This is not surprising, nor should one expect that such tension can ever be fully resolved here on earth. On the contrary, wherever there is genuine life, there will also be some tension. Such tension need not be interpreted as hostility or real opposition, but can be seen as a vital force and an incentive to a common carrying out of their respective tasks by way of dialogue. [109]

Jayne Hoose comments that "tradition must dialogue with what is contemporary in order to be credible." [110] The way of dialogue is more adequately developed and constructively formulated in Pope John Paul II's *Ut unum sint* than in the Congregation for the Doctrine of the Faith's *Instruction*. The encyclical provides a guide for transforming the opposition of charisms between theologians and the magisterium into a cooperation and complementarity of charisms as magisterium, theologians, and the entire body of the faithful journey together to the Holy Mystery in an ongoing dialogue of charity. We now proceed to consider this dialogue as it occurs specifically in the analysis of human sexuality.

QUESTIONS FOR REFLECTION

1. What do you understand by the word *charism*. Who is the source of charisms and who are their beneficiaries?
2. Cardinal Avery Dulles notes that the Church has two kinds of teachers: "a class of official teachers whose task is to establish the official doctrine of the Church and a class of theologians whose function is to investigate the questions concerning faith in a scholarly way." What do you think should be the relationship between these two classes of teachers?
3. In 1990, the Congregation for the Doctrine of the Faith published an *Instruction on the Ecclesial Vocation of the Theologian*. In that *Instruction* it taught that the Church needed its theologians and the truth of any theological proposal need to be discerned through "fraternal

dialogue." Do you see any signs of such fraternal dialogue in the Church between Magisterium and theologians or between Magisterium and laity? How do you think such dialogue could or should take place?

4. It is commonly held that theologians function in the Church in a two-way directional mediation, from the faith and questions of the laity to the teaching of the Magisterium and from the teaching of the Magisterium back to the laity. How do you think this two-way mediation might function? Were you aware that Pope Francis had commissioned a survey on the family to be answered by the whole Church for just such mediation? What could be the potential benefits for the Church of such a survey?

5. What do you understand by the terms *infallible* and *non-infallible* teaching? There is great polarity in the Church these days created by differing attitudes to these two kinds of teaching. The Second Vatican Council's *Constitution on the Church in the Modern World* taught that this polarity could be solved only by dialogue which "requires us first of all to create in the Church itself mutual esteem, reverence, and harmony, and to acknowledge all legitimate diversity" (n. 92). How do you envision this dialogue taking place? Do you see any sign of the required genuine dialogue in the Church today?

NOTES

An earlier version of this essay appeared in *Horizons* 36, no. 1 (2009): 7–31. It is reprinted here with permission.

1. In this essay, the term "the magisterium" with the definite article refers to both hierarchical officeholders and their teaching function in the Catholic Church.

2. Joseph Bernardin, "Magisterium and Theologians: Steps towards Dialogue," *Chicago Studies* 17, no. 2 (1978): 158.

3. Pope John Paul II, *Ut unum sint*, nn. 17, 51, and 60.

4. Pope Paul VI, *Ecclesiam suam*, esp. ch. 3.

5. Karl Rahner, S.J., "The Teaching Office of the Church in the Present-Day Crisis of Authority," in his *Theological Investigations*, vol. XII (New York: Crossroad, 1974), 3.

6. René Laurentin, "Charisms: Terminological Precision," in *Charisms in the Church, Concilium*, vol. 109, ed. Christian Duquoc and Casiano Floristan (New York: Crossroad, 1978), 8.

7. John C. Haughey, "Charismata: An Ecclesiological Exploration," in *Retrieving Charismata for the Twenty-First Century*, ed. Doris Donnelly (Collegeville: Liturgical Press, 1999), 10.

8. Yves Congar, "Theologians and the Magisterium in the West: From the Gregorian Reform to the Council of Trent," *Chicago Studies* 17, no. 2 (1978): 223.

9. Michael D. Place, "From Solicitude to Magisterium: Theologians and the Magisterium from the Council of Trent to the First Vatican Council," *Chicago Studies* 17, no. 2 (1978): 226.

10. Karl Rahner, S.J., "Observations on the Factor of the Charismatic in the Church," in his *Theological Investigations*, vol. XII (New York: Crossroad, 1974), 81.

11. See Thomas Aquinas, *Quodlibet* 3, 4, 1, ad 3; and *Contra Impugn. Caput 2.*

12. See Henricus Denzinger and Adolph Schonmetzer, *Enchiridion Symbolorum, Definitionum, et Declarationum de Rebus Fidei et Morum* (Freiburg: Herder, 1965), n. 3886.

13. Rahner, "Observations," 85.

14. *Lumen gentium*, n. 7.

15. Ibid., n. 12; emphasis added.

16. Francis A. Sullivan, *Charisms and Charismatic Renewal: A Biblical and Theological Study* (Ann Arbor: Servant Books, 1982), 13.

17. Avery Dulles, "The Two Magisteria: An Interim Reflection," in *Catholic Theological Society of America: Proceedings of the Thirty-Fifth Annual Convention*, ed. Luke Salm (Mahwah, NJ: CTSA, 1981), 155.

18. Ibid., 165.

19. Rahner, "Observations," 85.

20. Congregation for the Doctrine of the Faith, *Instruction on the Ecclesial Vocation of the Theologian* (Vatican City: Libreria Editrice Vaticana, 1990). Hereafter *Instruction.*

21. *Instruction*, n. 1.

22. See John P. Boyle, *Church Teaching Authority: Historical and Theological Studies* (Notre Dame: University of Notre Dame Press, 1995), 142–160; Francis A. Sullivan, *Creative Fidelity: Weighing and Interpreting Documents of the Magisterium* (Mahwah, NJ: Paulist, 1996), 15–27.

23. *Instruction*, n. 40.

24. Ibid., n. 6.

25. Ibid., n. 7.

26. Ibid., n. 9.

27. Ibid., n. 11.

28. Ibid., n. 13.

29. *Lumen gentium*, n. 12.

30. Congregation for the Doctrine of the Faith, *Mysterium ecclesiae*, n. 2.

31. *Instruction*, nn. 15, 16, 17, 23, and 33.

32. Ibid., n. 16.

33. Ibid., n. 17.

34. Ibid., n. 20.

35. Ibid., n. 21.

36. Ibid., n. 26.

37. Ibid., n. 32. See *Dignitatis humanae*, n. 10.

38. *Instruction*, n. 37.

39. Ibid., n. 40.

40. Ibid., n. 37.

41. See Denzinger-Schonmetzer, *Enchiridion Symbolorum*, nn. 3073–74.

42. *Instruction*, n. 40

43. *Christifideles laici*, n. 33; emphasis added.

44. *Instruction*, n. 7.

45. Yves Congar, "A Brief History of the Forms of the Magisterium and Its Relations with Scholars," in *The Magisterium and Morality: Readings in Moral Theology No. 3*, ed. Charles E. Curran and Richard A. McCormick (New York: Paulist, 1982), 314–15.

46. *Catechism of the Catholic Church*, n. 5; see also, United States Catholic Conference of Bishops, *Co-Workers in the Vineyard of the Lord* (Washington, DC: USCCB, 2005), n. 43.

47. Francis. A. Sullivan, *Magisterium* (Mahwah, NJ: Paulist Press, 1983), 193.

48. *Instruction*, n. 22.

49. Catholic Theological Society of America (CTSA), "Church Procedures and Authority," *Origins* 20, no. 29 (December 27, 1990), 464, n. 21.

50. Richard. A. McCormick, "Some Early Reactions to *Veritatis splendor*," in *John Paul II and Moral Theology: Readings in Moral Theology No. 10*, ed. Charles Curran and Richard A. McCormick (New York: Paulist Press, 1998), 9–10.

51. Ibid., 10. See also, Todd Salzman, *Deontology and Teleology: An Investigation of the Normative Debate in Roman Catholic Moral Theology* (Leuven: Peeters Press, 1995), 307.

52. Pope John Paul II, *Veritatis splendor*, *Origins* 23, no. 18 (October 14, 1993): n. 4.

53. Others have made this same point. See Francis A. Sullivan, "The Sense of Faith: The Sense/Consensus of the Faithful," in *Authority in the Roman Catholic Church: Theory and Practice*, ed. Bernard Hoose (Burlington, VT: Ashgate, 2002), 90; Paul Lakeland, *The Liberation of the Laity: In Search of an Accountable Church* (New York: Continuum, 2003), 67, 205–7; Bradford Hinze, *Practices of Dialogue in the Roman Catholic Church: Aims and Obstacles, Lessons and Laments* (New York: Continuum, 2006), 247.

54. See, for instance, *Lumen gentium*, n. 37; and *Gaudium et spes*, nn. 13, 21, 33, 37, 44, 46, and 52.

55. See *Veritatis splendor*, nn. 53, 86, and 98; *Redemptor hominis*, n. 17; *Familiaris consortio*, nn. 32 and 73.

56. This term is borrowed from Jorg Rieger, *Remember the Poor: The Challenge to Theology in the Twenty-First Century* (Harrisburg: Trinity Press International, 1998), 1–5. Rieger uses it to dramatize the situation of the poor and oppressed. The term is given greater import in Guttierez' description of Jesus as "God become poor." See Gustavo Guttierez, *The Power of the Poor in History* (New York: Orbis, 1983), 13.

57. Norbert Rigali, S.J., "The Ecclesial Responsibilities of Theologians, Forty Years after Vatican II," *Horizons* 33, no. 2 (2006): 299.

58. Ibid.

59. Roger Haight, *Jesus, Symbol of God* (Maryknoll, NY: Orbis, 1999).

60. "Statement of the Board of Directors, The Catholic Theological Society of America, with Respect to the Notification Issued by the Congregation for the Doctrine of the Faith Concerning the book, *Jesus: Symbol of God*, by Rev. Roger Haight, S.J. and Prohibiting Fr. Haight from Teaching Catholic Theology," http://www.ctsa-online.org/haight.html.

61. Rigali, "The Ecclesial Responsibilities," 301.

62. Ibid., 302.

63. *Lumen gentium*, nn. 10–13.

64. This is an apt point to recall Cardinal Newman's judgment about the laity during the Arian controversy, published in his famous essay "On Consulting the Faithful." Newman judged that it was not the bishops who saved the church from Arianism, for "the body of bishops failed in their confession of faith," but the laity who were "preeminent in faith, zeal, courage, and constancy." It was "mainly by the faithful people," judged Newman, "that paganism was overthrown." See John Henry Newman, *On Consulting the Faithful in Matters of Doctrine*, ed. John Coulson (New York: Sheed and Ward, 1961), 10.

65. Paul Lakeland, *Catholicism at the Crossroads: How the Laity Can Save the Church* (New York: Continuum, 2007), 99.

66. *Lumen gentium*, n. 12.

67. *Instruction*, n. 26.

68. Ibid., n. 15.

69. Ibid.

70. Sullivan, *Magisterium*, 192; "The Sense of the Faith," 90.

71. Bernardin, "Magisterium and Theologians," 153.

72. See CTSA, "Church Procedures," 14–18.

73. Nicholas Lash, "Authors, Authority and Authorization," in *Authority in the Roman Catholic Church*, ed. Hoose, 59, emphasis added.

74. Yves Congar, "Reception as an Ecclesiological Reality," in *Election and Consensus in the Church, Concilium* vol. 77, ed. Giuseppe Alberigo and A. Weiler (Freiburg: Herder and Herder, 1972), 62.

75. Walter Burghardt, *Long Have I loved You: A Theologian Reflects on his Church* (Maryknoll: New York, 2000), 332.

76. At this point, we are tempted to pause to consider the contribution of the entire body of the faithful to doctrinal formulations in the contemporary recovery of the theological notions of reception and *sensus fidei*, but space does not permit such a pause. Readers who wish information on that matter may consult Sullivan, "The Sense of Faith," 85–93; Richard R. Gaillardetz, "The Reception of Doctrine: New Perspectives," in *Authority in the Roman Catholic Church*, ed. Hoose, 95–114; Michael G. Lawler, *What Is and What Ought to Be: The Dialectic of Experience, Theology, and Church* (New York: Continuum, 2005), 119–42.

77. CTSA, "Church Procedures," 16.

78. Ibid., 13.

79. Ibid., 22.

80. *Instruction*, n. 37.

81. Ibid.

82. See *Ut unum sint*, nn. 17, 51, and 60.

83. Ibid., n. 31.

84. Ibid., n. 28.

85. Ibid., n. 29, emphasis in original.

86. *Gaudium et spes*, n. 92.

87. Jack Mahoney, *The Making of Moral Theology: A Study of the Roman Catholic Tradition* (Oxford: Clarendon, 1987), 218.

88. *Gaudium et spes*, n. 36.

89. Pope Benedict XVI's lifting of the excommunications of the Lefebvrite bishops is a recent example of this. See, for example, John L. Allen, "Vatican Lifts Excommunication," in *National Catholic Reporter* (February 6, 2009): 1.

90. See extensive examples and modes of dialogue exercised in and by the Catholic Church in Hinze, *Practices of Dialogue in the Roman Catholic Church*, passim.

91. *Instruction*, n. 37.

92. Bernardin, "Magisterium and Theologians," 158.

93. *Instruction*, n. 21.

94. Pope John Paul II, "How Authority is Conceived," *Origins* 25, no. 34 (February 15, 1996): 572–74, n. 3.

95. See John T. Noonan, *A Church that Can and Cannot Change: The Development of Catholic Moral Teaching* (Notre Dame, IN: University of Notre Dame Press, 2005).

96. See Ladislas Örsy, *The Church Learning and Teaching: Magisterium, Assent, Dissent, Academic Freedom* (Collegeville, MN: The Liturgical Press, 1991).

97. Peter Cantor, *Verbum abbreviatum*, 1, in *Patrologiae Cursus Completus: Series Latina*, vol. 205, ed. J. P. Migne (Paris: Garnier, 1844-1904), 25, emphasis added.

98. Vatican Synod Secretariat, "The Bishop: Servant of the Gospel of Jesus Christ for the Hope of the World," Working Paper for 10th Ordinary Assembly of the Synod of Bishops, *Origins* 31, no. 5 (June 14, 2001): 65, 67–104, 105.

99. John Henry Newman, *The Via Media of the Anglican Church*, vol. 1 (London: Longmans, 1906), xlvii.

100. Sullivan, "The Sense of the Faith," 90.

101. Michael G. Lawler and Thomas J. Shanahan, *Church: A Spirited Communion* (Collegeville, MN: Liturgical Press, 1995), 67.

102. See Geoffrey Robinson, *Confronting Power and Sex in the Catholic Church: Reclaiming the Spirit of Jesus* (Collegeville, MN: Liturgical Press, 2008).

103. The election of bishops in the early church by local clerics and laity is beyond doubt. See, for example, Hugh Lawrence, "Spiritual Authority and Governance: A Historical Perspective," in *Authority in the Roman Catholic Church*, ed. Hoose, 38–39; Pope Celestine decreed that "no bishop is to be imposed on people who do not want him" (*Epist. 45*, *Patrologia Latina*, vol. 50, 434); Pope Leo the Great is equally emphatic: "He who is to preside over all must be chosen by all. There is required the vote of the clergy, the testimony of honored witnesses, the consent of order and of the people" (*Ad Anas.*, *Patrologia Latina*, vol. 54, 634); Cyprian declared, contrary to Pope Stephen, that this is of divine origin (*Epist.* LXVII, 4, *Saint Cyprien: Correspondence*, ed. Louis Bayard (Paris: Belles Lettres, 1925), 229–30. See Patrick Granfield, "Episcopal Election in Cyprian: Clerical and Lay Participation," in *Theological Studies* 37, no. 1 (1976): 41–52.

104. Michael Himes, "Introduction," in J. S. Drey, *Brief Introduction to the Study of Theology: With Reference to the Scientific Standpoint and the Catholic System* (Notre Dame, IN: University of Notre Dame Press, 1994), xxvi.

105. Ibid., xxv.

106. See Karl Rahner, S.J., *Foundations of Christian Faith: An Introduction to the Idea of Christianity* (New York: Seabury, 1978), 65–71.

107. Angela Bonavoglia, *Good Catholic Girls* (New York: Reganbooks, 2005), 7.

108. *Ut unum sint*, n. 18; cites *Dignitatis humanae*, n. 3.

109. International Theological Commission, *Theses on the Relationship Between the Ecclesiastical Magisterium and Theology* (Washington: United States Catholic Conference, 1977), n. 7.

110. Jayne Hoose, "Dialogue as Tradition," in *Moral Theology for the Twenty-First Century*, ed. Bernard Hoose, Julie Clague, and Gerard Mannion (Edinburgh: T&T Clark, 2008), 65.

Chapter Three

The Mystery of Sexuality

Catholic Reflections

Having considered method in moral theology or theological ethics and the different ethical theories to which different methods give rise, we now proceed to apply this analysis to the reality of human sexuality, which the United States Catholic Conference of Bishops (USCCB) calls a "great mystery."[1] Mystery is a term that permeates and energizes the Catholic tradition. In its strictest terms, *mysterium verum et proprie dictum*,[2] it refers to the infinite incomprehensibility of God, even in the Beatific Vision. In common, analogical language, it connotes something beyond human understanding, something that is incomprehensible to humans unless revealed by some higher power. In this essay, briefly and only to establish the root Catholic theological meanings of the word *mystery*, we first consider the mystery of God and God's created *oikonomia*. We then consider what the USCCB calls in the second, analogical sense of mystery the mystery of sexuality in its physical, psychological/emotional, and spiritual/relational dimensions.[3] We offer a mystagogy of this great mystery, a science-based interpretation of it, leading to a theological understanding of its role as lower-case sacrament of the presence of the triune God in the present *oikonomia*. We conclude that human sexuality demands ongoing analysis to be, first, better understood physically, psychologically/emotionally, and spiritually/relationally in order, second, to be better understood theologically as lower-case sacrament revelatory of the incomprehensible God.

Before proceeding, however, we must make clear the difference between the words and concepts *sex* and *sexuality*. *Sex* differentiates an animal species into either male or female, and this with special attention to the animal's reproductive function. It is not to be confused, as it frequently is confused in

Catholic magisterial documents, with the social construct *gender*. Sex is a physiological reality which makes humans either man or woman. Gender is a culturally constructed reality which makes men and women masculine or feminine and shapes how they perceive, in general, the world in which they live and, in particular, how men and women relate to one another in a particular culture.[4] Sex is universally one among humans; gender is culturally plural. We mention here, but will not develop, a fact that usually surprises our students, namely, that the ancient world, in contrast to our taken-for-granted sexual dimorphism, judged that there was only one sex. That sex was male, and females were judged to be not fully developed males. Hence the still-used designation of humans as *man* or *mankind*, the prevalence of patriarchy and sexism, and the description of females as the weaker sex. Contemporary science, rather than seeing human sex on the dimorphic scale, a person is either male or female, sees it as a continuum between male and female. On that continuum lie heterosexual males and females, homosexual males and females, and bisexual males and females. Societies' and Churches' refusal to acknowledge this continuum has led to the almost universal scorn for and persecution of gay and lesbian men and women, which we will consider in Chapter Six. The dignity of each and every person created in the image and likeness of God (Gen 1:26) is at the very heart of Catholic morality. "God does not love someone any less," the USCCB teaches, "simply because he or she is homosexual."[5]

Sexuality, a term which came into use only in the 1860s as part of medical discourse and therefore not to be read back into pre-modern times, is an essential dimension of being human and shapes our approach to life in general and to relationships in particular. Sexuality, the Pontifical Council for the Family teaches, "concerns the intimate nucleus of the person."[6] The *Catechism of the Catholic Church* offers a more extended description: "Sexuality affects all aspects of the human person in the unity of his body and soul. It especially concerns affectivity, the capacity to love, and to procreate, and in a more general way the aptitude for forming bonds of communion with others."[7] Sexuality, the USCCB teaches along the same lines, "refers to a fundamental component of personality in and through which we, as male or female, experience our relatedness to self, others, the world, and even God."[8] In and through sexuality, humans enter relationships in and through which they become both whole and holy.

MYSTERY, *THEOLOGIA*, AND *OIKONOMIA*

In Catholic theological language, there are many understandings of the word *mystery*, but in this essay we collate them in two broad fundamental understandings. In the first understanding, mystery refers to God and God's absolute incomprehensibility. For all-too-finite humans, the infinite God is not just unknown, *Deus ignotus*, but also infinitely incomprehensible, *Deus absconditus*. The First Vatican Council, in its fight against a too-confident rationalism, taught that "surpassing those things to which natural reason can attain, there are proposed to our belief mysteries hidden in God, which cannot be known unless they are revealed by God."[9] It goes on to declare that, "by their very nature, the divine mysteries surpass the created intellect, so that even when they are communicated by revelation and received by faith they remain obscured by the veil of faith and shrouded in a quasi-darkness, as long as in this mortal life we are on pilgrimage far from the Lord."[10] The second understanding of mystery is biblical rather than philosophical. God, the Letter to the Ephesians tells the followers of Jesus, "has made known to us in all wisdom and insight the mystery [*musterion*] of his will, according to his purpose which he set forth in Christ as a plan [*oikonomian*] for the fullness of time, to unite all things in him, things in heaven and things on earth" (Eph 1: 9–10).

This plan, the Catholic tradition teaches, was definitively accomplished by the incarnation of God's Son and ever more clearly revealed in human history by the Spirit the Son sent. As a direct result of the saving incarnation of the Son and the gracing inspiration of the Spirit in it, human history is transformed into a history of revelation, of grace, and of salvation.[11] Trinity, incarnation, and grace, *mysteria proprie dicta*, are all embedded in human history and can, therefore, be discerned and darkly known from that history and the created realities that comprise it.[12] For this reason, the Greek and Latin Fathers located the biblical mystery, the saving plan of God worked out in human history, as *musterion* and *sacramentum* respectively. Those *musteria* and *sacramenta*, contemporary Catholic theologians explain,[13] are not only the seven upper-case, paradigmatic Sacraments the Catholic Church administers but also all those lower-case and recurring sacraments that men and women experience in their real history as real symbols of God.

The two understandings of mystery are not unrelated, and in contemporary Catholic theology their relationship is variously described. Karl Rahner relates the second understanding to the first. There is only one mystery, he argues, with two aspects, the mystery of the essential being of the incomprehensible God and of the saving presence of this God in human history. This assertion leads him to his basic thesis: "the 'economic' Trinity is the 'immanent' Trinity and the 'immanent' Trinity is the 'economic' Trinity."[14] This thesis, when established,

> first, takes into account the really binding data of the doctrine of the Trinity as presented by the magisterium; next can more naturally do justice to the biblical statements concerning the economy of salvation and its threefold structure, and to explicit biblical statements concerning the Father, the Son, and the

> Spirit, so that we are no longer embarrassed by the simple fact that in reality the scriptures do not explicitly present a doctrine of the 'immanent' Trinity; finally helps us to understand that in the Christian's act of faith, as s*alutary* faith, and in the Christian's life the Trinity is present and has to be present. [15]

The threefold structure of the economy of salvation is, of course, the revelation of God as Trinity, Father, Son, and Holy Spirit, a structure that could never have been known had God not revealed it in salvation history.

Catherine Mowry Lacugna also judges that the two understandings of mystery are united, but she explains them differently. The first she names *theologia*, the second *oikonomia*. *Theologia* is "the mystery of God as such;" *oikonomia* is "the economy of salvation, the self-communication of God in the person of Christ and the activity of the Holy Spirit." [16] All *theologia* is rooted in *oikonomia*, which "shows that the fundamental issue in trinitarian theology is not the inner workings of the 'immanent' Trinity, but the question of how the Trinitarian pattern of salvation history is to be correlated with the eternal being of God." [17] The pattern of the relationship between *theologia* and *oikonomia* may be described, as it is in contemporary Christology, as a pattern of *theologia* "from below," from the actual *oikonomia* of salvation, rather than "from above," from the speculated inner life of God.

SEXUALITY

Following the lead of the USCCB, and without suggesting in any way that it is a mystery in the proper and strict sense like the mystery of God, we consider human sexuality under the genus of mystery and the species of *oikonomia*. [18] "The gift of human sexuality can be a great mystery at times," the bishops teach. [19] Indeed it can, and perhaps must be, burdened and obscured as it is in another mystery in *oikonomia*, the finiteness and sinfulness of human life. The acknowledgment of mystery, however, does not free the theologian from the ongoing task of discerning the human as sexual person and of determining the meaning and morality of the sexuality and sexual acts of a person who is *simul iustus et peccator*.

The claim that human sexuality is a created element in God's *oikonomia* entails three theological claims. First, human sexuality is an integral part of the great sweep of salvation history and the triune God is incarnated in it. To illustrate this theological claim, a group commissioned by the USCCB boldly asserts that mutually pleasurable marital sexual acts are possibly the human experiences that most fully symbolize the loving communication between the divine Trinity. [20] Second, sexuality is one of those many lower-case sacraments in which God is incarnated in human lives, waiting to be discerned and revealed. It is, as Pope Paul VI once defined mystery, "a reality imbued with the presence of God." Third, as a reality imbued with the presence of the incomprehensible God, Paul VI further argued, sexuality is "of such a nature that there are ever-new and deeper explorations of it possible."[21] Not only is ever-new exploration possible, we suggest, it is also necessary, and Paul's successor, John Paul II, suggests how that exploration might be carried out.

"The Church values sociological and statistical research," John Paul asserts, "when it proves helpful in understanding the historical context in which pastoral action has to be developed and when it leads to a better understanding of the truth."[22] We suggest there is no doubt that, despite its well-known excesses, the sexual science of the twentieth century has led to a better understanding of the truth about human sexuality and, therefore also, after theological discernment, to a better understanding of God's *oikonomia* and ultimately of Godself. One of the things that science has taught us is that human sexuality is multi-dimensional; it has *physical, emotional, psychological, spiritual,* and *relational* dimensions. To those dimensions we now turn.

Physical Sexuality

We deal first with the embodiment of sexuality in physical sexuality, the joining of bodies in sexual intercourse. In their treatment of sexuality, Masters and Johnson explain four phases in the process of sexual intercourse. Phase One is the excitement phase, in which, for the man, the penis becomes erect due to the flow of blood into the penile tissues and, for the woman, there is moistening of the vagina, enlarged breasts, and tensing of the muscles with increased breathing and heart rate. Phase Two is the plateau phase, the entry of the penis into the vagina, further quickening of the heart and breathing, mounting erotic pleasure, and the appearance of a flush on both bodies. Frequently noted in this phase is the penetration of the female by the male; not so frequently noted, but true in every just and loving intercourse, is the welcoming envelopment of the male by the female. The male penetrates the female, not only physically but also psychologically and emotionally, and is physically enveloped by her who, in turn, enters emotionally and psychologically into the male. In their intercourse they become, in very deed, a two-in-one-bodiness.[23]

Phase Three, the climax, discharge of semen by the male and a number of orgasmic muscle spasms by the female, is the moment of greatest sexual pleasure. This pleasure is, of course, quite individual, and it is part of the ambiguity of sexuality and sexual intercourse that, in the climactic moments of orgasm, the act intended to be the giving of one person to the other throws each back on herself and himself in a solitude of pleasure. The act that is intended to be and is indeed fully unitive, at its peak moment, is also paradoxically divisive. Michel Foucault reminds us of the similarity the ancients saw between sexual orgasm and an epileptic fit,[24] both moments of being most alone and vulnerable. This is but one instance of the essential ambiguity of sexual activity; we will call attention to others as this section unfolds. Phase Four is the resolution phase, in which the couple relax and blood pressure and respiration return to normal.[25] Though these four phases are not to be "used as a 'check list' against which to measure sexual performance,"[26] every sexually active couple can, at least sometimes, identify them in their intercourse, a natural fact that offers profound evidence for the sexual *oikonomia* planned by the Creator-God.

Meanings of Physical Sexuality: Pleasure and Love-Making

There are two related meanings of these various physical stages of sexual intercourse. The first is the natural pleasure associated with it; the second is the human interpretation of it as love-making. Sexual pleasure has always been morally suspect in the Christian traditions, even though it is demonstrably an intrinsic dimension of both God's creation and just and loving sexual intercourse. Sexual pleasure is an obvious dimension of the mystery of God's *oikonomia*, a good created by God and gifted as grace to women and men. Like all gifts, it can be used for good and it can be used for evil, and the abuses of sexual pleasure and a hedonistic morality based *exclusively* on pleasure are fully evident in the historical past and present. The pleasure of the couple genuinely making love is good, the pleasure of the rapist is evil. The abuses of sex and pleasure, however, ought not and do not diminish the essential and valuable place of sexual pleasure as a natural component of human sexual morality.

As for Plato and Aristotle, so also for Augustine and Aquinas sexual activity and pleasure are "occupations with lower affairs which distract the soul and make it unworthy of being joined actually to God."[27] They are not, however, sinful at all times and in all circumstances. Augustine restricts moral sex to marriage and procreative intercourse: "Intercourse which is necessary for the purpose of generation is blameless, and only this kind belongs to marriage. But that which goes beyond this necessity follows not reason but lust [desire]."[28] Platonic Augustine, with his dualist hierarchy of body and soul, has no doubt what the problem with lust/desire is. "I feel that nothing more casts down the masculine mind from the heights than female allurements and that contact of bodies without which a wife cannot be had."[29] Note that it is the *masculine* mind that is cast down, loses control, and made irresponsible to the neglect of his duties; the *feminine* mind at the time simply did not count. Evil, however, "does not follow because marriages [and the sexual intercourse that characterizes them] are good, but because in the good things of marriage there is also a use that is evil. Sexual intercourse was not created because of the concupiscence of the flesh, but because of good. That good would have remained without that evil if no one had sinned."[30] Thomas Aquinas repudiated this Augustinian position that sexual pleasure was a bad thing, arguing that within marriage sexual intercourse is meritorious,[31] and to forego the pleasure and thwart the end would be sinful.[32] That said, however, he still held the Augustinian view that sex for the sole purpose of pleasure was sinful, and the later Catholic tradition followed him in this view. John Boswell documents the difficulty in the tradition, perhaps even the impossibility, of a heterosexual relationship based on mutual love because of the cultural, hierarchical value-differentiation between men and women.[33]

Ultimately, his more positive view of sex and pleasure led Aquinas and his teacher Albert the Great, for the first time in Catholic history to the further unequivocal judgment that marriage is an upper-case Sacrament of the incomprehensible God,[34] which means that those *oikonomia*-gifts so central to marriage, sexual activity, sexual pleasure, and sexual love-making are lower-case sacraments. Aquinas understood, at least inchoately, that the relationship between a husband and a wife should be one of friendship and that sexual intercourse enhances that friendship.[35] His contemporary and theological rival, the Franciscan Bonaventure, is more explicit, calling friendship between the spouses the lower-case sacrament of the relationship between God and the soul.[36] Basil Hume, the saintly twentieth-century Archbishop of Westminster, followed the line set by both. "When two persons love," he wrote after the death of a close friend, "*whether of the same sex or of a different sex*...they experience in a limited manner in this world what will be their unending delight when one with God in the next."[37] Or perhaps he was following his English compatriot, Aelred of Rievaulx, who in his classic treatise on friendship made the extraordinary, but defensible, claim: *Deus amicitia est*, God is friendship.[38] An essential component of any Christian sexual ethical principle, then, we suggest, must be a deeper understanding of sexual activity, sexual pleasure, and sexual love-making, with a major caveat.

We distinguish two types of pleasure in sexual intercourse: the pleasure of need and the pleasure of appreciation. The pleasure of need arises from the satisfying of the physical need a person has as the result of sexual desire. This pleasure is *taken* rather than *shared*, and it brings sexual release, which can just as easily be achieved alone. The pleasure of appreciation results not from *taking* pleasure in the fulfillment of a personal need but in justly and lovingly *sharing* pleasure with a loved partner, and it can never be achieved alone. The pleasure of appreciation is as much given as taken, and it brings not only physical relief but also personal, shared satisfaction and an enhanced sense of partnership. In sexual intercourse, both pleasures are available, but it is only when the pleasure of satisfaction is shared that the partners may be said to be "making love."[39]

The second meaning of sexual activity is love-making, a term that demands explanation. I have needs, and so do others: needs for trust, for respect, for affection, for safety, for understanding, for acceptance as I am. Some people commit themselves to respond to my needs and I commit myself to respond to theirs. We are, we say, friends. We companion one another on life's journey; we reveal ourselves mutually to one another; we assist one another and sustain one another when one or the other is weak; we provoke one another to realize our highest potential, to be the best we can be; we rejoice together when the best is achieved. In short, we will good to one another; in an ancient understanding, we love one another. [40] It is love that is willing good to one another we seek to clarify in this section.

As a freely willed act, love is a species of promise or commitment, the giving of my word to do something, namely, to will and to actively seek the good of another. The action in which my commitment is expressed, whether it be a promise to love until death do us part or a particular just and loving sexual action is the symbol of both my present love and my intention to love for the whole of life. This symbol so relates and bonds me to the one I love that she or he can legitimately object ever after: "but you promised." We mutually commit to one another as lovers to make our love permanent and to communicate it as permanent. In reality, of course, because of the finiteness and sinfulness of human lives, though we can *intend* our love to be indissoluble, we cannot actually *make* it indissoluble at any given moment of our lives, for love, as life, stretches out into the unknown and uncontrollable future. What we can do, in Margaret Farley's wise words, is "initiate in the present a new form of relationship that will endure in the form of fidelity or betrayal." Commitment, to both the one loved and to the loving relationship, she continues, "is love's way of being whole while it still grows into wholeness."[41]

The Greeks distinguished four kinds of love: *storge*, the love we call affection; *eros*, the love we call desire; *philia*, the mutual love we call friendship; *agape*, the love we call unconditional or self-sacrificing love. Though all four are legitimately called love, the good that is striven for in each is distinct. *Eros* is love of another person for my good; *agape* is love for another person for that person's good; *philia* is mutual love for the mutual good of both persons. Because *philia* is mutual love, seeking the good of both persons, we suggest it is the best foundation for a stable relationship. That is what Judith Wallerstein found in her study of the "good marriage."

"My marriage depends on friendship," one man told her. "Sex you can have with anyone, I got married for companionship and respect and most of all for friendship."[42] A woman agreed. "Let me describe what makes our marriage work. We like each other. We have mutual respect. We trust each other." Love is important, she explained, but what gives love stability is "a basic sense of real trust, of really knowing where that other person is at and knowing that whatever they are going to do is going to be in your best interest as well as theirs."[43] In relationship, when the mutuality of *philia* prepares the foundation on which the one-sidedness of both *eros* and *agape* are raised, spouses achieve mutual well-being through a love that is mutual (*philia*), unconditional (*agape*), and embodied (*eros*). When friendship is the foundation of a relationship, the friends or lovers recognize that the other's good is the only way to each individual's good and to their common good or communion.

Because *eros* and the sexual pleasure it desires is so powerful and so easily misconstrued as the pleasure of need to the detriment of the pleasure of mutual satisfaction, there must be parameters for its responsible and moral sexual expression.[44] We have outlined those parameters in detail elsewhere and here we give only a summary recitation. To be responsible and moral, every sexual activity must be just, that is, it must recognize and express the human freedom, equality, and mutuality of both partners, and it must be loving, that is, it must will and actively seek the good of both partners.[45] We conclude this section, then, by articulating a first thesis we believe to be sufficiently theologically established in it: physical sexuality, including the sexual pleasure of satisfaction, is part of the mystery of God's *oikonomia* and is a lower-case sacrament of the presence of the incomprehensible God in human history. As such, it demands ongoing analysis to be better understood in its physical sense so that it can be better understood also in its theological sense as revelatory of the incomprehensible God.

Psychological/Emotional Sexuality

Psychiatrist Jack Dominian presents an excellent synthesis of six psychological dimensions of human sexuality that further illuminate the sexual intercourse of a loving couple.[46] First, through sexual intercourse a couple affirms one another's identity. The sexual act is symbolic in that, when we become naked in front of another human person, we become totally and completely vulnerable. To make love in "a truly human manner"[47] is both a mutual affirmation and unconditional acceptance of the other with all her or his physical, emotional, psychological, and spiritual blessings and flaws. This affirmation and acceptance progresses through various stages.

As is well documented, sexual intercourse is more frequent early in a marriage,[48] and perhaps it is also more passionate. As a couple's relationship develops and deepens over the years, the routine of mutual affirmation and acceptance may lose its novelty and excitement, but this is not to be interpreted to mean that affirmation and acceptance cease. In reality, they increase as the couple comes to know and accept one another more profoundly and intimately over time. While the novelty and excitement of sexual intercourse may diminish with age, the affirmation and acceptance of the other person, a unique self created in the image and likeness of God and affirmed, accepted, and loved unconditionally, becomes more profound. Repetition may breed familiarity and a sense of routine, but it also deepens unconditional affirmation and acceptance of the other as he or she is.

Second, the sexual act reflects, affirms and creates gender identity, a fundamental dimension of sexual identity. Gender is concerned with the socially constructed meanings of femininity or masculinity. It is determined not simply by biology but also by culture, ethnicity, and rearing experience, and is expressed in actions, interactions, and social roles. Dominian describes gender expression as a liturgy of exchange, a divine language,[49] in which a couple communicates with each other through sexual desire. In the formation and development of sexual identity through a recognition and embodiment of gender roles, it is crucial that sexual activity be a form of just, loving, open, and honest human communication. If it is, then the act is humanly communicative at the deepest level, transforming simple communication into interpersonal communion and functioning as what Martin Buber called "the [lowercase] sacrament of dialogue," in which "one tastes God."[50] The sparks of genuine dialogue between lovers, in which each turns wholly toward the other, intends the other, receives the other, and affirms the other, illumines the presence of the dialogic God who in *oikonomia* turns toward the human other, intends the other, receives the other, and affirms the other. If sexual activity is not just, loving, open, and honest communication, then the same act can stagnate, or even block, future possibilities for communication and formation of healthy sexual identity. This is yet one more example of the essential ambiguity of human sexual activity.

Self-esteem is the third psychological dimension of human sexuality. Psychological studies indicate that one of the greatest threats to healthy human development, including sexual development, is poor self-esteem.[51] The Christian tradition has not always done a good job of emphasizing healthy self-love. Jesus' love-commandment is well known: "You shall love the Lord your God with all your heart, with all your soul, with all your mind, and with all your strength" and "You shall love your neighbor as yourself" (Mark 12:28–34; Matt 22:34–40,46b; and Luke 10:25–28). Not so well known is the fact that there are *three* commandments in this love-commandment: love God, love neighbor, *and* love self. Typically, the Christian tradition has interpreted neighbor love as altruistic and agapaic and self-love as egocentric and antithetical to the love of the gospel. This certainly *can* be the case, and those modern cultures that emphasize radical individualism encourage egocentric love, but egocentric love is not the healthy self-love demanded by the gospel. Authentic self-love first affirms oneself as a self-in-God, good, valuable, and lovable, and then, in alliance with neighbor-love, turns towards the other and offers this good, valuable, and lovable self-in-God unconditionally to the other. As Aquinas might argue: no one gives what he does not have. If a man does not truly and fully accept himself, in both his wholeness and his brokenness, he can neither give himself fully to another person nor fully accept the other person. So it is, too, with a woman.

Fourth, sexual intercourse is therapeutic and relieves distress. The human person is a psycho-somatic unity, an intrinsic union of body and spirit. There is distinction between body and spirit but there is no separation, and there is ongoing and constant dialogue between them. When a couple makes love, each person brings to that experience all the psychological burdens that accompany daily life including worries about relationship, possible conception, work, finances, and children. The act of sexual intercourse makes possible the suspension of those anxieties and worries, at least for the moment, and has a healing effect on the individual. This relief of distress, however, depends on the nature of the relationship. If the relationship is just, loving, committed, and honest, relief of distress is often an intrinsic component of sexual activity. If, however, the relationship is promiscuous, inauthentic, or dishonest, while the physical act can still suspend distress for the moment, the after effects of the experience can cause greater distress in the form of guilt, a sense of inauthentic or dishonest intimate communication, or objectification of the other.

Fifth, sexual intercourse is reconciling. There are no conflict-free relationships, not even in the most just and loving of relationships. Frictions, disagreements, misunderstandings are all inevitable aspects of any human relationship, and any and all of these experiences can create hurt, distress, and general distrust of the other in the relationship. One will find few couples who desire sexual intimacy at the peak of such quarrels, but intimacy returns after the resolution of the quarrel and may be an enhancing component of it. Some couples claim that the best sex they have is after the resolution of an argument. This is because sexual intimacy heals the wounds caused by the quarrel and reaffirms the trust, commitment, and communion that may have been threatened by it. The sparks of this real-life, loving and forgiving reconciliation illumine the presence in human life of the always reconciling and forgiving God. Again, just and loving sexual activity functions in the established *oikonomia* as a lower-case sacrament of the God present amid all the messiness of human life.

Finally, sexual intercourse is a profound act of thanksgiving or *eucharistia*. The embodied nature of the human person binds him or her to bodily expression which is best exemplified, though by no means limited to, verbal language. Alongside, and indeed beyond, verbal language there is body language, and alongside and beyond body language there is ritual language, symbolic action with socially-approved meanings. Couples can say to one another "I love you," or "I thank you," or "I forgive you," and in the spoken words they are reaching to meanings far beyond the words they speak. They can say the same things in socially-approved actions, by looks, by touches, by gifts, and in all of these actions they are similarly reaching far beyond the actions to express love, forgiveness, reconciliation, affirmation, and thanks-giving. In the physical action of sexual intercourse, an action as symbolic as any spoken word, they express all these things in the most intimate, pro-found, and total way available to an embodied human being, namely through the completely unmasked and, therefore, totally vulnerable body. They say to one another, in the words of the ancient Anglican wedding ritual, "with this *body* I thee worship."[52] They say, that is, in the etymological meaning of the word *worship*, I ascribe worth to you and to us, and for this worth I give thanks.

Couples who are Christian cannot help but link this moment of sexual and mutual thanksgiving for human relationship with that liturgical thanksgiving for divine relationship they call Eucharist.[53] "This is my body which is given for you," Jesus says to his disciples at the Supper;[54] "This is my body given for and to you," lovers say to one another in the act of intercourse. In both the Supper and the sex, the body and the person synonymous with it are vulner-able, even broken, but both body and person are given in love to the other, trusting that they will be received in love and handled with care. In the Supper, the Body of Christ is given to be eaten; so, too, are the bodies of the truly human lovers in sexual intercourse. Adrian Thatcher points out, legiti-mately, that "many of the intimacies of love-making are fairly literally an eating of the body of the person one loves. Kissing, especially deep kissing; the use of the tongue in caressing and stimulating; biting, sucking, and nib-bling; these are all patently ways in which we eat the bodies of our lovers."[55]

The central theological point here is a very Christian one. The God incar-nate in the Christ who gives his body in the Supper for the salvation of all is the same God incarnate in the lovers who give their bodies for the enhance-ment and salvation of their relationship. In the theology of *oikonomia*, the one ritual is as sacramental of God as the other, which is precisely why both eucharist and marriage are listed among the Catholic upper-case Sacraments. The spousal acts within marriage, especially the most intimate act of sexual intercourse, are fittingly lower-case sacraments of, in Cardinal Hume's felici-tous formulation, the "unending delight when one with God in the next."[56]

Any psycho-theological treatment of human sexuality and union must include their emotional dimensions. Emotions, strong, generalized feelings with both physical and psychological manifestations, apprehend value and disvalue for men and women. They are forms of evaluative judgments, Mar-tha Nussbaum argues, "that ascribe to certain things and persons outside a person's own control great importance for the person's own flourishing."[57] We caution that the evaluative judgment carried out by an emotion is not yet the rational judgment that affirms truth or the judgment of conscience that affirms moral action. We prefer to say, therefore, in partial agreement with Nussbaum, that emotions are *proto-judgments*, preliminary apprehensions of value or disvalue leading to personal flourishing, that become part of the experiential data that precedes judgment of truth or conscience.

Emotions may be either positive or negative. Positive emotions include love, joy, hope, humor, trust, happiness, satisfaction; negative emotions include hatred, sadness, despair, anxiety, distrust, unhappiness, and dissatisfaction. Beyond the obvious physical union of bodies, there is in play in the act of just and loving sexual intercourse a complex combination of emotions that unite two individuals into one partnered person, the *one body* of Genesis. That act, on one occasion, can express mutual love, openness, healing, comfort, reconciliation and, on another occasion, heal woundedness, neediness, anxiety, or brokenness. Either way, the sexual act entails and reveals through discernment a wide spectrum of both positive and negative emotions. The revelation of these God-created emotions and their interpersonal outcomes in just and loving sexual intercourse reveals also their nature as lower-case sacraments in the mystery of *oikonomia* in and through which the God who creates, loves, heals, comforts, reconciles, and saves humans is incarnated and to be discerned. Emotional sexuality, we suggest, is part of the mystery of *oikonomia* and demands, therefore, ongoing analysis to be better understood in an emotional sense so that it can be better understood also in a theological sense revelatory of the incomprehensible God.

Spiritual/Relational Sexuality

The theologically-construed communion between the three persons of the Trinity provides the model for every genuine human communion, and the grace of the Spirit enables each and every believer to share this communion with a loved other through a multitude of actions, including sexual actions. *The* characteristic of marriage, which distinguishes it from all other forms of friendship, is that it is expected to be an exclusive sexual relationship. From what we have already explained in this section, it is not difficult to conclude that the communion between the spouses expressed in the sexual intercourse that characterizes marriage is a lower-case sacrament of the divine communion. That is precisely what the Catholic Church intends when it teaches that marriage is an upper-case Sacrament, an efficacious sign in human history of the God who *is* communion.

The act of sexual intercourse allows humans a unique insight into the love and relationship shared within the Trinity. In intercourse there can be both the unconditional gift of self to the other and the unconditional reciprocation of the gift in return. Such mutuality, reciprocity, and unconditional acceptance reflect and reveal to careful discernment the total surrender of the Persons within the Godhead one to the others. "It is our capacity to love and be loved," Charles Gallagher notes, "that *makes* us most God-like."[58] The love, including the sexual love, shared by a couple in relationship draws them more and more into communion, and this human communion reflects and reveals the divine communion, draws them closer not only to one another but also to God, and overflows into all their other relationships. Most profoundly, this sexual communion always procreates new life, just as the loving communion between the Father and Son eternally leads to the procession of the Spirit. Even in cases where biological procreation is neither possible nor desired for "serious reasons,"[59] their sexual union procreates and enhances the couple's life in communion in imitation, and as lower-case sacrament, of God, the infinite source of loving communion.

This is not to suggest that, in the moment of orgasm when the partners are momentarily isolated in each individual self, the divine communion is immediately revealed. It is to suggest, with the Catholic tradition, that the intimate communion achieved in just and loving intercourse, on prayerful reflection and discernment, reveals both the communion within the Godhead and the communion yet to be achieved between God and God's human creatures in glory. The God who exists eternally in being incomprehensible to humans is sacramentally revealed to them on careful reflection on God's created *oikonomia.* The economic God, as Karl Rahner never tired of saying, is in very deed, the immanent God.

EMBODIED LOVE

As we have noted earlier, Platonic Augustine and Aristotelian Aquinas viewed the human person as a composite of body and soul. In that composite, soul and its faculties, intelligence and will, was the higher part and body, with its property, sexuality, was degraded, leading to the western and Christian general ambivalence towards both the body and sexuality. Feminist theologians of the past quarter century have consistently pointed out that ambivalence was greater toward the female body and female sexuality, seen as a source of temptation and sin for celibate males.[60] Peter Brown points out that third-century Origen believed that abstinence liberated the soul,[61] clearly a demeaning of marriage, sex, and the body. In the same century, Tertullian described women as "the devil's gateway" and demanded that the holy practice continence in marriage. Both men and women could reach sanctity by renouncing sex.[62] That ambivalence toward sex continues in the Catholic tradition and manifests itself in the modern world in a spiritualizing approach to sexuality and sexual intercourse. That approach locates the principal value of human sexuality on the spiritual level of human existence, a level judged to be superior to the bodily.

The objection we have to this spiritualizing approach to sex is well articulated by Giles Milhaven. "Man does do these spiritual, personal things in his sexual life (encounters, communicates, expresses love, etc.) and they do constitute the principal value of human sexuality, but not solely. The bodiliness and the sexualness with which he does them changes intrinsically their nature and therefore their value from what they would be in a nonbodied, nonsexual life."[63] The encounter, the interpersonal communication, the love-making between two human beings, are all essentially embodied activities. The integrated human self, as distinct from the Platonic dualist body-soul self, is essentially a bodyself.[64] The body can never be banished from the essential human; it grounds and expresses every human relationship. To attempt to spiritualize human sex out of its bodiliness is as untrue to the essential human as is reducing it to the merely animal.

It is not difficult to understand the underpinning of the spiritualizing tactic. Scorned bodiliness, always distrusted as either sinful or leading to sin, and specifically the bodiliness of human sexuality and sexual intercourse, is precisely what led Augustine to declare the original-sin-corrupted body "burdensome to the soul."[65] Modern Christians have inherited that distrust of their bodies and that has led them to doubt the goodness of their bodies, their sexualities, and their sexual intercourse even in marriage. The loving *consortium vitae* or life communion between a wife and a husband in marriage, however, and the sacrament of marriage which is grounded in it,[66] is a communion not only of spiritselves but also and essentially of bodyselves. Indeed, if the human is essentially as we have argued a bodyself, it is a communion of bodyselves *tout court*. Marital love is *agape*, the love of the spouse for the spouse's sake, but it is more than *agape*. It is also and importantly *philia*, the love of the spouse as a best friend, and *eros*, the love of the spouse for one's own satisfaction and fulfillment. This assertion must now be explicated.

CHRISTIAN MARITAL LOVE

Christian marital love is a species of neighbor-love. Christian spouses, like all Christians, are bound by the great commandment to "love your neighbor [spouse] as yourself" (Mark 12:21). That commandment in the Christian tradition is interpreted as grounding a wholly legitimate self-love: "love your neighbor *as yourself*." Marital love is never exclusively self-love but it is unquestionably in part self-love, which comes to be grounded in neighbor-love and friendship as the spouses gradually consummate their marriage and become best friends for life. In the life-long covenant communion that is marriage, spouses come to value one another as full and fully-esteemed partners, never as anything less than equal partners, and certainly never as objects to be used or abused for the benefit of either spouse alone. In such a life-long and deepening communion, "I love you" grows into "I love you and me" and eventually, as Milhaven puts it so beautifully, into "We love us."[67]

Though we do not wish to expand on the issue here, we do wish to state that the reason many Christian men and women have difficulty coming to genuinely love another human being is that they have difficulty coming to love themselves.

With self-love solidly grounded in neighbor-love, we can now consider *eros*-desire, that rambunctious, irrational, and selfish component of marital love. The spiritualizers always want to transform it into *agape*, but there is no alchemy for such transformation. *Eros* is an essential and inescapable element of human, embodied love. It is the foundation of all sexual attraction, of all friendship, of all love, and of all sexual relationship. What humans can do is not scorn it with fifth-century Augustine but embrace it, ground it, and give it a distinctively human form. That distinctive form appears, we submit, when the irrationality of *eros* becomes allied to the wisdom and grace of *agape*. When *eros* is allowed to dominate, there is neither mutuality nor equality; there is only the self-serving drive to use, which is effectively to abuse, another as a means to one's own selfish ends. That approach ultimately creates what it seeks to avoid, namely, loneliness, alienation, emptiness, everything but communion. When *agape* dominates, partners recognize that the other's well-being is the way to their common well-being and, therefore, also to each's individual well-being. When *eros* and *agape* are allied, partners seek their mutual well-being as partners and as a couple in a love that is always embodied even when those things that fuel *eros*, youth, beauty, grace, health, have long since passed away.

In a Catholic theological perspective, *eros*, sexuality, and sexual intercourse are all sacramental, not because of any human meaning attached to them but because they are all God's gifts to *'adam*, man and woman, in creation, and "God saw everything that he had made and, behold, it was very good" (Gen 1:31). To use them as good gifts in a marital relationship is to use them in a way that points to their origin in God. That is already to use them sacramentally, as outward signs of the presence of the God who is grace. In a Christian marriage, therefore, there is no need to be afraid of graced *eros* and sexual intercourse, there is no need to spiritualize them, there is certainly no need to abstain from communion in the Body of Christ because of them (as was once the common case). For concrete women and men, each of whom is an essential bodyself, entering into communion includes essentially, though not exclusively, body communion. This bodily communion, even in its most passionately erotic form, is an element in the embodied sacrament of marriage, it is graced, for in the use of God's good gift it makes explicit the presence of the God who is Giver. Bodily union is far from all there is to personal communion, but bodily union occupies a central place in a Christian relationship as symbol of the communion not only between the partners but also between them and the God who does not shrink from expressing his love for them and all humankind in that most beautiful and explicitly erotic of love songs, the biblical Song of Songs.

The Song has always posed difficulties for both Jewish and Christian interpreters, specifically the difficulty of deciding whether it was a paean to divine or human love. For centuries, unwilling to admit that erotic love could have any place in their sacred writings, commentators opted for an allegorical reading. The Song, they piously and prudishly explained, was about divine love. Embodied women and men, however, need only listen to the extraordinarily explicit words of erotic love to know otherwise.

"I am sick with love," the woman exclaims (2:5; 5:8). "Come to me," she cries out in desire for her lover, "like a gazelle, like a young stag upon the mountains where spices grow" (2:17; 8:14). When he comes and gazes upon her nakedness, he is moved to ecstasy. "Your rounded thighs are like jewels. Your vulva [68] is a rounded bowl that never lacks wine. Your belly is a heap of wheat encircled with lilies…. You are stately as a palm tree and your breasts are like its clusters. I say I will climb the palm tree and lay hold of its branches" (71–78). Her reply is far from coy. "I am my beloved's and his desire is for me. Come, my beloved, let us go forth into the fields…. There I will give you my love" (7:10–12). No woman or man who has ever been sick with love and desire can doubt the language or its intent.

Such explicitly erotic language has always cast doubts on the claim that the Song of Songs is about divine love. A growing consensus has emerged among contemporary interpreters that the meaning of the Song is its literal meaning, and that its literal meaning is the meaning of any human love song. The Song may be read as an allegory of divine love, but only indirectly. It is directly about love that includes *eros*, about love that is deliriously sick with passion and desire, the human love that so troubled Augustine. It is about the love of men and women who in love seek the presence of and bodily union with the lover. Christians celebrate this love as gift and, therefore, as sacrament of the presence in their lives of the God who loves women and men as the partners love one another. It is as explicit and intentional symbol that *eros* and the sexual relationship and intercourse to which it leads serve as outward signs, that is as sacraments, of the God who is Grace and gracious.

One final comment about embodied love. Pope John Paul II argued that human sexuality "is realized in a truly human way only if it is an integral part of the love by which a man and a woman commit themselves totally to one another until death. The total physical self-giving would be a lie if it were not the sign and fruit of a total personal self-giving."[69] The notion of a lie is well known; it is verbally stating something that we know to be untrue, like "I've never met her," when I know full well that I had dinner with her last night. The term *body language* is common in the contemporary world. Since the primary meaning of the word *language* refers to verbal communication, body *language* is a metaphorical use of the word, but it is still a use that is legitimate. Humans do communicate in bodily gestures as they do in words. Importantly, however, the meaning of both the words and the gestures are inherently contextual. I might use the word *chicken* to designate the bird or to accuse someone of being a coward, and the meaning I intend can be clarified only in the context in which I use it. Similarly, I might raise my arm to mean I want to ask a question in a class or to mean that I am exercising my arm muscles. Again, the meaning I intend by raising my arm is clarified and understood only from the context in which I raise it. Sexual gestures, like fondling, kissing, intercourse are also understood only in context. John Paul II, therefore, is correct. If the gesture of sexual intercourse commonly expresses total personal self-giving, any intercourse that is not expressive of total personal self-giving, rape for instance, is indeed a lie. And a bodily-gesture lie is as harmful to the social fabric as is a verbal lie.

OIKONOMIA AND THE SEXUAL PERSON

Spirituality is all about relationship. So, too, is human sexuality from which "the human person receives the characteristics which, on the biological, psychological, and spiritual levels, make that person a man or a woman, and thereby largely condition his or her progress toward maturity and insertion into society."[70] Human sexuality is a gift from God that draws persons towards interpersonal relationship and communion. It is an intrinsic, mysterious dimension of human beings that draws individuals out of self and towards another. "Sexuality is a dimension of one's restless heart, which continually yearns for interpersonal communion, glimpsed and experienced to varying degrees in this life, ultimately finding full oneness only in God, here and hereafter."[71] In and through human sexuality and relationships humans seek to become both whole and holy. This relational gift is at the core of human identity, and allows humans to enter into communion not only with one another but also with God.

Relationship with the gospel "neighbor" takes several forms. First, and primarily, neighbor is the partner or intimate other. Sexual acts are the most intimate communion between two people; in them two individuals become physically and personally a coupled one. Catholic tradition refers to this relationship in terms of a covenant and a communion of persons, and limits this covenantal communion to marriage between a man and a woman.[72] A second close neighbor is family. God's gift of sexuality provides women and men with the desire to unite as couple and to create, nurture, and educate new life out of their union, thereby creating family. The Catholic Church correctly describes family as the "original cell of social life"[73] and the "domestic church,"[74] a relational community of partnered life and love.

Neighbor also extends to the human community beyond the family. Too often in Christian history moral theology has focused on the individual's acts and their impact on the individual's relationship with God, while neglecting the broader social implications of those acts. For instance, whereas Catholic teaching has focused on the separation of the unitive and procreative dimensions of the individual sexual act as the basis for condemning artificial reproduction, some Catholic moral theologians have suggested, rather, a focus on the social justice issues of using such technology in terms of cost and the use of limited medical resources.[75] This shift in focus is especially relevant in sexual ethics. Too often, sexual and social ethics are seen in isolation from each other, each utilizing its own methodology and having its own point of reference. Whereas traditional Catholic sexual ethics tends to focus on acts and absolute norms that guide individuals and married couples, Catholic social ethics tends to focus on the network of human interrelationships that constitute a community and on general principles to guide these interrelationships towards a common good. Sexuality is a relational reality that challenges us to more fully integrate not only its individual but also its social moral dimensions.

CONCLUSION

In the mysterious God's mysterious *oikonomia*, human sexuality is a unique gift to each individual "from which the human person receives the characteristics which, on the biological, psychological, and spiritual levels, make that person a man or a woman, and thereby largely condition his or her progress toward maturity and insertion into society."[76] It is a gift of God that draws persons into relationship and communion. History demonstrates beyond doubt that, despite an intellectual and abstract acknowledgment that sexuality and sex are good because they are created by a good God,[77] much of the Christian tradition has not appreciated the goodness of this gift practically and concretely. This lack of real appreciation for the gift of human sexuality has created a great deal of guilt and self-loathing with the unfortunate consequence that Christians sometimes live out their sexuality in unhealthy ways.

Sexuality is intimately related to our attraction to other persons, to love, and committed relationships. For this natural attraction to be nurtured and manifested in responsible relationships, it must first be accepted and integrated in a healthy manner. Christians need to be conscious of and critically reflect upon perspectives that frustrate the personal acceptance and integration of sexuality, for at least one major theological reason. The frustration of the personal acceptance and integration of God's gift of sexuality leads to the theological frustration and obscuring of the gift of sexuality as a lower-case sacrament of God in God's created *oikonomia*. Having considered in this essay human sexuality in the light of contemporary social scientific data about it, we now proceed to consider another source of Catholic theological ethics, namely, human experience.

QUESTIONS FOR REFLECTION

1. What do you understand by the use of the word *mystery* in general and in this essay in particular? In what sense can the word be applied to human sexuality which is intimately related to our attraction to other persons, to interpersonal love, and to committed relationships?
2. What is the difference between *sex* and *gender*? What is your opinion of the ancient theory that holds that there is only one human sex which is male and that females are not fully developed males? What are the contemporary results of this theory?
3. What are the various dimensions of human sexuality dealt with in this essay? Do you find any of these dimensions in your personal life? Do you find the connection between sexual intercourse and eucharist convincing?
4. What do you understand by the word *oikonomia*? How do you see the human person as an essential part of that *oikonomia*? How do you see the sexual person as an essential part of that *oikonomia*?
5. Both Augustine and Thomas Aquinas taught that the human was a composite of a higher part named *soul* and a lower part named *body*, which included sexuality. The inferior nature of body, and therefore sexuality, led to their distrust in the Christian tradition. That distrust was particularly of the female body and female sexuality which was seen as a temptation to males to sin. Do you see any contemporary evidence of this attitude continuing? What do you think of it? Discuss examples.

NOTES

An earlier version of this essay appeared in *Theology and Sexuality* 17, no. 2 (2011): 161–80. It is reprinted here with permission.

1. United States Conference of Catholic Bishops, *Always Our Children* (Washington, DC: USCCB, 1997), n. 3.

2. First Vatican Council, Denzinger-Schoenmetzer, *Enchiridion Symbolorum Definitionum et Declarationum de Rebus Fidei et Morum*, editio XXXIII (Freiburg: Herder, 1965), n. 3041. Hereafter DS.

3. See United States Catholic Conference, *Human Sexuality: A Catholic Perspective for Education and Lifelong Learning* (Washington, D.C.: USCC, 1991), 7–8.

4. See Harriet Bradley, *Gender* (Cambridge, UK: Polity Press, 2007); Lisa Sowle Cahill, *Sex, Gender, and Christian Ethics* (Cambridge, UK: Cambridge University Press, 1996).

5. Committee on Marriage and Family, USCCB, "Always Our Children," in *Same-Sex Attraction: A Parents' Guide*, ed. John F. Harvey and Gerard V. Bradley (South Bend, IND: St. Augustine's, 2003), 215.

6. The Pontifical Council for the Family, "The Truth and Meaning of Human Sexuality: Guidelines for Education Within the Family" (December 8, 1995), http://www.vatican.va/roman_curia/pontifical_councils/family/documents/rc_pc_family_doc_08121995_human-sexuality_en.html, n. 3.

7. *Catechism of the Catholic Church*, n. 2332.

8. United States Conference of Catholic Bishops, *Human Sexuality*, 9.

9. DS, n. 3015.

10. Ibid., n. 3016.

11. See Karl Rahner, "History of the World and Salvation History," in *Theological Investigations*, vol. 5 (London: Darton, Longman, and Todd, 1966), 97–114.

12. DS, n. 3026.

13. See, for instance, Bernard Cooke, "Sacraments," in *The New Dictionary of Sacramental Worship*, ed. Peter E. Fink (Collegeville: Liturgical Press, 1990), 1119.

14. Karl Rahner, *The Trinity* (New York: Seabury, 1974), 22; *Foundations of Christian Faith: An Introduction to the Idea of Christianity* (New York: Seabury, 1978), 136–37; "The Mystery of the Trinity," in *Theological Investigations*, vol. 16 (New York: Crossroad, 1976), 258.

15. Ibid., emphasis in original.

16. Catherine Mowry Lacugna, *God for Us: The Trinity and Christian Life* (San Francisco: Harper, 1991), 2.

17. Ibid., 4.

18. While much of what we write in this essay on human sexuality under the genus of mystery and the species of *oikonomia* focuses on heterosexual marital relationships it applies, *mutatis mutandis*, to homosexual and bisexual relationships as well.

19. USCCB, *Always Our Children*, n. 3.

20. See Charles A. Gallagher, *et al.*, *Embodied in Love: Sacramental Spirituality and Sexual Intimacy* (New York: Crossroad, 1985), 21–37.

21. Pope Paul VI, *Acta Apostolicae Sedis* 55 (1963): 848.

22. Pope John Paul II, *Familiaris consortio*, n. 5.

23. These thoughts on Genesis 2:24 are developed from the section "Penetrer-Etre Penetre," in Xavier Lacroix, *Le Corps de chair: les dimensions éthiques, esthétiques, et spirituelles de l'amour* (Paris: Cerf, 1992), 111–14.

24. Michel Foucault, *L'Usage des plaisirs* (Paris: Gallimard, 1984), 142.

25. William H. Masters and Virginia E. Johnson, *Human Sexual Response* (Boston: Little, Brown, 1966), 3–8.

26. June M. Reinisch and Ruth Beasley, *The Kinsey Institute New Report on Sex: What You Must Know to be Sexually Literate* (New York: St. Martin's Press, 1990), 84.

27. Thomas Aquinas, *ST*, III (Suppl.), 41, 3.

28. Cited from Gareth Moore, *The Body in Context: Sex and Catholicism*, Contemporary Christian Insights (New York: Continuum, 2001), 43.

29. Cited from ibid., 47.

30. Augustine, *Contra Julianum Pelag.*, 3, 23, 53, *PL* 44, 729–30.

31. ST, III (Suppl.), 41, 4; 49, 5.

32. Ibid., II–II, 142, 1.

33. John Boswell, *Christianity, Social Tolerance, and Homosexuality* (Chicago: University of Chicago Press, 1980), chapter 5.

34. *Contra Gentiles*, 4, 78.

35. *ST*, II–II, 26, 11; See also *Contra Gentiles*, 3, II, 123, 6.

36. Bonaventure, *In Quart. Sent.*, 33, 1, 1.

37. Basil Hume, "Note" added after the death of a close friend to his "Observations on the Catholic Teaching Concerning Homosexual People," in his *Created Design*, 20–24. Cited in Alan Bray, *The Friend* (Chicago: University of Chicago Press, 2003), 298. Emphasis added.

38. Aelred of Rievaulx, *Spiritual Friendship*, trans. Mark E. Williams (Scranton: University of Scranton Press, 1994), 1:69.

39. See Evelyn Eaton Whitehead and James D. Whitehead, *A Sense of Sexuality: Christian Love and Intimacy* (New York: Doubleday, 1989), 103–5.

40. Aquinas, *ST*, 1, 20, 1 ad 3.

41. Margaret Farley, *Personal Commitments: Beginning, Keeping, Changing* (San Francisco: Harper and Row, 1990), 34. For a detailed analysis of commitment, see Scott M. Stanley, *The Power of Commitment: A Guide to Active, Lifelong Love* (San Francisco: Jossey-Bass, 2005).

42. Judith S. Wallerstein and Sandra Blakeslee, *The Good Marriage: How and Why Love Lasts* (Boston: Houghton Mifflin, 1995), 156.

43. Ibid., 169–70.

44. For an investigation of pleasure as an essential component of human sexuality, see Christine E. Gudorf, *Body, Sex, and Pleasure: Reconstructing Christian Social Ethics* (Cleveland: Pilgrim Press, 1995).

45. See Todd A. Salzman and Michael G. Lawler, *The Sexual Person: Toward a Renewed Catholic Anthropology* (Washington, DC: Georgetown University Press, 2008), 157–59.

46. See Jack Dominian, "Sexuality and Interpersonal Relationships," in *Embracing Sexuality: Authority and Experience in the Catholic Church*, ed. Joseph A. Selling (Burlington, VT: Ashgate, 2001), 12–15.

47. See *Gaudium et spes*, n. 49; *Code of Canon Law*, n. 1061.

48. See Tom W. Smith, *American Sexual Behavior: Trends, Socio-Demographic Differences, and Risk Behavior* (Chicago: University of Chicago Press, 2003), 74. Also at www.norc.uchicago.edu/issues/American_Sexual-_Behavior_2003.

49. Dominian, "Sexuality and Interpersonal Relationships," 20.

50. Martin Buber, *Between Man and Man* (New York: Macmillan, 1948), 17.

51. Dominian, "Sexuality and Interpersonal Relationships," 14.

52. Mark Searle and Kenneth W. Stevenson, eds., *Documents of the Marriage Ceremony* (Collegeville, MN: Liturgical Press, 1992), 151.

53. The connection of marriage and Eucharist is beautifully developed in Germain Martinez, *Worship: Wedding to Marriage* (Washington, DC: Pastoral Press, 1993).

54. Luke 22:19.

55. Adrian Thatcher, *Liberating Sex: A Christian Sexual Theology* (London: SPCK, 1993), 89.

56. Cardinal George Basil Hume, "Note on Church Teaching Concerning Homosexual People," *Origins* 24, no. 45 (April 27, 1995): 767–68.

57. Martha C. Nussbaum, *The Upheavals of Thought: the Intelligence of Emotions* (New York: Cambridge University Press, 2003), 22.

58. Charles Gallagher, *et al.*, *Embodied in Love* (New York: Crossroad, 1987), 108; emphasis in original.

59. Pope Pius XII, *Acta Apostolicae Sedis* 43 (1951): 846; Pope Paul VI, *Humanae vitae*, n. 10.

60. See Rosemary Radford Ruether, *New Woman/New Earth: Sexist Ideologies and Human Liberation* (New York: Seabury, 1975), esp. 186–211; Christine E. Gudorf, *Body, Sex, and Pleasure: Reconstructing Christian Sexual Ethics*; Lisa Sowle Cahill, *Sex, Gender and Christian Ethics* (New York: Cambridge University Press, 1996).

61. Peter Brown, *Body and Society: Men, Women, and Sexual Renunciation in Early Christianity* (New York: Columbia University Press, 1988), 170.

62. Ibid., 78–79.

63. John Giles Milhaven, "Conjugal Sexual Love and Contemporary Moral Theology," *Theological Studies* 35, no. 4 (1974): 700.

64. See Gudorf, *Body, Sex, and Pleasure*, 160–204.

65. Augustine, *City of God*, Bk. 13, Chap. 16 (New York: Image Books, 1958), 280.

66. See Michael G. Lawler, "The Mutual Love and Personal Faith of the Spouses as the Matrix of their Sacrament of Marriage," *Worship* 65 (1991): 339–61.

67. Milhaven, "Conjugal Sexual Love," 705.

68. The Revised Standard Version modestly translates *sorerek* as "navel." Its location in the poem between thighs and belly, however, suggests "vulva," as does the Arabic cognate of *sorerek*. Marcia Falk translates it as "hips" in her *Love Lyrics from the Bible: A Translation and Literary Study of the Song of Songs* (Sheffield, U.K.: Almond Press, 1982), 41; see her explanation, 127–28.

69. John Paul II, *Familiaris consortio*, n. 11.

70. CDF, *Persona humana*, "Declaration on Certain Questions Concerning Sexual Ethics," n. 1.

71. USCCB, *Human Sexuality*, 9.

72. See n. 1055, 1.

73. *Catechism of the Catholic Church*, n. 2207.

74. Pope John Paul II, *Familiaris consortio*, n. 21.

75. See Maura Ryan, *Ethics and Economics of Assisted Reproduction: The Cost of Longing* (Washington, DC: Georgetown University Press, 2001), 134.

76. CDF, *Persona humana*, n. 1.

77. See Clement of Alexandria, *Stromatum*, 3, 12, *Patrologia Graeca* (*PG*) 8, 1186; Irenaeus, *Adversus Haereses*, 1, 28, 1, *PG* 7, 690; Augustine, *De Bono Matrimonio*, passim, *PL* 40.

Chapter Four

Human Experience and Catholic Ethics

Catholic moral theology generally accepts a quadrilateral of sources of moral knowledge, scripture, tradition, reason, and experience.[1] In this chapter, we consider the relationship between human experience and Catholic theological ethics. In the next chapter, we consider the contribution of the sciences to the understanding of theological ethics in general and sexual anthropology in specific. The chapter develops in three sections. The first opens the discussion and situates human experience as one of the sources of Catholic moral theology. The second considers two realities that are dimensions of Catholic theological experience, namely, *sensus fidei* and reception. The third presents empirical sociology as a means to illuminate human, theological experience, thereby enabling the practical theological questions of what is and what ought to be.

HUMAN EXPERIENCE AND MORAL THEOLOGY

Any Catholic moral theology seeking to be normative will, of necessity, have to interpret, prioritize, coordinate and integrate the four sources of moral knowledge into a comprehensive and comprehensible moral theory. In the four hundred years preceding the Second Vatican Council, years in which the manuals dominated Catholic moral theology, Catholic moral theologians focused on tradition and reason to the neglect of scripture and experience. In its Declaration on Priestly Formation, the Council prescribed that "special attention needs to be given to the development of moral theology. Its scientific exposition should be more thoroughly nourished by scriptural teaching."[2] It needs also, we argue in this chapter, to be more thoroughly nourished by attention to human experience for, as the Council acknowledges, it is, "Thanks to the experience of past ages, the progress of the sciences, and the treasures hidden in the various forms of human culture, [that] the nature of man himself is revealed and *new roads to truth are opened.*"[3] In response to that conciliar judgment, in this chapter we focus explicitly on one dimension of the moral quadrilateral, namely, human experience, fully agreeing with Servais Pinckaers that human experience has "a very important function in moral theology."[4] So very important is experience that Aristotle judges that a young man cannot have the moral virtue of prudence, for prudence "includes a knowledge of particular facts, and this is derived from experience which a young man does not have." The young may be good at mathematics but, given their lack of experience, they cannot be good at natural philosophy or ethics.[5]

We note at the outset a division in contemporary Catholic moral theology, between theologians who are generally called traditionalists and theologians who are generally called revisionists. "Traditionalist" is the label assigned to moral theologians who support and defend absolute magisterial norms; "revisionist" is the label assigned to moral theologians who question and theologically challenge some absolute magisterial norms.[6] These two schools differ in their approach to experience in the construction of their moral theology. Traditionalists argue that human experience is to be *judged* by moral norms derived from moral principles; revisionists argue that experience can help to *formulate* moral norms and principles. The traditionalist approach to experience is deductive, from guiding principles and norms to judged experience; the revisionist approach is inductive, from interpreted and evaluated experience to formulated norms and principles. The Catholic natural law tradition teaches, and Pope John Paul II reaffirms, the relevance of experience for formulating moral norms and criteria to judge the rightness or wrongness of an act. For example, how do we know that adultery is intrinsically wrong? Is it because God says so? Is it because the magisterium says so? Or is it because human experience has demonstrated that performing such an act damages one's relationship to one's self, to one's spouse and family, to the spouse and family of another person, to the social or community fabric, and ultimately to God? We believe the latter option is true and that both the magisterium and God proscribe adultery as immoral because human experience clearly shows that it is harmful to human flourishing and, therefore, immoral.

Critically and theologically interpreted human experience, of both past and present, helps to formulate norms to judge experience; it serves as a window onto the morally normative. To deny the validity and moral relevance of human experience for assisting in the formulation of norms and criteria for judging the rightness or wrongness of acts reflects a reductionist methodology where the only legitimate human experience is that which conforms to, and confirms, established norms. It was such a methodology, in large part, which allowed the magisterium's approbation of slavery until

Pope Leo XIII's rejection of it in 1890 and the denial of religious freedom until the Second Vatican Council's approbation of it in 1965. John Noonan comments with respect to the magisterium's late condemnation of slavery, "it was the experience of unfreedom, in the gospel's light, that made the contrary shine clear."[7]

Both traditionalists and revisionists are challenged to discern what human experience may lead to the formulation, perhaps even the transformation, of moral principles and norms and what human experience is to be judged by those principles and norms. The former is authentic human experience that leads to human flourishing; the latter is inauthentic human experience that does not lead to human flourishing. We consider three types of experience as a concrete way of separating authentic and inauthentic experience.

One type of experience that provides a basis of reflection for the construction of a moral theory is cultural experience.[8] "Thanks to the experience of past ages, the progress of the sciences, and the treasures hidden in the various forms of human culture, the nature of man himself is more clearly revealed and new roads to truth are opened." Thus taught *Gaudium et spes*, adding that, "from the beginning of [the Church's] history, she has learned to express the message of Christ with the help of the ideas and terminology of various peoples;"[9] that is, with the help of interpreted human experience. It is undoubtedly true that the Church is called on occasion to be countercultural, to confront cultural theories and actions that do not lead to human flourishing, for example, the rabid individualism rampant in the contemporary culture of the United States. It is also undoubtedly true that reflection on cultural experience can lead to insight into moral truth and facilitate the communication of that truth within the culture and from one culture to another. This second case is especially true when a particular cultural context requires specific norms to address specific moral problems. The pastoral letters of the bishops of the United States on the economy and nuclear war are examples of the dialectic between culture and the development of moral norms. These letters draw on the traditional Catholic principles of justice and fairness to formulate culturally specific norms, but the understanding of justice and fairness they evince is transformed in light of the specific and cultural experiences to which they respond.

Another type of experience is contemporary scientific experience and the expansion of scientific knowledge, where new discoveries and technologies challenge traditional moral answers based on inaccurate or incomplete scientific knowledge and raise new moral questions that require new answers. Some answers will be drawn from traditional moral principles, but in a new, nuanced way that will lead to the formulation of new norms and criteria. A current and widely debated question is what is and what is not a moral use of medical technologies to begin, sustain, restore, or end life. The successful mapping of the human genome is making possible genetic engineering. Is it moral to use such engineering to eliminate, for instance, Huntington's disease? What about beginning of life decisions in the case of a foetus with an incurable defect or end of life decisions in the case of a person in a persistent vegetative state? What about health insurance issues for advancing health technologies and for those who can and cannot afford health insurance? What about the Catholic principle of the common good in such cases? Moral reflection on and responses to these questions may generate new moral insight and lead to new moral norms.

A third type of experience is the liberation theology that grew out of reflection on the experience of the socioeconomic oppression of the poor in Latin America and led to a variety of feminist theologies that grew out of reflection on the universal experience of gender oppression. [10] "Feminist ethics," Lisa Sowle asserts, "begins with the particular, with practice, with experience, with the situation – but out of the particular (not over against it) feminists recognize what furthers or damages 'full humanity' for women and men." [11] The experience of women, past and present, challenges the moral norms that oppress them by challenging the very definition of authentic personhood. Any norm that proscribes women, the impossibility of their ordination to the priesthood for instance, is a norm that requires, at the very least, serious reconsideration.

All three of these categories of experience require criteria for determining what is and what is not authentic experience that will further human flourishing and fulfillment. Do certain experiences require a more precise specification of a specific norm, or its adjustment, or its complete reversal, as happened in the case of slavery and religious freedom? The answer to these questions will be reached through careful discernment of the quadrilateral of sources of moral knowledge. Again, traditionalist and revisionist theologians aware of Catholic theological history, agree that adjustment or reversal of moral norms is possible, but they disagree about the ultimate criterion for such development. Traditionalists hold that the magisterium is the only authority to judge on such development. [12] No matter how rational the argument grounded in experience, scripture, tradition, and reason to reverse a gender-oppressive norm, the ordination of women to the priesthood, for example, traditionalists conform to magisterial teaching. [13] Revisionists, on the other hand, while acknowledging, respecting, and appreciating the role of the magisterium to speak on particular questions, do not acknowledge it as the ultimate determinant of moral truth regardless of contrary discernment of the sources of moral knowledge. Catholic history abundantly justifies such caution. [14]

A legitimate question at this point is whose experience is to be used in the formulation of a moral theology? We emphasize again that experience is only one part of the moral quadrilateral and never a stand alone source of moral theology. "My experience" alone is never a source at all. Moral authority is ecclesially granted only to "our experience," to *communal* experience, as a source of moral theology, and only in constructive conversation with the three other sources, scripture, tradition, and reason, as well as with the theological reality called *sensus fidei*, which we discuss in the next section. First, however, we must clarify what we mean by experience. There is little to be gained from simply encountering the world in which we live; many people have many such encounters and learn little from them. The experience we speak of in this chapter, with Neil Brown, intends "the human capacity to encounter the surrounding world consciously, to observe it, be affected by it, and to learn from it."[15] It is of the essence of such experience that it is never a raw, neutral, pure, unadulterated encounter with the world. It is always interpreted, construed, socially constructed by both individuals and communities in specific socio-historical contexts. It is, therefore, also dialectical, differently construed, perhaps, by "me," by "you," by "us," and by "them," by traditionalist and revisionist theologians, for instance. For genuine human experience as we have defined it, the dialectic is necessarily a "dialectic of reason *and* experience" and never a dialectic controlled by either reason or experience alone. It is also a dialectic that results not in an absolutist moral code but in "various revisable rules."[16] In a Church that is a communion of believers[17] the resolution of different construals of experience to arrive at moral truth requires an open, respectful, charitable, and prayerful dialogue, such as that lauded and rhetorically embraced by Pope John Paul II.[18] Charitable dialogue must occur internally, among the communion of believers, some of whom are laity, some of whom are theologians, and some of whom are bishops including the bishop of Rome,[19] all of whom, if feminist theologians are right, and we believe they are, acquire knowledge through practice or action,[20] that is, through experience, and externally, among all people of good will.

EXPERIENCE, *SENSUS FIDEI*,
RECEPTION AND MORAL THEOLOGY

Two specific dimensions of internal dialogue and Catholic theological experience are the interconnected theological realities called *sensus fidei* and reception. We consider each in turn.

Sensus Fidei

Sensus fidei, and its historical cognates, *sensus* or *consensus fidelium, sensus ecclesiae, sensus catholicus, communis ecclesiae fides*, is a theological concept which denotes, "the instinctive capacity of the *whole Church* to recognize the infallibility of the Spirit's truth,"[21] and the spontaneous judgment of loyal and faithful Catholics that has "theological weight."[22] *Sensus fidei* is a

spiritual charism of discernment, possessed by the whole Church, which
knows and receives a teaching as apostolic truth and, therefore, to be believed. The concept was sharply focused for moderns by John Henry Newman's famous essay *On Consulting the Faithful in Matters of Doctrine.*
Newman suggested that *sensus fidei* was, "a sort of instinct, or *phronema*,
deep in the bosom of the Mystical Body of Christ," and cited with approval
Moehler's opinion that the Spirit of God arouses in the faithful "an instinct,
an eminently Christian tact, which leads it to all true doctrine."[23] *Sensus fidei*
belongs in the realm of knowledge, but it is not rational, discursive knowledge. Whether one calls it "instinct" or "spontaneous judgment" or "intuition," its *locus* is the lived experience we articulated above, "the human
capacity to encounter the surrounding world consciously, to observe it, be
affected by it, and to learn from it." It "entails a structure of beliefs, opinions,
affective attractions, and behavioral tendencies" considered valid because "it
is testified to by the Spirit as a requirement and way of following Christ."[24]
Newman's careful effort to explain that *consult* meant simply establishing
what laity actually believed, what we will later call the *what is* of their faith,
and not their enthronement as sole judges of orthodoxy, did not forestall a
storm of protest from those whose perspective was that faith was gifted to the
apostles, transmitted by them to their bishop-successors, and transmitted by
them in turn to an unquestioningly obedient and passive faithful.[25]

The root of the theological concept *phronema*, which is foundational for
the *sensus fidei*, is in the New Testament. Paul exhorts the Philippians to
"have this [common] mind (*phroneite*) among yourselves, which is yours in
Christ Jesus" (Phil 2:5). The theological use of the concept is constructed
upon this scriptural foundation. For Newman, with his great reverence for
Christian tradition, the great teacher was Athanasius, who insisted that scripture should be interpreted according to tradition and cited "the *phronema* of
Catholics"[26] as a central component of the tradition. This *phronema*, Samuel
Femiano explains, is understood by him as "a type of prudential judgment by
which the faithful sense the truths of faith;" this judgment is externalized as
"the voice of the Christian people."[27] Truth is always achieved only in judgment; Catholic truth is achieved in the judgment not of any one Catholic
individual, not of any one Catholic group of believers, but of all three groups,
laity, theologians, and bishops in *consensus fidei.*

Sensus fidei, therefore, means a charism or gift of the Holy Spirit related
to the traditional objective and subjective realities of faith, what one believes,
fides quae creditur, and the act of faith by which one believes, *fides qua
creditur.* It relates to objective faith, the concepts, words, and the realities
they intend, that is handed on to the Church from the past and which the
Church, in turn, hands on to contemporary believers to be believed. It relates
also to subjective faith, the personal act of faith by which the individual
believer actually believes and embraces the beliefs proposed by the Church.

Both objective and subjective faith are necessarily influenced by and created in the socio-historical contexts of their times. Different socio-historical contexts might yield different experiences, understandings, and judgments of meaningfulness. Yves Congar insists that the content embedded in the concept of *sensus fidei*, and its historical variations, is a universal belief of the Fathers of the Church, the thirteenth-century scholastics, and the theologians of the sixteenth century. All acknowledged both the objective-abstract and subjective-practical side of faith and listed *sensus fidelium* "among the *loci theologici*, that is, among the criteria of Christian thought." [28]

The theological concept of *sensus fidei*, therefore, is much older than Newman and the nineteenth century. Vincent of Lerins formulated the ancient rule of faith in the fifth century: *quod ubique, quod semper, quod ab omnibus creditum est*, what is believed everywhere, always, and *by all*. [29] Thomas Aquinas explained *sensus fidei* in scholastic language. The faithful understand a teaching *per modum connaturalitatis,* that is, they incline naturally in subjective faith to believe what is in harmony with the true meaning of the word of God. [30] Christian apostolic faith connaturally knows a truth that belongs to it. Robert Bellarmine added his opinion that, "what *all the faithful* hold as a matter of faith is necessarily true and of faith." [31] In every development of both doctrinal and moral teaching that has taken place in the Church, and there have been many, Vincent of Lerins' rule was the essential factor in the reception or non-reception of a doctrine or moral norm as the faith of the universal Church. Though one could complain that Pius XII surveyed only the bishops of the world, and not the whole body of believers, before he defined as Catholic dogma the Assumption of Mary, it still never occurred to him to define the dogma on his own authority without somehow "consulting the faithful."

One of the sub-texts at the Second Vatican Council, and in the theological developments that followed it, was a debate over who precisely were the *all* in Vincent's rule of faith, "always, everywhere, and *by all*." Vatican theologians argued that it was only the magisterium who determined doctrine (including, by implication, moral doctrine) and that they, therefore, were the *all*, a claim that had become common only since the definition of papal infallibility by the First Vatican Council in 1870. Bishops who attended that council and theologians responded with the more historically accurate claim that the Church's faith was preserved in the faith of *all* the faithful, laity, theologians, and bishops in *consensus*. They argued that, although the magisterium ultimately spoke *for* the Church, it was also obliged to speak *from* the Church and that, when it structured doctrine along only magisterial lines, ignoring a clear *sensus fidei* in the two other divisions of believers, it was being unfaithful to the Church's primary rule of faith. Vatican I's Constitution *Pastor Aeternus* made it clear that, even on those rare occasions when he speaks infallibly, even the pope does not create objective faith *ex nihilo* but judges and declares what already is the faith of the Church and only when he does so does he enjoy, "that infallibility the Redeemer willed his Church to have in defining doctrine on faith and morals."[32] At Vatican II, the position of conciliar bishops and theologians prevailed.

The council declared, in words that could be considered a practical description of *sensus fidei*, that the teaching of the Catholic Church is preserved by the Holy Spirit in all the faithful, laity, theologians, and bishops together. "The body of the faithful *as a whole*, anointed as they are by the Holy One (cf. 1 John 2:20; 2:27), cannot err in matters of belief [they are infallible]. Thanks to a supernatural sense of the faith (*sensus fidei*) which characterizes the people *as a whole*, it manifests this unerring quality when, 'from the bishops to the last of the faithful,' it manifests universal agreement in matters of faith and morals."[33] Pope John Paul II adds his authority to this position in the case of marriage, teaching that the discernment of the full dignity of marriage "is accomplished through the *sensus fidei*, and is therefore the work of the *whole Church* according to the diversity of the various gifts and charisms."[34] He cites the above text from *Lumen Gentium* and 1 John 2:20 in support of this teaching. John could not be clearer: "You, no less than they, are among the initiated; this is the gift of the Holy One and by it you *all* have knowledge" (1 John 2:20). He is even clearer a few verses further on, "The anointing which you have received from him abides in you, and you have no need that anyone should teach you, as his anointing teaches you about everything, and is true, and is no lie" (1 John 2:27). Catholic tradition enshrines this belief in the doctrine that the Spirit of God is gifted to the whole Church.

These texts make two theological points clear. First, *sensus fidei* of virtually the whole Church is a gift of grace; its source is the Spirit of God. Second, this gift of grace is given to the *whole Church*, laity, theologians, and bishops alike; it is not a gift given only to a hierarchical few. "The entire People of God is the subject that receives."[35] The Church has always been convinced that authentic *sensus fidei* and reception require *universalis ecclesiae consensione* (consent of the whole Church),[36] *totius mundi reverentia* (the reverence of the whole world),[37] *universalis ecclesiae assensus* (the assent of the whole Church),[38] and that this reverence and assent is a sign of the presence of the Spirit in the whole Church.[39] This tradition supports Nathaniel Soede's claim that *sensus fidei* is actually *sensus fidelium ecclesiaeque*, sense of the faithful and of the whole Church.[40]

The continuation of the above-cited passage from *Lumen Gentium*, in Flannery's translation, introduces an important consideration. "By this sense of the faith...the People of God, guided by the sacred *magisterium* which it faithfully obeys (*cui fideliter obsequiens*), receives...truly the word of God."[41] The Latin word *magister*, the root of *magisterium*, literally means *master*, school-master, ship's master, master of a trade; in the medieval Church it came to mean one who has authority deriving from mastery of a subject. Thomas Aquinas, for whom the symbol of genuine authority was the *cathedra* or chair, distinguished two kinds of *magisterium*: that of a bishop, *magisterium cathedrae pastoralis*, and that of a theologian, *magisterium cathedrae magistralis*. The former derives from ordination as a bishop, the latter from mastery of the theological tradition. In the Catholic Church of the past two hundred years, *magisterium* has come to be restricted exclusively to the teaching authority of bishops.[42]

Austin Flannery's translation of the sentence from *Lumen Gentium* cited above underscores the ongoing understanding that Vatican theologians demand of believers toward the ecclesial magisterium: the People of God are to be guided by the *magisterium* and are to *obey* it.[43] The translation of the Latin *obsequium* by the English *obedience*, however, is seriously doubtful. In the official English translation of the Code of Canon Law, *debitum obsequium* is translated as *due respect* (Can 218), and *religiosum obsequium* as *religious respect* (Can 752 and Can 753). There is a difference between obedience and respect, and Flannery's translation tendentiously and falsely bridges the gulf in favor of passive obedience rather than active and mutually respectful dialogue.

Francis Sullivan's reading of *obsequium* appears to us more accurate theologically. "As I understand it, then, to give the required *obsequium religiosum* to the teaching of the ordinary *magisterium* means to make an honest and sustained effort to overcome any contrary opinion I might have, and to achieve a sincere assent of my mind to this teaching."[44] Jean-Marie Tillard comments that "those faithful who have no hierarchical responsibility cannot be seen as simply receiving what is determined by the heads of the Church...the faithful have a specific part to play in this knowledge by the whole Church of the truth given in Jesus Christ."[45] The recipient of the *sensus fidei*, and therefore the proper *locus* for its discernment, is the whole communion of believers. In a Church that is a communion of believers, *sensus fidei* and *consensus fidelium* are attained only through the open, respectful, charitable, and uncoerced dialogue of the entire communion, "from the bishops to the last of the faithful." Bernard Sesboue points out, and we agree, that such *consensus fidelium* takes time. It also requires legitimate magisterial authority to test it critically for ongoing theological meaningfulness, and thereby to fashion and discern it.[46]

Reception

Reception is an ecclesial process by which virtually[47] all the members of the Church assent to a teaching presented to them as apostolic truth and ecclesial faith, thereby assimilating the teaching into the life of the whole Church.[48] The teaching may come to them internally from their own Church, for instance, from an ecumenical council or a decision of the Magisterium, or it may come to them externally from another religious community, as ecumenism came to the Catholic Church from the Protestant traditions. In either case, though it is not what makes the teaching true or false, reception flows from a critical judgment of the existential data and a responsible and prudential decision that the teaching is good for the whole Church and is in agreement with the apostolic tradition on which the Church is built. It is important to be clear that reception is not necessarily a judgment about the truth or validity of a teaching, but a decision about its usefulness in the life of the Church. A non-received teaching is not *eo ipso* false or invalid; it is simply judged by a large majority of believers to be not recognized in, and therefore irrelevant to, their own lives and the life of the Church. As culture, time, and place necessarily inculturated the gospel, the good news of what God has done in Jesus Christ, so too do they also inculturate every doctrinal and moral teaching and every reception of that teaching.[49] The act of reception, therefore, cannot and does not receive the tradition of the past unchanged; the past is always re-appropriated or re-received in the present.[50] In Catholic history, there are many examples of both reception and non-reception.

There is an active dialectic in the Church over the process of reception; reception is a matter of either fiat or dialogue. Vatican theologians seek to reduce it to magisterial fiat and believers' obedience (as does the Flannery translation above), in keeping with the hierarchical model of church still favored by them, "a wholly pyramidal conception of the Church as a mass totally determined by its summit."[51] In the communion model of Church re-introduced into the Catholic world by the Second Vatican Council,[52] reception requires active dialogue, judgment, and consensus in the whole body of the communion's believers, laity, theologians, and bishops. Reception "is not a matter of blind obedience to formal authority, but of the divinely-assisted recognition of the truth of what is taught."[53] Congar points out that obedience is called for, "if the church is conceived as a society subject to monarchical authority," and dialogue and consensus are required, "when the universal church is seen as a communion of churches." "It is certain," he continues, "that this second conception was the one that prevailed effectively during the first thousand years of Christianity, whereas the other one dominated in the West between the eleventh-century reformation and Vatican II."[54] Edward Kilmartin agrees, emphasizing that the patristic and medieval notion of reception was, "a tributary of the dominant ecclesiology of that age: a communion ecclesiology."[55] If obedience to magisterial pronouncements is what is called for, then *sensus fidei* and reception become mere juridical realities; if dialogue and consensus is what is called for, then they become truly ecclesial and theological realities.

We argue that reception of magisterial teaching, both doctrinal and moral, is not the task of the magisterium alone but "of the *whole* people...from the Bishops to the last of the faithful."[56] In the case of infallible statements the "assent of the Church can never be lacking to such definitions on account of the same Spirit's influence, through which Christ's *whole* flock is maintained in the unity of the faith and makes progress in it."[57] If "Christ's whole flock" is involved in receiving *infallible* teaching, it is a safe theological conclusion that the whole flock is involved also in receiving non-infallible teaching. The instances of dramatic development in both Catholic doctrinal and moral teachings to be noted below suggest one obvious reason why this must be so: authoritarian pronouncements do not necessarily assure correct understanding or freedom from error.

There are many classic examples of non-reception in history. The Councils of Lyons II (1274) and Constance (1439), for instance, both produced decrees of union to heal the rift between the churches of the East and West, but both came to nothing when the laity and clergy of the Eastern churches refused to receive them. Closer to modern times there are three classic examples of non-reception leading to dramatic development of Catholic teaching. The first of these is the doctrine on usury. Between 1150 and 1550 the Catholic Church taught that "seeking, receiving, or hoping for anything beyond one's principal – in other words looking for profit – on a loan constituted the mortal sin of usury."[58] The Council of Vienne (1311–12) condemned the taking of interest in the most severe terms. "If anyone should fall into that error of pertinaciously persisting to affirm that interest taking is not a sin, we declare he should be punished as a heretic."[59] This doctrine, which forbade usury as contrary to the natural law, Church law, and the gospel, was taught by the ecumenical councils Lateran II (1139)[60] and Lateran III (1179),[61] and by popes and theologians unanimously. Its reception was altered by the historic experience of the rise of capitalist economies and the approval of interest by lay and clerical believers alike.

The second example is slavery. As late as 1860, the Catholic Church, "taught that it was no sin for a Catholic to own a human being; to command the labor of that other human being without paying compensation...to sell him or her for cash."[62] In 1866, the Holy Office, now the Congregation for the Doctrine of the Faith, issued an instruction about slavery. "Slavery itself, considered as such in its essential nature, is not at all contrary to the natural and divine law, and there can be several just titles of slavery."[63] Gradually, however, as modern European cultures came to understand and value the uniqueness and dignity of every human person, this teaching became non-received and it was abandoned in the final quarter of the nineteenth century.

The third example has to do with the teaching on religious freedom. From the middle of the fourth to the middle of the twentieth century, a 1600 year tradition, the Catholic Church taught that only Christian faith had the right to freedom of expression and worship, and that those who did not share that faith could be punished, even by death, for their false belief. In 1864, Pius IX condemned, "that erroneous opinion, most fatal in its effects on the Catholic

Church and the salvation of souls, called by our predecessor Gregory XVI *insanity*, namely, that freedom of conscience and worship is each man's personal right which ought to be proclaimed and asserted in every rightly constituted society."[64] Against the loud and contentious objections of a vocal minority, this tradition was un-received by the Second Vatican Council and re-received in a way that affirmed as a sacred religious right the freedom to believe as one freely chooses. "A sense of the dignity of the human person has been imposing itself more and more on the consciousness of contemporary man [that is, human experience].... This Vatican Synod declares that the human person has a right to religious freedom."[65] Brian Tierney comments that to argue that this shift in Church teaching is not a correction of a past error but a simple development of what was already implicit in the tradition is "to strain human credulity too far," and that anyone "who believes that will believe anything."[66]

Ladislas Örsy's description of the process of the reception of law is paradigmatic of all reception. He distinguishes two stages in the life of a law. In the first stage, the actor is the legislator, who conceives, formulates, and promulgates the law. In the second stage, the actors are the subjects of the law, who must understand the meaning and value of the law, decide to implement it, and then affirm it by observing it or, by not observing it, bring to the attention of the legislator the difficulty of the law. "When this process is completed and the law is observed throughout the community, its reception is achieved; it has become a vital force that shapes the life of the church."[67] Örsy points out that all this must be done under the umbrella of communion.

Margaret Farley asserts, correctly, that this two-stage process is not only useful but actually *needed* in the case of moral norms. "This is because understanding of moral choices cannot come merely from receiving laws or rules. It entails at the very least a discernment of the meaning of laws and rules in concrete situations."[68] Such discernment and understanding require reflection on human experience, personal, social, and religious, and the social sciences throw revealing light on that experience. We agree wholeheartedly with Farley's further assertion that "it is inconceivable that moral norms can be formulated without consulting the experience of those whose lives are at stake."[69] It is equally inconceivable that doctrines can be formulated without consulting the faith of the whole Church which is articulated in them. As has been already explained, before he defined the dogma of the Assumption of Mary, Pope Pius XII surveyed the Bishops of the world to find out whether or not their various churches received the doctrine. It never occurred to him to define the dogma without somehow "consulting the faithful."

SOCIOLOGY, EXPERIENCE, AND MORAL THEOLOGY

The English theologian-sociologist Robin Gill points out what every sociologist takes for granted, namely, that however much theologians may strive to influence society they themselves are inevitably first influenced by the society in which they live. Long before they start doing theology, and still while they are doing theology, theologians are persons living in and formed by a particular socio-historical experience. Their personal contexts, their very selves, and their theologies are all, at least in part, products of that experience and can, therefore, be "illuminated by the lighting apparatus of the sociologist."[70]

This same point has been made somewhat differently by Robert Doran in his monumental explication and extension of Bernard Lonergan's meta-methodology of theology. For Lonergan, the total enterprise of theology unfolds in two phases. A first phase, which includes the functional specialities of research, interpretation, history, and dialectic, is indirect discourse and mediates the past to the present. A second phase, which includes the specialties of foundations, doctrines, systematics, and communications, is direct discourse and mediates the present to the future. "There is a theology *in oratione obliqua* that tells what Paul and John, Augustine and Aquinas, and anyone else had to say about God and the economy of salvation. But there is also a theology *in oratione recta* in which the theologian, enlightened by the past, confronts the problems of his own day."[71] In Lonergan's intentionality analysis, the functional specialty *foundations* is "a fully conscious decision about one's horizon, one's outlook, one's world-view [and in what we called in a previous chapter perspective]. It deliberately selects the framework in which doctrines have their meanings."[72] Doran adds that an essential part of horizon is the self-appropriation of the theologian which results from self-reflection and possible intellectual, moral, or religious conversion.[73] Social science can illuminate the theologian's horizon and document his or her possible conversion.

Gill further suggests that sociology can illuminate not only the theologian's social horizon but also the social context of his or her theology in three different ways. First, if theologians wish to communicate to society at large, and not just to the choir of convinced believers, sociology can clarify for them the *social context* in which their theology is both construed and received. That social context includes both past and present experience. If they wish, however, to communicate only to the community of believers, they can ignore social context and communicate exclusively in the special, sometimes arcane, categories of traditional abstract theology. Second, in assessing the mutual correlation between faith and praxis, sociology can clarify what may be called the *social structure* of theology, the existential *is* of a religious or theological situation rather than the *ought to be*. As long as sociologists stay within the limits of their discipline to describe the *is* and do not intrude on theological prescription of the *ought to be*, they can be of great help to the theologian seeking to assess the presence of both faith and its existential practice. Third, sociology can also help the theologian assess the *social consequences* of theology as long as, again, it is restricted to assessing, and not evaluating, those consequences. Evaluation of theological consequences is the task of theology, but sociology can greatly assist theological evaluation by supplying detailed assessment of them.[74] Sociology, then, can illuminate theologians and their theologies in four different ways: by illuminating the theologian's existential horizon, by illuminating his or her socio-historical experience, by illuminating the social structure of the theologian's theology, and by illuminating the social consequences of that theology.

Karl Rahner presents practical theology as a descriptive and critical discipline, very much in line with Gill's presentation of sociological *description* followed by theological *prescription*. "Practical theology is that theological discipline which is concerned with the Church's self-actualisation here and now – both that which *is* and that which *ought to be*."[75] The task of practical theology embraces both description and evaluation of present theological experience, including here the present situation of both moral teaching and moral practice. For description, practical theology relies on social science. For evaluation, theology critically distills social scientific data through the established theological filters of scripture, tradition, reason, and described experience and, from this theological evaluation, proceeds the prescription of either dogmatic or moral norms. The assistance received from the social sciences is description of the present experience; theology alone then carries out the task of theological evaluation and prescription.

Rahner explains why theology needs the social sciences for description. Present theological or ecclesial experience cannot be deduced abstractly from prior dogmatic and theological knowledge; it can be concretely described only by practical analysis of the present experience. This is in accord with Lonergan's empirical principle, "there are no true *factual* judgments without a foundation in relevant data,"[76] and the relevant empirical data are supplied by social scientific research. The social sciences offer a range of scientific tools for that analysis, and theology, drawing on its own tradition and principles, can then suggest courses of action consonant with that tradition and those principles. The Second Vatican Council articulated the very same principle on, one can safely assume, the very same foundation. "In pastoral care, sufficient use should be made not only of theological principles but also of the secular sciences, especially sociology and psychology."[77]

This approach shows a resemblance to Don Browning's "descriptive theology." Descriptive theology is, broadly, "horizon analysis; it attempts to analyze the horizon of cultural and religious meanings that surround our religious and secular practices."[78] Since this horizon embraces the human actors in the practice, including the researcher-actor and his or her experience, what Boisen called "the human document,"[79] descriptive theology cannot be just a sociological task, if sociology is understood as a narrowly empirical science. If sociology, however, is understood as a hermeneutical discipline, as it is in the sociology of knowledge,[80] descriptive theology and hermeneutical sociology merge into one another. Hermeneutical sociology sees its task as dialogue between the concrete realities and practices which the researcher studies and the multiple theories and pre-understandings embedded in the human document. Material, psychological, and social realities that determine the researchers are placed within the larger meanings that direct their actions, research, and conclusions.[81] "These larger meanings that constitute the theory embedded in our practices," Browning argues, "invariably have a religious dimension. This is why hermeneutic sociology, when properly conceived, fades into descriptive theology."[82]

If, as Rahner argues, every human situation is actually a divinely graced situation, then every sociological effort to describe the present situation will ultimately have to move from sociological to theological analysis. The former will describe the empirical facets of the situation, the latter the theological facets. We argue that the moral life of real people is an authentic place for sociology to assess scientifically the social consequences of moral doctrine and norms. We suggest, with Gill, that sociology can illuminate the *social structure* of theology, the concrete *is* of the ecclesial and theological experience rather than the abstract *ought to be*. Sociology can provide empirical description of actual moral experience, the what *is*, which the theologian can take, distill through ecclesial and theological filters, and proceed to prescription of what *ought to be*. That prescription, history shows, may be either the validation of an existing moral norm or its transformation into a revised norm. This chapter reflects on that suggestion and attempts to concretize it theologically in two theological realities, namely, moral experience, specifically *sensus fidei moralis* and *reception*, and the moral praxis that flows from them.

The Catholic Church praises sociological research, teaching that "methodical research in all branches of knowledge...can never conflict with the faith, because the things of the world and the things of faith derive from the same God."[83] It asks its theologians "to seek out more efficient ways...of presenting their teaching to modern man: for the deposit and the truths of faith are one thing, the manner of expressing them is quite another."[84] John Paul II teaches that "the church values sociological and statistical research," but immediately adds the proviso that "such research alone is not to be considered in itself an expression of the *sensus fidei*."[85] The pope is correct. Neither empirical research nor public opinion polls are necessarily expressions of *sensus fidei*, but each may contribute to the illumination of *sensus fidei* and may manifest both *fides qua creditur* and *fides quae creditur*.[86]

Only when he received a virtually unanimous affirmative response to his quasi-sociological survey about whether the local churches believed that Mary was assumed into heaven, did Pius XII define in infallible judgment that Mary's Assumption was a universal belief, and therefore a dogma of the Catholic Church. Though his historico-theological horizon and experience was not that of a Church conceived as the communion of all believers, and therefore he did not consult *all* the faithful, from the bishops to the last of the faithful, it still never occurred to him, with all his papal authority, to define the dogma on his own without somehow seeking to determine the universal *sensus fidei.*

How could Vincent of Lerin's rule of faith, everywhere, always, and by all, ever be determined without sociological survey? Of course, such survey does not create either the faith of the individual, the traditional *fides qua creditur,* or what he or she believes, the traditional *fides quae creditur;* both of these are gifts from God. It may, however, and frequently does manifest and illuminate both these aspects of theological faith. "Doctrines," David Martin reminds us, "do not land like meteorites from outer space but grow organically where they have a supporting, fertile niche or cranny."[87] Sociological research illumines the niches and crannies and the doctrines that grow in them; without such empirical illumination the work of theologians tends to appear, at best, no more than interesting speculation or, at worst, abstract anachronism.[88] Gill delivers a judgment that all moral theologians should heed. Christian ethicists, he complains, have been "reluctant to admit that sociology has any constructive role to play in their discipline. It is rare to find a Christian ethicist prepared to examine data about the moral effects of church-going. Instead Christian communities have become far *too idealized.*"[89] What Gill asserts about ethicists we accept, and we assert also about the magisterium, which tends to talk about faith and beliefs as they *ought* to be, rather than as they *are.* If "the body of the faithful as a whole cannot err in matters of belief,"[90] then they must be infallible in the content of their actual faith, in what is in terms of their faith. It is that actual belief that can be illuminated by sociological research.

Pope John Paul's words cited above are intended to suggest that the theological reality, *sensus fidei,* is not reached *solely* by demonstrating sociologically majority reception or non-reception of a teaching or decision. The Church, as has so often been pointed out, is not a political democracy in which majority head count controls faith. Neither, however, is it a monarchy. The Church is, rather, a communion of believers, laity, clergy, and bishops, all of whom are called to listen to the word of God and to receive the apostolic faith as it is contextualized and revealed to them in their contemporary experience. The very scriptures in which the word of God is first communicated or, more precisely, the Christian interpretations of those scriptures, illustrate why majority rule can never be the rule of faith. Authentic

Catholic teaching concerning the reading of scripture today accepts a historical-critical approach; the literal meaning of the texts is the meaning intended
by the writers at a particular time, place, and culture.[91] The approach of a
large majority of Christians, Catholic and Protestant alike, is different; the
literal meaning of the text is the meaning they find in and through modern
language translations, ignoring the time, culture, and place of the writer.

Interpreting documents written in another time and another culture is
always a difficult task, requiring competence in languages, cultures, social
rules, and experiences that are not one's own. It would be disastrous to
permit only people unskilled in these competencies to judge what the gospel
writers did and did not mean. Only those believers trained in the necessary
competencies, that is, the Church's theologians, are qualified to be judges,
but not even them alone. The bishops, legitimately authorized to tradition the
apostolic faith, must challenge the faith of the laity and the theologians, and
their own faith, to discern the authentic faith of the Church in contemporary
times. Only when a respectful dialogue between these three categories of
believers is carried out, explicitly acknowledging the active and not passive
roles of all three, can one speak of authentic *consensus fidelium* and reception. A majority opinion of any one of the three will not necessarily be a
manifestation of the faith of the communion Church.

The same argument applies to Church doctrines. Such doctrines, which
Rahner correctly insists are not only ends but also beginnings of theological
debate,[92] are articulated in concise, technical language: *homoousios, hypo-
stasis* (incorrectly equated with the English *person*), substance, accident,
transubstantiation. They are best understood by believers who grasp the philosophical and theological precision of the language, and are as often as not
misunderstood by believers who do not understand either the language or its
precision. Theological doctrines and their meanings can be properly evaluated only by believers who understand the historical, philosophical, and theological competencies involved. Dulles argues that, to determine *sensus fidei*,
"we must look not so much at the statistics, as at the quality of the witnesses
and the motivation for their assent."[93] We agree.

Sensus fidei, the connatural capacity to discern the truth into which God
as Spirit is leading the Church, must itself be carefully discerned by all who
are competent, that is, in the case of moral teaching, competently trained
moral theologians. Pope John Paul II is correct: a simple head count does not
necessarily express the faith of the Church. A count, however, which includes virtually *all* the faithful, laity, theologians, and bishops alike, most
certainly does manifest the actual faith of the whole church. Contemporary
empirical sociology can and does show that, for instance, in the case of the
moral doctrines related to divorce and remarriage without annulment, contraception, and homosexuality, the contemporary *sensus fidei* of the majority of
both Catholic laity and theologians and, perhaps, pastorally-oriented bishops

shows dramatic development and transformed reception akin to the dramatic development and transformed reception of the doctrines on usury, slavery, and religious freedom. It remains for open, respectful, and challenging dialogue between laity, theologians, and bishops to fashion and attain an authentic *consensus fidelium*.

The understanding of reception propagated by magisterial bishops is historically correlated with their understanding of Church. Reception is most visible and effective when Church is understood to be a communion of believers; it is least visible and effective when Church is understood to be a hierarchically-ordered perfect society. Both these understandings of Church were in evidence at the Second Vatican Council, and a major task for the Council was to discriminate between them. There is no doubt that the prevailing Catholic ecclesiology of the time was the understanding of Church as a hierarchically-ordered perfect society. Ecclesiology, in Congar's judgment, was "practically reduced to a hierarchology."[94] The schema on the Church presented to the Council by Cardinal Ottaviani on November 13, 1962, was a summary of this ecclesial hierarchology: the Church is a perfect and unequal society, within which only clerics, not laity, are the recipients of God-gifted powers of sanctifying, teaching, and governing. This schema was overwhelmingly rejected by the Council's bishops and returned to the Preparatory Commission with a request for a new schema that would balance the institutional, juridical elements of the Church with its mystical, spiritual elements. The new schema's dominant teaching was of the Church as a communion.

The Council's teaching on communion as the essence of the Church was and continues to be greatly facilitated by the pronouncements of successive bishops of Rome, as the Council of Chalcedon's teaching on the two natures in Christ was greatly facilitated by the proclamations of successive bishops of Rome. In a 1971 audience, Paul VI explained that at the Council the Church rethought itself and offered an essential and accessible definition, "the Church is a communion."[95] In a 1976 audience, he explained that communion means, "unity with God...[and]...brotherly love in sharing the same faith, the same hope, and the same charity."[96] His successor, John Paul II, agrees with Paul VI's assessment of the Church as a communion.

In his important *Apostolic Exhortation on the Lay Faithful*, Pope John Paul teaches that "communion is the very mystery of the Church"[97] and, in an address to the bishops of the United States, he explains that "the concept of communion lies at the heart of the Church's self-understanding."[98] Papal reception of the doctrine of the Church as communion could not be clearer. That such reception of the doctrine is widespread also among the bishops of the universal Church is evident from the judgment of the 1985 Synod of Bishops: that the understanding of Church as *koinonia*-communion was the Council's most important teaching.[99] All these receptive judgments confirm the judgment immediately after the Council of Monsignor Gerard Philips, secretary of the Council's Central Theological Commission, that the guiding vision of the Council's concept of Church was its notion that the Church is a communion.[100] As this model of Church as a communion of believers, laity, theologians, and bishops together, takes root in the experience of the contemporary Church, and that rooting is already slowly happening, so also simultaneously will new models of *sensus fidei, consensus fidelium,* and reception take root. The changed experience of Church, *sensus* fidei, and reception will inevitably lead to a changed, re-received moral experience.

CONCLUSION

This chapter might be described as an exercise in Rahner's practical theology, the "theological discipline which is concerned with the Church's self-actualization here and now – both that which *is* and that which *ought to be.*"[101] Practical moral theology is *theological* reflection on and evaluation of the Church's actual moral theological experience. It seeks to explain that experience not in the classicist way, that is, by deduction from abstract theological principles, but in the historically conscious way, that is by induction from empirical description of actual experience critically tested for ongoing theological meaningfulness in light of both the received theological tradition and the actual experience. Practical theology grows out of the relationship between *theoria* and *praxis* which, for morality in the Church, is the relationship between moral faith and *praxis*. To recognize scientifically the Church's actual experience and to perform the required theological reflection, Rahner argues, "practical theology certainly requires sociology."[102]

Today, development in the way Catholics make moral choices and receive a variety of moral teachings, from remarriage after divorce without annulment, to contraception, non-marital sexual intercourse, and homosexual intercourse, is demonstrated by sociological research focused on both laity and theologians.[103] The theologian's task is to speak *from* the actual faith situation of the Church that this research indicates, not only to hand on traditional doctrine which comes from the past but also to evaluate it for theological meaningfulness in the present experience and to hand it on, unchanged or changed as required by critical theological judgment, to shape future theological and ecclesial experience. Charles Peguy, whose thought Congar claims as the root of the *ressourcement* theology which flourished in the middle of the twentieth century and provided the horizon for the theological developments at the Second Vatican Council, expresses the theologian's task well. It is "a call from a less perfect tradition to a more perfect tradition, a call from a shallower tradition to a deeper tradition, an overtaking of depth, an investigation into deeper sources; in the literal sense of the word a 'resource.'"[104] If that is the task, then sociology, which explores and manifests

the present doctrinal experience, can be as much a handmaid for contemporary theological reflection as philosophy was for Thomas Aquinas and his
followers in the medieval period.

No Catholic theologian would deny that ecclesial faith is the primary
source for theological reflection, [105] but that faith always includes *praxis* or
action. That is the pattern that stretches from Paul, who speaks of the *fruits* of
the Spirit (Gal 5:22–23), to Matthew, "you will know them by their *fruits*"
(7:16), and James, who insists that "faith by itself, if it has not works, is
dead" (2:14–17). These biblical texts are advanced not as proof-texts of the
connection between faith and *praxis* but as revealing a pattern that pervades
the New Testament and establishes the connection between faith and *praxis*
as a long-standing Catholic tradition. In the Catholic tradition, one has always been able to argue from the presence of genuine faith to appropriate
praxis and, conversely, from actual *praxis* to the faith that underlies it. Sociology can play an important part in that argument by illuminating present
action, making it possible for theologians to consider the faith behind the
praxis. That is probably why the Second Vatican Council taught that "in
pastoral care sufficient use should be made, not only of theological principles, but also of the findings of secular sciences, especially psychology and
sociology." By making use of these sciences, the Council goes on to assert,
"the faithful will be brought to a purer and more mature living of the
faith." [106] Our claim in this chapter is similar. Sociology has an important role
to play in assessing the moral experience of the entire communion-Church,
laity, theologians, and bishops, thereby providing important data for the entire Church to assess, evaluate, and prescribe a *consensus fidelium* of what
the entire Church ought to believe today, and what it ought to do and not do
in response to that belief. We repeat here our earlier assertion: the attainment
of such *consensus fidelium* takes time and requires ongoing dialogue and
charitable critique by magisterial bishops to fashion and establish.

Pope John Paul II proposed as a motto for our times *opus solidaritatis
pax*, peace as the fruit of solidarity. [107] In conclusion to this consideration of
experience in the communion Church, we adapt that motto to this form: *opus
solidaritatis pax communioque,* peace and communion as the fruit of solidarity. In the next chapter we consider how theology, specifically theological
ethics, and science might cooperate in peace and communion to construct a
realistic sexual anthropology.

QUESTIONS FOR REFLECTION

1. What are the four sources of moral knowledge of Catholic moral
   theology? How is each source to be correlated to the others? How

have they been correlated and prioritized in the past Catholic tradition?

2. How do you understand the word *experience* as used in this chapter? If experience is a source of moral theology, whose experience is to be used, mine, yours, or ours? Discuss criteria for evaluating authentic and inauthentic experience that should inform doctrinal teaching.

3. What do you understand by the word *reception*? What is its function in Catholic theology? Discuss some examples of reception and non-reception which have had serious impact on Catholic teaching. Who determines the reception or non-reception of a Catholic teaching?

4. What is the meaning of the phrase *sensus fidei*? Who are the subjects of this *sensus fidei*? Think of Vincent of Lerins' ancient rule of faith: what is believed everywhere, always, and by all. When, in 1950, Pope Pius XII defined Mary's assumption into heaven, how did he define the "all" in Lerins' rule of faith? How did the Second Vatican Council later define the "all"?

5. Two models of Church were in evidence at the Second Vatican Council: first, a model of Church as a hierarchically structured society; second, a model of Church as a communion of believers. The Council opted for the model of Church as a communion, so that Pope John Paul II could later declare that "communion is the very mystery of the Church." How did the Council understand both the notions of reception and *sensus fidei*? What are the implications of this understanding for all Catholics today?

NOTES

An earlier version of this essay appeared in *Irish Theological Quarterly* 76, no. 1 (2011): 35–56. It is reprinted here with permission.

1. See Charles Curran, *The Catholic Moral Tradition Today: A Synthesis* (Washington, DC: Georgetown University Press, 1999), 48.

2. *Optatam totius*, n. 16.

3. *Gaudium et spes*, n. 44, emphasis added.

4. Servais Pinckaers, *The Sources of Christian Ethics* (Washington, DC: Catholic University of America Press, 1995), 91.

5. Aristotle, *Nicomachean Ethics*, VI, viii, 5–6.

6. For a full explication and analysis of these two schools with respect to sexual norms, see Todd A. Salzman and Michael G. Lawler, *The Sexual Person: Towards a Renewed Catholic Anthropology* (Washington, DC: Georgetown University Press, 2008), 48–123.

7. John T. Noonan, "Development in Moral Doctrine," *Theological Studies* 54, no. 4 (1993): 674–75.

8. What follows in this section is dependent on Todd A. Salzman, *What Are They Saying About Catholic Ethical Method?* (New York: Paulist, 1989), 48–79.

9. *Gaudium et spes*, n. 44.

10. See, for instance, Charles E. Curran, Margaret A. Farley, and Richard A. McCormick, ed., *Feminist Ethics and the Catholic Moral Tradition: Readings in Moral Theology No. 9* (New York: Paulist, 1996).

11. Lisa Sowle Cahill, "Feminist Ethics, Differences, and Common Ground: A Catholic Perspective," in *Feminist Ethics in the Catholic Moral Tradition*, 185. See also Cahill's *Sex, Gender, and Christian Ethics* (Cambridge: Cambridge University Press, 1996) for her emphasis on experience in developing a credible sexual ethic.

12. See Germain Grisez, *The Way of the Lord Jesus. Volume One: Christian Moral Principles* (Chicago: Franciscan Herald, 1983), 10–11.

13. See Germain Grisez, *The Way of the Lord Jesus. Volume Two: Living a Christian Life* (Quincy, IL: Franciscan Herald, 1993), 387–89.

14. John T. Noonan, *A Church That Can and Cannot Change: The Development of Catholic Moral Teaching* (Notre Dame: University of Notre Dame Press, 2005).

15. Neil Brown, "Experience and Development in Catholic Moral Theology," *Pacifica* 14 (2001): 300.

16. Edward Collins Vacek, "Catholic 'Natural Law' and Reproductive Ethics," *Journal of Medicine and Philosophy* 17 (1992): 342–43.

17. For the explanation of church as communion, see Jerome Hamer, *The Church Is a Communion* (New York: Sheed and Ward, 1965); Gustave Martelet, *Les idees maitresses de Vatican II* (Paris: Desclee, 1966); Jean-Marie R. Tillard, *Church of Churches: The Ecclesiology of Church as Communion* (Collegeville: Liturgical, 1992); Michael G. Lawler and Thomas J. Shanahan, *Church: A Spirited Communion* (Collegeville: Liturgical, 1995).

18. John Paul II, *Ut unum sint*, nn. 28–39. See Todd A. Salzman and Michael G. Lawler, "Theologians and the Magisterium: A Proposal for a Complementarity of Charisms Through Dialogue," *Horizons* 36, no. 1 (2009): 7–31.

19. We shall use this tripartite division of believers throughout for purposes that will become apparent as we proceed.

20. Richard Bernstein, *Beyond Objectivism and Relativism* (Philadelphia: University of Pennsylvania Press, 1985), 74.

21. John E. Thiel, *Senses of Tradition: Continuity and Development in Catholic Faith* (New York: Oxford University Press, 2000), 47, emphasis added.

22. John W. Glaser, "Authority, Connatural Knowledge, and the Spontaneous Judgment of the Faithful," *Theological Studies* 29, no. 4 (1968): 742.

23. John Henry Newman, *On Consulting the Faithful in Matters of Doctrine* (New York: Sheed and Ward, 1961), 73.

24. Zoltan Alszegy, "The *Sensus fidei* and the Development of Dogma," in *Vatican II: Assessment and Perspectives Twenty-Five Years After*, ed. Rene Latourelle (New York: Paulist, 1988), 147.

25. For a history of the concept *sensus fidei* and a careful analysis of both its authority and its limitations, see William M. Thompson, "*Sensus fidelium* and Infallibility," *The American Ecclesiastical Review* 167 (1973): 450–86; and Daniel J. Finucane, *Sensus fidelium: The Use of A Concept in the Post-Vatican II Era* (San Francisco-London: International Scholars Publications, 1996). See also John J. Burkhard, "*Sensus fidei* Since Vatican II: I 1965–1984," *The Heythrop Journal* 34, no. 1 (1993): 41–59; "*Sensus fidei* Since Vatican II: II 1985–1989," ibid., no. 2 (1993): 123–36; "*Sensus fidei*: Recent Theological Reflection. Part I," ibid. 46, no. 4 (2005): 450–75; "*Sensus fidei*: Recent Theological Reflection. Part II," ibid., 47, no. 1 (2006): 38–54.

26. John Henry Newman, trans., *Select Treatises of Saint Athanasius in Controversy with the Arians* (London: Longmans Green, 1903), 261.

27. Samuel D. Femiano, *Infallibility of the Laity* (New York: Herder and Herder, 1967), 23.

28. Yves Congar, *Lay People in the Church* (Westminster, MD: Newman, 1967), 288.

29. Vincent of Lerins, *Commonitorium primum* 2, *Patrologia Latina* (*PL*) 50, 640, emphasis added.

30. Thomas Aquinas, *ST* II–II, 2. 3. ad 2. See J. de Guibert, "A propos des textes de Saint Thomas sur la foi qui discerne," *Révue des Sciences Religieuses* 9 (1919): 30–44; C. H. Joyce, "La foi qui discerne d'après Saint Thomas," *Révue des Sciences Religieuses* 6 (1916): 433–55.

31. Cited in Avery Dulles, "*Sensus Fidelium*," *America* 155, no. 1 (November 1, 1986): 240, emphasis added.

32. Denzinger-Schönmetzer, *Enchiridion symbolorum definitionum et declarationum de rebus fidei et morum*, ed. Peter Hünermann, 33rd edn. (Freiburg im Breisgau: Herder), n. 3074. Cited hereafter as DS.

33. *Lumen gentium*, n. 12, quoting Augustine, *De Praed. Sanct.* 14, 27 (*Patrologia Latina* 44, 980), emphasis added.

34. John Paul II, *Familiaris Consortio*, n. 5, emphasis added.

35. Herman J. Pottmeyer, "A New Phase in the Reception of Vatican II: Twenty Years of Interpretation of the Council," in *The Reception of Vatican II*, ed. Giuseppe Alberigo, Jean-Pierre Jossua, and Joseph A. Komonchak (Washington, DC: Catholic University of America Press, 1987), 30.

36. Augustine, *De Baptismo*, VII, 53, *PL* 43, 243.

37. Pope Leo the Great, *Epist.* 14, 2, *PL* 54, 672.

38. Pope Gelasius, *Epist.* 13, *PL* 59, 63.

39. See Gerard Bartelink, "The Use of the Words *Electio* and *Consensus* in the Church (Until about 600)," *Concilium* 77 (1972): 147–54.

40. Nathanael Yaovi Soede, "The *Sensus fidelium* and Moral Discernment," in *Catholic Theological Ethics in the World Church*, ed. James Keenan (New York: Continuum, 2007), 195.

41. *Lumen gentium*, n. 12, in *Vatican Council II: Constitutions, Decrees, Declarations*, ed. Austin Flannery (Dublin: Dominican Publications, 1996), 17.

42. See, for instance, DS, nn. 3011 and 3065; *Lumen gentium*, nn. 18, 22, 25.

43. Austin Flannery, *Vatican Council II,* 363.

44. Francis A. Sullivan, *Magisterium: Teaching Authority in the Catholic Church* (Dublin: Gill and Macmillan, 1985), 164.

45. Jean-Marie R. Tillard, "Le *sensus fidelium.* Reflection theologique," in *Foi populaire* (Paris: Cerf, 1976), 11–12.

46. Bernard Sesboüé, "Le *sensus fidelium* en morale a la lumiere de Vatican II," *Le Supplément* 181 (1992): 153–66.

47. In this essay we acknowledge the ambiguity of the word *virtual* and argue that it can be specified only by dialogue and consensus in the Church. We have no doubt that 86% of any population is virtually all of it, but is 80% or 75% or 68%? Only a dialogue of charity and peaceful consensus will decide.

48. The foundational work on reception was done by Yves Congar, "La réception comme réalité ecclésiologique," *Revue des Sciences Philosophiques et Théologiques* 56 (1972): 369–403; and Alois Grillmeier, "Konzil und Rezeption: Methodische Bemerkungen zu einem Thema der ökumenischen Discussion der Gegenwart," *Theologie und Philosophie* 45 (1970): 321–52. See additional bibliography in Richard R. Gaillardetz, *Teaching with Authority: A Theology of the Magisterium in the Church* (Collegeville: Liturgical, 1997), 252–53.

49. See Second Vatican Council, *Dei verbum*, nn. 11–20; Congregation for the Doctrine of the Faith, *Mysterium ecclesiae*, 5, *Acta Apostolicae Sedis* 65 (1973): 402–3; John Zizioulas, "The Theological Problem of Reception," *Centro Pro Unione* 26 (Fall 1984): 6.

50. Pottmeyer, "A New Phase in the Reception of Vatican II," 27–43.

51. Yves Congar, "Reception as an Ecclesiological Reality," *Concilium* 77 (1965): 60.

52. See, for example, Jean-Marie R. Tillard, *Church of Churches: The Ecclesiology of Communion* (Collegeville: Liturgical, 1992); Michael G. Lawler and Thomas J. Shanahan, *Church: A Spirited Communion*; Dennis M. Doyle, *Communion Ecclesiology* (Maryknoll: Orbis, 2000).

53. Sullivan, *Magisterium*, 112.

54. Congar, "Reception as an Ecclesiological Reality," 62.

55. Edward Kilmartin, "Reception in History: An Ecclesiological Phenomenon and Its Significance," *Journal of Ecumenical Studies* 21 (1984): 34.

56. *Lumen gentium*, n. 12, emphasis added.

57. Ibid., n. 25.

58. Noonan, "Development in Moral Doctrine," 662.

59. DS, n. 906.

60. DS, n. 716.

61. DS, n. 753.

62. Noonan, "Development in Moral Doctrine," 664.

63. Cited in Charles E. Curran, "Authority and Dissent in the Roman Catholic Church," in *Vatican Authority and American Catholic Dissent*, ed. William W. May (New York: Crossroad, 1987), 29.

64. Pius IX, *Quanta cura*, in *The Papal Encyclicals 1740–1878*, ed. Claudia Carlen (Raleigh: McGrath Publishing, 1981), 383.

65. *Dignitatis humanae*, nn. 1–2.

66. Brian Tierney, *Origins of Papal Infallibility 1150–1350: A Study on the Concepts of Infallibility, Sovereignty, and Tradition in the Middle Ages* (Leiden: Brill, 1972), 277.

67. Ladislas M. Örsy, "Reception of Law," in *Encyclopedia of Catholicism*, ed. Richard P. McBrien (San Francisco: Harper Collins, 1995), 1082.

68. Margaret A. Farley, "Moral Discourse in the Public Arena," in *Vatican Authority and American Catholic Dissent*, 177.

69. Ibid.

70. Robin Gill, *The Social Context of Theology: A Methodological Inquiry* (Oxford: Mowbrays, 1975), 7.

71. Bernard J. F. Lonergan, *Method in Theology* (New York: Herder and Herder, 1972), 133.

72. Ibid., 268.

73. Robert M. Doran, *Theology and the Dialectics of History* (Toronto: University of Toronto Press, 1990), 452.

74. Robin Gill, ed., *Theology and Sociology: A Reader* (London: Cassell, 1996), 229–30.

75. Karl Rahner, "Practical Theology Within the Totality of Theological Disciplines," *Theological Investigations* IX (London: Darton, Longman and Todd, 1972), 102, emphasis original.

76. Bernard J.F. Lonergan, "Moral Theology and the Human Sciences," *Method: Journal of Lonergan Studies* 15 (1997): 5–20, emphasis added.

77. *Gaudium et spes*, n. 62.

78. Don S. Browning, *A Fundamental Practical Theology: Descriptive and Strategic Proposals* (Minneapolis: Fortress, 1991), 47.

79. See Alison Stokes, *Ministry After Freud* (New York: Pilgrim Press, 1985), 51–62.

80. For further elucidation of this assertion, see Michael G. Lawler, *What Is and What Ought to Be: The Dialectic of Experience, Theology, and Church* (New York: Continuum, 2005), 44–66.

81. For further detail, see David Tracy, *The Analogical Imagination* (New York: Crossroad, 1981) and Paul Ricoeur, *Hermeneutics and the Human Sciences* (Cambridge: Cambridge University Press, 1981).

82. Browning, *A Fundamental Practical Theology*, 48.

83. *Gaudium et spes*, n. 36.

84. Ibid., n. 62.

85. *Familiaris consortio*, n. 5.

86. Here we disagree with Dario Vitali, "*Sensus fidelium e opinione pubblica nella Chiesa*," *Gregorianum* 82 (2001): 689–717, who seems to us to distinguish too rigidly between public opinion and *sensus fidei* in the Church he acknowledges as a communion.

87. David Martin, *Reflections on Sociology and Theology* (New York: Oxford University Press, 1997), 69.

88. This is the argument made in Richard Dawkins, *The God Delusion* (Boston: Mariner, 2008) and Christopher Hitchens, *God is Not Great: How Religion Poisons Everything* (New York: Twelve, 2009).

89. Robin Gill, *Churchgoing and Christian Ethics* (Cambridge: Cambridge University Press, 1999), 1. Emphasis added.

90. *Lumen Gentium*, n. 12.

91. Pius XII, *Divino afflante spiritu* (*Acta Apostolicae Sedis* 35 [1943]:297–325); Pontifical Biblical Commission, *Instructio de historica evangeliorum veritate* (*Acta Apostolicae Sedis* 56 [1964]: 712–18); Second Vatican Council, *Dei verbum*; Pontifical Biblical Commission, *The Interpretation of the Bible in the Church* (*Origins* 23, no. 29 [January 6, 1994]: 497–524).

92. See Karl Rahner, "Current Problems in Christology," *Theological Investigations*, Vol. 1 (London: Darton, Longman, and Todd, 1965), 150.

93. Avery Dulles, "*Sensus fidelium*," 242.

94. Yves Congar, *Lay People in the Church* (London: Chapman, 1957), 51.

95. Cited from *L'Osservatore Romano*, English Edition, 29 July, 1971. This phrase, "the Church is a communion," was the title of an earlier treatise by Jerome Hamer (New York: Sheed and Ward, 1965).

96. Ibid., 28 July, 1976.

97. John Paul II, *Christifideles laici*, n. 18.

98. *Catholic International*, 3 (1992): 761, n. 1.

99. See its final report, "The Church, in the Word of God, Celebrates the Mysteries of Christ," in *Origins* 15, no. 27 (1985), 444–50, at 2, C, 1.

100. Gerard Philips, *L'Eglise et son mystère au IIe Concile du Vatican* (Paris: Desclée, 1966), I: 7, 59; II: 24, 54, 159.

101. Karl Rahner, "Practical Theology within the Totality of Theological Disciplines," 102, emphasis original.

102. Ibid., 105.

103. See, for instance, Michael Hornsby-Smith, *Roman Catholicism in England* (Cambridge: Cambridge University Press, 1991); William V. D'Antonio, James D. Davidson, Dean R. Hoge, and Ruth A. Wallace, *Laity American and Catholic: Transforming the Church* (Kansas City: Sheed and Ward, 1996); James D. Davidson, Andrea S. Williams, Richard A. Lamanna, Jan Stenftenagel, Kathleen Maas Weigert, William J. Whalen, and Patricia Wittenberg, *The Search for Common Ground: What Unites and Divides Catholic Americans* (Huntington, IN: Our Sunday Visitor, 1997); John Fulton, ed., *Young Catholics at the New Millennium: The Religion and Morality of Young Catholics in Western Countries* (Dublin: University College Press, 2000); William V. D'Antonio, James D. Davidson, Dean R. Hoge, and Katherine Meyer, *American Catholics: Gender, Generation, and Commitment* (Lanham, MD: Rowman and Littlefield, 2001); Dean R. Hoge, William D. Dinges, Mary Johnson, and Juan L. Gonzales, Jr., *Young Adult Catholics: Religion in the Culture of Choice* (Notre Dame: University of Notre Dame Press, 2001); William V. D'Antonio, James D. Davidson, Dean R. Hoge, and Mary L. Gauthier, *American Catholics Today: New Realities of Their Faith and Their Church* (Lanham, MD: Rowman and Littlefield, 2007).

104. Cited in Yves M. J. Congar, *Vrai et fausse réforme dans l'église* (Paris: Cerf, 1950), 43, n. 35.

105. See, for instance, Joseph Doré, "De la responsabilité des théologiens dans l'église," *Nouvelle Revue Théologique* 125 (2003): 3–20.

106. *Gaudium et spes*, n. 62.

107. *Sollicitudo rei socialis*, n. 39.

Chapter Five

Theology, Science, and Sexual Anthropologies

An Investigation

In the previous chapter, we considered the place of human experience in constructing a Catholic theological ethics. In this chapter, we consider another source of theological ethics, namely, science, as a source for developing a sexual anthropology. Practical theology, according to Karl Rahner, is "that theological discipline which is concerned with the church's self-actualization here and now – both that which *is* and that which *ought to be*."[1] Practical theology embraces both description and evaluation of the present situation. For description, theology relies on the sciences; for evaluation, it critically distils the scientific data through its own theological filters. The present situation, social or theological, cannot be deduced abstractly from prior theological theories; it can only be described concretely by the sciences. "There are no true *factual* judgments," Lonergan declares, "without a foundation in relevant data,"[2] and the relevant data are supplied by scientific research and analysis. The sciences offer a range of scientific tools for that research and analysis and theology, drawing on its own traditions and principles, can then suggest a moral course of action consonant with those traditions and principles. This kind of relationship between science and theology is surely what the Second Vatican Council's *Gaudium et spes* had in mind when it taught that, "in pastoral care, sufficient use should be made not only of theological principles but also of the secular sciences, especially sociology and psychology."[3]

Throughout his distinguished career, Joseph Selling, who considers *Gaudium et spes* "a manifesto for contemporary moral theology,"[4] has contributed extensively to fundamental moral theology and theological anthropology, especially by continuing to develop the personalist method—the human person adequately considered—of his mentor Louis Janssens. In this chapter, we hope to contribute to the ongoing development of the personalist method by exploring the interrelationship between science and theology, what is and what ought to be, to adequately consider the sexual person. Historically, much of what has been written and passed on as accepted tradition about theological anthropology has been grounded in a distorted view of creation in general and of sexuality in specific, creating an incomplete theological anthropology at best and an erroneous theological anthropology at worst. Josef Fuchs' judgment on the history of human sexuality throughout the Christian tradition is incontrovertible: "one cannot take what Augustine [or Plato] or the philosophers of the Middle Ages knew about sexuality as the *exclusive* basis of a moral reflection."[5] Christian ethics should be grounded in a comprehensive theological anthropology of the human person adequately considered. Such an anthropology is dependent on theology informed by the sciences. Exploring and analyzing the interrelationship between theology and science can further the renewal of a comprehensive theological sexual anthropology. This chapter, then, has three cumulative sections. First, it explores models of the interrelationship between theology and science. Second, it investigates current Catholic theological sexual anthropologies. Third, it indicates future directions for the investigation and development of a comprehensive sexual anthropology through scientific and theological discourse.

THEOLOGY AND SCIENCE:
MODELS OF THE INTERRELATIONSHIP

Pope John Paul II highlights the need for intense dialogue between science and theology.[6] Theology and science must enter into a "common interactive relationship" whereby, while maintaining its own integrity, each discipline is "open to the discoveries and insights of the other." Physicist Ian Barbour proposes a fourfold typology of the relationship between theology and science: conflict, independence, dialogue and integration.[7] Particularly germane to our topic are dialogue and integration.

The *dialogue* typology explores methodological parallels, content, and boundary questions. Methodological parallel seeks out similarities and dissimilarities between the methods of each discipline that may either complement or serve the method of the other. Boundary questions delimit the capabilities of each discipline and stipulate how far each may go in explaining reality. The *integration* typology encompasses natural theology, theology of nature, and a systematic synthesis of science and religion. For natural theology, the world is the point of departure and the goal is to deepen theological understanding by integrating theological insights. For theology of nature, a particular theological tradition is the point of departure and the goal is to seek to integrate scientific insights into that tradition. For systematic synthesis, the point of departure is the methods, knowledge, and language of theology and science and the goal is to integrate the two into a single system. [8]

Barbour's dialogue and integration typologies parallel Pope John Paul II's proposal for a "community of interchange" between theology and science to expand the partial perspectives of each and "form a new unified vision." An important caveat should be heeded, however: theology should not seek to become science and science should not seek to become theology in terms of either method or content. "Unity always presupposes the diversity and the integrity of its elements."[9] Neither science nor theology should become less itself but, rather, more itself in a dynamic interchange. Each discipline retains its own autonomy and language and yet draws knowledge and insight from the other. [10]

The unity between theology and science that John Paul calls for has common threads with Ted Peters' hypothetical consonance model. Peters posits that consonance "indicates that we are looking for those areas where there is a correspondence between what can be said scientifically about the natural world and what the theologian understands to be God's creation."[11] Consonance may be either strong or weak. Strong consonance means virtual accord or harmony between theology and science. This type of consonance can be misleading, Peters suggests, because the insights of theology and science are often thoroughly dissonant. Weak consonance identifies "common domains of question-asking" and proposes hypothetical answers to these common questions. For theologians, weak consonance invites a shift from rigidity and absolute truth claims, and calls for willingness to subject theological assertions to ongoing investigation and confirmation or disconfirmation. [12]

Gavin D'Costa places John Paul II's stance on the interrelationship between science and theology "squarely within" Peters' hypothetical consonance, where it corresponds more closely with strong than with weak consonance.[13] D'Costa disagrees with the inferences for theology and theological method that Peters draws from strong consonance. For Peters, progress in human knowledge and understanding requires a new theological method in which inviolable theological truth claims are considered actually hypothetical and subject to ongoing "illumination" through the contribution of the sciences and theology in dialogue. Truth claims should not be determined by ecclesial fiat. For D'Costa, "Theology, on a Roman Catholic model, can make no 'progress' without reference to scripture, tradition, and ecclesial authority, even if in practice 'progress' may sometimes be hampered by the latter authority, or probably more often, wisely guided."[14]

We argue that D'Costa's defense of strong consonance and critique of Peters is correct in one sense and incorrect in another. He is correct to the extent that, in the ongoing discernment of truth, theology must certainly utilize scripture and tradition but it must also utilize science in dialogue with ecclesial authority. Peters would certainly accept the revelatory aspects of theology and its contribution to consonance both methodologically and in terms of content, including its need to dialogue with ecclesial authority. What he is rejecting is another model of the relationship between science and theology, namely, "*Ecclesiastical Authoritarianism.*" This authoritarianism, which perceives science as a threat, is evident throughout history but especially in the post-enlightenment period. Peters does not reject theological method *per se*. What he rejects is ecclesiastical authority "sailing past the port" of science in the same way that D'Costa would reject theology "sailing past the port" of scripture, tradition, and ecclesial authority. In light of the historical record and current ecclesiastical suspicion of the contributions of science, especially if those contributions challenge the truth-claims of magisterial moral teaching, D'Costa's view of ecclesiastical authority as a "wise guide" on the incorporation of science into theology might be overly optimistic. Such authority might be more a flight from a critical realism into a naïve ecclesiological realism.

On moral issues such as artificial nutrition and hydration and the permanent vegetative state patient,[15] population control and contraception,[16] homosexuality and same-sex parenting,[17] and sexual anthropology, as we shall see, ecclesial authority has not always served as a wise-guide in incorporating the insights of science. Furthermore, the "dialogue in charity" that Pope John Paul II proposed in *Ut unum sint*[18] has often been lacking when it comes to openness to exploring "inviolable truths."[19] Historically, ecclesial suspicion of the sciences and their perception as a threat gives credence to Peters' (as well as Pannenberg's and Popper's) option for weak consonance. Despite Peters and D'Costa's disagreements on whether strong consonance or weak consonance is the preferred model for the theology-science dialogue, the epistemological method for determining confirmation or disconfirmation affirmed by John Paul II, Peters, and many other theologians and scientists is critical realism.

CRITICAL REALISM IN SCIENCE AND THEOLOGY

Critical realism builds a bridge between science and theology in the process of discerning the meaning of reality and its implications for human flourishing. Critical realism is distinguished from naïve realism. Naïve realism "invokes the correspondence theory of truth to presume a literal correspondence between one's mental picture and the object to which this picture refers."[20]

Critical realism, John Haught suggests, "maintains that our understanding, both scientific and religious, may be oriented toward a real world, whether the universe or God, but that precisely because the universe and God are always too colossal for the human mind to encompass, our thoughts in both science and religion are also always open to correction."[21] By definition, critical realism realizes that human understanding is partial, revisable, and evolving. This insight is what the theologian-scientist Bernard Lonergan labeled an historically conscious worldview, distinguishing it from a classicist worldview.

A classicist worldview asserts that reality and knowledge of it is static, necessary, fixed, and universal. The method utilized, anthropology formulated, and norms taught in this worldview are timeless, universal, and immutable, and the acts condemned by those norms are always so condemned without exceptions. Historical consciousness fundamentally challenges this view of reality and knowledge and asserts that they are both dynamic, evolving, changing, and particular. The method utilized, anthropology formulated, and norms taught in this worldview are contingent, particular, and changeable, and the acts condemned by those norms are morally evaluated in terms of evolving human knowledge, understanding, and circumstances. An historically conscious worldview is dependent upon critical realism; a classicist worldview is dependent upon naïve realism.

Lonergan systematically formulates a version of critical realism. He begins by distinguishing between two kinds of objects. There is the object in the immediate exterior world, the reality that is there before anyone asks "what is it?" and before anyone answers with a name, "it is an apple" or "it is sexual intercourse." Such an object is "already, out, there, now, real." It is *already* for it is prior to any human attention to it; it is *out* for it is outside human consciousness; it is *there* for it is spatially located; it is *now* for it exists and is attended to in time; it is *real* for it is bound up with human living and acting "and so must be just as real as they are."[22] There is also the object in the inner world mediated by meaning. This object is what becomes scientifically and socially understood, judged, and decided by the answer to the question: What is it? "To this type of object we are related immediately by our questions and only mediately by the [intellectual] operations relevant to the answers."[23] There are, in short, objects independent of any human cognitive activity and objects that are the result of human cognitive activity. The two should never be confused.

To these two meanings of the word *object* correspond two meanings of the word *objectivity*. In the world of immediacy, objectivity has one component; it is a characteristic of the object already, out, there, now, and real. In the world mediated by meaning, however, objectivity has three components. First, there is the experiential objectivity constituted by the facticity of objects that are already, out, there, now, and real. Second, there is the normative objectivity constituted by the human knowing and naming of these factual objects through attending, understanding, judging, and deciding about them. Third, there is the absolute objectivity that results from the combination of the two. Through experiential objectivity conditions for already, out, there, now, real objectivity are fulfilled, and through normative objectivity those conditions are truly linked by an attending, understanding, judging, and deciding subject to the object they condition. "The combination yields a conditioned [object] with its conditions fulfilled and that, in knowledge, is a fact and, in reality, is a contingent being or event."[24] This same conclusion is articulated in the philosophy of science as "all facts are theory-laden."[25] The eminent physicist, Werner Heisenberg, formulated this position as an Uncertainty Principle: our knowledge of reality is never exclusively objective but is always mediately conditioned by the knowing subject. The theory-laden nature of facts distinguishes critical realism from naïve realism.

The tension between critical and naïve realism in theological method is well illustrated in ecclesial moral statements on human sexuality. On the one hand, the United States' Bishops have noted, "the gift of human sexuality can be a great mystery at times."[26] The acknowledgment of mystery, however, does not free theologians or the magisterium from the ongoing task of attempting to discern the human as sexual being and of determining the "nature," meaning, and morality of sexuality and sexual acts in the context of human relationships. This acknowledgment of the mysterious nature of human sexuality indicates a commitment to critical realism and hypothetical consonance whereby we must be cautious and tentative in our assertions about human sexuality. On the other hand, in spite of that mysterious nature, ecclesial teaching asserts absolute norms to control sexual behavior. The disconnect between human sexuality as a great mystery and sexual norms that imply a comprehensive understanding of that mystery reflects naïve realism and literal correspondence between a mental picture of human sexual nature and all sexual persons to whom this picture refers. Critical realism's non-literal, though referential, picture allows normative claims for human sexuality to be subjected to confirmation or disconfirmation.

Wolfhart Pannenberg argues that theological hypotheses must be tested and verified indirectly, based on the hypotheses' ability to facilitate increased intelligibility of our experience of finite reality.[27] In light of human experience, a number of absolute sexual norms deduced from ecclesial hypotheses on the nature of the sexual person do not seem to facilitate intelligibility in terms of understanding the mystery of human sexuality. In fact, they seem to assail much of the knowledge gained through the sciences and human experience. The disconnect between ecclesial hypotheses on the nature of the sexual person and the capacity of those hypotheses to make the mysterious nature of human sexuality more intelligible reflects the tensions between naïve realism and critical realism. This tension is evident in the sexual anthropologies that ignore, reduce, or distort the contributions of science (and experience) to theological discourse about human sexuality.

The theory-laden nature of facts, both their compilation and their interpretation, poses challenges for both theologians and scientists, and distinguishes traditionalist and revisionist theologians.

SEXUAL ANTHROPOLOGY AND THE SCIENCES

While many traditionalist and revisionist theologians espouse critical realism, their use of science in the process of constructing a sexual anthropology reflects different models of the theology-science interrelationship.

Traditionalists and Sexual Anthropology

Pope John Paul II laments the fact that theology in general has not fully utilized the sciences in exploring theological questions.[28] This lament seems to apply particularly to traditionalist sexual anthropologies such as New Natural Law Theory (NNLT), developed by Germain Grisez, John Finnis, *et al.*[29]

NNLT and the Basic Good of Marriage

According to NNLT, the person is essentially *homo rationalis*, a rational agent whose choices are to actualize and realize basic or intelligible goods. NNLT's sexual anthropology is based upon the basic good of heterosexual marriage and its fulfillment through parenthood. NNLT's argument for marriage as a basic good and the absolute norms that follow from that basic good develops in three steps. The first step defines heterosexual marriage as a basic good; the second defines marital, reproductive-type sexual acts in terms of that basic good; the third judges all non-reproductive-type sexual acts to be non-marital and, therefore, unnatural, unreasonable, and immoral.

The sexual anthropology that arises from NNLT's understanding of basic goods can be summarized as follows. Basic goods are aspects of human personhood. Marriage, defined as a communion of life requiring consent and consummation, is such a basic good, actualized through marital sexual acts that have two intrinsic meanings, parenthood and friendship. There is a strict hierarchy in the relation between the biological and the personal meaning of the marital act. The biological aspect is the *sine qua non* for the personal meaning of the sexual act. Marital acts of a reproductive kind, Finnis claims, are "biologically *and thus* personally one."[30] All non-marital sexual acts, including non-reproductive acts within marriage, are merely acts of personal gratification and are unnatural, unreasonable, and immoral.[31] NNLT argues that the absolute norms of the magisterium condemning artificial contraception, homosexual sex, masturbation, and reproductive technologies are grounded in the basic good of marriage. These norms are absolute, even infallible,[32] and cannot be changed.

Martin Rhonheimer and the Heterosexuality of Virtue

Rhonheimer's unique contribution to a traditionalist sexual anthropology is his development of an "intimate connection" between moral virtue and the precepts of the natural law.[33] His "integral/personal anthropology" is grounded in moral virtue.[34] Rhonheimer defines the "truth of human sexuality" as married love, "a free, mutual self-giving of indissoluble permanence between two persons of the opposite sex."[35] At the core of human sexuality is freedom, autonomy in the "nature" of the human being, to be drawn to the good of marriage. The truth of human sexuality lies necessarily between male and female and this truth is dependent, not on physical or natural functions but on the personal function of autonomous human beings in relation to one another.

Rhonheimer argues that sexual acts that stand outside this truth contradict it and are objectively immoral, not because they are unnatural "but because they contradict the (practical) truth of the natural, as it appears on the horizon of apprehension and regulation by the reason."[36] We know human "nature," Rhonheimer argues, by the inclination towards the goods through practical reason. Humans are inclined towards the good of married love, and it is this inclination that reveals their true "nature" and the truth of human sexuality. This objective truth is specified by the inseparability of the unitive and procreative meanings of the sexual act, and is affirmed by the virtue of chastity, or "mastery of one's own sexual drives so as to integrate them into the order of personal love."[37] Rhonheimer's virtue-based anthropology condemns as objectively immoral all acts that contradict this truth, including homosexual acts, non-marital sexual acts, and contraceptive acts.

Pope John Paul II and Ontological Complementarity

John Paul II attempted to move the Catholic tradition beyond a procreationist, biological model and to develop the unitive dimension of human sexuality by more fully developing personalist insights into human relationality. For John Paul, "sexuality, by means of which man and woman give themselves to one another through the acts which are proper and exclusive to spouses, is by no means something purely biological, but concerns the innermost being of the human person as such." This is said to be a sign of "a total personal self-giving."[38]

John Paul develops his philosophical personalism in conjunction with an idiosyncratic reading of scripture to construct a theological anthropology, which others have called a theology of the body.[39] This theology is grounded in a theological anthropology, developed from Genesis, of the communion between man and woman.[40] Masculinity and femininity are "two 'incarnations' of the same metaphysical solitude before God and the world." These two ways of "'being a body'…complete each other" and are "two complementary ways of being conscious of the meaning of the body."[41] It is through the complementarity of male and female that a "communion of persons" can exist and that the two "become one flesh."[42]

Complementarity has become a foundational concept in both John Paul II's theological anthropology and magisterial teaching on human sexuality. Complementarity intends that certain realities belong together and produce a whole that neither can produce alone. We note the following characteristics of John Paul's complementarity. First, complementarity is nearly always classified along masculine and feminine lines.[43] Second, complementarity is often formulated as a "nuptial hermeneutics" in terms of bridegroom and bride.[44] Third, in his theological anthropology John Paul posits an "ontological complementarity" whereby men and women, though fundamentally equal and complete in themselves,[45] are incomplete as a couple.[46] Sexual complementarity completes the couple in marriage and reproductive-type sexual acts by bringing the masculine and feminine biological and psychological elements together in a unified whole. All non-reproductive-type sexual acts damage this complementarity and are immoral.

Traditionalists, Sexual Anthropology, and Science: A Critique

In traditionalist anthropologies, we are struck by the reductionist use of scientific knowledge. For NNLT, the basic good of marriage is grounded in a heterogenital, biological criterion where marital, reproductive-type acts are "biologically *and thus* personally one." For Rhonheimer, the virtue of chastity and its requirement for heterosexual, non-contraceptive, reproductive-type sexual acts intrinsically links chastity to openness to procreation and heterogenitality. For John Paul II, there is only one theology of the body, heterogenitally complementary bodies open to biological reproduction. Scientific knowledge appears to be either totally lacking or used selectively in these anthropologies in at least three ways.

First, traditionalist anthropologies posit that heterosexuality is ordered or "natural" and homosexuality is "objectively disordered"[47] or unnatural. Such a move is problematic metaphysically and scientifically. Metaphysically, when traditionalists shift "the ground of moral debate from the inter-personal (e.g., human relationships) to the biological (e.g., objective disorder), it sounds like an admission of defeat. It's a materialistic argument which elevates the biological to the metaphysical."[48] Scientifically, it is a misrepresentation. Peer-reviewed scientific literature has documented same-sex sexuality in over 300 species of vertebrates as a natural component of the social system.[49] Based on such studies, James Allison challenges the claim that a homosexual orientation is objectively disordered. "There is no longer any reputable scientific evidence of any sort: psychological, biological, genetic, medical, neurological – to back up the claim."[50] There is, in fact, substantial scientific evidence to the contrary. Though homosexuals make up a very small minority of the human population, the homosexual orientation of this population is still an intrinsic dimension of human sexual identity.[51]

Second, the scientific knowledge of homosexual orientation has implications for assessing the morality of homosexual acts. What is "natural" sexual behavior for homosexuals and heterosexuals must be determined in terms of the sexual orientation of a given person and the meaning of the sexual act for that person in relationship. Just as it would be "unnatural" for a heterosexual person to engage in homosexual acts, so too, it would be "unnatural" for a homosexual person to engage in heterosexual acts. These acts are judged unnatural, not because of a foundational heterogenital, biological criterion but because of an inadequate consideration of the sexual human person. There is no scientific evidence to substantiate the claim that homosexual acts (or non-reproductive heterosexual acts) assault human dignity and are destructive of relationships. In fact, there is substantial scientific evidence to the contrary. Michael Hartwig notes "the overwhelming convergence of [scientific] evidence is that gay men and lesbians, as a group, display levels of health, family functioning and strength, personal development, mutuality, commitment, and, dare we say, love, similar to heterosexuals."[52]

Third, complementarity arguments, in which the biological, heterogenital sexual differences are *sine qua non* for the personal characteristics that enable male and female to be "ontologically complementary," are not substantiated by biology. "Biology is no longer a prop," Christine Gudorf comments, "but a problem" for such arguments. "Whether we speak of sexual orientation, sexual identity, or sex differences," she continues, "biology and related sciences present us with complex data that cannot be reduced simply to a dimorphic, complementary human sexuality."[53] This scientific data demonstrates that male-female sex differences may frustrate personal complementarity in a relationship rather than facilitate it. Traditionalists have not gone far enough in incorporating "biology" or other scientific insights into their anthropologies. Human sexuality is influenced and shaped not only by biology but also by society, culture, religion, and experience.[54] Traditionalist sexual anthropologies tend to reduce the scientific contribution to actual or possible biological reproduction in reproductive-type sexual acts. This reductionist use of science fails to adequately consider the sexual human person.

Where do NNLT, Rhonheimer, and John Paul II fall in the science-theology dialogue? Peters notes that John Paul II has "a serious interest in fostering dialogue between theology and the natural sciences" in an attempt to negotiate "a new peace between faith and reason."[55] In the use of science in formulating a sexual anthropology, however, there seems to be at best a disconnect between scientific knowledge and doctrinal claims, or at worst an actual misuse of scientific claims. Stephen Pope notes that, in the writings of Pope John Paul II, scientific discoveries and information are expected to confirm what the magisterium claims to know from scripture and the natural law.[56] In terms of human sexuality and anthropology, traditionalists engage in scientific proof-texting, i.e., they accept a heterosexual, reproductive anthropology as the sole "truth" of human sexuality and judge any scientific contributions in light of that "truth." This approach to the theology-science dialogue seems to be a cross between strong consonance and ecclesiastical authoritarianism.

Strong consonance means virtual accord or harmony between theology and science. While traditionalist supporters of John Paul claim that their position represents strong consonance,[57] there is not accord or harmony between science and theology on a number of anthropological sexual claims, including sexual orientation, the "objective disorder" of homosexual orientation, and the damaging impact on human dignity of all non-reproductive type sexual acts. Given the history of ecclesial responses to those theologians who disagree with their normative claims regarding human sexuality, ecclesiastical authoritarianism seems to dominate the theology-science relationship for traditionalists. Ecclesiastical authoritarianism seems to perceive science as a "threat," especially when science challenges Catholic doctrine.[58]

Revisionists and Sexual Anthropology

While traditionalist theologians make limited and selective use of science in constructing their theological anthropologies, revisionist theologians seek to construct a theological anthropology by integrating scientific knowledge in a way that reflects Peters' weak hypothetical consonance model.

Christine Gudorf: Body, Pleasure, and Relationship

Gudorf cautions against the absolutization of science and acknowledges its limitations for discerning meaning in human sexuality, but still claims that the biological and social sciences have "revolutionized" our understanding of sexuality.[59] She suggests they can facilitate "restructuring Christian sexual ethics" by deepening our understanding of human sexuality.[60] Her proposal for a revised sexual anthropology evinces a profound appreciation for embodied sexuality and recognizes pleasure as a fundamental good within responsible, meaningful, sexual relationships and acts. That requires, however, that we give greater weight than has been given in the past to the sciences.

Traditionally, biological science posited that there were only two sexes indicated by two sets of chromosomes, either XX or XY. This dimorphic sexual classification has been used to defend a heterosexual, procreationist sexual anthropology. More recently, however, scientists have discovered that there are over 70 sex chromosomal variations containing chromosomal combinations such as XXX, XYY, and single X make-ups.[61] This information profoundly challenges the simple dimorphic male-female distinction. Masters and Johnson pointed out years ago that sexual identification actually lies on a continuum. Contemporary biology and social science support this hypothesis and suggest a changed understanding of not only the biological dimorphism of male/female but also the relationships that embody different sexual orientations and their cultural assimilation.

The social sciences provide further information on human sexuality, especially on the social construction of the understanding of human sexuality and its structures, organization, and practices throughout history. They can also provide data to guide our discussion of human sexuality and to evaluate its experience in scripture, in tradition, and in contemporary relationships. The analysis and interpretation of this data is crucial for the construction of a holistic sexual anthropology, which recognizes that, as our scientific understanding of what it means to be a sexual person evolves and changes, so too assertions about the normative expression of sexuality that leads to human dignity and flourishing may change.

The United States' Catholic Bishops note that "the gift of human sexuality can be a great mystery at times."[62] That acknowledgment of mystery suggests caution in formulating and propagating absolute prohibitions of certain types of sexual acts, allied to continued commitment to further discern the mystery of human sexuality through the dialogue between the sciences and theology. It is on the basis of dialogue that seeks to integrate knowledge gained through the sciences with scripture and tradition that Gudorf proposes expanding the traditionalist procreative, act-centered model of human sexuality. This expanded model focuses on the *meaning* of sexual acts for human relationships, rather than on the acts themselves. Focusing on the *meaning* of sexual acts and not on the naked acts *in se* enables Gudorf to consider the morality of homosexual and heterosexual reproductive and non-reproductive type sexual acts, depending on a person's biological makeup and cultural context.

Lisa Sowle Cahill: Family, Kinship, and Gender

Whereas Gudorf's sexual anthropology emphasizes pleasure and intimacy, Cahill asserts that these dimensions need to be complemented by a critical analysis of the "social ramifications of sex." Cahill writes from a feminist perspective, "a commitment to equal personal respect and social power for women and men."[63] Her method is grounded in Aristotle and Aquinas and is critically realist, inductive, experientially based, and historically conscious. She uses social sciences to dialogue with other cultures to discern substantive universal goods associated with embodied personhood, including sex, gender, marriage, parenthood, and family.[64] While she is committed to the Catholic natural law tradition, a universalist ethic grounded in human flourishing reflected in basic goods or fundamental values, Cahill differs from traditionalists on the definition of the goods and their normative implications for human relationships.

Cahill posits goods that are both universal and particular. Goods are universal as "shared framing experiences and moral common ground,"[65] indicating "shared human being in the world."[66] Goods are particular, in that the "'shared' is achieved not beyond or over against particularity but in and through it."[67] Particularity is discerned through social analysis and intercultural dialectic.[68] While the emphasis on marriage and family as a universal good is shared with traditionalists, Cahill provides an interpersonal model of marriage that particularizes this good and goes beyond traditionalists' emphasis on biologism and procreationism over relationship. She espouses an interpersonal sexual anthropological model, but argues that it "should be placed in a deeper and more nuanced social context, with better attention both to the familial ramifications of sexual partnerships, and to differences and similarities in cross-cultural experiences of sex, gender, and family."[69] This cultural and historically conscious sensitivity fundamentally distinguishes Cahill's method and definition of the goods of marriage and family from traditionalist methods and definitions. She highlights the importance of children as an aspect of that good, but also emphasizes the need to see marriage and family as a complex interrelationship between relational, sexual, and social dimensions. In light of this complexity and totality, some absolute magisterial norms, such as the prohibition of artificial birth control, need to be refined and redefined.

Margaret Farley: Just and Loving Sexual Acts

Farley emphasizes that the sciences or "secular disciplines" and human experience have contributed to our understanding of human sexuality by correcting past mistakes and by generating new insights that clarify sexual ethics and call into question long-taken-for-granted but unverifiable conclusions. Although the secular disciplines "give us a kind of 'access' to reality," they do require a sort of "exegesis" and interpretation to discern their relevance to sexual anthropology and sexual ethics.[70] This exegesis should be carried out through responsible and respectful dialogue that involves diverse voices seeking to discern and formulate a credible sexual anthropology. Diversity must include gender, sex, sexual orientation, socio-economic, ethnic, cultural and historical dimensions. To explore diversity, Farley investigates the biological and the social sciences.

First, the biological sciences indicate that there are chromosomal, hormonal, and anatomical differences among human beings classified as male and female. One should be aware, however, that both biological studies on human sexual differentiation and the use of those studies in constructing "sextypes" are subject to cultural interpretation and bias. Biological studies can be helpful for informing an anthropology, but one "should not expect more from them than they can deliver."[71] Farley's cautionary note reflects the position many scholars espouse, a non-reducible hierarchy in scientific disciplines. This non-reducible hierarchy begins with the hard-sciences and moves upwards to the soft sciences and the speculative sciences. On the one hand, the lower level sciences place "constraints" on upper level sciences; on the other hand, they allow for authentic "emergence" of upper-level laws, processes, and properties.[72] Many scholars locate theology at the top of the scientific hierarchy since it attempts to integrate the entirety of knowledge, but they also insist that it must be "maximally constrained" by the other scientific disciplines.[73]

Second, Farley uses the social sciences to explore cross-cultural and interreligious understandings of human sexuality "in which sexuality gains its meaning in profoundly different ways of living and believing."[74] She cautions, however, against drawing strong conclusions from these investigations. The conclusion she does draw recognizes "the very plasticity of human sexuality, its susceptibility to different meanings and expressive forms."[75] Such sociological studies "belong to the map of human sexual meanings."[76]

Though she recognizes the importance of biological, sociological, and anthropological insights, which alert theologians to the multifaceted historical, cultural, and religious understandings and expressions of human sexuality, Farley rejects a reductionist, absolutist, "one-size-fits-all" anthropology and normativity for human sexuality. Instead, relying upon the sciences and experience, she constructs a complex vision of the sexual person and proposes justice in love as a principled approach to determine "when sexuality and its expressions are appropriate in human relationships."[77] She asserts that for sexual acts to facilitate human flourishing, they must be just and loving. Such acts go far beyond the narrow and limited normative spectrum of the traditionalists based on a reproductive anthropology. "Today we also know that the possibilities of mutuality exist for many forms of relationship—whether heterosexual or gay, whether with genital sex or the multiple other ways of embodying our desires and our loves."[78]

Todd Salzman and Michael Lawler: Holistic Complementarity and the Human Person Adequately Considered

In an effort to move a seemingly stalled Catholic sexual anthropology forward, Salzman and Lawler have recourse to both scientific and theological resources, employing biological and social sciences along with scripture, tradition and human experience to do two things. First, to engage dialogically, critically, and historically consciously normative Catholic principles guiding sexual morality and reigning traditionalist and revisionist analyses of those principles in order, second, to construct a renewed Catholic sexual anthropology and to formulate a new foundational principle for sexual ethics, namely, holistic complementarity.[79] They appropriate to themselves Pope John Paul II's judgment that dialogue "is rooted in the nature and dignity of the human person. . . . [I]t is an indispensable step along the path toward human self-realization, the self-realization of each individual and of every human community."[80] Following the direction mapped out by that papal judgment, Salzman and Lawler enter into dialogue with both traditionalist and revisionist positions on normative sexual morality in order to articulate a renewed and critically realist Catholic anthropology.

The biological sciences challenge the rigid magisterial dimorphism of human sexuality and complementarity and indicate the naturalness of heterosexual, homosexual, and bisexual orientations, and experience shows that a variety of sexual expressions facilitate human flourishing and the love of God, neighbor and self.[81] The social sciences provide no data to support the claim, made again recently in the United States Catholic Bishops' letter on Marriage, that non-reproductive type sexual acts, heterosexual or homosexual, are destructive of human dignity.[82] Indeed, they supply a large volume of data to support the contrary claim.[83] Integrating scientific studies with scripture and tradition, Salzman and Lawler seek to renew the traditionalist, primarily procreationist, Catholic sexual anthropology and complement it with a more adequately considered sexual anthropology that prioritizes the unitive over the procreative meaning of human sexuality. They develop a holistic complementarity that includes orientation, personal, and biological complementarity, and the integration and manifestation of all three in just, loving, committed sexual acts that promote human flourishing and facilitate a person's ability to love God, neighbor, and self in a more personally profound and holy way.[84]

Joseph Selling: Meanings of Human Sexuality

In addition to his focus on historical studies tracing the "meanings" of human sexuality throughout Christian tradition,[85] Selling emphasizes the need to complement tradition with other sources of moral knowledge, namely experience, science, and scripture, to construct a personalist, holistic meaning of human sexuality. Regarding human experience, Selling notes that sexuality is not reducible to physical or biological meaning. Rather, meaning "is the result of personal-social construction that is attributed to experience uniquely by human beings."[86] Discerning meaning is always in process historically and contextually. Selling has recourse to various scientific disciplines, which are essential complements in this process of discernment. He approvingly cites *Persona humana's* statement on the findings of the sciences:

> According to contemporary scientific research, the human person is so pro-
> foundly affected by sexuality that it must be considered as one of the factors
> which give to each individual's life the principle traits that distinguish it . . .
> make that person a man or a woman, and thereby largely condition his or her
> progress towards maturity and insertion into society. [87]

Reviewing the findings of sexologists, psychiatrists, [88] and sociologists on the meanings of human sexuality, Selling concludes that a holistic under-standing of those meanings include, among other dimensions, "not only inti-macy ('unitive') and fertility ('procreative') but also pleasure, recreation (play), relief, affirmation, receptivity, self-acceptance, forgiveness, reconcili-ation, gratitude and, of course, respect." These meanings extend beyond the experience of the couple-in-relationship "to the social, institutional, political and religious meanings that can only be appreciated in those respective con-texts."[89] While scripture does not give us a blueprint for a timeless meaning of human sexuality, it "always begins with a relational context and is only concerned with specific sexual behavior insofar as it has a bearing on the integrity of individual and social relationships."[90]

Combined, the sources of moral knowledge—scripture, tradition, reason (sciences), and experience—point to relationality as "the primary character-istic of human sexuality." If relationality is the primary characteristic of human sexuality in all its meanings, and we accept that it is the primary characteristic, then, Selling suggests, perhaps we should shift the focus of the discussion of appropriate sexual behavior from the virtue of temperance, which has traditionally served as the guiding virtue in sexual behavior, to the virtue of justice, which "respects persons and renders what is their due." Sexual justice and the objective criteria for discerning whether or not respect-ing and rendering persons-in-relationship their due have been realized, must be based on "a total vision of 'the human person integrally and adequately considered.'"[91] This total vision is not reducible to the biological or physical but is discerned through the meanings of sexual acts for relationality.

Revisionists, Anthropology, and Science: A Critique

All the revisionist theological anthropologies we explored above have differ-ent nuances, but they share four things in common. First, they view the traditionalist, procreationist sexual anthropology as too narrow and reduc-tionist. Second, they engage more comprehensively the sciences and human experience, especially as this is revealed through the social sciences, and seek both to facilitate dialogue between theology and science and to integrate scientific knowledge into a comprehensive theological anthropology. This project is ongoing and evolving and requires care and humility in making normative assertions. Revisionists fully affirm Pope John Paul II's invitation that theology and science must search for truth through "critical openness and interchange" and that this interchange "should not only continue, but also grow and deepen in its quality and scope."[92] This process of dialogue will require openness to exploring positions that may challenge a traditional anthropology and the norms that are deduced from it. Third, revisionists manifest a degree of tentativeness towards the contributions of both the sciences and theology and they insist on the need for ongoing dialogue and discernment in constructing a sexual anthropology. Fourth, this tentativeness demands that all hypotheses be subjected to confirmation and/or disconfirmation, as in Peters' weak hypothetical consonance.[93]

FUTURE DIRECTIONS

Theology

How can Catholic theology, in dialogue with science, move forward in constructing a holistic sexual anthropology? In the space remaining, we sketch in outline some important considerations. First, more theologians "should be sufficiently well versed in the sciences to make authentic and creative use of the resources that the best-established theories may offer them."[94] Second, for authentic dialogue to take place, the magisterium must include in the dialogue both "safe" theologians, those whose use of science supports ecclesial teachings, and "unsafe" theologians, those whose use of science may challenge ecclesial teachings. Current magisterial practice limits consultation to only safe theologians, a practice that implicitly endorses one school of theology over others and provides implicit ecclesial sanction for that school's theological method and sexual anthropology. The result is harmful in two ways. Debates are frequently settled by the exercise of authority rather than by rational argument and constructive dialogue; responses from theologians who have not been consulted is sometimes critical, which then permits them to be labeled, unfairly, as dissenters.[95]

Third, discerning the impact of science on theological doctrine may reveal an ecclesiology guiding the discernment process. Yves Congar, arguably the greatest Catholic ecclesiologist of the twentieth century, accurately described two attitudes required of Catholics on the basis of two distinct theological models of church. Obedience to church authority is required when the church is modeled as a society subject to monarchical authority, and dialogue and consensus are required when the church is modeled as a communion.[96] A theologian's ecclesiology does not necessarily determine the scientific theories and data he will select to construct an anthropology, but it can influence

the selection of such theories and data. Ecclesiology, therefore, must be part
of the science-theology dialogue. Fourth, human experience, especially as
this is revealed through the social sciences, must be given due consideration
in analyzing any doctrinal teaching. While experience alone is never determinative of doctrine, history shows that it has often influenced changes in
doctrine.[97] *Sensus fidelium*, an essential aspect of Catholic tradition and a
source of moral knowledge, is often manifested in and through experience
documented by the social sciences..

Fifth, there must be consistency in the use of science to inform church
teaching. In *Caritas in veritate*, Pope Benedict XVI affirms the importance
of scientific contributions to discern the impact of economics on peoples and
the environment and invites creative responses in light of those contributions.[98] Creative responses based on scientific contributions have long been a
hallmark of Catholic social ethics, but not of Catholic sexual ethics. Sixth,
the use of science should be consistent *and* accurate. The CDF argues against
same-sex unions based on the premise that "allowing children to be adopted
by persons living in [same-sex] unions would actually mean doing violence
to these children."[99] The CDF provides no scientific evidence, here or elsewhere, to substantiate this claim. The social sciences, however, provide
abundant evidence to the contrary. Already in 1995, Charlotte Patterson summarized the evidence in a 20-year retrospective. "There is no evidence to
suggest that lesbians and gay men are unfit to be parents or that psychosocial
[including sexual] development among children of gay men or lesbians is
compromised in any respect relative to that of heterosexual parents."[100]

Anne Brewaeys' 1997 study in the Netherlands[101] and Raymond Chan's
1998 study in the United States[102] confirmed that there was no reason to be
concerned about the psychological development of children raised by lesbian
mothers. Tasker and Golombok[103] and Bailey and Dawood[104] reported from
Britain and North America respectively that the vast majority of children of
homosexual parents grow up to be heterosexual young adults. On the basis of
the scientific evidence, the American Academy of Pediatrics judged in 2002
that children of gay parents "fare as well in emotional, cognitive, social, and
sexual functioning as do children whose parents are heterosexual."[105] The
American Psychological Association rendered the same judgment in 2004.[106]
In 2009, a major study by Paige Averett demonstrated that there is no significant difference in emotional problems experienced by children adopted by
heterosexual, gay, and lesbian parents, and that the children of gay and lesbian parents had strength levels equal to or exceeding scale norms. Gay and
lesbian parents also fell into the desirable range of the Parent-as-Teacher
Inventory.[107]

Finally, James Gustafson highlights three questions that each theologian
must address when using the empirical sciences in theological discourse.
First, "What data and concepts are relevant to the moral issue under discus-

sion?"[108] While such determinations are often implicit, they should be formulated and justified explicitly. Second, "What interpretation of a field should be accepted? And on what grounds?"[109] This question requires clear criteria to evaluate methods and knowledge claims. Third, "How does the moralist deal with the value biases of the studies that he [or she] uses?"[110] "All facts are theory-laden" not only for scientists but also for theologians. The challenge is to be honest about the values, principles, and biases of both the scientific data selected and the theologian who selects them, and to critically evaluate the anthropological and normative implications of those biases for any moral norm.

Science

In its pursuit of truth, science can facilitate dialogue, first, by suspending the traditional suspicions surrounding religious belief. Second, science can promote funding that not only furthers political and economic agendas (e.g., the military complex or drugs that only benefit wealthy nations) but also promotes human dignity among the powerless and oppressed.[111] Third, scientists and theologians, recognizing that "all facts are theory-laden," should seek to uncover and suspend biases that distort research methods and data results.[112] Fourth, researchers must have freedom from coercion to have research findings conform to the presuppositions or desires of people who can reward or punish the researcher's work. Fifth, private and public funding for scientific research should be flexible in implementing research protocols for religious institutions.

Tensions exist, for example, for clinical investigators in Catholic medical institutions when research protocols for externally funded research projects require subjects to use artificial contraception as a requisite for participation. The FDA recognizes abstinence as a legitimate form of birth control when testing drugs that have potential teratogenic effects that may cause severe birth defects, but some pharmaceutical companies often require additional forms of contraception that are proscribed by magisterial teaching.[113] This places researchers in Catholic institutions at a severe disadvantage for funded research, which has institutional ramifications. Such conflicts require dialogue and compromise both on the side of funding organizations pursuing scientific knowledge and on the side of religious institutions providing the researchers.

Interrelationship between Theology and Science

On the interrelationship between theology and science, John Paul II notes "the unprecedented opportunity we have today is for a common interactive relationship in which each discipline retains its integrity and yet is radically open to the discoveries and insights of the other."[114] Mooney notes, and addresses, many of the obstacles to realizing this radical openness, and posits a focus that will make the interrelationship meaningful and productive for both participants.[115] Theology must recognize the impact of matter and culture on human understanding and self-transcendence; science must recognize the complexity of the human person that transcends the merely material. Exploring the interrelationship between the transcendent and material, soul and body, requires ongoing dialogue, in which, John Paul II asserts, "science can purify religion from error and superstition [and] religion can purify science from idolatry and false absolutes."[116] We add that science can also purify religion from false absolutes. Traditionalist absolute claims about human sexuality, for instance, need to be parsed in dialogue with the data of the biological and social sciences to investigate their truth or falsity.

CONCLUSION

Even though Pope John Paul II and traditionalists claim to rely on data from the sciences and experience to construct a sexual anthropology and justify absolute norms,[117] they proceed from a misdefined, and therefore inadequate, sexual anthropology to judge the validity of what science and experience discover concerning human sexuality. In effect, the truth-claims of magisterial statements on human sexuality and the epistemology used to justify those claims are used to judge the truth-claims and epistemologies of other types of discourse, science and experience, without any attempt at dialogue with scientific conclusions that challenge magisterial statements. Such an approach risks committing the "fallacy of epistemological imperialism," that is, "seeking to nullify another discourse from within one's own."[118] True development and insight into human understanding requires authentic dialogue between theology and science.[119] Pope Benedict's statement on the moral use of condoms for male prostitutes to prevent the spread of HIV may signal a positive move towards such a dialogue that recognizes the complexity of human sexuality and the moral norms guiding sexual behavior. We hope that such authentic dialogue might become normative, rather than exceptional, in the theological-scientific evaluation of not only what *is* but also what *ought to be,* and might ultimately lead to the construction of a credible and coherent Catholic sexual anthropology. In the next chapter, we move on to consider such a sexual anthropology.

QUESTIONS FOR REFLECTION

1. Bernard Lonergan judges that "there are no true factual judgments without a foundation in relevant data." Do you think this applies to

theology? Where would theology find a foundation for its factual judgments about, for instance, sexuality and sexual activity?

2. Pope John Paul II highlights theology's need for dialogue with the sciences, the need for "a community of interchange" between the two. What would be the basis and what would be the rules for such dialogue?

3. What do you understand by the phrase *critical realism*? What do you understand by the claim that "all facts are theory laden?" How do you see the two as related? What does it mean to claim that the challenge for both theology and science is to be honest about the biases of each and of the biases of the theologian or scientist dealing, for instance, with sexual data?

4. What do you understand by the terms *traditionalist theologian* and *revisionist theologian*? How do they differ? What do you think of their various sexual anthropologies?

5. Pope John Paul II asserts that "science can purify religion from error and superstition and religion can purify science from idolatry and false absolutes." How could such mutual purification take place and what would be the rules for its functioning?

NOTES

An earlier version of this essay appeared in *Louvain Studies* 35, no. 1 (2011): 69–97. It is reprinted here with permission.

1. Karl Rahner, "Practical Theology Within the Totality of Theological Disciplines," *Theological Investigations*, vol. 9 (London: Darton, Longman and Todd, 1972), 102; emphasis in original.

2. Bernard Lonergan, "Moral Theology and the Human Sciences," in *Method: Journal of Lonergan Studies* 15 (1997): 6; emphasis added.

3. *Gaudium et spes*, n. 62.

4. Joseph A. Selling, "*Gaudium et spes*: A Manifesto for Contemporary Moral Theology," in *Vatican II and Its Legacy*, ed. Mathijs Lamberigts and Leo Kenis (Leuven: Leuven University, 2002), 145–62.

5. Joseph Fuchs, *Moral Demands and Personal Obligations* (Washington: Georgetown University Press, 1993), 36; emphasis added.

6. John Paul II, "The Relationship of Science and Theology: A Letter to Jesuit Father George Coyne," in *Origins* 18, no. 23 (17 November 1988): 375–78.

7. Ian G. Barbour, *Nature, Human Nature, and God* (Minneapolis, MN: Fortress Press, 2002), 1–2.

8. Ibid. See also, Robert John Russell and Kirk Wegter-McNelly, "Science and Theology: Mutual Interaction," in *Bridging Science and Religion*, ed. Ted Peters and Gaymon Bennett (Minneapolis: Fortress Press, 2003), 19–34.

9. John Paul II, "The Relationship of Science and Theology," 377.

10. Ibid. See also Michael J. Buckley, "Religion and Science: Paul Davies and John Paul II," in *Theological Studies* 51, no. 2 (1990): 310–24.

11. Ted Peters, *Science, Theology, and Ethics* (Burlington, VT: Ashgate, 2003), 19.

12. Peters, "Science and Theology: Toward Consonance," in *Science and Theology: The New Consonance*, ed. Peters (Boulder, CO: WestviewPress, 1998), 18.

13. Gavin D'Costa, *Theology in the Public Square: Church, Academy and Nation* (Oxford: Blackwell Publishing, 2005), 209.

14. Ibid., 211.

15. See Kevin O'Rourke, O.P., "Reflections on the Papal Allocution Concerning Care for Persistent Vegetative State Patients," *Christian Bioethics* 12 (2006): 92.

16. See Todd A. Salzman and Michael G. Lawler, "Experience and Moral Theology: Reflections on *Humanae vitae* Forty Years Later," *INTAMS Review* 14, no. 2 (2008): 160–62.

17. Compare the CDF's, "Considerations Regarding Proposals to Give Legal Recognition to Unions between Homosexual Persons," *Acta Apostolicae Sedis* 100 (2004): 41–57 and Paige Averett, B. Nalavany, and S. Ryan, "Does Sexual Orientation Matter? A Matched Comparison of Adoption Samples," in *Adoption Quarterly* 12 (2009): 129–51. See also the publications cited below in note 100, many of which were published prior to the publication of the CDF's document.

18. Pope John Paul II, *Ut unum sint*, nn. 17, 36–39.

19. Compare, for example, the attitude towards dialogue in Pope John Paul's *Ut unum sint* and the CDF's *Donum veritatis*. See Todd A. Salzman and Michael G. Lawler, "Theologians and the Magisterium: A Proposal for a Complementarity of Charisms through Dialogue," *Horizons* 36, no. 1 (2009): 7–31.

20. Peters, *Science, Theology, and Ethics*, 24.

21. John F. Haught, *Science and Religion: From Conflict to Conversation* (Mahwah, NJ: Paulist Press, 1995), 20.

22. Robert M. Doran, *Theology and the Dialectics of History* (Toronto: University of Toronto Press), 263.

23. Ibid., 262.

24. Ibid., 263. For a fuller exposition, see Bernard J. F. Lonergan, *Insight: A Study of Human Understanding* (London: Longmans, 1958), 375–83.

25. See, for example, Norwood Russell Hanson, *Patterns of Discovery: An Inquiry into the Conceptual Foundations of Science* (Cambridge: Cambridge University Press, 1958) and *Observation and Explanation: A Guide to Philosophy of Science* (New York: Harper and Row, 1971).

26. United States Conference of Catholic Bishops, *Always Our Children* (Washington, DC: USCCB, 1997), n. 3.

27. Wolfhart Pannenberg, *Theology and the Philosophy of Science* (Louisville: Westminster/John Knox, 1976). See Peters, *Science and Theology*, 24–25.

28. Pope John Paul II, "The Relationship of Science and Theology," 377.

29. The sources for the new natural law are extensive. Among them are the following: Germain Grisez, *The Way of the Lord Jesus, Volume One: Christian Moral Principles* (Chicago: Franciscan Herald Press, 1983); *The Way of the Lord Jesus, Volume Two: Living a Christian Life* (Quincy, IL: Franciscan Herald Press, 1993); Grisez and Russell Shaw, *Fulfillment in Christ* (Notre Dame, IN: University of Notre Dame Press, 1991); John Finnis, *Natural Law and Natural Rights: Fundamentals of Ethics* (Washington, DC: Georgetown University Press, 1983); *Moral Absolutes: Tradition, Revision, and Truth* (Washington, DC: The Catholic University Press of America, 1991); Grisez, Joseph M. Boyle, and Finnis, *Nuclear Deterrence, Morality and Realism* (Oxford: Clarendon Press, 1987); and, "Practical Principles, Moral Truth and Ultimate Ends," *American Journal of Jurisprudence* 32 (1987): 99–151. For a synthesis of NNLT, see Jean Porter, "Basic Goods and the Human Good in Recent Catholic Moral Theology," *Thomist* 57 (1993): 28–42; and, " The Natural Law and the Specificity of Christian Morality: A Survey of Recent Work and an Agenda for Future Research," *Method and Catholic Moral Theology: The Ongoing Reconstruction*, ed. Todd A. Salzman (Omaha, NE: Creighton University Press, 1999), 209–29.

30. Finnis, "Law, Morality, and 'Sexual Orientation'," *Notre Dame Law Review* 69, no. 5 (1994): 1067. Emphasis added.

31. See ibid., 1066–67.

32. Grisez and Ford, for example, claim that the Magisterium's teaching against artificial contraception is infallible. See Grisez and John C. Ford, S.J., "Contraception and the Infallibility of the Ordinary Magisterium," *Theological Studies* 39, no. 2 (1978): 258–312; and Grisez,

"Infallibility and Specific Moral Norms: A Review Discussion," *Thomist* 49 (1985): 248–87; and, *"Quaestio Disputata*: The Ordinary Magisterium's Infallibility: A Reply to Some New Arguments," *Theological Studies* 55, no. 4 (1994): 720–32, 737–38.

33. Martin Rhonheimer, "The Cognitive Structure of the Natural Law and the Truth of Subjectivity," *Thomist* 67 (2003): 38.

34. Rhonheimer, *Natural Law and Practical Reason: A Thomist View of Moral Autonomy*, trans. G. Malsbary (New York: Fordham University Press, 2000), 117. For another traditional-ist attempt to ground sexual ethics in virtue, see John Grabowski, *Sex and Virtue: An Introduction to Sexual Ethics* (Washington, DC: Catholic University of America Press, 2003). This is an admirable attempt to formulate a sexual anthropology grounded in scripture, personalism, and virtue, but Grabowski's theory is subject to some of the same classicist critiques of human "nature," intentionality, and a univocal correlation between acts and virtues.

35. Rhonheimer, *Natural Law*, 569.

36. Ibid., 569–70.

37. Rhonheimer, "Contraception, Sexual Behavior, and Natural Law: Philosophical Foundation of the Norm of '*Humanae Vitae*,'" *Linacre Quarterly* 56, no. 2 (1989): 39.

38. *Familiaris consortio*, n. 11.

39. Pope John Paul II developed this position in a series of general audience talks he gave from 1979–1981. These talks are published in a single volume, *The Theology of the Body: Human Love in the Divine Plan* with a Foreword by John S. Grabowski (Boston, MA: Pauline Books and Media, 1997).

40. John Paul II, *Theology of the Body*, 48.

41. Ibid.

42. Ibid., 49.

43. It is important to note that the distinction between biological sex (male/female) and socially constructed gender (masculine/feminine) is frequently absent in magisterial discussions of complementarity. See Susan A. Ross, "The Bridegroom and the Bride: The Theological Anthropology of John Paul II and Its Relation to the Bible and Homosexuality," in *Sexual Diversity and Catholicism: Toward the Development of Moral Theology*, ed. Patricia Beattie Jung with Joseph A. Coray (Collegeville, MN: Liturgical, 2001), 56 n. 5.

44. Ross, "Bridegroom and the Bride"; and David M. McCarthy, "The Relationship of Bodies: A Nuptial Hermeneutics of Same-sex Unions," in *Theology and Sexuality: Classic and Contemporary Readings*, ed. Eugene F. Rogers (Oxford: Blackwell, 2002), 206–10.

45. John Paul II, "Authentic Concept of Conjugal Love," *Origins* 28, no. 37 (March 4, 1999): 655.

46. John Paul II, "Letter to Women," *Origins* 25, no. 9 (27 July 1995): 141.

47. CDF, *Persona humana*, n. 8; and *Catechism of the Catholic Church*, n. 2357.

48. Owen Sullivan, "On Including Gays," *The Furrow* 61 (2010): 170.

49. See Bruce Bagemihl, *Biological Exuberance: Animal Homosexuality and Natural Diversity* (New York: St. Martin's Press, 1999).

50. James Allison, "The Fulcrum of Discovery Or: How the 'Gay Thing' is Good News for the Catholic Church," unpublished essay, 8.

51. See William Paul, *et al.*, eds. *Homosexuality: Social, Psychological, and Biological Issues* (Beverly Hills: Sage, 1982); Pim Pronk, *Against Nature? Types of Moral Argumentation Regarding Homosexuality* (Grand Rapids, MI: Eerdmans, 1993); Richard C. Pillard and J. Michael Bailey, "A Biological Perspective on Sexual Orientation," *Clinical Sexuality* 18 (1995): 1–14; Lee Ellis and Linda Ebertz, *Sexual Orientation: Toward Biological Understanding* (Westport, CN: Praeger, 1997); Richard C. Friedman and Jennifer I. Downey, *Sexual Orientation and Psychoanalysis: Sexual Science and Clinical Practice* (New York: Columbia, 2002). For a contrary perspective see Robert L. Spitzer, "Can Some Gay Men and Lesbians Change Their Sexual Orientation? 200 Participants Reporting a Change from Homosexual to Heterosexual Orientation," *Archives of Sexual Behavior* 32 (2003): 403–17.

52. Michael J. Hartwig, "The Use of Sociological Studies to Confirm or Critique Roman Catholic Sexual Ethics," in *Applied Ethics in a World Church*, ed. Linda Hogan (Maryknoll, NY: Orbis Books, 2008), 257.

53. Christine Gudorf, "Gendered Identity Formation and Moral Theology," in *Applied Ethics in a World Church*, 114.

54. See Michael G. Lawler and Todd A. Salzman, "Human Experience and Catholic Moral Theology," *Irish Theological Quarterly* 76, no. 1 (2011): 35–56; and "Experience and Moral Theology," 156–69.

55. Peters, *Science, Theology, and Ethics*, 17.

56. Stephen Pope, "Sexual Diversity and Christian Moral Theology," in *God, Science, Sex, Gender: An Interdisciplinary Approach to Christian Ethics*, ed. Patricia Beattie Jung and Aana Vigen, with John Anderson (Chicago, IL: University of Illinois Press, 2010), 189.

57. See, for example, D'Costa, *Theology in the Public Square*, 209–12.

58. Ted Peters, *Science and Theology: The New Consonance* (Boulder, CO: Westview Press, 1998), 15.

59. Christine E. Gudorf, *Body, Sex, and Pleasure: Reconstructing Christian Sexual Ethics* (Cleveland: Pilgrim Press, 1994), 7.

60. Ibid., 3.

61. Ibid., 4.

62. United States Conference of Catholic Bishops, *Always Our Children*, n. 3.

63. Lisa Sowle Cahill, *Sex, Gender, and Christian Ethics* (Cambridge: Cambridge University Press, 1996), 1; and "Feminist Theology and Sexual Ethics," in *A Just and True Love: Feminism at the Frontiers of Theological Ethics: Essays in Honor of Margaret Farley*, ed. Maura Ryan and Brian Linnane (Notre Dame, IN: University of Notre Dame, 2007), 21–46.

64. Cahill, *Sex, Gender, and Christian Ethics*, 13.

65. Ibid., 54.

66. Ibid., 51.

67. Ibid., 55.

68. Martha Nussbaum, "Introduction," in *The Quality of Life*, ed. Martha Nussbaum and Amartya Sen (Oxford: Clarendon Press, 1993), 4. See Lisa Sowle Cahill, "Feminist Ethics, Differences, and Common Ground: A Catholic Perspective," in *Feminist Ethics and the Catholic Moral Tradition*, ed. Charles E. Curran, Margaret Farley, and Richard A. McCormick (NY: Paulist Press, 1996), 195; and, *Sex, Gender, and Christian Ethics*, 55–61.

69. Cahill, Sex, *Gender, and Christian Ethics*, 10.

70. Margaret Farley, *Just Love: A Framework for Christian Sexual Ethics* (New York: Continuum, 2008), 188–89.

71. Ibid., 148.

72. Russell and Wegter-McNelly, "Science," in *The Blackwell Companion to Modern Theology*, ed. Gareth Jones (Oxford: Blackwell Publishing Co., 2007), 516.

73. Ibid.

74. Farley, *Just Love*, 103.

75. Ibid., 104.

76. Ibid., 105.

77. Ibid., 311.

78. Ibid., 221.

79. Todd A, Salzman and Michael G. Lawler, *The Sexual Person: Toward a Renewed Catholic Anthropology* (Washington, DC: Georgetown University Press, 2008).

80. John Paul II, *Ut unum sint, Acta Apostolicae Sedis* 87 (1995): n. 28.

81. Farley, "An Ethic for Same-Sex Relations," in *A Challenge to Love: Gay and Lesbian Catholics in the Church*, ed. Robert Nugent (New York: Crossroad, 1983), 99–100.

82. USCCB, *Marriage: Love and Life in the Divine Plan* (Washington, DC: USCCB, 2009), 19.

83. Lawrence A. Kurdek, "What Do We Know about Gay and Lesbian Couples?" *Current Directions in Psychological Science* 14 (2005): 251; "Differences between Partners from Heterosexual, Gay, and Lesbian Cohabiting Couples," *Journal of Marriage and Family* 68 (May 2006): 509–28; "Lesbian and Gay Couples," in *Lesbian, Gay and Bisexual Identities over the Lifespan*, ed. Anthony R. D'Augelli and Charlotte J. Patterson (New York: Oxford University, 1995), 243–61; "Are Gay and Lesbian Cohabiting Couples *Really* Different From Heterosexual Married Couples?" *Journal of Marriage and Family* 66 (2004): 880–900. See also,

Ritch C. Savin-Williams and Kristin G. Esterberg, "Lesbian, Gay, and Bisexual Families," in *Handbook of Family Diversity*, ed. David H. Demo, Katherine R. Allen, and Mark A. Fine (New York: Oxford University, 2000), 207–12; and Philip Blumstein and Pepper Schwartz, *American Couples: Money, Work, Sex* (New York: Morrow, 1983).

84. Salzman and Lawler, *The Sexual Person*, 124–61.

85. See Joseph A. Selling, "Evolution and Continuity in Conjugal Morality," in *Personalist Morals: Essays in Honor of Prof. Louis Janssens. Bibliotheca Ephemeridum Theologicarum Lovaniensum*, 83, ed. Selling (Leuven: University Press, 1988), 243–64; "The History of Conjugal Morality," in *Human Sexuality and Family Health Sciences, Leuven Monographs on Sexology*, ed. Alfons Vansteenwegen (Leuven: Peeters, 1990), 58–76; "Magisterial Teaching on Marriage 1880–1968: Historical Constancy or Radical Development?," in *Historia: memoria futuri Mélanges Louis Vereecke, 70e anniversaire de naissance*, ed. Réal Tremblay and Dennis Billy (Rome: Ed. Academiae Alphonsianae, 1991), 351–402; reprinted in Charles Curran and Richard McCormick, ed., *Readings in Moral Theology, 8: Dialogue about Catholic Sexual Teaching* (New York: Paulist, 1993), 93–97, and in Curran, ed., *Readings in Moral Theology, 13: Change in Official Catholic Moral Teachings* (New York: Paulist, 2003), 248–52; "The Development of Catholic Tradition and Sexual Morality," in *Embracing Sexuality: Authority and Experience in the Catholic Church*, ed. Selling (Aldershot, UK: Ashgate, 2001), 149–62; and "Magisterial Teaching on Marriage 1880–1968: Historical Constancy or Radical Development?," *Studia Moralia* 28 (1990): 439–90.

86. Joseph A. Selling, "The 'Meanings' of Human Sexuality," *Louvain Studies* 23, no. 1 (1998): 32.

87. CDF, *Persona humana*, n. 1.

88. See Jack Dominian, "Sexuality and Interpersonal Relationships," in *Embracing Sexuality*, 12–15.

89. Selling, "The 'Meanings' of Human Sexuality," 35.

90. Ibid., 36.

91. Ibid., 37.

92. John Paul II, "The Relationship of Science and Theology," 376.

93. Peters, "Science and Theology: Toward Consonance," 18.

94. John Paul II, "The Relationship of Science and Theology," 377.

95. For a full analysis of this situation, see Todd A. Salzman and Michael G. Lawler, "Theologians and the Magisterium: A Proposal for a Complementarity of Charisms through Dialogue," *Horizons* 36, no. 1 (2009): 7–31.

96. Yves Congar, "Reception as an Ecclesiological Reality," in *Election and Consensus in the Church*, ed. Giuseppe Alberigo and Anton Weiler, *Concilium* 77 (1972), 72.

97. John T. Noonan, Jr., "Development in Moral Doctrine," *Theological Studies* 54, no. 4 (1993): 662–77; and id., *A Church that Can and Cannot Change: The Development of Catholic Moral Teaching* (Notre Dame, IN: University of Notre Dame Press, 2005).

98. Pope Benedict XVI, *Caritas in veritate*, nn. 31–32.

99. CDF, "Considerations Regarding Proposals to Give Legal Recognition to Unions between Homosexual Persons," n. 7.

100. Charlotte J. Patterson, "Lesbian and Gay Parenting" (APA, 1995), http://www.apa.org/pi/parent.html, para. D. Emphasis added. See also Charlotte J. Patterson, M. Fulcher, and J. Wainright, "Children of Lesbian and Gay Parents: Research, Law, and Policy," in *Children, Social Science, and the Law*, ed. Bette L. Bottoms, Margaret B. Kovera, and Bradley D. McAuliff (Cambridge: Cambridge University Press, 2002), 176–202; Marybeth J. Mattingly and Robert N. Bozick, "Children Raised by Same-Sex Couples: Much Ado about Nothing," paper presented at the Conference of the Southern Sociological Society, 2001; Isiaah Crawford and Brian D. Zamboni, "Informing the Debate on Homosexuality: The Behavioral Sciences and the Church," in *Sexual Diversity and Catholicism*, 216–42; Serena Lambert, "Gay and Lesbian Families: What We Know and Where Do We Go from Here," *Family Journal* 13 (2005): 43–51.

101. Anne Brewaeys, I. Ponjaert, and E. V. Van Hall, "Donor Insemination: Child Development and Family Functioning in Lesbian Mother Families," *Human Reproduction* 12 (1997): 1349–59.

102. Raymond W. Chan, B. Raboy, and C. Patterson, "Psychological Adjustments Among Children Conceived via Donor Insemination by Lesbian and Heterosexual Mothers," *Child Development* 69 (1998): 443–57.

103. Fiona Tasker and Susan Golombok, *Growing Up in a Lesbian Family* (New York: Guilford Press, 1997).

104. J. M. Bailey and K. Dawood, "Behavior Genetics, Sexual Orientation, and the Family," in *Lesbian, Gay, and Bisexual Identities in Families*, ed. C. J. Patterson and A. R. D'Augelli (New York: Oxford University Press, 1998), 3–18.

105. American Academy of Pediatrics.

106. APA, "Resolution on Sexual Orientation and Marriage," (2004) http://www.apa.org/releases/gaymarriage_reso.pdf.

107. Paige Averett, B. Nalavany, and S. Ryan, "Does Sexual Orientation Matter? A Matched Comparison of Adoption Samples," *Adoption Quarterly* 12 (2009): 129–51.

108. James Gustafson, "The Relationship of Empirical Science to Moral Thought," in *From Christ to the World: Introductory Readings in Christian Ethics*, ed. Wayne G. Boulton, Thomas D. Kennedy, and Allen Verhey (Grand Rapids: Wm. B. Eerdmans Publishing Co., 1994), 170.

109. Gustafson, "The Relationship of Empirical Science to Moral Thought," 171.

110. Ibid., 171.

111. John B. Cobb, Jr., "One Step Further," in *John Paul II on Science and Religion: Reflections on the New View from Rome*, ed. Robert John Russell, William R. Stoeger, and George V. Coyne (Notre Dame, IN.: University of Notre Dame Press, 1990), 5.

112. See Joan Roughgarden, "Evolutionary Biology and Sexual Diversity," *God, Science, Sex, Gender*, 89–105; and *Evolution's Rainbow: Diversity, Gender, and Sexuality in Nature and People* (Los Angeles, CA: University of California Press, 2004).

113. See Marc Rendell, *et al.*, "Ethical Dilemma of Mandated Contraception in Pharmaceutical Research at Catholic Medical Institutions," *American Journal of Bioethics* 12, no. 7 (July 2012): 34–37.

114. John Paul II, "The Relationship of Science and Theology," 377.

115. Christopher Mooney, *Theology and Scientific Knowledge: Changing Models of God's Presence in the World* (Notre Dame, IN: Notre Dame University Press, 1996), 28.

116. John Paul II, "The Relationship of Science and Theology," 378.

117. See John Paul II, *Familiaris consortio*, n. 32.

118. Luke Timothy Johnson, "Human and Divine: Did Jesus Have Faith?" *Commonweal* 135, no. 2 (31 January 2008): 15.

119. Lonergan, "Moral Theology and the Human Sciences," 5–18.

Chapter Six

Sexual Ethics

Complementarity and the Truly Human

The previous two essays revolved around two sources of Catholic theological ethics, experience and science. This essay considers science again, this time in dialogue with a third source, namely, magisterial tradition. This essay enters the discussion on the (im)morality of homosexual acts by focusing on two important and related terms, "truly human" and "complementarity," that have recently been introduced by the magisterium into the discussion of sexual morality in the Catholic tradition. Vatican II's *Gaudium et spes*, which Joseph Selling describes as "a manifesto for contemporary moral theology,"[1] declared that the sexual intercourse in and through which spouses symbolize their mutual gift to one another is to be *humano modo*, "in a manner which is [*truly*] *human*."[2]

Unfortunately, the Council offered no definition of what it meant by "truly human" and, when the phrase was introduced into the specification of marital consummation in the revised Code of Canon Law in 1983, it was again added without definition. Ten years before the revision of the code, in 1973, the subcommission that drafted the revision of the canons on marriage recognized the difficulty of including *humano modo* in law without definition and noted the lack of a verifiable criterion "to prove that a consummating act has not been done in a human manner." Given that lack, the commission unanimously recommended that the words *humano modo* be included in the text within parentheses "so that their doubts on the matter may be on record."[3] This recommendation was ignored and the revised code decrees that a marriage is "ratified and consummated if the spouses have *humano modo* engaged together in a conjugal act in itself apt for the generation of offspring."[4] The problem noted by the subcommission, the lack of a verifiable criterion for nonconsummation, remains unresolved today, leaving legislators with no sure criterion for verifying that a marriage has been truly humanly consummated and is, therefore, indissoluble.

Efforts have been made to provide canonical description of intercourse *humano modo*, but they have been minimalist. John Beal suggests the act of intercourse must be "a natural and voluntary act";[5] Thomas Doyle argues that intercourse must be engaged in "willingly and lovingly on the part of each party."[6] Beal's concluding comment, however, remains true. "The precise determination of what constitutes sexual relations in a human fashion will have to be determined gradually in the jurisprudence of the Congregation for the Sacraments."[7] This judgment remains especially true for any *theological* reflection on *humano modo*, and this article seeks to contribute to that reflection.

Since we intend this essay to be a *disputatio* in the Scholastic mode, we offer a word about the nature and importance of the *disputatio*. The Scholastic Master had three tasks: *lectio* or commentary on the Bible; *disputatio* or teaching by objection and response to a theme; *praedicatio* or theology and pastoral application.[8] Peter Cantor speaks for all Scholastics when he declares that "it is after the *lectio* of scripture and after the examination of the doubtful points, thanks to the *disputatio, and not before*, that we must preach."[9] This essay intends a *disputatio* that seeks to uncover and elucidate the Catholic truth that necessarily precedes *theologia* or *praedicatio* about moral sexual activity.

MAGISTERIUM AND THE MEANINGS OF COMPLEMENTARITY

The idea of complementarity, if not the term itself, is used throughout magisterial documents and applies to eschatological,[10] ecclesiological,[11] vocational,[12] and anthropological realities. Basically complementarity intends that certain realities belong together and produce a whole that neither produces alone. While space does not permit an exploration of how complementarity is applied to all these realities, we can note the following characteristics of its use. First, complementarity is nearly always classified along masculine and feminine lines,[13] and this classification is used metaphorically, biologically, or in combination of both. Second, it is often formulated as a "nuptial hermeneutics," in terms of bridegroom and bride.[14] So, God, Jesus, and husband are masculine and bridegroom; and creation, church, and wife are feminine and bride. Third, in its theological anthropology, the magisterium posits an "ontological complementarity" whereby men and women, though fundamentally equal and complete in themselves,[15] are incomplete as a couple.[16] Sexual complementarity completes the couple in marriage and sexual acts by bringing the masculine and feminine biological and psychological elements together in a unified whole.

While complementarity serves as a foundational sexual ethical concept in Pope John Paul II's theology of the body[17] and in magisterial pronouncements on human sexuality,[18] there are difficulties in discerning the specific meaning of the term in these writings and concerns arise regarding its plausibility as a foundational sexual principle. First, there are various *types* of complementarity depending on the context; complementarity is used, often without distinction, to refer to marriage, the sexual act, and parenthood. It is not clear, for example, how or if complementarity in parenthood differs from complementarity in the sexual act. Second, many authors have argued that the magisterium's conceptualization of complementarity cannot adequately consider the human sexual person, serve as a foundational sexual ethical principle, or define a truly human sexual act.[19] We believe, however, that a "reconstructed complementarity"[20] can serve as a foundational sexual ethical principle. This article will first explain and critique the various types of sexual complementarity used in magisterial writings and then propose revised types of complementarity and demonstrate their implications for a truly human sexual act.

SEXUAL COMPLEMENTARITY

The Congregation for the Doctrine of the Faith (CDF), in its "Considerations Regarding Proposals to Give Legal Recognition to Unions between Homosexual Persons" (CRP), has recently sought to clarify the meaning of truly human sexual acts. It first states that homosexual unions lack "the conjugal dimension which represents the human and ordered form of sexuality," and then articulates the principle that "sexual relations are human when and insofar as they express and promote the mutual assistance of the sexes in marriage and are open to the transmission of new life."[21] This is the standard unitive-procreative principle that, in the 20th century, became the foundational principle for all Catholic marital teaching. According to this principle, truly human sexual acts are acts within marriage that are simultaneously unitive of the spouses and open to procreation, and only such acts are judged to be "truly human."[22] CRP uses the term *sexual complementarity* in relation to this principle, which includes parenting or the education of children and, on this foundation, defends heterosexual marriage and condemns homosexual unions. The term *complementarity* has appeared only relatively recently in magisterial sexual teaching, in Pope John Paul II's *Familiaris consortio* (1981),[23] and its types and implications for defining truly human sexual acts have yet to be fully explored. In the next section we investigate and critique several types of complementarity to advance the understanding of both it and its implications for the "truly human" sexual act.

BIOLOGICAL AND PERSONAL COMPLEMENTARITY

There are two general types of sexual complementarity in the CDF's document, biological and personal, with subtypes within each (Table 6.1). The definition of what constitutes truly human sexual acts depends on how biological and personal complementarity are defined in themselves and in relation to one another. We will consider each definition in turn.

Biological Complementarity: Heterogenital and Reproductive

Biological complementarity is divided into what we label *heterogenital* and *reproductive complementarity*. The CDF describes heterogenital complementarity this way: "Men and women are equal as persons and complementary as male and female. Sexuality is something that pertains to the physical-biological realm."[24]

Table 6.1.   Types of Sexual Complementarity in Magisterial Teaching

I. Biological Complementarity

Title	Definition
Heterogenital Complementarity	The physically functioning male and female sexual organs (penis and vagina).
Reproductive Complementarity	The physically functioning male and female reproductive organs used in sexual acts to biologically reproduce.

II. Personal Complementarity

Title	Definition
Communion Complementarity	The two-in-oneness within a heterogenital complementary marital relationship that is created and sustained by truly human sexual acts.
Affective Complementarity	The integrated psycho-affective, social, relational, and spiritual elements of the human person grounded in heterogenital complementarity.
Parental Complementarity	Heterogenitally complementary parents who fulfill the second dimension of reproductive complementarity, namely, the education of children.

Heterogenital complementarity pertains to the biological, genital distinction between male and female. The mere possession of male or female genitals, however, is insufficient to constitute heterogenital complementarity; genitals must also function properly. If they cannot function complementarily, neither heterogenital nor reproductive complementarity is possible, and in that case canon law prescribes that a valid marriage and sacrament are also not possible. "Antecedent and perpetual impotence to have intercourse, whether on the part of the man or of the woman, which is either absolute or relative, of its very nature invalidates marriage."[25]

Heterogenital complementarity is the foundation for reproductive complementarity and "therefore, in the Creator's plan, sexual complementarity and fruitfulness belong to the very nature of marriage."[26] Heterogenital and reproductive complementarity, however, are to be carefully distinguished for, while the magisterium teaches that a couple must complement each other heterogenitally, it also teaches that, "for serious reasons and observing moral precepts," it is not necessary that they biologically reproduce.[27] Infertile couples and couples who choose for serious reasons not to reproduce for the duration of the marriage can still enter into a valid marital and sacramental relationship. In light of this teaching, Pope Paul VI's statement that "each and every marriage act must remain open to the transmission of life"[28] is *morally* ambiguous in the cases of infertile couples, couples in which the wife is postmenopausal, and couples who practice permitted natural family planning with the specific intention of avoiding the transmission of life. We may reasonably ask in what way are sexual acts between such couples "open to the transmission of life"?

Biological Openness to the Transmission of Life

First, magisterial teaching, following Thomas Aquinas, distinguishes between reproductive acts that are essentially (*per se*) closed to reproduction and reproductive acts that are accidentally (*per accidens*) nonreproductive.[29] Contraceptive (including natural family planning with a contraceptive will), nonreproductive heterosexual (oral sex, for example) and homosexual sexual acts are types of sexual acts that are essentially closed to reproduction. Sterile, either permanently or temporarily during the infertile period of a woman's cycle, and postmenopausal sexual acts are accidentally nonreproductive and belong to the same type of reproductive acts. Accidentally nonreproductive sexual acts are essentially of the same type as reproductive sexual acts and thus fulfill sexual complementarity, the unitive and procreative meanings of the sexual act. We ask, however, is it really the case that all such sexual acts are essentially the same type of act?

Gareth Moore notes that whether or not two acts are of the same type depends on how we classify acts according to our interest. The interest here

is reproduction ("open to the transmission of life"). We call vaginal intercourse and not anal intercourse a reproductive type of act because we know
that, under the right conditions, pregnancy can result in the former case and
can never result in the latter case. Science and knowing the biological facts of
reproduction enables us to classify certain sexual acts as reproductive types
of acts and other sexual acts as nonreproductive types of acts. If science is
relevant in distinguishing between vaginal intercourse that is open to reproduction and anal intercourse that is not open to reproduction, it would seem
that this consideration would apply equally to the distinction between potentially fertile and permanently or temporarily sterile reproductive acts. As
Moore correctly notes, "vaginal intercourse which we know to be sterile is a
different type of act from vaginal intercourse which, as far as we know, might
result in conception."[30]

If potentially fertile reproductive acts and permanently or temporarily
non-reproductive acts are essentially of a different type in terms of the
"openness to the transmission of life," then we must ask what distinguishes
infertile heterosexual acts from homosexual acts. The answer seems to reside
in heterogenital complementarity. That is, leaving aside personal complementarity for the moment, heterogenital complementarity, not reproductive
complementarity, seems to serve as an essential categorization for potentially
reproductive and permanently or temporarily sterile nonreproductive heterosexual acts.

Grounding the essential act-type of heterosexual potentially reproductive
and permanently or temporarily nonreproductive sexual acts in heterogenital,
rather than reproductive, complementarity raises two sets of questions. First,
it raises questions about the morality of other types of nonreproductive
heterosexual acts, such as oral sex, which are permanently nonreproductive
though heterogenital complementarity is present. Second, the magisterium's
claim that homosexual acts are intrinsically disordered because they are
closed to the transmission of life can be challenged. Permanently infertile
reproductive acts are as biologically closed to the transmission of life as are
homosexual acts. From the point of view of reproduction, nonreproductive
heterosexual acts *may* have more in common with homosexual acts in terms
of personal complementarity and relationality than with infertile reproductive
sexual acts in terms of reproductive complementarity. While homosexual
acts do not exhibit heterogenital or reproductive complementarity, it remains
to be seen whether or not they exhibit personal complementarity.

Metaphorical Openness to the Transmission of Life

Second, rather than arguing biologically and scientifically for an essential
type classification of reproductive acts that are open to the transmission of
life, one can argue metaphorically for this openness. James Hanigan, for

instance, argues for this metaphorical openness in terms of an "iconic signifi-cance of one's sexuality," whereby "one's maleness or femaleness in all its embodied reality must be taken with full seriousness."[31] Male and female sexuality are created to be spousal in that they are ordered towards interper-sonal union. Furthermore, male sexuality is "paternal in its ordination to the maternal, to the female, and to the raising up of new life." Similarly, female sexuality is "maternal in its ordination to the paternal, the male, and to the birthing and nurturing of new life."[32] In their genital maleness and female-ness, their paternity and maternity, postmenopausal and other infertile heterosexual couples represent this openness to the transmission of life to the community in the very reality of their relationship, and this representation has moral significance. Hanigan's claim has moral credibility by interpreting "openness to the transmission of life" in a metaphorical rather than a biologi-cal sense.

A question to be posed to Hanigan, however, is this: In what way is an infertile heterosexual couple's sexuality iconically significant in a way that a homosexual couple's sexuality is not? The most obvious answer is that a homosexual couple does not have the heterogenital complementarity neces-sary to reproduce. Aside from heterogenital complementarity and potential biological reproduction, however, it is not clear that a homosexual couple's sexuality cannot be iconically significant. Referring to Paul VI, Hanigan himself notes that marriage is "*one* way God has of realizing in human history the divine plan of love." And while there may be other ways to achieve this plan, "conjugal union is the way that *fully* enacts human sexual-ity."[33]

One response to Hanigan's claim of iconic significance of male and fe-male sexuality is that, while we may agree that conjugal acts of a reproduc-tive kind fully enact human sexuality, it does not follow that acts that fall short of that full enactment, such as nonreproductive heterosexual or homo-sexual acts, are immoral and, therefore, impermissible. To say that an act is inferior is not to say that it is immoral.[34] One must demonstrate this immoral-ity in terms of personal complementarity and the affective, relational, and spiritual dimensions of the human sexual person. Many would deny that nonreproductive heterosexual or homosexual acts violate personal comple-mentarity and are, therefore, immoral.

Such an interpersonal response in the case of homosexual acts, however, too easily concedes heterogenital complementarity as normative, and by-passes the moral significance of bodiliness to argue on the interpersonal significance of homosexual acts within a homosexual relationship. David McCarthy takes a different approach, arguing theologically for a nuptial metaphor of *both* homosexual *and* heterosexual unions grounded in the hu-man body. He does so in four steps. First, the beginning of all theological reflection is "God's reconciliation with the world, which, in the gathering of the Church, constitutes a body."[35] Second, the Church or Body of Christ generates a relationship of bodies to create a network of communion or common life. Within this network there is a "desire of the body" to enter into permanent unions, "which is drawn to God's faithfulness and patterned in mimesis of God's enduring love." Third, this desire is "matched by a thoroughgoing hermeneutics of the body" whereby, "through marriage, the body is given an identity that does not merely bring its agency to fulfillment but also locates the communicative acts of the body at the axis of a community's whole life."[36] Up to this point, McCarthy and Hanigan would agree.

Fourth, McCarthy argues that, although the hermeneutics of the body and the nuptial metaphor it justifies is limited to heterosexual marriage in the Catholic tradition, as it is in Hanigan, it can be extended to homosexual unions as well. It can be so extended by integrating an adequate definition of sexual orientation into a theology of the body to develop a "nuptial hermeneutics of same-sex unions."[37] The magisterium defines heterosexual orientation as normative, the "natural" explanation of the nuptial metaphor, and defines homosexual orientation as objectively disordered. Homosexual orientation is objectively disordered in the *desire* for a person of the same sex ("A homosexual orientation produces a stronger emotional and sexual attraction toward individuals of the same sex, rather than toward those of the opposite sex"),[38] and because it creates a "strong tendency" towards homosexual *acts* that are intrinsically evil.[39] This emphasis on desire and act highlights the underlying disparity in magisterial teaching in the term "orientation" when it comes to heterosexual or homosexual orientation. Whereas heterosexual orientation focuses on the affective complementarity of two embodied persons, biologically, psycho-affectively, socially, and spiritually,[40] homosexual orientation focuses on desire and acts.

McCarthy, however, provides a definition of homosexual orientation, which, aside from heterogenital complementarity, is consistent with the magisterium's understanding of heterosexual orientation. "Gay men and lesbians are persons who encounter the other (and thus discover themselves) in relation to persons of the same sex. This same-sex orientation is a given of their coming to be, that is, *the nuptial meaning of human life emerges* for a gay man in relation to other men and a woman when face to face with other women."[41] In a steadfast interpersonal union, then, homosexual couples give their bodies to one another and are "theologically communicative," that is, they are witnesses to the community of God's "constancy and steadfast fidelity."[42] In their witness, homosexual couples have "iconic significance" in their sexuality through embodied interpersonal union, just as heterosexual couples, both fertile and infertile, have "iconic significance" in their sexuality in their embodied interpersonal union. Heterogenital complementarity is not a determining factor. Rather, two genitally embodied persons, heterosexual or homosexual, in permanent interpersonal union, who reflect God's constant love and steadfast fidelity are the determining factor.[43] In the case of fertile heterosexual couples, embodied interpersonal union is potentially procreative; in the case of infertile heterosexual and homosexual couples, embodied interpersonal union is not potentially procreative. Embodiment and the nuptial metaphor, however, are essential to all three interpersonal unions.

To summarize: if one explores "openness to the transmission of life" in biological terms, then potentially reproductive and permanently or temporarily nonreproductive heterosexual acts are essentially different types of acts, and heterogenital complementarity becomes the essential difference that distinguishes nonreproductive heterosexual acts from homosexual acts. If one explores "openness to the transmission of life" in metaphorical terms, following McCarthy, both homosexual and heterosexual couples can exhibit "iconic significance" in their embodied interpersonal unions and sexual acts. For Hanigan, heterogenital complementarity becomes the essential difference that distinguishes "iconic significance" in heterosexual and homosexual interpersonal unions, allowing "iconic significance" to be morally determinative in the sexual act for heterosexual unions, but not for homosexual unions.

It is to be noted that, although reproductive complementarity always entails heterogenital complementarity, heterogenital complementarity does not always entail reproductive complementarity. Heterogenital complementarity is distinct from and can stand alone from reproductive complementarity in the service of personal complementarity. Reproductive complementarity can also stand alone from parental complementarity, for a couple may choose to adopt rather than to reproduce offspring.

Personal Complementarity

Communion Complementarity

The CDF also refers to sexuality on the "personal level—where nature and spirit are united." We refer to the personal level of sexuality as personal complementarity, which can be divided into several subcategories. First, there is *communion complementarity* in the marital relationship, "a communion of persons is realized involving the use of the sexual faculty."[44] The male and female genitals, the penis and vagina, contribute to the realization of a communion of persons in marriage expressed in truly human sexual acts. Without heterogenital complementarity, communion complementarity is not possible, a point implied by the CDF's statement on the morality of homosexual unions. "There are absolutely no grounds for considering homosexual unions to be in any way similar or even remotely analogous to God's plan for marriage and family. Marriage is holy, while homosexual acts go against the natural moral law. Homosexual acts 'close the sexual act to the gift of life.

They do not proceed from a genuine affective and sexual complementarity. Under no circumstances can they be approved.'"[45]

Affective Complementarity

Second, there is "natural,"[46] "ontological,"[47] or *affective complementarity.* This type of complementarity is at the crux of magisterial teaching on sexual complementarity because it intrinsically links biological and personal complementarity. Citing the *Catechism of the Catholic Church,* the CDF notes that affective complementarity is lacking in homosexual acts and, therefore, these acts can never be approved. It does not clarify here what it means by affective complementarity, but we can glean some insight from other magisterial sources. The Congregation for Catholic Education (CCE) teaches that, "in the Christian anthropological perspective, affective-sex education must consider the totality of the person and insist therefore on the integration of the biological, psycho-affective, social and spiritual elements."[48] Since affective sex education seeks to integrate the biological, psycho-affective, social, and spiritual elements of the human person, affective complementarity must similarly integrate these elements in a truly human sexual act. Important questions for magisterial understanding of affective complementarity are how it understands these elements in the individual person, in the person in relationship, and in a truly human sexual act.

First, John Paul II claims that "even though man and woman are made for each other, this does not mean that God created them incomplete."[49] Each individual has the potential to be complete by integrating the biological, psycho-affective, social, and spiritual elements of affective complementarity. Claiming that men and women are complete in themselves seems to respond to the concerns expressed by some theologians that the idea of complementarity implies that celibate religious or single people are somehow not complete and lack something in their humanity.[50] Second, when he moves from individual to couple, even though man and woman are "complete" in themselves, the pope argues that "for forming a couple they are incomplete."[51] He further notes that "woman complements man, just as man complements woman. . . . Womanhood expresses the 'human' as much as manhood does, but in a different and complementary way."[52] We may reasonably ask, however, where the incompleteness and the need for complementarity reside in an individual that is complete in himself or herself, but is incomplete for forming a couple? Where in the human person does this incompleteness exist that needs complementing by the opposite sex in order to complete it? John Paul II responds that "Womanhood and manhood are complementary *not only from the physical and psychological points of view,* but also from the *ontological.* It is only through the duality of the 'masculine' and the 'feminine' that the 'human' finds full realization."[53] Kevin Kelly accurately notes that "ontological complementarity maintains that the distinction between men and women has been so designed by God that they complement each other, not just in their genital sexual faculties but also in their minds and hearts and in the particular qualities and skills they bring to life, and specifically to family life."[54] The masculine and feminine complement each other to create a "unity of the two," [55] a "psychophysical completion,"[56] not only in sexual acts but also in marital life. Finally, beyond heterogenital complementarity for the purpose of reproduction, John Paul's claim of affective complementarity leaves ambiguous and undeveloped *how* these elements are integrated in a truly human sexual act.

To summarize: magisterial teaching on affective complementarity, the affective (biological, psycho-affective, social, and spiritual) elements are strictly divided according to gender and comprise essential male and female human natures; only when they are brought together in marriage and heterogenital sexual acts is the human couple complete.

There are two important points to note in John Paul's explanation of affective complementarity. First, there is an intrinsic relationship between heterogenital and personal complementarity, between body and person (heart, intelligence, will, soul).[57] Second, given the magisterium's teaching on the immorality of homosexual acts, it is clear it regards heterogenital complementarity as a *sine qua non* for personal complementarity in truly human sexual acts. Without heterogenital complementarity, the other elements of affective complementarity in the sexual act cannot be realized.

Several points need to be made regarding the claims that God created individuals complete in themselves but are incomplete when they come to form a couple and that this incompleteness is made complete through the (biological, psycho-affective, social, and spiritual) affective complementarity of male and female. First, to claim that a person is complete in him- or herself indicates that the person is complete biologically, psycho-affectively, socially, and spiritually, at least when the person is in relationship with God and neighbor. Second, while it is clear that male and female complete one another biologically in terms of genitalia for reproduction, it is not clear how they are incomplete and complete each other psycho-affectively, socially, and spiritually. John Paul II claims that "It is only in the union of two sexually different persons that the individual can achieve perfection in a synthesis of unity and mutual psychophysical completion."[58] Biological and psycho-affective, social, and spiritual elements of the human person are ontologically divided along masculine and feminine lines, however, without justification, save that these are God-given from the very beginning.[59] It is reasonable to question, however, whether the psycho-affective, social, and spiritual elements are intrinsically divided along masculine and feminine lines and find completion only in male-female unity.[60] Besides genitalia, what are the "feminine" affective elements a man lacks and what are the "masculine" affective elements a woman lacks?

One finds certain gender stereotypes in magisterial documents where femaleness is defined primarily in terms of motherhood, receptivity, and nurturing, and maleness is defined primarily in terms of fatherhood, initiation, and activity.[61] With the exception of biological motherhood and fatherhood, the ontological claim of gendered psychological traits does not seem to recognize the culturally conditioned and defined nature of gender, and does not adequately reflect the complexity of the human person and relationships. Within individuals and relationships psycho-affective, social, and spiritual elements are not "natural" to either gender as such, but may be found in either gender, may vary within a relationship, and may express themselves differently depending on the relational contexts.[62] Psycho-affective, social, and spiritual traits are variously distributed among males and females and are not intrinsic to either nature. For instance, some males are more nurturing and some females more dominant and analytical. These traits also vary within relationships in which there may be two dominant people or two nurturing people. In these cases, do we want to claim that these two people do not complement each other? The "masculinity" and "femininity" of the nonbiological elements are largely conditioned and defined by culture,[63] and are not "essential" components of masculine and feminine human nature mysteriously creating a "unity of the two."

All that can be claimed with certainty in the magisterium's version of affective complementarity is that heterogenital complementarity is necessary for reproduction. Even heterogenital complementarity is of only relative importance, however, for infertile couples where reproduction is physically impossible, and may become increasingly insignificant as a fertile couple matures.[64] The further claim that there is an intrinsic difference between male and female whereby the male and female find psycho-affective, social, and spiritual completion in one another only in marriage is unsubstantiated.

Since there are reasonable grounds for questioning the magisterium's claim that affective complementarity entails certain psycho-affective, social, and spiritual elements intrinsic to the male and female and strictly divided on gender lines and, further, that these can be realized only in heterosexual marriage and heterosexual acts, the absolute claim prohibiting homosexual acts because they lack affective complementarity is substantially weakened. While homosexual persons cannot realize the biological element of affective complementarity (heterogenital and reproductive complementarity), it remains a question whether or not they can realize its personal elements.

Granted that there is an important sense in which affective complementarity integrates the biological and personal elements in a truly human sexual act, we believe that the magisterium's account relies primarily on heterogenital complementarity, entails an incomplete, if not distorted, vision of gender, and neglects an adequate consideration of the experiential and relational dimensions of human sexuality. [65]

Parental Complementarity

Third, the CDF refers to *parental complementarity*. It argues against same-sex unions based on the claim that, "as experience has shown, the absence of sexual complementarity in these unions creates obstacles in the normal development of children who would be placed in the care of such persons. . . . Allowing children to be adopted by persons living in such unions would actually mean doing violence to these children."[66] The congregation, however, provides no scientific evidence, here or elsewhere, to substantiate its claim that homosexual union is an obstacle to the normal development of children. There is, however, abundant evidence to the contrary.

While acknowledging that research on gay and lesbian parents is still evolving, especially with respect to gay fathers, Charlotte Patterson summarizes the evidence available from 20 years of studies. "There is no evidence to suggest that lesbians and gay men are unfit to be parents or that psychosocial [including sexual] development among children of gay men or lesbians is compromised in any respect relative to that among offspring of heterosexual parents. *Not a single study* has found children of gay or lesbian parents to be disadvantaged in any significant respect relative to children of heterosexual parents."[67] In her overview of the research, Joan Laird goes further to suggest that the scientific data indicate that homosexual parents are somewhat more nurturing and tolerant than heterosexual parents, and their children are, in turn, more tolerant and empathetic.[68] This preponderance of evidence led the American Psychological Association (APA) to approve and disseminate an important resolution. Since "lesbian and gay parents are as likely as heterosexual parents to provide supportive and healthy environments for their children . . . [and since] research has shown that the adjustment, development, and psychological well-being of children is unrelated to parental sexual orientation and that the children of lesbian and gay parents are as likely as those of heterosexual parents to flourish," the APA opposes any discrimination based on sexual orientation.[69]

The important and thoroughly child-centered Child Welfare League of America (CWLA) is also convinced by the data that there are no significant differences between the parental attitudes and skills of heterosexual, gay, and lesbian parents.[70] In 1994, the league's policy statement recommends that "Gay/lesbian adoptive applicants should be assessed the same as any other adoptive applicant. It should be recognized that sexual orientation and the capacity to nurture a child are separate issues." The league further recommends that factual information about gays and lesbians should be provided "to dispel common myths about gays and lesbians."[71] It is not the sexual orientation of gay and lesbian parents that produce negative outcomes in their children but the social discrimination towards them generated by myths propagated against them.

The Second Vatican Council praises the advances of the social sciences that bring the human community "improved self-knowledge" and "influence on the life of social groups."[72] Pope John Paul II teaches that "the Church values sociological and statistical research when it proves helpful in understanding the historical context in which pastoral action has to be developed and when it leads to a better understanding of the truth."[73] The present question, namely, the effect of homosexual parents on their children, is a classic case in which the social sciences have clearly led to a better understanding of the truth. Given that the CDF's premise is manifestly false, the question whether parental complementarity is as intrinsically linked to heterogenital complementarity as the CDF claims is unavoidable. Parental complementarity, however, does serve to remind us that truly human sexual acts have implications beyond the couple's act of sexual intercourse, and that intercourse that leads to conception demands long-term caring, nurturing, and authentic familial relationships. There is abundant social scientific data to support the claim that communion and affective complementarity between the parents greatly facilitate both parental complementarity and the positive nurture of children.[74]

Interrelationship between Heterogenital and Personal Complementarity

Heterogenital complementarity alone is insufficient to justify truly human sexual acts. Heterosexual rape and incest take place in a heterogenitally complementary way, but no one would claim they are also personally complementary. Truly human complementarity is not either/or—either heterogenital complementarity alone or personal complementarity alone—but both/ and, heterogenital and personal complementarity together. The magisterium posits an intrinsic relationship between biological (heterogenital and possibly reproductive) and personal (communion, affective, and parental) complementarity, but there is a misplaced prioritization of heterogenital over personal complementarity.

For the magisterium, male and female genitals and their "natural" functioning are always the point of departure for personal complementarity in truly human sexual acts. Heterogenital complementarity, of course, must always be situated within the appropriate marital, interpersonal, and relational context, but if heterogenital complementarity is not present, as it is not present in homosexual acts, the act is by definition "intrinsically disordered."[75] There is no possibility of personal complementarity in sexual acts that do not exhibit heterogenital complementarity.

An important question for the theological understanding of truly human sexual acts is whether or not there can be such acts without heterogenital complementarity. Is heterogenital complementarity the primary, foundational, and *sine qua non* component of truly human sexual acts, or must genital and personal complementarity be more thoroughly integrated to found a truly human sexual act? If the latter is the case, then might a just and loving homosexual act fulfill the criteria for a truly human sexual act? We approach this question via what we call *sexual orientation complementarity*.

SEXUAL ORIENTATION COMPLEMENTARITY AND TRULY HUMAN SEXUAL ACTS: A RECONSTRUCTED COMPLEMENTARITY

An important psycho-social dimension of the human person, and therefore of the sexual human person, is the person's integrated relationship to self. To be truly human, a sexual act must be integrated with the whole self. The Congregation for Catholic Education asserts what is widely taken for granted today, namely, that sexuality "is a fundamental component of personality, one of its modes of being, of manifestation, of communicating with others, of feeling, of expressing and of living human love. Therefore it is an integral part of the development of the personality and of its educative process."[76] The congregation goes on to cite the CDF's *Persona humana* and its teaching that it is "from sex that the human person receives the characteristics which, on the biological, psychological, and spiritual levels, make that person a man or a woman, and thereby *largely condition his or her progress towards maturity and insertion into society*."[77] If it is true that a person's sexuality and sexual characteristics largely condition her or his insertion into society, and we agree that it is true, then the question naturally arises about the nature and meaning of what is called today sexual orientation, that dimension of human sexuality that directs a person's sexual desires and energies and draws him or her into deeper and more sexually intimate human relationships. To define "truly human" sexual acts, we must first understand sexual orientation.

The meaning of the phrase "sexual orientation" is complex and not universally agreed upon, but the magisterium offers a description. It distinguishes between "a homosexual 'tendency,' which proves to be 'transitory,' and 'homosexuals who are definitively such because of some kind of innate instinct.'" It goes on to declare that "it seems appropriate to understand sexual orientation as a *deep seated* dimension of one's personality and to recognize its *relative stability* in a person. A homosexual orientation produces a stronger emotional and sexual attraction toward individuals of the same sex, rather than toward those of the opposite sex."[78] Following Robert

Nugent, we define sexual orientation as a "psychosexual attraction (erotic, emotional, and affective) toward particular individual *persons*"[79] of the opposite or same sex, depending on whether the orientation is heterosexual or homosexual. Sexual orientation is produced by a mix of genetic, hormonal, psychological, and social "loading."[80]

Concerning the genesis of homosexual and heterosexual orientations, the bishops note what is agreed on in the scientific community, namely, that there is as yet no single isolated cause of a homosexual orientation. The experts point to a variety of loading factors, genetic, hormonal, psychological, and social from which the orientation may derive and develop. There is a growing agreement also in the scientific community that sexual orientation, heterosexual or homosexual, is a psychosexual attraction that the person does not choose and that she or he cannot change.[81] In addition, since homosexual orientation is experienced as a given and not as something freely chosen, it cannot be considered sinful, for morality presumes the freedom to choose. This judgment is not to be understood as a claim that, according to the magisterium, a homosexual orientation is morally good or even that it is morally neutral, for elsewhere it teaches that "this inclination . . . is objectively disordered," and homosexual acts that flow from the orientation are intrinsically disordered.[82] Homosexual acts are intrinsically disordered because "they are contrary to the natural law. They close the sexual act to the gift of life. They do not proceed from a genuine affective and sexual complementarity."[83] Again, heterosexuality is the norm against which all sexual acts are judged.

The magisterium condemns homosexual acts because they do not exhibit heterogenital and reproductive complementarities and, because they do not exhibit these biological complementarities, they are ontologically incapable of realizing personal complementarity, regardless of the meaning of the act for a homosexual couple. Since the sexual act is frequently closed to reproductive complementarity, sometimes essentially and sometimes accidentally even for fertile heterosexual couples, as we have already explained, heterogenital complementarity is established as *the* litmus test for determining whether or not a sexual act can fulfill personal complementarity, and thus be "truly human." There is no doubt that truly human sexual acts necessarily include personal complementarity but, for the magisterium, personal complementarity is not sufficient for a truly human sexual act. Heterogenital complementarity is the primary, foundational, *sine qua non* condition for what defines a truly human sexual act. Since homosexual acts lack heterogenital complementarity, they can never be truly human.

While the magisterium consistently condemns homosexual acts on the grounds that they violate heterogenital and reproductive complementarity (that is the so-called "natural law" argument), it does not explain why they also violate personal complementarity other than to assert that homosexual acts "do not proceed from a genuine affective and sexual complementarity."[84] This statement, however, begs the question whether or not such acts can ever be truly human on the level of sexual and personal complementarity. Though the magisterium has not confronted this question, monogamous, loving, committed, homosexual couples have confronted it experientially and testify that they do experience affective and communion complementarity in and through their homosexual acts, a claim amply supported by scientific research.[85] They add that these acts also facilitate the integration of their human sexuality and bring them closer to self, to neighbor, and to God.

We suggest that the needed complementarity for a truly human sexual act is *holistic* complementarity that unites people bodily, affectively, spiritually, and personally in light of a person's sexual orientation. Heterogenital complementarity is needed for reproduction, but it is not needed for the sexual, affective, spiritual, and personal connection between two people that the recent Catholic tradition acknowledges as an end of marriage equal to procreation.[86] Though they cannot exhibit genital complementarity, homosexual individuals can exhibit this holistic complementarity.

Some 20 years ago, while acknowledging that the question of same-sex relations is a question of dispute, Margaret Farley noted this homosexual experience from anecdotal sources and commented that we "have some clear and profound testimonies to the life-enhancing possibilities of same-sex relations and the integrating possibilities of sexual activity within these relations. We have the witness that homosexuality can be a way of embodying responsible love and sustaining human friendship." She concludes, logically, that "this witness alone is enough to demand of the Christian community that it reflect anew on the norms for homosexual love."[87] Her judgment is in line with John Courtney Murray's principle that practical, as distinct from theoretical, intelligence is preserved from ideology by having "a close relation to concrete experience."[88] As we saw above regarding the scientific studies of children being raised by gay and lesbian parents, magisterial positions on gays and lesbians tend to be theoretical hypotheses unsubstantiated by the practical experience of those gays and lesbians.

As we have already noted, the relationship between biological and personal complementarity is both/and. Truly human sexual acts require human genitals. In couples of heterosexual orientation, personal complementarity is embodied, manifested, nurtured, and strengthened through the use of their genitals; in couples of homosexual orientation, it is equally embodied, manifested, nurtured, and strengthened through the use of their genitals. Orientation complementarity integrates genital complementarity into personal complementarity.

Orientation complementarity reconstructs the magisterium's definitions of affective complementarity and genital complementarity. First, orientation complementarity cannot espouse the magisterium's heterogenital point of departure for affective complementarity. As we have seen, for the magisterium the point of departure for affective complementarity is an ontological unity between the biological (heterogenital) and the personal that can find completion only in heterosexual marriage and conjugal acts. The definition of affective complementarity is the "unity of the two" where the masculine and feminine affective elements (biological, psycho-affective, social, and spiritual), which for forming a couple are incomplete, find completion in heterogenitally complementary sexual acts. In our model, the point of departure for affective complementarity is not the heterogenital but the sexual human person of either a homosexual or heterosexual orientation. The definition of affective complementarity in truly human sexual acts is the "unity of the two" where the affective elements (biological, psycho-affective, social, and spiritual), complement one another.[89] In the case of persons with a homosexual orientation, these acts will be genitally male-male or female-female; in the case of persons with a heterosexual orientation, these acts will be genitally male-female; in the case of persons with a bi-sexual orientation, these acts may be genitally male-male, female-female, or male-female.[90]

Orientation complementarity also requires us to redefine heterogenital complementarity in relation to affective complementarity. Severing the male-female ontological complementarity of the affective elements includes the genitals. No longer is heterogenital complementarity the foundational, *sine qua non* for personal complementarity. Genital complementarity, indeed, can be determined only in light of orientation complementarity. In a truly human sexual act, the genitals are at the service of personal complementarity, and they may be male-male, female-female, or male-female, depending on whether the individual person's orientation is homosexual or heterosexual. Our principle of sexual orientation complementarity embraces the entirety and complexity of the human person, and reconstructs genital complementarity to be in dialogue with, and totally at the service of, personal and orientation complementarity. The genitals may be said to be complementary when they are used in a truly human sexual act that realizes the psycho-affective, social, and spiritual elements of affective complementarity.

Truly human sexual acts can be morally evaluated, not simply as isolated acts, but only in the context of this complex orientation, personal, and genital interrelationship. When we shift the foundation for a truly human sexual act from heterogenital complementarity to an integrated orientation, personal, and genital complementarity, the principle for what constitutes a truly human sexual act can be formulated as follows.

A truly human sexual act is an *actus humanus* in accord with a person's sexual orientation that facilitates a deeper appreciation, integration, and sharing of a person's embodied self with another embodied self. Genital complementarity is always a dimension of the truly human sexual act, and reproductive complementarity may be a part of it in the case of fertile, heterosexual couples who choose to reproduce. Reproductive complementarity will not be a possibility in the case of homosexual couples (or infertile heterosexual couples), but genital complementarity, understood in an integrated, embodied, personal, orientation sense, and not just in a biological, physical sense, will be. This personalist interpretation of genital complementarity, which sees the physical genitals as organs of the whole person, allows us to expand the definition of a "truly human" sexual act to apply to both heterosexuals and homosexuals.

The foundation for this definition and its moral evaluation rest, not primarily on heterogenital complementarity, but on the integrated relationship between orientation, personal, and genital complementarity. Given that complex dialogical relationship, it remains to ask whether or not a particular sexual act facilitates or frustrates the partners' human flourishing, their becoming more affectively and interpersonally human and Christian. We agree with Stephen Pope. "Interpersonal love is here the locus of human flourishing," [91] especially that love which fulfills the three requirements of the great commandment: love God, love neighbor, and love self (Mk 12:31).

HOLISTIC COMPLEMENTARITY, SEXUAL MORAL NORMS, AND THE TRULY HUMAN

In light of the various types of complementarity explored in the foregoing, a truly human sexual act must be an authentic integration and expression of holistic complementarity as set forth in the Figure 6.1.

Holistic complementarity integrates orientation, personal, and biological complementarity, and the integration and manifestation of all three in just, loving, committed sexual acts that facilitate a person's ability to love God, neighbor, and self in a more profound and holy way.

Two immediate implications for Catholic sexual ethics follow if we espouse holistic complementarity as our foundational principle for truly human sexual acts. The first is that the magisterium's absolute moral norm prohibiting all homosexual acts must, at least, be reexamined. Without a prior consideration of one's sexual orientation, a sexual act that violates heterogenital complementarity can no longer be considered *ipso facto* intrinsically or objectively disordered. Genital complementarity is relevant in determining the morality of truly human sexual acts, but it is not the primary factor. The morality of the use of the genitals in sexual acts must be determined primarily in light of orientation and personal complementarity.

The second implication for Catholic sexual ethics follows from the first, the foundation for sexual moral norms may need to be redefined. Current magisterial teaching posits, for both homosexuals and heterosexuals, an intrinsic relationship between biological and personal complementarity in

HOLISTIC COMPLEMENTARITY

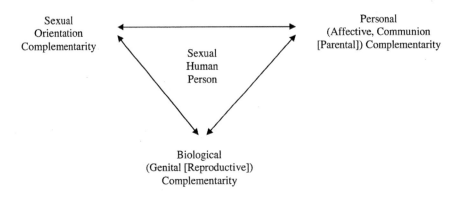

Figure 6.1.

which heterogenital complementarity is primary and foundational. On this foundation, certain sexual acts are *ipso facto* immoral because they violate heterogenital complementarity, regardless of sexual orientation and the relational meaning of the act for personal complementarity. In holistic complementarity, there is an integrated relationship between orientation, personal, and biological complementarity that serves as the foundation for sexual norms. In this relationship, for both heterosexuals and homosexuals, orientation and personal complementarity are primary, and they determine what constitutes authentic genital complementarity in a particular sexual act. If orientation complementarity indicates that a person is of heterosexual orientation, then personal complementarity would indicate that authentic genital complementarity would be male-female. If orientation complementarity indicates that a person is of homosexual orientation, then personal complementarity would indicate that authentic genital complementarity would be male-male or female-female. In current magisterial teaching, heterogenital complementarity is the primary foundational dimension for the essential relationship between biological and personal complementarity. In our holistic complementarity model, orientation and personal complementarity are the foundational dimensions for the integrated relationship between orientation, personal, and biological complementarity.

In light of these two considerations, we advance the following with regard to sexual moral norms and truly human sexual acts. Sexual moral norms must be formulated and truly human sexual acts must be defined in light of a revised theological anthropology grounded in holistic, not heterogenital, complementarity. A person's sexual orientation is a fundamental dimension of the concretely and normatively human, and sexual norms that prescribe or proscribe specific sexual acts must be formulated and applied in light of that orientation. Sexual moral norms must seek to facilitate the integration of holistic complementarity, orientation, personal, and biological complementarity. This integration does not allow for the absolute condemnation of particular sexual acts without due consideration of a person's sexual orientation and the meaning of this sexual act for persons in relationship—that is, in personal complementarity—which is expressed in and through genital complementarity. Whereas the magisterium's model posits the absolute norm forbidding homosexual acts for all people, our model cannot justify this absolute norm for people with a homosexual orientation. It does, however, posit a formally absolute norm in relation to truly human sexual acts.

Formal absolutes are norms that emphasize character and/or virtue in relation to acts. A formal absolute norm, for instance, might state the following: a not-truly-human, abusive, unjust, uncommitted, unloving sexual act, heterosexual or homosexual, is morally wrong; a truly human, caring, just, committed, loving, sexual act, heterosexual or homosexual, is morally right. [92] The integration of holistic complementarity, that is, the integration of orientation, personal, and biological complementarity, determines whether or not a sexual act is moral or immoral. In the case of a person with a homosexual orientation, a truly human, caring, just, committed, loving, sexual act will be expressed with male-male or female-female genitalia. In the case of a person with a heterosexual orientation, a truly human, caring, just, committed, loving, sexual act will be expressed with male-female genitalia. Some theorists have proposed this shift to formal absolutes in terms of a virtue-based sexual ethic in which the cardinal virtues of prudence, justice, fortitude, and temperance, always allied with the theological virtues of faith, hope, and charity, would be the guiding "norms" for what constitute truly human sexual acts. [93]

The challenge presented by this shift from predominantly act-centered norms to formal, holistic relation-centered norms is that the latter may not always be as clear as we would like. They may not always give clear guidelines for what we may or may not do. Especially when it comes to morality, humans often desire clarity, simple and unambiguous answers to complex questions. Unambiguous answers, unfortunately, sometimes oversimplify complex human relationships and the questions they raise. They may also be achieved at the expense of preempting the responsible discernment required for every *actus humanus*, every truly human moral act. It is, in fact, that responsible discernment in the area of sexual activity, and not the naked fact of "nature," that makes possible the mature integration of a person's sexuality, heterosexual or homosexual, and the living out of that sexuality in a manner that facilitates a truly human flourishing in relationship with those we love, including the God who created all people sexual in the first place.

CONCLUSION

This *disputatio* is an inquiry into the nature of the truly human sexual act. We inquired, first, into the types of complementarity—heterogenital, reproductive, communion, affective, and parental—that the magisterium finds in a truly human sexual act and challenged the primacy granted to heterogenital complementarity as the *sine qua non* of such a truly human sexual act. We suggested that the scientific evidence for the genetic, physiological, psychological, and social loading that creates either heterosexual or homosexual orientation as part of a person's sexual constitution requires the addition of orientation complementarity to the equation. This addition yielded our conclusion that an integrated orientation, personal, and biological complementarity is a more adequate *sine qua non* of truly human sexual acts. The truly human sexual act is doubly defined, therefore, as an act that is in accord with a person's sexual orientation *and* leads to the human flourishing of both partners. If accepted, that definition will lead to the abandonment of the absolute norm prohibiting homosexual acts for persons with a homosexual orientation. We repeat, the integration and expression of holistic complementarity, that is, the integration of orientation with personal and biological complementarity, determines whether or not a sexual act is moral or immoral.

We offer a final word about the theologian's task. It is not for theologians to establish the doctrine or the practice of their Church. That is a task for the communion-Church, "the body of the faithful as a whole [who], anointed as they are by the Holy One (cf. John 2:20, 27), cannot err in matters of belief."[94] The theologian's task is different, but critical in every sense of that word. It is the task of "interpreting the documents of the past and present magisterium, of putting them in the context of the whole of revealed truth, and of finding a better understanding of them by the use of hermeneutics," and it "brings with it a somewhat critical function which obviously should be exercised positively rather than destructively."[95] It is that hermeneutical task we seek to fulfill critically, but positively and not destructively, in this *disputatio*. We expect and invite criticism in the same vein so that an important discussion may move forward. We now move forward in this book to consider our preferred method for doing theological ethics, namely, virtue ethics.

QUESTIONS FOR REFLECTION

1. What do you understand by the term *complementarity*? How is it to be understood in the sexual union between two persons? In your opinion do those two persons need to be male and female, or can two persons

of the same sex be complementary? Is there any scientific data to confirm your answer?

2. What are the types of complementarity mentioned in the pronouncements of the Church? What is your opinion of the heterogenital basis on which the Church bases all marital and sexual morality?

3. Pope John Paul II's theology of the body evolves in an exclusively heterogenital context. What do you think of McCarthy's counter arguments developing a theology of the body that opens to homosexuality and "a nuptial hermeneutics of same-sex unions?"

4. How do you understand the difference between sex and gender? It has frequently been noted, especially by feminist theologians, that there are gender stereotypes posing as sexual absolutes in Church documents on sexual morality. What do you think, for instance, of the Church's claim that allowing same-sex unions is actually doing violence to children? Is there any evidence to the contrary?

5. In this essay, we offer a *holistic complementarity* in contrast to the Church's *heterosexual complementarity*. What is the distinction between the two? If our theory of holistic complementarity is correct, then two conclusions follow. First, the Church's moral norms prohibiting all homosexual acts must be reexamined; second, the foundation of these norms must be especially reexamined. What do you think of the Church's approach to complementarity and our approach, and which theory do you think meets the facts of human sexuality and sexual activity?

NOTES

An earlier version of this essay appeared in *Theological Studies* 67, no. 3 (2006): 625–52. It is reprinted here with permission.

1. Joseph A. Selling, "*Gaudium et Spes*: A Manifesto for Contemporary Moral Theology," in *Vatican II and Its Legacy*, ed. Mathijs Lamberigts and Leo Kenis (Leuven: Leuven University, 2002), 145–62.

2. *Gaudium et spes*, n. 49, emphasis added. "*Humano modo*" is frequently translated in magisterial documents and canon law as "truly human," but its more literal translation is simply "in a human manner."

3. Commissio Pontificia Codici Iuris Canonici Recognoscendo, "De Matrimonio," *Communicationes* 5 (1973): 79.

4. Canon 1061, 1.

5. John P. Beal, "Title VII: Marriage," in *New Commentary on the Code of Canon Law*, ed. John P. Beal, James A. Coriden, and Thomas J. Green (New York: Paulist, 2000), 1258.

6. Thomas P. Doyle, "Title VII: Marriage," in *The Code of Canon Law: A Text and Commentary*, ed. James A. Coriden, Thomas J. Green, and Donald E. Heintschel (New York: Paulist, 1985), 745.

7. Beal, *et al.*, *New Commentary on the Code*, 1364.

8. See Jean-Pierre Torrell, *Saint Thomas Aquinas*, vol. 1, *The Person and His Work*, trans. Robert Royal (Washington: Catholic University of America, 1996), 54–74.

9. Peter Cantor, *Verbum abbreviatum* 1, *Patrologia Latina* 205, 25, emphasis added.

10. John Paul II, *Redemptoris mater*, *Acta Apostolicae Sedis* 79 (1987): 20, 23.

11. John Paul II, *Mulieris dignitatem*, *Origins* 18, no. 17 (October 6, 1988): 278–80, nn. 26, 27.

12. John Paul II, *Familiaris consortio*, n. 11 (hereafter *FC*), in *The Post-Synodal Apostolic Exhortations of John Paul II*, ed. J. Michael Miller (Huntington, Ind.: Our Sunday Visitor, 1998), 148–233; and *Mulieris dignitatem*, nn. 17, 21.

13. It is important to note that the distinction between biological sex (male/female) and socially conditioned gender (masculine/feminine) is frequently absent in magisterial discussions of complementarity (see Susan A. Ross, "The Bridegroom and the Bride: The Theological Anthropology of John Paul II and Its Relation to the Bible and Homosexuality," in *Sexual Diversity and Catholicism: Toward the Development of Moral Theology*, ed. Patricia Beattie Jung with Joseph Andrew Coray [Collegeville: Liturgical, 2001], 56 n. 5).

14. Ross, "Bridegroom and the Bride"; and David Matzko McCarthy, "The Relationship of Bodies: A Nuptial Hermeneutics of Same-sex Unions," in *Theology and Sexuality: Classic and Contemporary Readings*, ed. Eugene F. Rogers, Jr. (Oxford: Blackwell, 2002), 206–10.

15. John Paul II, "Authentic Concept of Conjugal Love," *Origins* 28, no. 37 (March 4, 1999): 655.

16. John Paul II, "Letter to Women," 7, *Origins* 25, no. 9 (July 27, 1995): 141.

17. See John Paul II, *The Theology of the Body: Human Love in the Divine Plan*, foreword by John S. Grabowski (Boston: Pauline, 1997), 48–49, 58, 69–70, 276–78, 298–99, 368–70.

18. See, for example, John Paul II, *Familiaris consortio*; "Letter to Women;" "Authentic Concept of Conjugal Love," 654–56; *Catechism of the Catholic Church* (Vatican City: Libreria Editrice Vaticana, 2000; CDF, *Considerations Regarding Proposals to Give Legal Recognition to Unions between Homosexual Persons*, *Acta Apostolicae Sedis* 100 (2004): 41–49 (hereafter, *CRP*); United States Conference of Catholic Bishops (hereafter USCCB), "Between Man and Woman: Questions and Answers about Marriage and Same-Sex Unions," *Origins* 33, no. 25 (2003): 257, 259.

19. See, for example, Charles E. Curran, *The Moral Theology of Pope John Paul II* (Washington: Georgetown University, 2005), 190–93; Cristina L. H. Traina, *Feminist Ethics and Natural Law: The End of the Anathemas* (Washington: Georgetown University, 1999), 1–2, 9, 31, 311–12; *idem*, "Papal Ideals, Marital Realities: One View from the Ground," in *Sexual Diversity and Catholicism*, 280–82; Ross, "Bridegroom and the Bride," 39–59; Edward Collins Vacek, "Feminism and the Vatican," *Theological Studies* 66, no. 1 (2005): 173–76; Gareth Moore, *The Body in Context: Sex and Catholicism*, Contemporary Christian Insights (New York: Continuum, 2001), 117–39, 203–8; and Christine E. Gudorf, "Encountering the Other: The Modern Papacy on Women," in *Feminist Ethics and the Catholic Moral Tradition, Readings in Moral Theology 9*, ed. Charles E. Curran, Margaret A. Farley, and Richard A. McCormick (New York: Paulist, 1996), 74–79.

20. Ross, "Bridegroom and the Bride," 53, 59, 37.

21. CDF, *CRP*, n. 7.

22. Ibid.; John Paul II, *Familiaris consortio*, n. 11.

23. Ibid., n. 19. The pope speaks of a "natural complementarity."

24. *CRP*, n. 3.

25. Canon 1084, 1.

26. *CRP*, n. 3.

27. Pope Paul VI, *Humanae vitae*, n. 10; see also Pope Pius XII, "The Apostolate of the Midwife," in *The Major Addresses of Pope Pius XII*, vol. 1, *Selected Addresses*, ed. Vincent A. Yzermans (St. Paul, MN.: North Central Publishing, 1961), 169.

28. Paul VI, *Humanae vitae*, n. 11.

29. Aquinas, *Summa contra gentiles* 3, chap.122.

30. Moore, *The Body in Context*, 162.

31. James P. Hanigan, "Unitive and Procreative Meaning: The Inseparable Link," in *Sexual Diversity and Catholicism*, 33.

32. Ibid., 35.

33. Ibid., 30, emphasis added.

34. Moore, *The Body in Context*, 200–1.

35. McCarthy, "Relationship of Bodies," 201.

36. Ibid., 210.

37. Ibid., 212.

38. USCCB, *Always Our Children* (Washington: USCCB, 1997), nn. 4–5; CDF, *Persona humana:* Declaration on Certain Questions concerning Sexual Ethics, n. 8, http://www.vatican.va/roman_curia/congregations/cfaith/documents/rc_con_cfaith_doc_19751229_persona-humana_en.html.

39. CDF, "Letter to the Bishops of the Catholic Church on the Pastoral Care of Homosexual Persons," *Origins* 16, no. 22 (November 13, 1986): 379, n. 3; CDF, "Vatican List of Catechism Changes," *Origins* 27, no. 15 (September 25, 1997): 257.

40. Congregation for Catholic Education (hereafter CCE), *Educational Guidance in Human Love: Outlines for Sex Education* (hereafter *EGHL*) (Rome: Typis Polyglottis Vaticanis, 1983), n. 35.

41. McCarthy, "Relationship of Bodies," 212–13; emphasis added.

42. Ibid., 213.

43. We will address "orientation complementarity" in more detail below.

44. CDF, *CRP*, n. 3.

45. Ibid., n. 4; *Catechism of the Catholic Church*, n. 2357.

46. John Paul II, *Familiaris consortio*, n. 19.

47. John Paul II, "Letter to Women," n. 7.

48. CCE, *EGHL*, loc. cit.

49. John Paul II, "Women: Teachers of Peace, Message of His Holiness Pope John Paul II for the XXVIII World Day of Peace" (January 1, 1995), n. 3, http://www.vatican.va/holy_father/john_paul_ii/messages/peace/documents/hf_jp-ii_mes_08121994_xxviii-world-day-for-peace_en.html.

50. Gudorf, "Encountering the Other," 75; and Curran, *Moral Theology*, 192–93.

51. Vacek, "Feminism and the Vatican," 173–74, referring to John Paul II, "Authentic Concept of Conjugal Love," 655.

52. John Paul II, "Letter to Women," n. 7.

53. Ibid., emphasis original; *Familiaris consortio*, n. 19.

54. Kevin Kelly, *New Directions in Sexual Ethics* (London: Cassell, 1999), 51. He goes on to critique ontological complementarity as ultimately "oppressive and deterministic" (52).

55. John Paul II, "Letter to Women," n. 8; *Mulieris dignitatem*, n. 6.

56. John Paul II, "Authentic Concept of Conjugal Love," n. 5.

57. John Paul II, *Familiaris consortio*, n. 19.

58. John Paul II, "Authentic Concept of Conjugal Love," n. 5.

59. John Paul II, "Letter to Women," nn. 7–8.

60. Moore, *Body in Context*, 121–27.

61. See John Paul II, *Familiaris consortio*, n. 23; "Letter to Women," n. 9; *Mulieris dignitatem*; and "Women: Teachers of Peace."

62. Traina, "Papal Ideals," 280–82.

63. See Elaine L. Graham, *Making the Difference: Gender, Personhood, and Theology* (Minneapolis: Fortress, 1996).

64. See Traina, "Papal Ideals," 281.

65. Ibid., 282.

66. CDF, *CRP*, n. 7.

67. Charlotte J. Patterson, "Lesbian and Gay Parenting" (APA, 1995), http://www.apa.org/pi/parent.html, para. D; see also Marybeth J. Mattingly and Robert N. Bozick, "Children Raised by Same-Sex Couples: Much Ado about Nothing," paper given at the Conference of the Southern Sociological Society, 2001.

68. Joan Laird, "Lesbian and Gay Families," in *Normal Family Processes*, ed. Froma Walsh (New York: Guilford, 1993), 316–17.

69. APA, "Resolution on Sexual Orientation and Marriage" (2004), http://www.apa.org/releases/gaymarriage_reso.pdf.

70. Ann Sullivan, ed., *Issues in Gay and Lesbian Adoption: Proceedings of the Fourth Annual Peirce-Warwick Adoption Symposium* (Washington: Child Welfare League of America, 1995), 24–28.

71. Sullivan, *Issues in Gay and Lesbian Adoption*, 41.

72. *Gaudium et spes*, n. 5.

73. John Paul II, *Familiaris consortio*, n. 5.

74. For a review of these data, see Osnat Erel and Bonnie Burman, "Interrelatedness of Marital Relations and Parent-Child Relations: A Meta-Analytic Review," *Psychological Bulletin* 118 (1995): 108–32; Paul R. Amato and Alan Booth, *A Generation at Risk: Growing Up in an Era of Family Upheaval* (Cambridge, MA: Harvard University, 1997), 67–83; Stacy J. Rogers and Lynn K. White, "Satisfaction with Parenting: The Role of Marital Happiness, Family Structure, and Parents' Gender," *Journal of Marriage and Family* 60 (1998): 293–316; David H. Demo and Martha J. Cox, "Families With Young Children: A Review of the Research in the 1990s," *Journal of Marriage and Family* 62 (2000): 876–900.

75. *Catechism of the Catholic Church*, n. 2357.

76. CCE, *EGHL*, n. 4.

77. CDF, *Persona humana*, n. 1, emphasis added.

78. USCCB, Always Our Children (Washington: USCCB, 1997), nn. 4–5; CDF, *Persona humana*, n. 8.

79. Robert Nugent, "Sexual Orientation in Vatican Thinking," in *The Vatican and Homosexuality: Reactions to the "Letter to the Bishops of the Catholic Church on the Pastoral Care of Homosexual Persons"*, ed. Jeannine Gramick and Pat Furey (New York: Crossroad, 1988), 55.

80. This terminology has been borrowed from John E. Perito, *Contemporary Catholic Sexuality: What Is Taught and What Is Practiced* (New York: Crossroad, 2003), 96.

81. See William Paul, *et al.*, ed. *Homosexuality: Social, Psychological, and Biological Issues* (Beverly Hills: Sage, 1982); Pim Pronk, *Against Nature? Types of Moral Argumentation Regarding Homosexuality* (Grand Rapids, MI: Eerdmans, 1993); Richard C. Pillard and J. Michael Bailey, "A Biological Perspective on Sexual Orientation," *Clinical Sexuality* 18 (1995): 1–14; Lee Ellis and Linda Ebertz, *Sexual Orientation: Toward Biological Understanding* (Westport, CN: Praeger, 1997); Richard C. Friedman and Jennifer I. Downey, *Sexual Orientation and Psychoanalysis: Sexual Science and Clinical Practice* (New York: Columbia, 2002). For a contrary perspective see Robert L. Spitzer, "Can Some Gay Men and Lesbians Change Their Sexual Orientation? 200 Participants Reporting a Change from Homosexual to Heterosexual Orientation," *Archives of Sexual Behavior* 32 (2003): 403–17.

82. CDF, "Vatican List of Catechism Changes," 257.

83. *Catechism of the Catholic Church*, n. 2357; CDF, *CRP*, n. 4.

84. Ibid.

85. Lawrence A. Kurdek, "Differences between Partners from Heterosexual, Gay, and Lesbian Cohabiting Couples," *Journal of Marriage and Family* 68 (May 2006): 509–28; "What Do We Know about Gay and Lesbian Couples?" *Current Directions in Psychological Science* 14 (2005): 251–54; "Lesbian and Gay Couples," in *Lesbian, Gay and Bisexual Identities over the Lifespan*, ed. Anthony R. D'Augelli and Charlotte J. Patterson (New York: Oxford University, 1995), 243–61; "Are Gay and Lesbian Cohabiting Couples *Really* Different From Heterosexual Married Couples?" *Journal of Marriage and Family* 66 (2004): 880–900; Ritch C. Savin-Williams and Kristin G. Esterberg, "Lesbian, Gay, and Bisexual Families," in *Handbook of Family Diversity*, ed. David H. Demo, Katherine R. Allen, and Mark A. Fine (New York: Oxford University, 2000), 207–12; and Philip Blumstein and Pepper Schwartz, *American Couples: Money, Work, Sex* (New York: Morrow, 1983).

86. See *Gaudium et spes*, nn. 48–50; *Code of Canon Law*, canon 1055, 1; Michael G. Lawler, *Marriage in the Catholic Church: Disputed Questions* (Collegeville: Liturgical, 2002), 27–42.

87. Margaret A. Farley, "An Ethic for Same-Sex Relations," in *A Challenge to Love: Gay and Lesbian Catholics in the Church*, ed. Robert Nugent (New York: Crossroad, 1983), 99–100.

88. John Courtney Murray, *We Hold These Truths: Catholic Reflections on the American Experience* (New York: Sheed & Ward, 1960), 106.

89. Though it is beyond the scope of this paper, as in the magisterium's model, *how* these elements complement one another in a "truly human sexual act," heterosexual or homosexual, needs to be more fully developed.

90. While we recognize the reality of bisexual persons, space does not allow us to address this orientation in detail.

91. Stephen J. Pope, "Scientific and Natural Law Analyses of Homosexuality: A Methodological Study," *Journal of Religious Ethics* 25 (1997): 111.

92. The formal criteria listed for what constitutes a morally right or wrong truly human sexual act, though not the specific acts themselves, are common in magisterial and moral theological discourse.

93. See Alasdair MacIntyre, *After Virtue: A Study in Moral Theory* (Notre Dame: University of Notre Dame, 1981); Martha Nussbaum, *The Fragility of Goodness: Luck and Ethics in Greek Tragedy and Philosophy* (New York: Cambridge University, 1988); *idem*, "Non-Relative Virtues: An Aristotelian Approach," in *Ethical Theory: Character and Virtue*, ed. Peter A. French, Theodore E. Uehling, Jr., and Howard K. Wettstein (Notre Dame: University of Notre Dame, 1988), 32–53; James F. Keenan, "Proposing Cardinal Virtues," *Theological Studies* 56, no. 4 (1995), 709–729; *idem*, *Virtues for Ordinary Christians* (Kansas City: Sheed & Ward, 1996); and *idem*, "Virtue Ethics and Sexual Ethics," *Louvain Studies* 30 (2005): 183–203.

94. *Lumen gentium*, n. 12.

95. International Theological Commission, *Theses on the Relationship between the Ecclesiastical Magisterium and Theology* (Washington: USCCB, 1977), thesis 8.

Chapter Seven

Virtue Ethics

Natural and Christian

A man was going down from Jerusalem to Jericho, and he fell among robbers who stripped him and beat him and departed, leaving him half dead. Now by chance a priest was going down that road, and when he saw him he passed by on the other side. So likewise a Levite, when he came to the place and saw him, passed by on the other side. But when a Samaritan, as he journeyed, came to where he was and saw him, he had compassion and went up to him and bound up his wounds, pouring on oil and wine. Then he set him on his own beast and brought him to an inn, and took care of him. (Luke 10: 29–34)

It is one of Jesus' best known parables. As parable it is open to many interpretations, but Christians have long privileged one moral interpretation by naming the Samaritan in the story the "Good Samaritan." By implication the priest and the Levite are, at least, less good. We suggest, from within our perspective of virtue ethics, that all three agents in the story might be good and moral according to the principles and actions imitated and learned in their own communities. That alternative interpretation of the story demands explanation.

In contemporary ethics there are three normative approaches to determining the morality of an action. There is the utilitarian approach; the moral action is the one that maximizes utility. There is the deontological approach, which emphasizes rules, obligations, and duties. There is the "new" virtue-ethical approach, which gives precedence, not to the actions of the agents but to their personal characters formed in their respective moral communities and learned through the imitation of respected role models in those communities. We share with Philippa Foot and Alasdair MacIntyre the judgment that neither utilitarianism nor deontology offers an adequately comprehensive moral

theory, indeed that, because of them, "We have—very largely if not entirely—lost our comprehension, both theoretical and practical, of morality."[1] We
join with them and the many other modern ethicists who advance virtue
ethics as a normative ethics more promising to the moral life than utilitarianism or deontology.[2] In what follows we give an account, due to space restric-
tions not a full-blown theory, of virtue ethics (and our suggested interpretation of the parable of the Good Samaritan). That requires, first, a virtue
theory and, then, based on that theory, a virtue *ethics*.

VIRTUE THEORY

Since the notion of *virtue* is central to this essay, we need to be clear from the
outset what we mean by *virtue*. We need a virtue theory. We may begin, as
one may frequently begin in the Western tradition, generally with the great
Greeks, specifically in this essay with Aristotle. He defines virtue as "a state
of character concerned with choice, lying in a mean."[3] Aquinas follows
Aristotle's tradition but rephrases Aristotle's definition. A virtue, he argues,
is a habit or a disposition[4] ordered to an act.[5] Mennonite theologian Joseph
Kotva's contemporary definition is similar, if slightly more specific: virtues
are "those states of character [habits or dispositions] that enable or contribute
to the realization of the human good." Virtues are involved in "both the
intellectual and rational part of the self and the affective or desiring part of
the self."[6]

As character state or habit, virtue not only explains why a person acts this
way on this particular occasion but also why the person can be relied on to
act this way always or, given human frailty, at least most of the time. Immediately, then, we can isolate three dimensions of a virtue: it is a character
state, habit, or disposition; it involves a judgment of truth and choice of
action; and it lies in a mean between excess and defect. These three dimensions of virtue are agreed by most proponents of virtue and virtue ethics as
essential to its definition. "Each of the virtues involves getting things right,
for each involves *phronesis*, or practical wisdom, which is the ability to
reason correctly about practical matters."[7] Without *phronesis*, no right action, and therefore no virtue, is possible. We will have much to say about
practical wisdom and practical judgment in the next section.

Common to all theories of virtue, including Aristotle's, is the essential
notion that virtues are not only preconditions for human flourishing but also
constituents of that flourishing. "A virtue is a character trait that human
beings, given their physical and psychological nature, *need* to flourish (or to
do and fare well)."[8] The person who has the virtues of benevolence and
justice will be a benevolent and just person who acts benevolently and justly.
This direction was mapped out by Aristotle, who names the ultimate human

good *eudaimonia*,[9] happiness or fulfillment and was Christianized by Aquinas, who names the ultimate Christian good union with God achieved through the virtue of *caritas*,[10] charity or self-sacrificing love. Given their different ends, happiness in the case of Aristotelian virtue ethics and union with God in Christian virtue ethics, we would expect the two ethics to be different, and we will argue later that they are different.

A central element of Aristotle's definition of virtue is that it is the result of deliberation and choice; it is rational as man himself is rational (and for Aristotle it is always *a man* who is rational, never a woman, a gender inequality that contemporary ethicists rightly do not accept). Deliberation is of possible choice and action, and choice is of one action in preference to others. Choice involves reason, thought,[11] and *phronesis* or practical wisdom and judgment. The choice of one action in preference to others is made of the mean that is appropriate and proportionate for this particular person, on this occasion, and for the right reason.

The mean that is virtuous action, it is important to note, is not an arithmetic mean but a mean relative to the individual and the circumstances in which he finds himself. The arithmetic mean between ten and two pounds of food is six pounds, but six pounds would be "too little for Milo" (a famous wrestler of Aristotle's day) and too much for "the beginner in athletic exercises." The mean to be chosen, therefore, is "not in the object but relatively to us."[12] Importantly, deliberation is about means, never about ends; ends are given and not to be deliberated. Aristotle's virtue ethics is thoroughly teleological; the final end is human happiness or flourishing. Virtuous actions are means to that end, and deliberation and choice are about those means and their contribution to the end. We deliberate only about what lies in our power to do or not to do;[13] actions we are forced to do are not freely chosen and, therefore, cannot be either virtuous or vicious, moral or immoral. It is because we are rational that we can know, first, that action is called for and, second, that we can choose this virtuous action or this vicious action. Virtue is ineluctably a rational activity and to fully understand it a theory of rationality and knowledge is required. To that we now turn.

KNOWLEDGE

That virtue includes a rational, intellectual, deliberative, and decisive dimension means that some epistemological theory is required for its full understanding. To act rightly is not only to act rightly in choice and action, it is also to know rightly and to feel rightly. To understand rightly the process of human knowing, we espouse the epistemology established by Bernard Lonergan in his magisterial *Insight*, and we believe that epistemology fully elucidates both the process of coming to know and the process of coming to virtue. "All human beings," Aristotle teaches, "desire to know by nature."[14] Lonergan agrees, arguing that human knowing begins in wonder and question, in the "pure desire to know."[15] There is no human knowledge, no genuine answer, without a prior question. Human knowing is not simply "taking a look" at reality. It is endlessly discursive, that is, it cycles and recycles through various levels of cognitive activity until knowledge and truth are reached in the judgment, deliberated on, and a decisive choice is made for action according to truth. It begins with attention and cycles on through perception, imagination (sometimes as memory), insight, conceptualization, deliberation and weighing of evidence, and culminates in the judgment of truth.[16] It is in the judgment of truth and only in the judgment of truth that genuine human knowledge and truth are achieved. This judgment may be followed by decision and action and it is only at the moment of decision and action that morality enters in.

Perception is critical in the process of coming to know. Perception, Lonergan argues, is a function of a subject's relationship to an object, the subject's active patterning of the object, a dialectical interaction between the personal subject and the object in the phenomenal world. The phenomenal object does not simply impress itself upon rational subjects, as it impresses itself upon non-rational animals, nor do rational subjects simply construct or project it. Rather, the appearances of the phenomenal world are already shaped by the subjects' attention, short-term and long-term interests, loves of varying intensity, immediate and ultimate goals, the intensity of their emotional interactions, and in general the character lens through which they view the object.[17] The phenomenal world persons encounter and attend to is not a world of naked sense data that is "out, there, now, real,"[18] but a world already shaped by their subjective interpretations called perceptions. Perception is an exercise of practical reason leading to choice; what we "see" is a function of who we are. This claim will later have implications for virtue ethics.

William James puts the cognitive psychology nicely. "My experience is what I agree to attend to. Only those items which I notice shape my mind – without selective interest experience is an utter chaos."[19] The Good Samaritan and his two clerical compatriots had the same retinal sensations of the same body on the same road, but because of different perceptual, that is, personally interpreted, sensations they really "saw" and "experienced" two different realities lying on the road. Character states or habits explain not only why a person acts this way on this particular occasion but also why the person acts this way always. Character is a set of enduring states or habits that affect how a person perceives, judges, acts, and ultimately lives. That is why philosopher of science Norwood Russell Hanson notes that "there is more to seeing than meets the eyeball."[20]

What, we may ask, does perception have to do with virtue? Aristotle writes that "we become just by first performing just acts."[21] We pose two questions to that assertion. First, how do we know which actions are just and, therefore, to be performed? Second, what motivation might we have for performing those actions? The first question is easily answered. We learn what are just acts or acts of any other virtue from respected others, parents, teachers, mentors, friends, "saints," whom we hold as virtuous and moral. We judge an action right and moral if it is one that a virtuous person would do in the circumstances, and it is by imitation of the virtuous person that we learn which actions are right, moral, and virtuous. We need to be careful, however, how we understand the word *learning*.

Words, expositions, arguments will never make anyone virtuous, for virtues are habits or states learned only by repeated and habitual performance. It is via such habituation, critically questioned and requestioned in the cycle of attention, perception, insight, judgment, decision, and action, that we come to learn and value the goodness of justice and love and of just, loving, and virtuous actions in general. The perception of moral relevance is the product of both experience and habituation but, we repeat, there is no real morality until that moral relevance is judged to be true in the judgment of truth and then followed by personal decision and action. Aristotle is pointing at this critical approach to learning virtues when he claims that "a morally praiseworthy act must be done in full awareness of *what* we are doing and *why* we do it. It must be an act freely chosen and not done from coercion."[22] We have already pointed out the universal Catholic position that morality enters the process of knowing only at the stage of decision and action. There is no moral action prior to my choice to do this action, nor is there any moral praise to be earned from simply imitating another person. "We are morally obliged not only to *act* well but also to *think* well."[23] That thinking well, Aristotle and Lonergan agree, requires moral agents to be open to ongoing inquiry and consequent reflective grasp of their attention, perception, understanding, judgment, and decision, for personal bias and pleasure can distort them and will need to be corrected.[24]

The second question about motivation is also easily answered. MacIntyre situates virtues within a broad category he names *practice*, a "coherent and complex form of socially established cooperative human activity through which goods internal to that form of activity are realized in the course of trying to achieve those standards of excellence which are appropriate to, and partially definitive of, that form of activity."[25] That complex definition requires instantiation for clarification. That a practice is a "socially established cooperative human activity" signals the importance of membership in, and the influence of, a community and culture on the individual learning virtue. The form of "socially established cooperative human activity" in focus here is the search for virtue or goodness; "goods internal to that form of activity" are the virtues themselves as defined in the community and culture; the desire "to achieve those standards of excellence [in that culture] appropriate to" being virtuous provides motivation to strive to achieve those virtuous goods. It is a central claim of virtue theory from Aristotle to MacIntyre that virtues are shaped in a community and culture by narratives and role models judged to be virtuous.

Virtues are *learned* and can be learned only within particular communities; they can be *sustained* only in those communities; they get their *content* from communities; they get their *worth* and convey worth only from and in community; and they act back on communities to sustain them.[26] Virtuous people, both past and present, have learned and learn from virtuous communities. Humans are not absolutely the autonomous and self-determining persons they are claimed to be. Persons who are "role-figures"[27] first exemplify what it means to be just, loving, and so on, and then by personal repetition of acts of justice and love an individual establishes those virtues as personal habits and dispositions. As habits are stabilized, both the virtuous exemplars and the acts of virtue learned from them need to be more and more focused and "purified" by critical examination and re-examination in the process of knowing that issues in the judgment of truth, value, decision, and action. This process of critical examination and re-examination not only purifies the agent and his virtues but also leads him nearer to the self-determination and authenticity which enable his full morality.[28] MacIntyre is still correct, however, when he asserts the sociologically-accepted position that "separated from the *polis* [community and culture] what could have been a human being becomes instead a wild animal."[29]

Caroline Walker Bynum enters an important caveat to this discussion of role models, warning us that "medieval hagiographers pointed out repeatedly that saints are not even primarily 'models' for ordinary mortals; the saints are far too dangerous for that."[30] The saint, Keenan judges, "has always been an original, never an imitation,"[31] a judgment that is empirically supported by a quick scan of what Jennifer Herdt calls "the rainbow cast of saints.... All are understood as having imitated Christ, but they are nevertheless a far cry from carbon copies of one another."[32] Augustine is not Maria Goretti, Therese of Lisieux is not Theresa of Calcutta, Francis is not Dorothy Day. The saints are all originals; they became virtuous and morally excellent in their own way, and so too must all moral agents become virtuous and morally excellent in their own way. They must become authentically, virtuously, and morally themselves, not simply clones of Augustine or Therese or Maria Goretti. Yet we do learn from those whom we judge to be virtuous and moral. The virtuous role model from whom we learn virtue, first, by *mimesis* or imitation offers a historical, living, and respected account of human flourishing and a demonstration that the virtues are both means and constituents of that flourishing. "We ought to attend to the undemonstrated sayings and opinions of experienced and older people or of people of practical wisdom not less than to demonstrations; for, because experience has given them an eye, they see aright."[33]

As we learn from role models, we must also submit them, their character, and their flourishing to critical attention, perception, insight, and the judgment that this role model is or is not a flourishing, virtuous person and his virtues are means to his flourishing and will be to ours *in our own ways*. The child's virtue is not *his* virtue but the virtue of the one who is his role model or is in authority over him. To become authentic and authentically virtuous the child must develop into *his* authenticity, *his* virtue and *his* adulthood. The virtuous life, like human life itself, is essentially developmental. As each person has an original way of being human, so also each has an original way of being virtuous. Neither the original human nor the original virtuous character can be ultimately created by imitating past models. They can be shaped by imitating past models but finished only by a fresh articulation. The dynamic of virtue begins with imitation of role models but concludes with authentic morality though personal decision and responsibility.

Though we are not told anything about the various motivations of the protagonists in the parable of the Good Samaritan, it is not difficult to understand that the characters of the Hebrew priest and Levite would be shaped by their Hebrew culture, perhaps by the laws and customs about purity and uncleanness, and that of the good Samaritan would be shaped by his quite different Samaritan culture, in which "neighbor" might be defined other than in the contemporary Hebrew culture. Motivations, of course, are always ambiguous and, therefore, need to be examined in the self-correcting and upwardly spiraling process of attention, perception, insight, judgment, decision, and action. The Good Samaritan could have acted out of genuine pity and compassion for the injured man or, like the hypocrite in Jesus' saying, out of the desire to be "praised by men" (Matt 6:2). His morality or goodness would be different in either case. Not only the Samaritan needs to challenge his motivations; so too does every person seeking virtue. Such challenges can be powered by the examples of virtuous role models, themselves critically challenged in the self-correcting and upwardly spiraling cognitive process. The search for right motivation and purity of virtue is a never-ending search; we are never the virtuous persons we could become. The human search for virtue, goodness, happiness, flourishing, and union with God is ineluctably historical, developing, and ultimately eschatological.

EMOTIONS

Since Kant and his categorical imperative of invariant duty, it has been philosophically fashionable to dismiss human emotions as partial and, therefore, unreliable and of no ethical value. The discussions are "arbitrary and fractious" and "puzzlingly pulled in what appears to be opposing directions."[34] Only rationality, especially will, it is said, is of importance for morality. Modern virtue ethicists judge that to be a mistake. Martha Nussbaum, for instance, argues that emotions "involve judgments about important things, judgments in which, appraising an external object as salient for our own being, we acknowledge our own neediness and incompleteness before parts of the world that we do not fully control."[35] Emotions, she continues, "are forms of *evaluative* judgments that ascribe to certain things and persons outside a person's own control great importance for the person's own flourishing."[36] Robert Roberts defines emotions along the same lines as "concern-based construals."[37] Emotions, then, 1) have a share in rationality, they convey cognitive content as value judgments of things and persons as 2) salient or critical for 3) a person's own happiness or flourishing. We agree with these three claims relative to the cognitive function of emotions, but not with the language in which they are articulated.

Lonergan has no consideration of emotions in *Insight*, but by 1972 and *Method in Theology* he holds that emotions are "central to the apprehension of value and the judgment of value."[38] Fitterer makes the Lonerganian distinction we believe must be made between the *apprehension* of value and the *judgment* of truth and value. Given the epistemology we have elaborated above, we cannot entirely agree with Nussbaum's description of emotion as a *judgment* of value, for we restrict the word *judgment* to the judgment of truth. That judgment is not merely an apprehension of a situation or object but the outcome of the cognitive process of attention, perception, reflection, and judgment that this is truly so, that this emotion, compassion for or distrust of the man on the road to Jericho, is not just a mere passing feeling but is a feeling that signals something salient for my happiness and fulfillment. We are willing to describe emotion as a *prima facie judgment* or a *proto-judgment*,[39] but such *prima facie* or *proto* judgments are no more than immediate apprehensions of *possible* value that must be refined through the cognitive process before any judgment of truth or *actual* value can be made and acted upon. Only in the judgment of truth and value can the possible value that emotion initially signals be judged a genuine value or disvalue for my good and flourishing.

Let us assume that, when he first saw the body on the road, the Samaritan was moved to feel compassion for the injured man. The movement from feeling and apprehending compassion as a *possible* value to the judgment that compassion is a *real and true* value for his good and flourishing is effected in the cognitive process we have outlined. Let us assume that, when he first saw the body by the side of the road, the priest was moved to feel distrust for the injured man as a possible source of impurity. The movement from feeling and apprehending distrust as a possible value to the judgment that distrust is an actual value or disvalue for his good and flourishing is effected in the same cognitive process. The one cultural and psychological difference is that the Samaritan and the priest bring different perceptual lenses to the situation and those different lenses lead initially to different apprehensions and perceptions of the situation and ultimately to different truth and value judgments about it.

Aristotle makes a distinction between the person he calls the "continent" or "self-controlled" and the one who is fully virtuous. The continent character is the one who, knowing what he should do, does it, but contrary to his own desires. The fully virtuous character is the one who, knowing what he should do, does it and desires to do it; his desires are in accord with his reason, and what he should do he does gladly.[40] Hence, Aristotle concludes, "just acts give pleasure to the lover of justice and in general virtuous acts to the lover of virtue."[41] The names Aristotle gives to the two characters in this distinction, the continent and the fully virtuous, reveal his evaluation of the distinction; the fully virtuous person is morally superior to the simply continent one. The fully virtuous person is the one whose emotions and desires are ultimately under the control of reason. The child and the animal do not have the capacity to be fully virtuous, Aristotle tells us, for they do not have the deliberative capacities for decision and action required for virtue.[42] They lack the judgment that can control desires.[43] No one, therefore, "would choose to live with the intellect of a child throughout his life, however much he were to be pleased at the things that children are pleased at."[44]

We believe this continent/fully virtuous distinction needs qualification. Take, for instance, this situation: a woman, without noticing it, drops her purse in a crowded shopping mall and walks on; a man picks up her purse and runs to return it to her. We would surely judge he is an honest man. But consider two possible circumstances that might qualify our judgment. The first is that the man who returns the woman's purse is an honest multi-millionaire; the money in her purse means nothing to him. He wants to act honestly and does act honestly, but it is in no sense hard for him to do so. The second circumstance is that the man who returns the purse is a poor man whose wife has breast cancer and they have no money to buy the drugs necessary for her treatment. He also wants to act honestly and does act honestly, but we can imagine how hard it is for him to restore the purse, how much it is against a deep-seated desire to keep the money and buy drugs for his sick wife. When he returns the purse to its owner, against his desires, he qualifies as Aristotle's continent man, but surely in this situation he is more honest than the multi-millionaire for whom restoring the purse was easy and totally in accord with his own desires. We believe this same sort of argument can be constructed for situations in which other virtues are in question, and as a result we offer our own axiom: the harder it is to act virtuously, the more it is against our personal emotion and desire, the more virtue is required to act virtuously.[45]

The second and third assertions above, that emotions are salient for a person's own individual goodness and flourishing are central to any consideration of virtue. The value I initially apprehend in an emotion is not just a general value for every human person but a particular value apprehended as a salient value for *my* particular good and flourishing. Emotions, Nussbaum claims and we agree, "contain an ineliminable reference to me."[46] They are the world seen and interpreted specifically through the lens of *my* perception. It is a culturally universal value, let us assume, that all mothers are to be loved. When *your* mother dies, then, I might feel emotions of love and grief, but my love and grief will be nothing compared to yours. Nor will my love and grief at the death of your mother be as powerful as my love and grief when *my* mother dies. The fact that it is *my* mother who has died is not just an accidental fact of *my* life but a fact that essentially structures the entire experience for me, and concentrates my keen attention on it. When that attention is cognitively processed through to the judgment of truth, my emotions reveal my deepest values and goals not only to me but also to any attentive observer.

If emotions are so self-centered, some ask, does training individuals to be attentive to them and the values they reveal not promote selfishness? It does promote selfishness, we respond, but not a selfishness that is exclusively self-centered and inward-looking but a self-ishness that is self-attention, self-understanding, self-judgment and self-responsibility that might lead to self-correction and greater outward-looking towards neighbors in the world. MacIntyre's *After Virtue* raised three questions that have become famous among virtue ethicists: Who are we? Who ought we to become? How do we get there? The self-understanding, self-judgment, and self-correction enabled by the cognitive processing of my emotions helps answer the first of those questions: who am I? That self-knowledge, in turn, contributes to any conversion from who I presently am to who I am to become, and the more I become who I am to become, the more I become of good character and virtue, the more I am enabled to deal virtuously with the injured man on the road, whenever, wherever, and in whatever condition I might find him. The person who has the virtue of benevolence may not always act benevolently, but she will always be, at least, prone to acting benevolently, and to feeling the emotions associated with benevolence. The virtues and vices "are all dispositions not only to act, but to feel emotions, as *r*eactions as well as impulses to action…[and]…in the person with the virtues, these emotions will be felt on the right occasions, towards the *right* people or objects, for the *right* reasons, where 'right' means 'correct.'"[47]

There is another consideration here, a specifically Christian one. When asked which commandment was the first of all, Jesus replied: "You shall love the Lord your God with all your heart…the second is this, you shall love your neighbor as yourself" (Mk 12:30–31). That injunction is well-known, but perhaps not so well understood. It contains three separate injunctions: love God, love your neighbor, and love yourself. Since Augustine, Jesus' saying has been interpreted in Christian teaching as grounding a wholly legitimate and virtuous self-love.[48] Self-love that locks me into myself is certainly not virtuous, for it ignores all the real relationships I have in the real world, but self-love that empowers me to the understanding of myself and my right place in those real relationships, and inserts me justly and lovingly into those relationships, is as virtuous as any love of neighbor and is, indeed, a necessary precondition for genuine neighbor-love.

We are in complete agreement with Margaret Farley: "love is the problem in ethics, not the solution."[49] It is the problem, however, because it is usually contentless, and so we give it content. We begin with an ancient definition: *amare est velle bonum*, to love is to will the good of another.[50] Love is an activity of the will, a will and a decision for the good of another human being. Love of another person is ecstatic, that is, in love I go out of myself to seek the good of another equal and unique self. That there are two equal selves in any loving relationship introduces the cardinal virtue of justice, "the virtue according to which, with constant and perpetual will, someone renders to someone else her or his due rights."[51] There is, therefore, in right love always an integration of love and justice. There is always, in Farley's apposite phrase, "just love."[52] In self-love, willing my own good, I go, not out of myself, but into myself to come to self-awareness, self-knowledge, and self-acceptance, not to stay imprisoned in my self-love but to go out of myself to another, equal person with full self-knowledge and responsibility. There is, we suggest, an ancient Latin axiom in play here: *nemo dat quod non habet*, no one gives what he does not have. We argue that not only is right self-love both humanly and Christianly legitimate but also that it is the basis of all other right love, of neighbor-love and God-love, for if a person does not fully accept himself, in both his wholeness and his brokenness, neither can he give himself fully to another person or fully accept that other person.[53]

We summarize our position on the moral significance of emotions in a passage borrowed from Hursthouse: "1. The virtues (and vices) are morally significant. 2. The virtues (and vices) are all dispositions not only to act, but to feel emotions, as *re*actions as well as impulses to action…. 3. In the person with the virtues, these emotions will be felt on the *right* occasions, towards the *right* people or objects, for the *right* reasons, where 'right' means 'correct.'"[54] We return to the agents on the road to Jericho. When they saw the man lying on the road, what were their reactions? Let us assume the Samaritan acted out of the virtue of benevolence. What did he feel before he decided to act benevolently? He felt possibly love for the injured man, possibly compassion and empathy as he imagined what he would want people to do if he were injured, and these feelings disposed him to act as virtuously as he did. It was certainly the right occasion for compassion, the injured man was the right person for compassion, and let us assume (though we are not told) that he acted and felt for the right reason, let us say to fulfill the Golden Rule. And what did the two clerics feel before they acted? They felt possibly distrust towards a man who might compromise their purity and, therefore, also their religious obligations, possibly fear that it might be a ruse that would place them in danger. It was the right occasion, we would surely say, to act out of the love command in Leviticus, though they might have wondered did this man qualify as a "neighbor" (Lev. 19:18). In their own minds, though not in Jesus', they might have acted for the right reason. No matter. The point is not to know the reasons for which the three agents acted. The point is to understand that emotions are morally significant, sometimes as morally significant as the virtues with which they are associated.

VIRTUE ETHICS

In the preceding section we discussed virtue *theory*, which is concerned neutrally with the nature of virtue in general; in this section, we discuss virtue *ethics*, which is more an advocacy of virtue and virtuous action. In the post-enlightenment period virtue was distrusted, largely because of anxiety over both the authenticity of virtues humanly acquired through imitation of role models and questions of divine and human agency.[55] In *After Virtue*, however, MacIntyre makes the "disquieting suggestion" that in the contemporary world the language of morality is in a state of disorder. "We possess indeed," he argued, "simulacra of morality; we continue to use many of the key expressions. But we have—very largely, if not entirely—lost our comprehension, both theoretical and practical, of morality."[56] Herdt comments that "contemporary revivers of virtue ethics, in contrast [to the distrust of virtue] have enthusiastically embraced the notion that habituation in virtue takes place within the context of a community and its practices."[57] Post-Kantian moral philosophers concentrated their attention on specific acts which are mandated by laws, rules, or consequences. Post-Tridentine Catholic moral theologians also concentrated their attention on acts mandated by laws and rules, and they created a taxonomy of *sins* arising from the violation of laws and obligations. Such an approach ignored questions of personal, and therefore also social, virtue, character, happiness, flourishing. It ignored, Louis Janssens argued in an oft-quoted article, "the human *person* integrally and adequately considered."[58]

Janssens developed a personalism rooted, he argued, in the methodological transformation in the Second Vatican Council's *Gaudium et spes* from an exclusively biological to a personalist perception of natural law. "When there is a question of harmonizing conjugal love with the responsible transmission of life," the Council decreed, "the moral aspect of any procedure…must be determined by objective standards. These [are] *based on the nature of the human person and his acts.*"[59] At the same time, other moral philosophers and theologians, not all of them challenged by the Second Vatican Council, were also paying increasing attention to the human person, her character, habits, dispositions, feelings, perceptions, judgments, and perhaps above all her flourishing. Virtue ethics was coming, not so much to birth as to *re*birth, for it had already flourished in the Greece of Plato and Aristotle and in the medieval Europe of Aquinas, not to mention in the Christian New Testament of the first centuries. That latter we shall consider at the end of this essay.

Focus on the human person rather than on her acts led to the common assertion that virtue ethics focuses on *being* and *character*, the being of a personal subject, and that the deontological ethics of duty or utilitarian ethics of consequences focuses on the subject's *doing* or actions. That assertion is true enough, but it is not particularly clarifying of virtue ethics and, indeed, if it is understood to mean that virtue ethics ignores *doing*, it is demonstrably untrue, for surely we expect the virtuous person to *do* or *act* virtuously. We expect the human being and character with the virtue of benevolence to *do* benevolent actions; we expect the human being and character with the virtue of justice to *do* just actions; and so on for all the other virtues.

Contrary, therefore, to critics who suggest that virtue ethics does not offer ethical directions or rules, it surely does offer rules. Virtue ethics offers prescriptive rules: do benevolently when benevolence is called for, do justly when justice is called for, and do them all on the right occasions, towards the right people, and for the right reasons. It offers also prohibitive rules: do not do what is mean, unjust, or dishonest. Moral action is action according to some virtue, vicious action is action according to some vice. The ethics of Aristotle and Aquinas was, and contemporary virtue ethics is, indeed, an ethics of virtue, character and being, but there was and there is always the axiom: *agere sequitur esse*, action follows being. It is, in fact, as we argued earlier, the habitual doing of acts of benevolence, justice, honesty, and so on that first instills and then reinforces the instilled habits that are virtues and the actions to which they are ordered. "Morality is ultimately in this view not about actions but about the acting subject."[60]

Rather than say, then, that virtue ethics focuses on being and character and deontological ethics focuses on action or doing, we prefer to say that virtue ethics gives precedence to virtue, character, and being over action and doing. Broadly speaking, deontological ethics holds that only judgments about right action are basic in morality and that virtue, and the virtuous character, are always derivative from right action. In virtue ethics the converse is the case; only judgments about virtue and the virtuous character are basic in morality and right action is derivative from virtue and the virtuous character. In virtue ethics, the moral agent and his character come first and his moral actions come second; in virtue ethics, that is, *agere vere sequitur esse*. Moral actions are as important in virtue ethics as in any other ethical system, but the basic judgment in virtue ethics is not about actions but about character.[61]

In virtue ethics, "the project of the moral life is to become a certain kind of person,"[62] a virtuous person, one who, in Aristotle's language, knows how to act and feel in ways appropriate to the circumstances. This approach, John McDowell argues, means that the moral question "How should one live" is approached from the notion of the virtuous person, so that the notion of right and moral behavior "is grasped, as it were, from the inside in."[63] The right action in any particular circumstances is what a virtuous person would characteristically do in those circumstances. We believe this approach to and articulation of virtue ethics is correct and provides greater insight into and understanding of the nature of virtue ethics than the bald statement that virtue ethics is an ethics of being rather than doing. The precedence of virtue over action in contemporary ethical theory is no small shift. It is, in Thomas Kuhn's sense, a paradigm shift and has led and will lead to a struggle of minds and morals between those committed to the older deontological ethics and those committed to the *renewed* virtue ethics.[64]

That conclusion can be elucidated by a critical consideration of the personal subject. A subject is a rational, attending, perceiving, understanding, judging, choosing, and acting person, and one who carries out these rational operations not only on objects external to him but also on his own internal self. A subject operates freely and consciously; he is an agent, the cause of his own actions in the sense that he has the power to produce the results he chooses, wills, and intends to produce. Subjects "are in essence self-determining beings, who act upon and through their nature and environment to give their lives particular form. In a sense [subjects] control their futures by becoming the kind of men [and women] they are through their present choices and actions."[65]

English poet John Donne wrote that "No man is an island;"[66] no human subject/agent is a completely isolated person. He is essentially a social subject; he lives in a specific community and culture. From his community and culture, he initially learns all sorts of meanings, including for our purpose here meanings of what, in general, constitutes the good and, in specific, what is the right thing to do on this occasion, towards this person, and for this right reason. In short, he learns rules and reasons for virtuous and moral behavior. When he is a child, he follows those rules to be a good boy in the sense that he does what adults want him to do, to be praised by others, or simply, unthinkingly, and legalistically to follow the rules he has learned.[67] We can say two things about the child's "moral" actions.

First, he acts, not out of any genuine desire or intention to do good because it is the right thing to do on this occasion, towards this right person, for this right reason, but because of his selfish desire for praise or fear of punishment. He acts inauthentically, doing the right things for the wrong reasons; he is far from acting virtuously or morally. Secondly, however, those less than virtuous actions learned and habitually done in his community become the dispositions and habits leading to genuine adult virtuous actions. Their habitual repetition and his ongoing critical attention to them, perception, understanding, and judgment of them, and his personal choice of them ultimately leads him to do the right thing on the right occasion, towards the right person, and for the right reasons out of a personal habit or virtue. Habitually doing the right things for the right reasons transforms his very being and develops his character from one that has the simulacrum of a virtuous and moral person to one that is an authentically virtuous and moral person.

Michael Slote charges that virtue ethics "appears to obliterate the common distinction between doing the right thing and doing the right thing for the right reasons."[68] We reject this charge and argue that virtue ethics does not obliterate that distinction but, rather, marks it as a stage in the psychological, moral development of the subject on his way to becoming a virtuous and moral adult. The child, just learning virtue, may do the right thing for the wrong reason, but the adult who has learned virtue is capable of doing the right thing, towards the right person, for the right reason. He is capable of acting self-responsibly and authentically. The focus of virtue ethics on character is sometimes referred to as an elitist view of human excellence; only a small group of people are capable of reaching authentic virtue. Our view of this accusation is in agreement with that of Jeffrey Stout: commitment to an ethics of virtue that, through a continuous critique in the cognitive process, "is *always* in the process of projecting a higher conception of self to be achieved and leaving one's achieved self (but not its accumulated responsibilities) behind."[69]

Slote raises, but does not accept, another objection to virtue ethics and its agent-based approach. If morality is to be judged on the basis of the inner state an agent has reached, if he *is* an agent of virtuous character, does it not follow that *every* action he does will be automatically an act of virtue, whether it be an action accepted as virtuous or vicious in his community of meaning? In other words, does the transition from an act-based morality to a being-based morality mean that anything goes, that any and every act of the virtuous person will be automatically deemed an act of virtue? There are, we suggest, two answers to this question. The first is the one that Slote suggests.[70]

Let us assume the Good Samaritan possesses the virtue of compassion or the virtue of benevolence. To the extent that compassion and benevolence are accepted as good in his community of meaning, which is where he came to learn and know them, and to the extent that because he possesses these virtues he is judged in his community to be a man of virtue, he cannot simply do any action and name it compassion or benevolence. There is a generally agreed-upon vision of compassion and benevolence in his community and his action will be judged compassionate or benevolent, and therefore virtuous and moral, on the basis of that vision. Since every agent, including the virtuous agent, is endowed with free will, each is perfectly capable of choosing a variety of actions that may or may not be compassionate or benevolent. If we assume that the Good Samaritan acted with compassion and benevolence toward the injured man, he still could have chosen to act as did the two clerics, that is, without compassion or benevolence. In virtue ethics, virtuous acts, not merely the virtuous character state of the person doing the acts, are important. As the intellectual virtues of wisdom and prudence are hard to achieve, so also is moral virtue hard to achieve. Many, acting only in mimesis of virtuous models, may well have the simulacra of virtue, but history shows that fewer are capable of reaching authentic and consistent virtue.

There is a second answer to the question Slote raises: the human subject adequately considered is a historical, always-developing being. Lonergan delineates what he calls "the theoretical premises from which there follows the historicity of human thought and action." They are as follows: "(1) that human concepts, theories, affirmations, courses of action are expressions of human understanding.... (2) That human understanding develops over time and, as it develops, human concepts, theories, affirmations, courses of action change...(3) That such change is cumulative, and (4) that the cumulative changes in one place or time are not to be expected to coincide with those in another."[71] From these premises flows the conclusion that the meanings, values, moral norms, virtues, and virtuous actions of one socio-historical era are not necessarily the articulations of another era or, indeed, of different groups in the same era. The world, both the world free of every human intervention, the corporeal world, and the human world fashioned by socially constructed meanings, is in a permanent state of change and evolution. It is essentially for this reason that Fuchs argues, correctly in our judgment, that anyone wishing to make a moral judgment about any human action in the present on the basis of its givenness in the past has, at least, two facts to keep in mind.

First, the past did not know either the entire reality and development of the human person or its individual elements hidden in human biology and psychology. "If one wishes to make an objective moral judgment today," Fuchs points out, "then one cannot take what Augustine or the philosophers of the Middle Ages knew about sexuality as the exclusive basis of a moral reflection." Second, "we never simply 'have' nature or that which is given in nature." We know "nature," rather, "always as something that has already been interpreted in some way."[72] The careful attention to, the perception, understanding, and judgment of, and responsible decision and choice of rational persons about "*nature*" and what it demands is what constitutes *natural law*,[73] never simply the pure givenness of "*nature*" alone. In the moral tradition, argument is never from "nature" alone or reason alone, but always from "nature" *interpreted by* reason. For the human person subject to historicity, moral decision making and virtuous action is always the outcome of a process controlled by reason. It is never the outcome of merely looking at the out, there, now, and real givenness of nature.

Lonergan was convinced that something new was happening in history in the twentieth century and that, since a living morality and virtuous life ought to be part of what was taking place in history, humans were living in a new age that required a new moral approach. That new approach, he prophesied correctly, would be necessarily historical and empirical. Lonergan's distinction between a classicist and an historical or empirical notion of culture has itself become classical. "The classicist notion of culture was normative: at least *de iure* there was but one culture that was both universal and permanent." The empirical notion of culture was "the set of meanings and values that informs a way of life. It may remain unchanged for ages. It may be in the process of slow development or rapid resolution."[74] Classicist culture is static, historical culture is dynamic. Ethics, which is necessarily part of culture, mirrors this distinction.

In its classicist mode ethics is a static, permanent achievement that anyone can learn as they learn algebra; in its historical mode it is a dynamic, ongoing process requiring a rational, attentive, perceptive, insightful, understanding, judging, and decisive subject. The classicist understanding, Fuchs writes, conceives of the person as "a series of created, static, and thus definitively ordered temporal facts." The historical understanding conceives of the person as a subject in process of "self-realization in accordance with a project that develops in God-given autonomy, that is, along a path of human reason and insight, carried out in the present with a view to the future."[75] Classicist ethics sees moral norms coming from the past as once and for all definitive; moral norms enunciated in the fifth or sixteenth centuries continue to apply absolutely in the twenty-first century. Historical ethics sees the moral norms of the past, not as facts for uncritical acceptance but as partial insights that provide bases for critical attention, perception, understanding, judgment, decision, and choice in the present. What Augustine and his medieval successors knew, for instance, about human sexuality cannot be the exclusive basis for a moral judgment about sexuality today.

So it is that persons deemed virtuous may on occasion act less than virtuously. As subjects in history, they have not yet finished their journeys to virtue; they may be deemed already virtuous but they are not yet as authentically or consistently virtuous as they could be. Aristotle recognized this problem and solved it by arguing that a person is not to be judged virtuous except "in a complete life. For one swallow does not make a summer... and so too one day, or a short time, does not make a man blessed and happy," or virtuous.[76] Contemporary theologians say that subjects-in-history, along with their virtues and morality, are ineluctably eschatological. Poet Rainer Maria Rilke, perhaps, says it best: "Just keep going. No feeling is final."[77]

CHRISTIAN VIRTUE ETHICS

We have argued that virtue, virtue ethics, and the learning of both are rooted in some community and culture, and up to this point we have been developing a virtue ethics rooted broadly in the human community. We have, that is, been developing a natural virtue ethics. We turn our attention now briefly to a Christian virtue ethics, one rooted in belief in Jesus Christ and the God he reveals.[78] In the 1970s, some Catholic moralists were tempted to argue that Christian morality was not distinctively different from natural morality.[79] They meant by that claim that virtuous actions were the same in both natural and Christian ethics. We, and most Christian ethicists today, do not accept their argument. Those earlier ethicists were locked into an ethics that focused on actions as moral or immoral, and they meant that natural ethics and Christian ethics held many of the same actions as moral. We grant that many of the virtues and the moral actions they demand and enable are the same in natural and Christian ethics, but the community in which Christians learn virtues, the rainbow of role models they have for the imitation and habituation of virtuous actions, the proximate and final ends to which their virtuous actions tend, the vision out of which they are done, all are entirely different in natural and Christian ethics. That, we submit, creates major differences between natural and Christian ethics.

The Christian vision, which will control our subsequent discussion, shines out as backdrop throughout the New Testament, but we call attention to two specific texts, one in the conclusion to the parable of the Good Samaritan, the other in Paul's letter to the Philippians. After offering his parable, Jesus asks the lawyer who initiated the discussion "Which of these do you think proved neighbor to the man who fell among robbers?" The lawyer answered "the one who showed mercy on him." And Jesus said to him "go and do likewise" (Luke 10:36–37). That "go and do likewise" controls everything moral that Christians are called to do. Paul articulated the same vision, if in different language: "Have this mind among yourselves which is yours in Christ Jesus, who though he was in the form of God did not count equality with God a thing to be grasped, but emptied himself, taking the form of a servant, being born in the likeness of men" (Phil 2:5–7). Self-sacrificing love for God and neighbor and obedience to God's known will: these specifically distinguish the person the Christian is called to be.

Virtue ethics, we have argued, offers an answer to the question "Who am I to become?" The New Testament invites the followers of Jesus to *become* and *be* like Jesus and, because they *are* like him, to *do* like him. The controlling principle of Christian virtue ethics is *imitatio Christi*: first, *be* like Jesus and, then, *do* like Jesus. That principle roots a specifically Christian virtue ethics. Note that it is, as is all virtue ethics, agent-centered; who Christians are and are called to be takes precedence over what they are called to do. The imitation of Christ is not some means external to characters that makes being and doing like Christ possible; it is something that is an internal, essential constituent of their specifically Christian character. It is what Karl Rahner called an *existential* of their Christian character, "an ontological modification…added indeed to nature by God's grace and therefore 'supernatural,' [which protects the Catholic priority of God's grace] but in fact never lacking in the real order."[80] Having the mind of Christ as an essential specification of their character, Christians habitually act out of that mind, so that not only do they become and act more and more like Christ, but also, like Aristotle's fully virtuous man, they do like Christ gladly. They act, as the New Testament regularly says, out of their "heart" (e.g. Matt 5:8, 28; 6:21; 12:34, 40; 13:15; 15:8, 18, 19; 22:37), in Jewish anthropology the zone of "intelligence, mind, wisdom, folly, intention, plan, will, affection, love, hate, sight, regard, blindness."[81]

Consideration of the "heart" leads us immediately to the virtue Aquinas called "the mother and root of all virtues"[82] and "the most excellent of the virtues,"[83] namely, *caritas*, charity or self-sacrificing love. Mark reports that a scribe asked Jesus "which commandment is the first of all?" Jesus answered that the first is "you shall love the Lord your God with all your heart" and "the second is this, you shall love your neighbor as yourself." "There is no other commandment," he added, "greater than these" (Mark 12:29–31). Nor, in the Christian vision, is there any other virtue greater than charity or self-sacrificing love, for all other virtues are informed or, as Aquinas says, "quickened" by charity and receive from charity their full complement as virtues. Virtues, we already explained, are both means to and constituents of human flourishing or happiness. Now Aquinas argues that man's happiness is twofold. "One is proportionate to human nature, a happiness, to wit, which man can obtain by means of his natural principles. The other is a happiness surpassing man's nature, and which man can obtain by the power of God alone." It is necessary, then, "for man to receive from God some additional principles, whereby he may be directed to supernatural happiness…. Such principles are called *theological virtues:* first, because their object is God, inasmuch as they direct us aright to God; secondly, because they are infused in us by God alone."[84] Charity is such an infused theological virtue, and so are faith and hope.

"Charity is the theological virtue by which we love God above all things for his own sake, and our neighbor as ourselves for the love of God."[85] Jesus' greatest commandment invites us to do acts of love towards God and neighbor. "Faith is the theological virtue by which we believe in God and believe all that he has said and revealed to us."[86] Paul insisted on the necessity of theological faith for salvation (Rom 1:16–17; 3:26–30; 5:1; Gal 3:6–9), and that theological tradition flowered on both sides of the Reformation controversies. Martin Luther took his stand on "faith alone" and the Council of Trent taught that faith is "the beginning of human salvation…without which it is impossible to please God."[87] Neither doubted that faith must issue in works, that is, acts in accord with faith. Another notable difference appears here between natural and Christian ethics: the natural man practices virtue according to reason; the Christian practices virtue through reason quickened by charity and faith. "Hope is the theological virtue by which we desire the kingdom of heaven [or God] and eternal life as our happiness, placing our trust in Christ's promises."[88] Hope too must issue in action. There is a critical caveat, however, to which we must attend when we talk of virtues, even God-infused virtues, and their contribution to supernatural flourishing or happiness.

All virtues, including theological virtues, are qualities that are dispositions or habits[89] ordered to acts.[90] A virtue is a necessary prerequisite to its corresponding act, but it is not the act nor does it ineluctably lead to the act. Translation from the virtue to the act requires the agent to be rational, to be attentive, perceptive, insightful, understanding, judgmental, and decisive, and again it is only at the point of judgment, decision, and action that morality enters in. The Catholic tradition holds that the virtues of charity, faith, and hope are infused into the new Christian at baptism. For any of those virtues to become personal acts of love, faith, or hope, however, they must be translated by the believer into free and therefore moral action.

In Thomistic terms, one might argue, both acquired and infused virtues are more potency than act. Jean Porter notes correctly that infused virtues are "present only potentially in those who lack the use of reason, and…present only in a minimal degree even in some of those who possess the use of reason."[91] For a person to be self-responsible and personally moral, that is, even "infused virtue must blossom out in a personal act."[92] As we have seen, "a habit of virtue cannot be caused by one act, but only by many."[93] Repeated acts of charity, faith, and hope, therefore, on the right occasions, towards the right people, and for the right reasons, habituate the theological virtues in the Christian character, as repeated acts of acquired virtue habituate it in any agent's character. Thus does the Christian become and do more and more like Christ. Even the theological virtues, infused by God though they are, need to be exercised over and over by the agent, to habituate the character to Christian excellence and ultimate happiness.

Besides the three God-infused virtues, there are four "cardinal virtues" important to Christians, cardinal because they are pivots around which all other human virtues turn. They are prudence, justice, fortitude, and temperance, described by Aquinas as principles of integration of both the agent and his action.[94] Aristotle argued that prudence is "A true and *reasoned* state of capacity to act with regard to the things that are good or bad for man."[95] Aquinas followed him, arguing that prudence is a special virtue[96] by which "right reason is applied to action."[97] Prudence is a virtue of the practical intellect which discerns and applies universal principles to particular situations and enables agents to make practical judgments that this is the right thing to do on this occasion, towards this right person, and for this right reason. Its moral importance is evident from the fact that practical judgment is what the Catholic tradition calls "conscience."

The pivotal position of prudence can be seen by a consideration, again, of the parable of the Good Samaritan. The Samaritan finds the injured man on the road; it appears that this is the right occasion, and the injured man is the right person, for the Samaritan to exercise compassion for the right reason. It is the task of prudence to go through the rational process to reach the judgment and decision that this is, indeed, the right occasion, the right person, and the right reason for compassion. Here prudence controls the right exercise of compassion; it similarly controls and integrates the right exercise of all other moral virtues. It is precisely because *phronesis* or *prudentia* controls the practical judgments that precede, and must precede for them to be moral, the exercise of all other moral virtues that both Aristotle and Aquinas hold that without it no other virtuous state or action can be achieved. Prudence is crucially important for both the natural and the Christian agent.

Justice is "the perpetual and constant will to render to each one his right."[98] Justice is essentially about equality,[99] for the natural man equality as human, for the Christian that too but also equality as child of God. Since it is about rendering to each person his right, it is also essentially about human relationships, for persons must be somehow related to other persons in order to render them their rights. Indeed, in relations between equal agents, Aristotle writes, "justice is often thought to be the greatest of virtues."[100] Aquinas agrees: justice "excels the other moral virtues," and it excels them for two reasons: first, it is "in the more excellent part of the soul, viz. the rational appetite or will;" second, "justice is somewhat the good of another person."[101] Is it because justice excels the other moral virtues that the paradigmatic virtuous man is often called simply the "just man," as is Joseph (Matt 1:19), or "righteous man," as is Noah (Gen 6:9)? "Keep justice and do righteousness," preaches Isaiah, "blessed is the man who does this" (56:1); and Jesus condemns the scribes and Pharisees who, he judges, "have neglected the weightier matters of the law, justice and mercy and faith" (Matt 23:23). The virtuous or excellent Christian, thus far in our analysis, is the one who *is* prudent and just and *does* prudence and justice quickened by charity.

Aristotle argues that virtue is "the state of character which makes a man good and which makes him do his own work well."[102] Aquinas agrees, and argues further that virtue must be in accord with reason. The human will, however, "is hindered in two ways from following the rectitude of reason. First, by being drawn by some object of pleasure to something other than what the rectitude of reason requires; and this obstacle is removed by the virtue of temperance. Secondly, through the will being disinclined to follow that which is in accord with reason, on account of some difficulty that presents itself." Fortitude of mind is required to remove this difficulty.[103]

Fortitude and temperance are cardinal virtues required to clear away difficulties for the practice of other moral virtues. "Fortitude is the moral virtue that ensures firmness in difficulties and constancy in the pursuit of the good."[104] It strengthens an agent to overcome obstacles that present themselves to the practice of the virtues and the moral life. Humans easily understand physical fortitude or courage in the face of a physical challenge, but Aquinas emphasizes "fortitude of mind," which is required in the face of intellectual difficulties. When he found the injured man on the road, the Samaritan might have had all sorts of thoughts: what can I do to help, it's not my problem, what will it do to my bank account if I help him, what will "they" think of me if I stop to help this man? It is mental fortitude that enables him to overcome these obstacles and clears the way for him to exercise the virtues, for instance, of charity and compassion. His act of charity and compassion hinges on his prior act of mental fortitude; that makes fortitude a cardinal virtue.

Aristotle and Aquinas also agree that temperance is a virtue, and Aquinas argues that it is a cardinal virtue.[105] It withholds "the appetite from those things that are most seductive to man,"[106] especially pleasures of touch.[107] Temperance "is the moral virtue that moderates the attraction of pleasures and provides balance in the use of created goods."[108] Temperance is about balance, the mean between excess and defect that prudence finds to indicate where virtue lies. From the Christian perspective, the behavior of the two clerics on the road to Jericho is a series of excesses: disdain instead of charity, contempt instead of compassion, injustice instead of justice toward an equal child of God. Temperance, quickened by charity and illuminated by prudence, clears the way for the balanced act of charity, compassion, and justice. Temperance, then, is a cardinal virtue. Since it, however, "moderates only the desires and pleasures which affect man himself," it is not as excellent as justice and fortitude, which regard more the common good. "Prudence and the theological virtues are more excellent" than any of the other virtues.[109]

James Keenan suggests that we "think of the virtues not in the classicist expression as perfecting individual powers within an individual person [to do acts] but rather [in the empirical expression] as rightly realizing the ways that we are related."[110] "Our identity," he further argues, empirically, "is relational in three ways: generally, specifically, and uniquely." [111] For a reason that will become apparent, we prefer a different trinity: generally, particularly, and self-ishly. In general, we are beings in relation to other beings who, as humans, are our equals and, as Christian, are equal to us as children of God. This essential human and religious equality demands the virtue of justice as we have explained it. In specific, we are in relation to particular persons with bonds of family or friendship. Christians, the Letter to Timothy instructs, are to provide for these particular persons, and "especially for family members" (1 Tim 5:8). We are, of course, in general, Augustine enjoins, to love all within our reach,[112] but we are, Aquinas further specifies, to love those nearest to us most of all.[113] Justice is about universality and impartiality; fidelity is about legitimate particularity and partiality. John Henry Newman endorses legitimate partiality when he argues that "the best preparation for loving the world at large, and loving it duly and wisely [under the guidance of prudence], is to cultivate an intimate friendship and affection toward those who are immediately about us."[114] All these relationships demand the virtue of fidelity and its cognates, loyalty and constancy.

Each of us is also in essential relationship to our unique self; we are in a relationship that is self-ish and/or self-loving. Everything we said earlier about the Christian legitimacy of self-love recurs here, and this legitimate and moral relationship of self-love demands what Keenan calls the virtue of self-care. Self-care includes, but is by no means limited to, self-awareness, self-knowledge, self-acceptance, self-disclosure, and self-love. Psychological studies repeatedly indicate that one of the greatest threats to healthy human flourishing is poor self-esteem[115] and, despite Jesus' injunction to "love your neighbor *as yourself*" (Mark 12:31), the Christian tradition has not been a noted promoter of healthy self-love.[116] Self-care is the virtue that permits healthy self-love and invites reflection on my unique self as a gift of God that summons me to recognize, accept, appreciate, and use that gift in the Christian task of drawing closer in self-sacrificing love to neighbor and to God. The three virtues of justice, fidelity, and self-care, neither of which precedes the others in importance, clear the ground for the practice of other virtues in each relationship. They are, that is, Keenan argues, cardinal virtues. They are, however, all preceded in importance by a fourth cardinal virtue, prudence, which discerns and judges which acts qualify as just, faithful, and self-caring, just as it discerns and judges which acts are just, courageous, and temperate for the traditional cardinal virtues. Whether one numbers the cardinal virtues with the tradition or with Keenan, it remains critical that they be habituated by repeated exercise in imitation of role models respected in one's community.

An obvious and much-raised objection to the very notion of a Christian virtue ethics is the fact that it is *Christian* and, therefore, not universally applicable. It is applicable, so runs the objection, only to Christians and is, therefore, relative. The answer to this objection stretches in a line from MacIntyre and Lonergan all the way back to Aristotle: meaning systems, including ethical meaning systems, are learned in a specific community and are indeed, therefore, all community-relative. Such a claim, of course, raises in many minds both the specter of relativism and the unwarranted conclusion from it, namely, the untruth of every community-relative meaning system.

With Lonergan, however, we prefer to speak of perspectivism rather than relativism. While relativism concludes to the falsity of a judgment, perspectivism concludes to its partial truth. Lonergan advances three reasons for perspectivism in human knowledge. First, human knowers are finite, the information available to them at any one time is incomplete, and they seldom attend to all the data available to them. Second, the knowers are selective, given their past socialization and personal experience. Third, knowers are individually different and we can expect them to make different selections of data. The individual trained in the philosophy of Plato, Augustine for instance, will attend to different data, achieve different understandings, make different judgments, and act on different decisions than the individual trained in the philosophy of Aristotle, Aquinas for instance. Each will produce a different theological system, both of which will be partial and incomplete explanations of an infinitely complex reality. Augustine and Aquinas are like two individuals at fourth-story and thirteenth-story windows of a skyscraper; each gets a different but no less partial view of the total panorama that unfolds outside the building. There are no meaning systems, including no ethical systems, that are universal and non-perspectivistic. "So far from resting on knowledge of the universe, [a judgment] is to the effect that, no matter what the rest of the universe may prove to be, at least *this* is so."[117]

It is, of course, inevitable that different groups of equally rational human beings, attending, perceiving, understanding, judging, and deciding from different social visions, may derive different interpretations of "nature" and moral obligation deriving from "nature," and that any given interpretation may be right or wrong. That is a fact which has been demonstrated time and again in history, including Christian history.[118] It is also something taken for granted in the social scientific enterprise known as the sociology of knowledge. One of the founders of this discipline, Alfred Schutz, presents its taken-for-granted principle: "It is the *meaning* of our experiences and not the *ontological structure* of the objects that constitute reality."[119] "The potter, and not the pot," Alfred North Whitehead adds metaphorically, "is responsible for the shape of the pot."[120] The uninterpreted experience of "nature," as of every other objective reality, is restricted to its mere facticity. Nature is indeed out, there, now, and real, but is void of meaning, a quality that does not inhere in "nature" but is assigned to it by rational and social beings in interpretive acts. Meaning is what is or was meant by the *agent*, who is always to be understood not as an Enlightenment radical *individual* but as an Aristotelian-Thomistic radically *social being*. MacIntyre is inarguably correct: "Separated from the *polis* [community and culture] what could have been a human being becomes instead a wild animal."[121]

A second answer to the objection is a genuinely empirical one. For all their undoubted perspectivisms, the great ethical systems reach conclusions that are not as different as is supposed. What we have called their "visions" may be different, but they agree broadly on core ethical values, norms, and behaviors, as evidenced by their various, and uncommonly similar, versions of the Golden Rule. For Christians it is: "Whatever you wish that men would do to you do so to them; for this is the law and the prophets" (Matt 7:12); for Jews: "What is hateful to you do not do to your fellowman. This is the entire law; all the rest is commentary" (Talmud, Shabbat, 3id); for Muslims: "No one of you is a believer until he desires for his brother that which he desires for himself" (Sunnah); for Buddhists: "Hurt not others in ways that you yourself would find hurtful" (Udana-Varga 5,1); for Hindus: "This is the sum of duty; do naught unto others what you would not have them do unto you" (Mahabharata 5, 1517). The saints in these various religious traditions, the paradigmatically virtuous persons to be imitated for the habituation of virtue, all endorse and exhibit a common core of behaviors. Since *agere sequitur esse*, it is easy to conclude to similar character states and virtues that are shaped and limited, but in no way nullified, because they derive from particular perspectives. In the next essay, we outline a sexual anthropology to sustain both a virtuous sexual person and virtuous sexual ethics.

QUESTIONS FOR REFLECTION

1. What do you understand by the word *virtue*? What are Aristotle's and Thomas Aquinas' definitions of virtue? Are they in any way related? How?

2. What do you understand by the claim that virtues are habits or states learned only by repeated and habitual performance? How is such performance learned?

3. How do you understand the claim that emotions are "evaluative judgments?" How do you understand the claim that emotions are *prima facie* or *proto-judgments*? How does a person proceed from an emotional proto-judgment to the intellectual judgment of truth or value?

4. What are the implications for ethics in the claim that "the project of the moral life is to become a certain kind of person?" What are the implications of the assertion that virtue ethics focuses on a person's *being* and *character*? Does this mean that virtue ethics has nothing to say about virtuous acts? How do you understand the claim that the notion of the right and moral act "is grasped...from the inside in?"

5. Is there such a thing as "Christian virtue ethics?" If there is, what would it be? (Remember that all virtues are learned in a specific community in imitating respected women and men.)

6. How do the cardinal virtues of prudence, justice, fortitude, and temperance or, in Keenan's numeration, justice, fidelity, self-care, and prudence, function in your life?

7. Since virtue ethics is an ethical meaning system learned in a specific community, does this mean that virtue ethics is a form of ethical relativism?

NOTES

An earlier version of this essay appeared in *Theological Studies* 74, no. 2 (2013): 442–73. It is reprinted here with permission.

1. Alasdair MacIntyre, *After Virtue,* 2nd edition (Notre Dame: University of Notre Dame, 1984), 2. See also G. E. M. Anscombe, "Modern Moral Philosophy," *Philosophy* 33 (1958): 1–19; Philippa Foot, "Moral Beliefs," *Proceedings of the Aristotelian Society* 59 (1958–9): 83–104.

2. In addition to Foot, and MacIntyre, whom most judge to be the preeminent modern virtue theorists, other important theorists in the field of virtue ethics will be introduced as the essay unfolds.

3. Aristotle, *Nicomachean Ethics*, trans. David Ross (Oxford: Oxford University, 2009), II, 6, 1106b, 36. Hereafter cited as NE. See Rosalind Hursthouse, *On Virtue Ethics* (Oxford: Oxford University, 1999), 11.

4. *Summa Theologiae* I-II, 49, 1. Hereafter cited as ST.

5. Ibid. 49, 3.

6. Joseph J. Kotva, Jr., *The Christian Case for Virtue Ethics* (Washington, DC: Georgetown University, 1996), 23.

7. Hursthouse, *On Virtue Ethics*, 12.

8. Hursthouse, "Applying Virtue Ethics," in *Virtues and Reason: Philippa Foot and Moral Theory*, ed. Rosalind Hursthouse, Gavin Lawrence, and Warren Quinn (Oxford: Clarendon, 1995), 68; emphasis added. See also Hursthouse, *On Virtue Ethics*, 13; Gregory Trianosky, "Supererogation, Wrongdoing, and Vice: On the Autonomy of the Ethics of Virtue," *Journal of Philosophy* 83 (1986): 26–40; Brad Hooker, "Does Moral Virtue Constitute a Benefit to the Agent?" in *How Should One Live?: Essays on the Virtues*, ed. Roger Crisp (Oxford: Clarendon, 1998), 141–55.

9. NE I, 4, 1095a, 17–20.

10. ST I, 23, 6.

11. NE III, 2, 1112a, 17.

12. Ibid. II, 6, 1106b, 3–8.

13. Ibid. III, 3, 1112a, 31.

14. Aristotle, *Metaphysics*, ed. Joseph Sachs (Santa Fe: Green Lion Press, 1990), 980a, 20.

15. Bernard J. F. Lonergan, *Insight: A Study of Human Understanding* (London: Longmans, 1957), 74, 372–75.

16. Ibid., 273–74.
17. Ibid., 190.
18. Ibid., 251; see also Lonergan, *Method in Theology* (New York: Herder, 1972), 263.
19. William James, *The Principles of Psychology* (Cambridge, MA: Harvard University, 1983), 380–81.
20. Norwood Russell Hanson, *Patterns of Discovery: An Inquiry into the Conceptual Foundations of Science* (Cambridge: Cambridge University, 1958), 7.
21. NE II, 1103a31–1103b2.
22. Robert J. Fitterer, *Love and Objectivity in Virtue Ethics: Aristotle, Lonergan, and Nussbaum on Emotions and Moral Insight* (Toronto: University of Toronto, 2008), 6, emphasis in original.
23. Ibid., emphasis in original.
24. NE II, 1109b1–12; Lonergan, *Insight*, 225–42.
25. MacIntyre, *After Virtue*, 187.
26. See Lawrence Bloom, "Community and Virtue," in *How Should One Live?*, 231–50.
27. Daniel Statman, "Introduction to Virtue Ethics," in *Virtue Ethics: A Critical Reader*, ed. Daniel Statman (Washington, DC: Georgetown University, 1997), 15.
28. Jennifer Herdt, in her *Putting on Virtue: The Legacy of the Splendid Vices* (Chicago: University of Chicago, 2008), gives a splendid account of the historical travails of this mimetic approach to learning virtue and ultimately comes down in its favor.
29. Alasdair MacIntyre, *Whose Justice? Which Rationality?* (Notre Dame: University of Notre Dame, 1988), 98.
30. Caroline Walker Bynum, *Holy Feast and Holy Fast* (Berkeley: University of California, 1987), 7.
31. James F. Keenan, "Proposing Cardinal Virtues," in *Theological Studies* 56, no. 4 (1995): 713.
32. Herdt, *Putting on Virtue*, 8.
33. NE VI, 11, 1143b10–13. The Council of Trent also urged the imitation of the lives and morals of saints for the cultivation of personal piety and virtue. See Denzinger-Schönmetzer, n. 1824.
34. Amelie Rorty, *Review of Metaphysics* 38 (1984): 521.
35. Martha C. Nussbaum, *Upheavals of Thought: The Intelligence of Emotions* (Cambridge: Cambridge University, 2001), 19. For more, see her *The Therapy of Desire: Theory and Practice in Hellenistic Ethics* (Princeton, NJ: Princeton University, 1994); Robert C. Roberts, *Spiritual Emotions: A Psychology of Christian Virtues* (Grand Rapids: Eerdmans, 2007) and *Emotions: An Essay in Aid of Moral Psychology* (Cambridge: Cambridge University, 2003).
36. Nussbaum, *Upheavals of Thought*, 22, emphasis added. For more on the evaluative character of emotions, see Michael Stocker, "How Emotions Reveal Value and Help Cure the Schizophrenia of Modern Ethical Theories," in *How Should One Live?*, 173–90.
37. Robert C. Roberts, *Emotions: An Essay in Aid of Moral Psychology* (Cambridge: Cambridge University, 2003), 64. See also his *Spiritual Emotions*.
38. Fitterer, *Love and Objectivity*, 64.
39. Ibid., 80.
40. NE, I, 8 and III, 9.
41. NE, I, 9, 1099a12.
42. NE, III, 2, 1111a25–26, 1111b8–9; VI, 13, 1144b8.
43. NE, VII, 3, 1147b5.
44. NE, X, 4, 1174a1–2.
45. The ideas expressed in the preceding passage, though not Philippa Foot's, were sparked by a reading of her penetrating discussion of a famous passage of Kant's in her *Virtues and Vices* (Oxford: Blackwell, 1978), 1–18. We are happy to acknowledge here our general debt to Foot, a debt we share with almost all contemporary virtue ethicists.
46. Nussbaum, *Upheavals of Thought*, 52.
47. Hursthouse, *On Virtue Ethics*, 108, emphases in original.
48. See, for example, Aquinas, ST II-II, 25, 4.

49. Margaret A. Farley, "An Ethic for Same-Sex Relations," in *A Challenge to Love: Gay and Lesbian Catholics in the Church*, ed. Robert Nugent (New York: Crossroad, 1983), 100.

50. See Thomas Aquinas, ST I-II, 28, 1c.

51. ST II-II, 58, 1.

52. Margaret Farley, *Just Love: A Framework for Christian Sexual Ethics* (New York: Continuum, 2006).

53. For more detail on the question of self-love, see Stephen Pope, "Expressive Individualism and True Self-Love: A Thomistic Perspective," in *Journal of Religion* 71 (1991): 384–99; *The Evolution of Altruism and the Ordering of Love* (Washington, DC: Georgetown University, 1994); Edward Vacek, *Love, Human and Divine: The Heart of Christian Ethics* (Washington, DC: Georgetown University, 1994), 239–73.

54. Rosalind Hursthouse, "Virtue Ethics and the Emotions," in *Virtue Ethics*, 108, emphases in original.

55. See Herdt, *Putting on Virtue*, passim.

56. MacIntyre, *After Virtue*, 2.

57. Herdt, *Putting on Virtue*, 350.

58. Louis Janssens, "Artificial Insemination: Ethical Considerations," *Louvain Studies* 8 (1980): 4, emphasis added.

59. *Gaudium et spes*, n. 51, emphasis added.

60. John Mahoney, *The Making of Moral Theology: A Study of the Roman Catholic Tradition* (Oxford: Clarendon Press, 1984), 220.

61. See Daniel Statman, "Introduction to Virtue Ethics," in *Virtue Ethics*, 7; Michael Slote, "Virtue Ethics and Democratic Values," *Journal of Social Philosophy* 24 (1993): 15; Peter Van Inwagen, "Response to Slote," *Social Theory and Practice* 16 (1990): 392.

62. Paul Waddell, *Friendship and the Moral Life* (Notre Dame: University of Notre Dame, 1989), 136.

63. John McDowell, "Virtue and Reason," *Monist* 62 (1979): 331.

64. Thomas S. Kuhn, *The Structure of Scientific Revolutions* (Chicago: University of Chicago, 1996).

65. Stanley Hauerwas, *Character and the Christian Life: A Study in Theological Ethics* (San Antonio, TX: Trinity University, 1979), 18. For the turn to the subject in contemporary philosophy and theology, see Michael Himes, "The Human Person in Contemporary Theology: Human Nature to Authentic Subjectivity," in *Introduction to Christian Ethics: A Reader*, ed. Ronald Hamel and Michael Himes (New York: Paulist, 1989), 49–62; Bernard J. F. Lonergan, *A Second Collection* (Philadelphia: Westminster, 1974); *The Subject* (Milwaukee: Marquette University, 1968).

66. John Donne, "Devotions Upon Emergent Occasions," in *The Works of John Donne*, ed. Henry Alford (London: John Parker, 1839), III, 574–75.

67. Lawrence Kohlberg has schematically outlined the child's moral development in his two-volume work *Essays on Human Development* (San Francisco: Harper and Row, 1981 and 1984). Along with a host of contemporary ethicists, we judge Kohlberg's scheme to be too rigid and reductive. It does, however, illustrate the point we are making here. For critique of Kohlberg and other approaches to moral education, see Sharon Parks, *Big Questions, Worthy Dreams: Mentoring Young Adults in their Search for Meaning, Purpose, and Faith* (San Francisco: Jossey-Bass, 2000) and Owen Flanagan, *Varieties of Moral Personality: Ethics and Psychological Realism* (Cambridge, MA: Harvard University, 1991).

68. Michael Slote, "Agent-Based Virtue Ethics," in *Virtue Ethics*, ed. Roger Crisp and Michael Slote (Oxford: Oxford University, 1997), 241.

69. Jeffrey Stout, *Democracy and Tradition* (Princeton University, 2004), 29, emphasis in original.

70. Slote, "Agent-based Virtue Ethics," in *Virtue Ethics*, ed. Crisp and Slote, 243–44.

71. Lonergan, *Method*, 325.

72. Joseph Fuchs, *Moral Demands and Personal Obligations* (Washington, DC: Georgetown University, 1993), 36.

73. See Aquinas, *In Duo Praecepta Caritatis*, ed. Taurinem (1954), 245; John Paul II, *Veritatis splendor*, nn. 40, 42, 44; Martin Rhonheimer, *Ethics of Procreation and the Defense of Human Life*, ed. William F. Murphy, Jr. (Washington, DC: Catholic University, 2010), 3–7.

74. Lonergan, *Method*, xi.

75. Fuchs, *Moral Demands*, 39.

76. NE, I, 7, 1098a, 18–19.

77. Rainer Maria Rilke, "Let Everything Happen," *The Book of Hours: Love Poems to God*, www.inwardoutward.org/author/rainer-maria-rilke.

78. For modern treatments of Christian virtue ethics, see Gilbert Meilaender, *The Theory and Practice of Virtue* (Notre Dame: University of Notre Dame, 1984); Klaus Demmer, *Leben in Menschenhand* (Freiburg: Universitatsverlag, 1987); Joseph Fuchs, *Essere del Signore* (Rome: Gregorian University, 1981); *Personal Responsibility and Christian Morality* (Washington, DC: Georgetown University, 1983); Richard McCormick, *Notes on Moral Theology, 1981 through 1984* (Lanham, MD: University Press of America, 1984); Bruno Schüller, *Wholly Human* (Washington, DC: Georgetown University, 1985); Joseph J. Kotva, Jr., *The Christian Case for Virtue Ethics*; William C. Spohn, "Notes on Moral Theology: 1991. The Return of Virtue Ethics," *Theological Studies* 53, no. 1 (1992): 60–75; and *Go and Do Likewise: Jesus and Ethics* (New York: Continuum, 1999); James F. Keenan, "Proposing Cardinal Virtues"; Daniel J. Harrington and James F. Keenan, *Jesus and Virtue Ethics: Building Bridges between New Testament Studies and Moral Theology* (Lanham: Sheed and Ward, 2002); and *Paul and Virtue Ethics: Building Bridges between New Testament Studies and Moral Theology* (Lanham, MD: Rowman & Littlefield, 2010). Though not specifically about virtue ethics, H. Richard Niebuhr, *An Essay in Christian Moral Philosophy* (New York: Harper and Row, 1963) is well worth consulting.

79. See Norbert J. Rigali, "On Christian Ethics," *Chicago Studies* 10 (1971): 227–47.

80. Karl Rahner and Herbert Vorgrimler, *Concise Theological Dictionary* (London: Burns Oates, 1965), 161. See also Karl Rahner, "The Dignity and Freedom of Man," in *Theological Investigations*, vol. 2 (London: Darton, Longman, Todd, 1967), 239–40.

81. Bruce, J. Malina, *The New Testament World: Insights from Cultural Anthropology* (Louisville: Westminster/John Knox, 1993), 74.

82. ST I-II, 62, 4.

83. ST II-II, 23, 6.

84. ST I-II, 62, 1, emphasis added.

85. *Catechism of the Catholic Church* (New York: Paulist, 1994), n. 1822.

86. Ibid., n. 1814.

87. Denzinger-Schönmetzer, n. 1532.

88. *Catechism*, n. 1817.

89. ST III, 69, 4.

90. ST I-II, 49, 3.

91. Jean Porter, "The Subversion of Virtue: Acquired and Infused Virtues in the *Summa Theologiae*," *Annual of the Society of Christian Ethics* (1992): 30.

92. Ladislas Örsy, "Faith, Sacrament, Contract, and Christian Marriage: Disputed Questions," *Theological Studies* 43, no. 2 (1982): 383, n.7. See also Michael G. Lawler, "Faith, Contract, and Sacrament in Christian Marriage: A Theological Approach," *Theological Studies* 52, no. 4 (1991): 712–31.

93. ST I-II, 51, 3.

94. ST I-II, 61, 2 and 3.

95. NE, VI, 5, 1140b, 5, emphasis added.

96. ST II-II, 47, 5.

97. ST II-II, 47, 2.

98. ST II-II, 58, 1 and 11.

99. See Paul Ricoeur, "Love and Justice," in *Radical Pluralism and Truth: David Tracy and the Hermeneutics of Religion*, ed. Werner G. Jeanrond and Jennifer L. Rike (New York: Crossroad, 1991), 195. Ricoeur argues that from Aristotle to Rawls justice has always been about equality.

100. NE, V, 1, 1129b, 27.

101. ST II-II, 58, 12.

102. NE, II, 6, 1106a, 22–23.

103. ST II-II, 123, 1.

104. *Catechism*, n. 1808.

105. ST, II-II, 141, 7.

106. ST II-II, 141, 2.

107. ST II-II, 141, 4.

108. *Catechism*, n. 1809.

109. ST II-II, 141, 8.

110. Harrington and Keenan, *Jesus and Virtue Ethics*, 122.

111. Ibid., 123.

112. Augustine, *The City of God*, trans. Marcus Dods (New York: Modern Library, 1994), 693.

113. ST II-II, 26, 6, 7, and 8.

114. John Henry Newman, *Parochial and Plain Sermons* (San Francisco: Ignatius, 1987), Sermon 5, 258.

115. See Jack Dominian, "Sexuality and Personal Relationships," in *Embracing Sexuality: Authority and Experience in the Catholic Church*, ed. Joseph Selling (Burlington, VT: Ashgate, 2001), 13.

116. In his "Proposing Cardinal Virtues," Keenan eschews both self-love and self-esteem in favor of self-care (727). We have no problem with the notion of self-love as we have earlier explained it.

117. Lonergan, *Insight*, 344, emphasis added. For a fuller explanation of perspectivism, see Todd A. Salzman and Michael G. Lawler, *Sexual Ethics: A Theological Introduction* (Washington, DC: Georgetown University, 2012), xxi–xxiii.

118. See John T. Noonan, Jr., *A Church That Can and Cannot Change: The Development of Catholic Moral Teaching* (Notre Dame: University of Notre Dame, 2005); Michael G. Lawler, *What Is and What Ought to Be* (New York and London: Continuum, 2005), 127–29.

119. Alfred Schutz, *Collected Papers* (The Hague: Martinus Nijhoff, 1964–67) I, 230.

120. Alfred North Whitehead, *Symbolism: Its Meaning and Effect* (New York: Putnam's, 1959), 8.

121. MacIntyre, *Whose Justice?*, 98.

Chapter Eight

Sexual Anthropology and Virtue Ethics

With the contemporary resurgence of virtue ethics, ethicists have been focusing on its application to specific ethical issues, including sexual ethics.[1] James Keenan proposes a sexual virtue ethic that goes beyond the traditional virtue of chastity and includes justice, fidelity, self-care, and prudence, shaped by mercy. He concludes his essay by noting that "we need at least to elaborate on who we ought to become as a community of faith, and from there develop an anthropology for a sexual ethics."[2] There is a dialectical relationship between virtue ethics and sexual anthropology, but sexual anthropology precedes and specifies the meaning and nature of the virtues and the "particular practices attendant to the virtues" that should be cultivated and prescribed.[3] In this chapter, we argue that virtue ethics assumes a theological anthropology and that sexual orientation is an intrinsic dimension of sexual anthropology and, therefore, also of an adequate theological anthropology. We do so in three cumulative sections. First, we explore the relationship between sexual anthropology and virtue ethics. Second, we explore the scientific justification for, and theological integration of, sexual orientation as an intrinsic anthropological dimension. Third, we investigate the implications of this anthropology for the virtues ordering human sexuality.

SEXUAL ANTHROPOLOGY AND VIRTUE ETHICS

Throughout history, much has been written on theological anthropology and its implications for ethics in general and sexual ethics in particular. However, much of what has been written and passed on as "tradition" has been grounded in a distorted metaphysics that, in turn, was grounded in an incomplete theological anthropology. Though there has been a resurgence of virtue ethics in the theological tradition, the traditional sources for this resurgence,

such as Aristotle and Aquinas, based their virtue theories on incomplete and
even inaccurate metaphysical perspectives and theological anthropologies.
Josef Fuchs' judgment on the history of human sexuality throughout the
Christian tradition is incontrovertible: "one cannot take what Augustine [or
Aristotle] or the philosophers of the Middle Ages knew about sexuality as the
exclusive basis of a moral reflection."[4] Virtue ethics, which orders human
beings to human flourishing, must be grounded in a holistic theological
anthropology.[5]

According to Keenan, virtue ethics asks three questions: "Who are we?
Who ought we to become? How are we to get there?"[6] These three questions
cannot be answered until we first acknowledge and understand who we are as
sexual beings. For contemporary Catholic theologians sexual anthropology
in the Catholic tradition has shifted from a primarily biological, reproductive
anthropology to a personalist, relational anthropology, and an essential guide
to discourse about sexual virtue ethics is the definition of the nature of the
relational, sexual being. Theories of sexual virtue ethics differ depending on
the dimensions of the human person emphasized in a particular sexual
anthropology. Traditional Catholic sexual anthropology is grounded in
heterogenital and reproductive complementarity and insists that heterosexual
orientation is objectively ordered and homosexual orientation is objectively
disordered.[7] The Church's definition of chastity as the foundational virtue
guiding all human sexual activity to reach human flourishing reflects this
sexual anthropology.

The *Catechism of the Catholic Church* defines the virtue of chastity as
"the successful integration of sexuality within the person and thus the inner
unity of [the hu]man in his [and her] bodily and spiritual being. Sexuality, in
which [the hu]man's belonging to the bodily and biological world is expressed, becomes personal and truly human when it is integrated into the
relationship of one person to another *in the complete and lifelong mutual gift
of a man and a woman.*"[8] Chastity, then, is the authentic integration of a
person's sexuality into human relationship and the practical living out of that
relationship in fidelity and commitment to another person. The focus is on
integrating one's sexuality bodily and spiritually. The final clause of this
definition, which we have underscored, limits this integration to heterosexual
relationships, and reveals a tension between this limitation and insights on
homosexual orientation widely accepted in the scientific community and
stated in the *Catechism*[9] and other magisterial documents.[10] These sources
agree that homosexuals do not choose their sexual orientation, which is a
result of a combination of physiological (nature) and social (nurture) factors.
What, then, does it mean for a homosexual person to integrate his or her
sexuality? Does it require celibacy or is there the possibility of a virtuous
expression of sexual activity between two people of the same sex?

Like the Congregation for Catholic Education (CCE), we accept that a Christian anthropological perspective "must consider the totality of the person and insist therefore on the integration of the biological, psycho-affective, social and spiritual elements."[11] Unlike the CCE, however, we accept that this integration can take place for homosexuals and bisexuals, as well as for heterosexuals, in sexually intimate relationships and that the virtues guiding these relationships can facilitate and inform this integration. To justify this claim, we first explore the science behind sexual orientation and then propose a theological justification for its integration into sexual anthropology. Finally, we explain the virtues that are deduced from this reconstructed anthropology.

SCIENCE, THEOLOGY, AND SEXUAL ORIENTATION

Critical Realism: A Methodological Relationship between Science and Theology

Pope John Paul II proposed a "community of interchange" between theology and science to expand partial perspectives and to "form a new unified vision." He cautioned, however, that theology should not become science and science should not become theology in terms of method or content. "We are asked to become one. We are not asked to become each other." In the community of interchange, neither science nor theology should become less itself but more itself. "Science can purify religion [theology] from error and superstition; religion [theology] can purify science from idolatry and false absolutes."[12] While expanding their partial perspectives and learning from the other, both science and theology should retain their own autonomy.

The unity between theology and science that John Paul calls for reflects Ted Peters' hypothetical consonance model of this relationship. Peters posits that consonance "indicates that we are looking for those areas where there is a correspondence between what can be said scientifically about the natural world and what the theologian understands to be God's creation."[13] Consonance can be either strong or weak. Strong consonance, virtual accord between theology and science, Peters argues, can be misleading, since the insights of theology and science are often dissonant. Weak consonance, which names "common domains of question-asking," proposes hypotheses to answer these questions. For theologians, weak consonance invites a shift from the rigidity and absolute truth claims of theological assertions and calls for willingness to subject theological assertions to ongoing investigation that leads to either confirmation or disconfirmation.[14] The epistemological method for determining confirmation or disconfirmation affirmed by John Paul II, Peters, and many other theologians and scientists is critical realism.

Bernard Lonergan contrasts naïve and critical realism. Naïve realism assumes that knowing is just like sensing, seeing, hearing, touching, tasting, or smelling, thus confusing the world of sensation with the world of understanding. But knowing is not at all like looking; it is not just sensing what is out there. It begins with sensation, as does all knowing of external reality, but proceeds beyond sensation to understanding, judging, and deciding. This process is what Lonergan calls critical realism.[15] Critical realism builds a bridge between theology and science in the search for the true meaning of reality and its implications for human fulfillment. Critical realism "maintains that our understanding, both scientific and religious, may be oriented toward a real world, whether the universe or God, but that precisely because the universe and God are always too colossal for the human mind to encompass, our thoughts in both science and religion are also always open to correction."[16] Critical realism realizes that human understanding is always partial, evolving, and revisable; it is what Lonergan called historically conscious. According to this worldview, our knowledge of reality is dynamic, evolving, changing, and particular. The method utilized, anthropology constructed, and virtues formulated in this worldview are contingent, particular, and changeable, and are morally evaluated in terms of evolving human knowledge and understanding of human flourishing. The contingency of human knowledge and understanding recognized by critical realism and historical consciousness require what Lisa Fullam describes as "epistemological humility" in constructing a sexual anthropology.[17]

John Paul asserts that "while needing to make use of the behavioral and natural sciences," moral theology "does not rely on the results of formal empirical observation or phenomenological understanding *alone*.... It is the Gospel which reveals the full truth about man and his moral journey."[18] Moral theology most certainly does not rely on the observations of science *alone*, but neither does it rely on the observations of theology *alone*. True science and theology demand mutual complementation to discern the truths of natural law. This complementation is *partially* exemplified in the Church's discussion of sexual orientation.

Sexual Orientation and Anthropology

Christian theology is an incarnate or embodied theology. The embodied sexual person is a psycho-somatic unity, an intrinsic union of *soma* and *psyche*, body and spirit. The dualism between these two realities the Western Church learned from the Greek philosophers is false;[19] there is no dualism. There is distinction between body and spirit in the human being but there is no separation, and there is ongoing dialogue between body and spirit in the biological, physical, emotional, relational, affective, and spiritual realms. A holistic sexual anthropology must conceptualize the sexual person in the person's multiple dimensions and integrate those dimensions into a comprehensive and comprehensible anthropology. The interpretation and prioritization of these realities and the various dimensions within each reality define human flourishing and the virtues that facilitate its attainment. Sexual orientation is an essential, intrinsic, and foundational dimension of sexual anthropology.

The interrelationship between the somatic and psychic dimensions of the sexual person is manifested in *eros*, sexual attraction and desire, what Sebastian Moore describes as "love trying to happen,"[20] draws us towards another person, and sexual orientation specifies the sex of the person to whom we are drawn. An important psycho-social dimension of the human person, and therefore of the sexual human person, is the person's integrated relationship to self. To be fully human, persons must be integrated with the whole self, including the sexual self. The CCE asserts what is widely taken for granted today, namely, that sexuality "is a fundamental component of personality, one of its modes of being, of manifestation, of communicating with others, of feeling, of expressing and of living human love. Therefore it is an integral part of the development of the personality and of its educative process."[21] The United States Bishops concur. In and through sexuality, "we, as male or female, experience our relatedness to self, others, the world, and even God."[22]

The CCC goes on to cite the CDF's *Persona humana* and its teaching that it is "from sex that the human person receives the characteristics which, on the biological, psychological, and spiritual levels, make that person a man or a woman, and thereby *largely condition his or her progress towards maturity and insertion into society.*"[23] If it is true that a person's sexuality and sexual characteristics largely condition her and his insertion into society, and we agree that it is true, then the question naturally arises about the nature and meaning of sexual orientation, that dimension of human sexuality that directs a person's sexual desires and energies and draws him or her into deeper and more sexually intimate human relationships. To fully discern the anthropological dimensions of the sexual person we must first understand sexual orientation.

The meaning of the phrase "sexual orientation" is complex and not universally agreed upon, but the magisterium offers a description. It distinguishes between "a homosexual 'tendency,' which proves to be 'transitory,' and 'homosexuals who are definitively such because of some kind of innate instinct.'" It goes on to declare that "it seems appropriate to understand sexual orientation as a *deep-seated* dimension of one's personality and to recognize its *relative stability* in a person. A homosexual orientation produces a stronger emotional and sexual attraction toward individuals of the same sex, rather than toward those of the opposite sex."[24] We define sexual orientation, following Robert Nugent, as a "psychosexual attraction (erotic, emotional, and affective) toward particular individual *persons*"[25] of the opposite sex, the same sex, or both sexes, depending on whether the orientation is heterosexual, homosexual, or bisexual.

The bishops note what is agreed on in the scientific community, namely, that there is as yet no single isolated cause for the genesis of sexual orientation. The experts point to a variety of "loading factors,"[26] genetic, hormonal, psychological, and social from which the orientation may derive and develop. There is a growing agreement also in the scientific community that sexual orientation, heterosexual, homosexual, or bisexual, is a psychosexual attraction that the person does not choose and that she or he cannot change.[27] Since homosexual orientation is experienced as a given and not as something freely chosen, it is premoral and cannot be considered sinful, for morality and immorality presume the freedom to choose. This judgment is not to be understood as a claim that, according to the magisterium, a homosexual orientation is morally good or neutral, for elsewhere it teaches that "this inclination . . . is objectively disordered," and homosexual acts that are an expression of this orientation are intrinsically disordered.[28] These judgments on homosexual orientation and homosexual acts entail a prioritization of doing over being and assume that, by definition, homosexual acts frustrate human flourishing. They are based on a normative anthropology that claims that only reproductive sexual acts between married heterosexual couples can facilitate human fulfillment and realize chastity. All other sexual acts, including non-reproductive sexual acts between married heterosexual couples, it is claimed, frustrate human flourishing and violate chastity. Scientific studies do not support these judgments.

Regarding the judgment that homosexual orientation is "objectively disordered," credible science finds that homosexual orientation is very much a natural reality. Peer-reviewed scientific literature has documented same-sex sexuality in over 300 species of vertebrates as a natural component of the social system.[29] Based on such studies, James Allison challenges the claim that a homosexual orientation is objectively disordered. "There is no longer any reputable scientific evidence of any sort: psychological, biological, genetic, medical, neurological – to back up the claim."[30] In fact, there is substantial scientific evidence to the contrary. Homosexuals make up a small minority of the human population, some 3-5% across all cultures, and homosexual orientation is an intrinsic dimension of their sexual identity. Such evidence leads evolutionary biologist Joan Roughgarden to assert the following: "To the extent that information about nature can inform theological discourse on human and biological diversity, the message for full and proper inclusion of gay, lesbian, and transgender persons is clear and unequivocal."[31] This full inclusion includes recognizing that gay, lesbian, and bisexual sexual relationships can be fully and authentically human.

Regarding the judgment that homosexual acts, by definition, are intrinsically disordered and therefore violate chastity and frustrate human flourishing, credible scientific studies indicate that this is not the case. Lawrence Kurdek, who has carried out extensive research on gay and lesbian couples, notes the following characteristics of their relationships compared to heterosexual relationships. Gay and lesbian couples tend to have a more equitable distribution of household labor, demonstrate greater conflict resolution skills, have less support from family members but more support from friends, and most significantly experience similar levels of relationship satisfaction. [32] A growing body of social scientific data demonstrates that committed, stable, and justly loving gay and lesbian unions are as *personally* complementary and fulfilling as heterosexual ones. Gay and lesbian acts of making just love are as unitive as heterosexual acts of making just love.

We are aware of John Paul II's concern about the relationship between the sciences and theology that, while the behavioral sciences may "develop an empirical and statistical concept of 'normality'....the Gospel...reveals the full truth about man [sic] and his moral journey." [33] In light of this concern, we explore theological arguments that integrate scientific insights on homosexual orientation and its manifestation in desire into a holistic sexual anthropology. These arguments provide a theological justification to reconstruct the traditional, exclusively heterosexual anthropology to include heterosexual, homosexual, and bisexual orientations. Two theologians, David Matzko McCarthy and Rowan Williams, provide an adequate theological integration of science's insights on homosexual orientation and desire. We consider each in turn.

David Matzko McCarthy: Sexual Orientation and Nuptial Hermeneutics

McCarthy proposes "a nuptial hermeneutics of same-sex unions," which expands traditional heterosexual nuptial hermeneutics to include homosexual nuptial hermeneutics. He does this on the basis, at least in part, of acknowledging the givenness of homosexual orientation and reflecting theologically on the meaning and nature of that givenness in a human being created in the image and likeness of God. In so doing, he argues theologically, in four steps, for a nuptial metaphor of *both* homosexual *and* heterosexual unions grounded in the human body. First, the beginning of all theological reflection is "God's reconciliation with the world, which, in the gathering of the Church, constitutes a body." [34] Second, the Church or Body of Christ generates a relationship of bodies to create a network of consortium-communion or common life. Within this network there is a "desire of the body" to enter into permanent unions, "which is drawn to God's faithfulness and patterned in mimesis of God's enduring love." Third, this desire is "matched by a thoroughgoing hermeneutics of the body" whereby, "through marriage, the body is given an identity that does not merely bring its agency to fulfillment but also locates the communicative acts of the body at the axis of a community's whole life."[35]

Fourth, although the traditional hermeneutics of the body and the nuptial metaphor it justifies is limited to heterosexual marriage in the Catholic tradition, it can be extended to homosexual unions by integrating an adequate definition of sexual orientation into a theology of the body, thereby developing a "nuptial hermeneutics of same-sex unions."[36] The magisterium accepts and defines heterosexual orientation as normative, the "natural" explanation of the nuptial metaphor, and defines homosexual orientation as objectively disordered. Homosexual orientation is objectively disordered in the *desire* or *attraction* for a person of the same sex ("A homosexual orientation produces a stronger emotional and sexual attraction toward individuals of the same sex, rather than toward those of the opposite sex"[37]), and because it creates a "strong tendency" towards homosexual *acts* that are intrinsically evil.[38] This emphasis on attraction and act highlights an underlying disparity in magisterial teaching about heterosexual and homosexual orientation. When that teaching deals with heterosexual orientation, it focuses on the affective complementarity of two embodied persons, biologically, psycho-affectively, socially, and spiritually.[39] When it deals with homosexual orientation, it focuses on objectively disordered attraction and acts.

McCarthy, however, provides a definition of homosexual orientation which, aside from heterogenital complementarity, is consistent with the magisterium's understanding of heterosexual orientation. "Gay men and lesbians are persons who encounter the other (and thus discover themselves) in relation to persons of the same sex. This same-sex orientation is a given of their coming to be, that is, *the nuptial meaning of human life emerges* for a gay man in relation to other men and for a woman when face to face with other women."[40] In a steadfast and just interpersonal union, then, homosexual couples give their bodies to one another and are "theologically communicative," that is, they are witnesses to their own and also God's "constancy and steadfast fidelity."[41] In their witness, homosexual couples have "iconic significance" in their sexuality through embodied interpersonal union, just as heterosexual couples, both fertile and infertile, have "iconic significance" in their sexuality in their embodied interpersonal union. Heterogenital complementarity is not a determining factor. Rather, two embodied sexual persons, heterosexual, homosexual, or bisexual, in permanent interpersonal union, who reflect God's constant love and steadfast fidelity are the determining factor.[42] In the case of fertile heterosexual couples, embodied interpersonal union is at times *potentially* procreative; in the case of infertile heterosexual and homosexual couples, embodied interpersonal union is never potentially procreative. Embodiment and the nuptial metaphor, however, are essential to all three interpersonal unions.

For the homosexual person, steadfast love is manifested when the gay or lesbian person "comes out" and is authentically true to herself or himself, in particular and general sexual relationships. For McCarthy, "in its most significant occurrence, coming out is telling who we are to people who are a fundamental aspect of who we are and who we are becoming."[43] This ongoing self-knowledge, self-acceptance, and self-disclosure to another person are all expressions of Keenan's virtue of self-care.

Rowan Williams: Desire and "The Body's Grace"

In his introduction to William's essay, Eugene Rogers notes "sexuality, like grace, involves the transformation that comes from seeing oneself as desired by another."[44] *Eros* or desire is at the very root of Christian identity and, therefore, of theological anthropology. We desire to enter into the potentially most profound of human relationships as sexual, relational beings because God has implanted that desire within each one of us. Just as God first loved us so that we can love one another, God first desired us so that we can desire one another. This desire is a manifestation of grace that invites us to enter into relationship with God and others individually and communally. According to Williams, "grace...is a transformation that depends in large part on knowing yourself to be seen in a certain way: as significant, as wanted.... God desires us, *as if we were God*, as if we were that unconditional response to God's giving that God's self makes in the life of the Trinity." The life of the Christian community, he adds, has as its rationale "the task of teaching us to so order our relations that human beings may see themselves as desired, as the occasion of joy."[45] Embodied sexual desire is a matter of grace. It is in and through that grace that we, in response to God's will, take the risk to become vulnerable, loving, faithful, and committed in sexual relationships, just as the gospel Christ, in response to his Father's will, took the risk to be infinitely vulnerable, loving, faithful, and committed.

Williams notes that the Christian community has been reluctant to see sexual desire as a matter of grace. We add that it has been, following in the footsteps of Augustine, reluctant to see anything sexual as a matter of grace. As they were for Plato and Aristotle, so also for Augustine and Aquinas sexual activity and pleasure are "occupations with lower affairs which distract the soul and make it unworthy of being joined actually to God."[46] Augustine restricts moral sex to marriage and procreative intercourse: "Intercourse which is necessary for the purpose of generation is blameless, and only this kind belongs to marriage. But that which goes beyond this necessity follows not reason but lust [desire]."[47] Platonic Augustine, with his dualist hierarchy of body and soul, has no doubt what the problem with lust/desire is. "I feel that nothing more casts down the masculine mind from the heights than female allurements and that contact of bodies without which a wife cannot be had."[48] Note that it is the *masculine* mind that is cast down, loses control, and made irresponsible to the neglect of his duties; the *feminine* mind at the time simply did not count. Evil, however, "does not follow because marriages [and the sexual intercourse that characterizes them] are good, but because in the good things of marriage there is also a use that is evil. Sexual intercourse was not created because of the concupiscence of the flesh, but because of good. That good would have remained without that evil if no one had sinned."[49] Thomas Aquinas repudiated this Augustinian position that sexual pleasure was an evil thing, arguing that within marriage sexual intercourse is meritorious,[50] and to forego the pleasure and thwart the end would be sinful.[51] That said, however, he still held the Augustinian view that sex for the sole purpose of pleasure was sinful, and the later Catholic tradition followed him in this view. John Boswell documents the difficulty in the tradition, perhaps even the impossibility, of a heterosexual relationship based on mutual love because of the cultural, hierarchical value-differentiation between men and women.[52]

Williams speculates that the reason for this Christian reluctance is that the Christian tradition has failed to understand the nature of sexual desire as risk and to discern the full meaning of being the loving delight of God. Heterosexual marriage has been presented as the sole moral context of sexuality, desire, and sexual intercourse and, within marriage, desire has been presented primarily as instrumental to procreation. However, celibates, homosexual couples, and infertile married couples, all challenge us to ask questions of the meanings of sexuality, desire, and intercourse beyond their procreative instrumentality. All three can both create and enhance new and joyous life, not only the life of a new human being but also, and perhaps primarily, the communion-life of the partners together. An answer to the questions of meaning, Williams suggests, can be found in scripture and Trinitarian theology.

In scripture, we discover a more productive ground for reflecting on the transformative power of sexual desire as grace. Sexual metaphors for God's relationship with humanity are notably non-biological, emphasizing instead God's vulnerability to enter into a covenant with human beings. "When looking for a language that will be resourceful enough to speak of the complex and costly faithfulness between God and God's people, what several of the biblical writers turn to is sexuality understood very much in terms of the process of 'entering the body's grace.'"[53] The emphasis in these accounts is on gift, vulnerability, and fidelity, not on a natural, biological, normative order. The inequality of covenant language in scripture, God and humans are simply not equal, and its implications for desire are evident, but a Trinitarian metaphor can complement and correct these shortcomings.

Trinitarian theology helps us to formulate a language of grace which uses a language of creation and redemption. We discover this language if we are able to see ourselves as "the object of the causeless, loving delight of God, being the object of God's love for God through incorporation into the community of God's Spirit and the taking-on of the identity of God's child."[54] Sexuality, heterosexual, homosexual, and bisexual is a gift from the creator God to facilitate women's and men's task of becoming authentically human in and through interpersonal relationship with others. Humans seek both wholeness or human flourishing and holiness or closeness to God in their journey to becoming fully integrated, relational, just, and loving sexual persons. This requires them to embrace sexuality, to seek to define, develop, and perfect those dimensions that facilitate its authentic development, and to resist those that frustrate this development. In a world of original, personal, and social sin, this is not an easy project.

The world humans inhabit, however, is not only a world of sin, it is a world of grace abounding. It is a world into which the God of all has sent his Son to be incarnated, making it thereby essentially holy. It is a world into which the Son has sent the Spirit-Paraclete to lead it into all truth. It is a world in which that Spirit is abroad, freely giving gifts of all kinds to all men and women of good will.[55] It is a world in which the search for full humanity, and therefore also for God, is pursued sexually by heterosexuals, homosexuals, and bisexuals. Any formulation of virtues to order sexuality, therefore, must include all three groups.

From scriptural and Trinitarian perspectives, sexuality, understood as an embodied, graced desiring, can move us beyond a strictly heterogenital, reproductive anthropology to a more holistic, relational anthropology. This revised anthropology, grounded in theological meaning beyond the instrumentality of reproduction, recognizes the multiple incarnations of desiring the sexual other. The sciences indicate that a person's sexual orientation is not a choice and that homosexual couples have authentic, meaningful, committed, loving, sexual relationships in the same way that heterosexual couples have authentic, meaningful, committed, loving, sexual relationships. Theological reflection on sacrament, scripture, and Trinitarian theology yields a theological hermeneutical lens to integrate these scientific and experiential data. Sexual orientation directs our sexual desire towards another sexual being and invites a return desire from that other sexual being. We ask now what are the implications of this theological anthropology for a virtue sexual ethic?

ORIENTATION COMPLEMENTARITY AND SEXUAL VIRTUE ETHICS

If our scientific and theological accounts of sexual orientation and desire have any merit, then traditional Catholic, exclusively heterosexual anthropology must be revised. Concomitant to this revised anthropology, there must also be a revised understanding of the virtues to facilitate human flourishing. We propose a revised anthropology grounded on the principle of holistic complementarity, which includes orientation (heterosexual, homosexual, or bisexual), personal (affective, emotional, psychological, relational, spiritual), and biological (genital, hormonal, chromosomal) complementarities, and the integration and manifestation of all three in just, loving, committed sexual relationships that facilitate a person's ability to love God, neighbor, and self in a more profound and holy way.[56]

Holistic complementarity includes essentially the personal integration of the biological and personal dimensions of the sexual person. Virtuous sexual relationships, heterosexual, homosexual, or bisexual, require human genitals, whether fertile or infertile. In couples of heterosexual orientation, personal complementarity is embodied, manifested, nurtured, and enhanced through the use of their genitals in stable, just, and loving relationships; in couples of homosexual and bisexual orientations, it is equally embodied, manifested, nurtured, and enhanced through the use of their genitals in stable, just, and loving relationships. Orientation complementarity suggests genital complementarity as an instrument primarily of personal complementarity, not necessarily of reproductive complementarity and procreation.

Orientation complementarity revises the magisterium's definitions of affective complementarity and heterogenital complementarity and cannot espouse the magisterium's heterogenital point of departure for affective complementarity. For the magisterium, the point of departure for affective complementarity is an ontological unity between the biological (heterogenital) and the personal that can find completion only in heterosexual marriage and reproductive conjugal acts. In our anthropology, the point of departure for affective complementarity is not the *genital* but the *sexual* person of a homosexual, bisexual, or heterosexual orientation. The definition of affective complementarity in virtuous sexual relationships is the "unity of the two" where the affective dimensions (psycho-affective, social, and spiritual) complement one another.[57] In the case of persons with a homosexual orientation, sexual acts will be genitally male-male or female-female; in the case of persons with a heterosexual orientation, they will be genitally male-female; in the case of persons with a bisexual orientation, they may be genitally male-male, female-female, or male-female.[58]

Holistic complementarity, which prioritizes orientation complementarity, redefines chastity and specifies the virtues to guide sexual persons in particular and general relationships. First, chastity that orders sexual relationships can no longer be defined exclusively heterogenitally as it is in the *Catechism* and throughout Christian tradition. We offer the *Catechism's* definition of chastity, minus the final clause that limits it to heterosexual relationships, as our definition of chastity in light of holistic and sexual orientation complementarity. Chastity is "the successful integration of sexuality within the person and thus the inner unity of [the hu]man in his [and her] bodily and spiritual being. Sexuality, in which [the hu]man's belonging to the bodily and biological world is expressed, becomes personal and truly human when it is integrated into the relationship of one person to another."[59]

Second, following James Keenan, our renewed sexual anthropology complements chastity with supplemental virtues to guide self-ish, particular, and general relationships.[60] By self-ish relationship we intend relationship with self and it requires what Keenan refers to as the virtue of self-care. Self-care includes, but is not limited to, self-knowledge, self-acceptance, self-respect, self-esteem, and self-disclosure. Psychological studies repeatedly indicate that one of the greatest threats to healthy human development and flourishing, including sexual development and flourishing, is poor self-esteem.[61] Despite the injunction in Leviticus and Mark to "love your *neighbor as yourself*" (Lev 19:18; Mark 12:31), with its double commandment to love self and neighbor, the Christian tradition has not done an adequate job of empowering healthy self-love, especially in the area of sexuality. Self-care is the virtue that invites reflection on human sexuality as a unique gift to each individual and that summons every woman and man to recognize, accept, appreciate, and integrate the gift in the Christian task of drawing closer to God in Christ and neighbor.

History demonstrates beyond doubt that, with the exception of an intellectual and abstract acknowledgment that sexuality and sex are good because they are created by a good God, much of the Christian tradition has not appreciated the goodness of this gift practically and concretely. We have already illustrated this historical fact in Augustine who has been a huge influence on the later Christian traditions. This lack of appreciation for the gift of sexuality has created a great deal of guilt and self-loathing with the unfortunate consequence that heterosexuals, homosexuals, bisexuals, and celibates sometimes live out their sexuality in unhealthy ways. The sexual abuse of women by men, of children by pedophiles, and less commonly of men by dominatrix women, is a most common and obvious example of widespread unhealthy sexuality. This may be truer for men and women with a homosexual or bisexual orientation who feel personally rejected by the Church in what Mark Jordan refers to as the "rhetoric of moral management."[62] This rhetoric is grounded in exclusion and is exemplarily manifested in the magisterium's designation of homosexual inclination as "objectively disordered,"[63] a designation which inhibits many gay, lesbian, and bisexual Catholics from revealing their sexual orientation.[64] Negatively labeling them as "objectively disordered" does not facilitate homosexuals' integration of their sexuality. Sexuality and desire are most intimately related to our attraction to other persons, to love, and to committed relationships but, for this natural attraction to be nurtured and manifested in responsible relationships, it must be acknowledged, accepted, and integrated in a healthy manner. It may be true that no human person has ever *fully* integrated his or her sexuality, but Christians still need to be conscious of and critically reflect upon perspectives that, consciously or unconsciously, frustrate the personal acceptance and integration of sexuality.

Self-care first affirms self as a created self-in-God, good, valuable, and lovable, and then, informed by neighbor-love, turns towards and gives this good, valuable, and lovable self-in-God unconditionally to an other in particular and to others in general. Aquinas argued that *nemo dat quod non habet*; no one gives what he does not have. If a man or a woman does not truly and fully accept himself or herself, in both wholeness and brokenness, neither can they give themselves fully to another person nor fully accept the other person. This is a concrete example of Jesus great commandment to love, first, oneself and, then, the neighbor (Mark 12:31). As he adds, "there is no other commandment greater than these." The virtue of self-care, rooted in properly ordered self-love, calls for the emotional, psychological, biological, and spiritual integration of one's sexuality, especially of one's sexual orientation, to foster self-knowledge and relationship to others as sexual beings.

Given their spatial and temporal finitude, men and women must prioritize their relationships and respond to them in a manner appropriate to the nature of the relationship. Fidelity and justice, informed by mercy, call us to faithful and mutually just sexual expression in particular sexual relationships. Fidelity or faithfulness (from the Latin *fides*/faith) has its Christian roots in God's fidelity to, his *hesed* or faithful love of, Israel. God and Israel entered into a covenant to which Israel was not overly faithful. God, however, in spite of Israel's every provocation, remains faithful to God's covenant promise, for God "is a God merciful and gracious, slow to anger, and abounding in steadfast love *(hesed)* and faithfulness" (Ex 34:6; see also Deut 7:9). These words are a perfect program for humans, both in their relationship with God and their relationships with one another. God's promise of faithfulness and his faithfulness to the covenant stands as the assurance that reconciliation and redemption are possible, not only in relationship with God but also in relationships in general between women and men and in the particular relationship between sexual partners. Fidelity requires both responsible and appropriate sexual expression in those relationships and also requires abstinence from sexual expression in other relationships where it is inappropriate. The primary, but by no means exclusive, Christian context for sexual expression is within marriage, a committed, loving, faithful, mutually just, and for Catholics sacramental, relationship. Within fruitful marriages, ongoing fidelity assures the future of the relationship, strengthens the bond of intimacy between the spouses, and extends that bond to any children born of the relationship.

Fidelity in and to a particular sexual relationship permits partiality to the sexual other in that relationship. Justice, on the other hand, demands appreciating all people and their equal and inalienable dignity as creatures created in the image and likeness of the Creator-God. Realizing another's human dignity always entails treating the other as subject, never as object, and rendering to them, as Aquinas argued, their "due rights."[65] Justice applies to all of our relationships, but it applies particularly to our relationship with the common good. Social justice, informed and prompted by mercy, invites us to seek out those who are most marginalized, to work towards a more just society, and to confront structures of oppression, including the sexual oppressions ingrained in homophobia, the commercialization and commodification of human sexuality in prostitution and pornography, sexism, and gender and orientation discrimination. It goes without saying that social justice is an essential virtue in the sexual relationships between women and men, between women and women, and between men and men. "Every sign of unjust discrimination" toward gay men and lesbian women, the *Catechism* teaches,[66] is to be avoided. Working towards justice for all men and women in the general realm of human sexuality will enable us to recognize and realize mutual justice in unique particular sexual relationships as well.

Three virtues, then, self-care, fidelity, and justice inform relationships to oneself, to the particular other, and to the general others respectively. A fourth virtue, love, defined by Aquinas as *velle bonum*, to will the good of another,[67] is a decision to will the good of another human being. It informs all the other virtues and facilitates their integration in human relationships. For Christians, two things are critical about love. First, as John says, "God is love (*agape*)" (1 John 4:8). Second, as he goes on to say, "In this is love, not that we loved God but that he first loved us and sent his Son to be the expiation of our sins" (4:10). God first loved women and men by willing for them creation, providence, and redemption. There is no good for God, who needs nothing, in these loving actions; the good is entirely for God's creatures. Hence the word chosen for God's love is *agape*, the love of another for the other's sake. That Greek word became the Latin word *caritas* which then became the English word *charity. Agape/caritas/charity* are central in the teachings of the Fathers of the Church and in the traditions that followed them, but the Second Vatican Council brought to the fore a dimension of love that was not always in the forefront of the tradition, namely, the social dimension. Charity is to be practiced not only in the individual, one-to-one relationships but also for the common, social good.[68] That enlargement of the function of charity applies in all human relationships, first of all in the one-to-one loving relationships which are expressed and enhanced in appropriate sexual relationships, and then in the extension of that love to the world and culture in which the partners love. No individual and no couple can respond to all the needs of the world, but they can and must, where they live, feed the

hungry, shelter the homeless, clothe the naked, visit the sick, visit the imprisoned, bury the dead, give alms to the poor, the so-called corporal works of
mercy. Jesus' great commandment to love our neighbor as ourself begins
with the partner in an intimate relationship and diffuses out into the world in
which the partners live.

There is a fifth, overarching virtue, prudence, which both Aristotle and
Aquinas agree is required for the exercise of all the other virtues.[69] Prudence
"is the virtue that disposes practical reason to discern our true good in every
circumstance and to choose the right means of achieving it."[70] It is "right
reason in action," judges Aquinas following Aristotle.[71] Prudence is sometimes called *auriga virtutum*, the charioteer of the virtues, for it guides all the
other virtues by determining how they are to be exercised in every particular
circumstance. In keeping with the virtue axiom, *in medio stat virtus*, virtue
stands in the middle, it is not be understood, as it is sometimes understood in
Western culture, with timidity or fear on the one hand or with hasty, uncon-
sidered, and careless action.[72] It provides the control over a person's actions
that is required for all other virtuous activity and enables women and men to
attain human flourishing and to take their proper place in the world, thereby
humanizing themselves, their relationships, and the world in which they live.
It goes without saying that prudence is essential in a relationship to love or
will the good of and to avoid hurting the other. This integrated vision of the
virtues recognizes the inevitable tension in morality between the universal
and particular, impartiality and partiality, other and self. These virtues are
universal in that all people share in the relationships that call them forth.
They are particular in that they are defined and realized in a particular,
historical, cultural, relational context. They are uniquely Catholic when they
realize that they are gifts of God which, as Jean Porter correctly notes, "must
blossom out in a personal act."[73] The Catholic tradition is longstandingly
firm: every good is from God, given not as a reward but as pure gift with
which women and men must cooperate and which they must personally
activate in their lives.[74]

The virtues are Catholic also when their particularity is informed by a
sixth virtue, mercy, "the willingness to enter into the chaos of another so as
to respond to their need,"[75] especially of the other who has no obvious claim
to kindness. In the Hebrew Bible, mercy is a designation for God who is
"merciful and gracious" (Exod 34:6). In the New Testament, God is "the
Father of mercies and the God of all comfort" (2 Cor 1:3). Jesus explains to
the Pharisees that "I desire mercy and not sacrifice (see Hosea 6:6). For I
came not to call the righteous but sinners" (Matt 9:13), and declares blessed
those who are merciful (Matt 5:7). He offers the parable of the Good Samaritan as exemplar of the virtue of mercy, and makes the ultimate point of the
parable perfectly clear: "Go and do likewise" (Luke 10:37). The followers of
Jesus are called to be merciful like the good Samaritan, ultimately because

they recognize that they themselves need the mercy of God for their frequent violations of the covenant. Mercy empowers them to seek the common good, especially for those who are most needy in society, like the injured man on the road from Jerusalem to Jericho. It guides them also in their particular relationships where forgiveness and reconciliation are the cornerstones of relationship for the whole of life. Mercy heals them and, informed by prudence, guides them in caring for themselves, so that they can give themselves to, care for, and nurture particular loving relationships and thereby also nurture the common good.

CONCLUSION

A Christian sexual virtue ethic must be in ongoing dialogue with an evolving understanding and definition of sexual anthropology that is credible not only theologically but also scientifically. This dialogue recognizes that the nature and meaning of the virtues will evolve as a sexual anthropology evolves. In this essay we have attempted a partial anthropological reconstruction, emphasizing the centrality of sexual orientation, its expression in desire, and its implications for the virtues of chastity, self-care, fidelity, and justice, informed by love, guided by prudence, and tempered by mercy unto human fulfillment in self-ish, particular, and general relationships. We admit that it is as yet an incomplete anthropology, but we insist that critical realism demands the ongoing attention, understanding, judgment and decision of the communion church about what it means, in the present age, to be a virtuous sexual person. In the final two essays, we consider the virtuous Catholic in the contexts of civil divorce and remarriage without an annulment and artificial reproductive technologies.

QUESTIONS FOR REFLECTION

1. What is the relationship between a sexual anthropology and a sexual virtue ethic? What is the root of Fuchs' claim that "one cannot take what Augustine or the philosophers of the Middle Ages knew about sexuality as the exclusive basis for a moral reflection?" How is the sexual ethics of Augustine or Thomas Aquinas to be corrected today?
2. The *Catechism of the Catholic Church* defines the virtue of chastity as "the successful integration of sexuality within the person and thus the inner unity of [the hu]man in his [and her] bodily and spiritual being." How do you understand this definition? What do you think of the *Catechism's* restriction of chastity to the relationship between a man and a woman with the implication that chastity for gays and lesbians is a life of sexual abstinence?

3. What do you understand by the term *sexual orientation*? What does science teach about its origin? What does it have to do with sexual anthropology and virtue ethics? Is it true, do you think, given the scientific evidence, that a homosexual orientation is, as the Catholic Church teaches, "objectively disordered?"

4. What do you think of David Matzko McCarthy's treatment of sexual orientation and his demonstration that "the nuptial meaning of human life emerges for a gay man in relation to other men and for a woman when face to face with other women?" And what about Archbishop Rowan Williams' account?

5. The claim is made that, given scientific discoveries about sexual orientation, the Catholic Church's traditionally exclusive heterosexual anthropology must be revised and, if that anthropology is revised, there must also be a revision of the virtues and norms that facilitate human flourishing. How do you react to this claim? Why do you react in this way?

6. What do you think of our proposal of a sexual anthropology grounded in *holistic complementarity*? If such a proposal were to be accepted, what would be the result for a sexual virtue ethic, including the virtue of chastity?

NOTES

An earlier version of this essay appeared in *INTAMS Review* 17, no. 2 (2011): 174–86. It is reprinted here with permission.

1. See James F. Keenan, "Virtue Ethics and Sexual Ethics," *Louvain Studies* 30, no. 3 (2005): 180–97; "Notes on Moral Theology: Contemporary Contributions to Sexual Ethics," *Theological Studies* 71, no. 1 (2010): 148–67; Lisa Fullam, "Sex in 3-D: A *Telos* for a Virtue Ethics of Sexuality," *Journal of the Society of Christian Ethics* 27, no. 2 (2007): 151–70; Margaret A. Farley, *Just Love: A Framework for Christian Sexual Ethics* (New York: Continuum, 2006); John Grabowski, *Sex and Virtue: An Introduction to Sexual Ethics* (Washington, DC: Catholic University of America Press, 2003); Martin Rhonheimer, *Natural Law and Practical Reason: A Thomist View of Moral Autonomy*, trans. G. Malsbary (New York: Fordham University Press, 2000); "The Cognitive Structure of the Natural Law and the Truth of Subjectivity," *Thomist* 67 (2003): 1–44.

2. Keenan, "Virtue Ethics," 197.

3. Ibid. The *Catechism of the Catholic Church's* (CCC) teaching on the virtue of chastity (n. 2337) well illustrates this prioritization.

4. Joseph Fuchs, *Moral Demands and Personal Obligations* (Washington: Georgetown University Press, 1993), 36.

5. Keenan, "Virtue Ethics," 187.

6. Ibid., 182–83.

7. Congregation for the Doctrine of the Faith (CDF), *Persona humana*, n. 8; *CCC*, n. 2357.

8. *CCC*, n. 2337, emphasis added.

9. *CCC*, n. 2358.

10. United States Catholic Conference of Bishops (USCCB), *Always Our Children* (Washington, DC: USCCB, 1997), n. 5.

11. Congregation for Catholic Education (CCE), *Educational Guidance in Human Love: Outlines for Sex Education (EGHL)* (Roma: Typis Polyglottis Vaticanis, 1983), n. 35.

12. John Paul II, "Our Knowledge of God and Nature: Physics, Philosophy and Theology," *Journal of Interdisciplinary Studies*, XVII (2005): 163–72; see Michael J. Buckley, "Religion and Science: Paul Davies and John Paul II," *Theological Studies*, 51, no. 2 (1990): 310–24.

13. Ted Peters, *Science, Theology, and Ethics* (Burlington, VT: Ashgate, 2003), 19.

14. Ibid., 18.

15. See Bernard J. F. Lonergan, *Method in Theology* (New York: Herder and Herder, 1972) and *Doctrinal Pluralism* (Milwaukee: Marquette University Press, 1971).

16. John F. Haught, *Science and Religion: From Conflict to Conversation* (Mahwah, NJ: Paulist Press, 1995), 20.

17. Lisa Fullam, "Sex in 3-D: A Telos for a Virtue Ethics of Sexuality," 160.

18. John Paul II, *Veritatis splendor,* nn. 111–12, emphasis added.

19. See Michael G. Lawler, *Marriage and Sacrament: A Theology of Christian Marriage* (Collegeville: Liturgical Press, 1993), 52–56.

20. Sebastian Moore, *The Contagion of Jesus: Doing Theology as if it Mattered*, ed. Stephen McCarthy (Maryknoll, NY: Orbis, 2007), 143.

21. CCE, *EGHL*, n. 4.

22. USCCB, *Human Sexuality: A Catholic Perspective for Education and Lifelong Learning* (Washington: USCCB, 1991), 9.

23. CDF, *Persona humana*, n. 1, emphasis added.

24. USCCB, *Always Our Children*, nn. 4–5; CDF, *Persona humana*, n. 8.

25. Robert Nugent, "Sexual Orientation in Vatican Thinking," in *The Vatican and Homosexuality: Reactions to the 'Letter to the Bishops of the Catholic Church on the Pastoral Care of Homosexual Persons,'*" ed. Jeannine Gramick and Pat Furey (New York: Crossroad, 1988), 55.

26. This terminology has been borrowed from John E. Perito, *Contemporary Catholic Sexuality: What is Taught and What is Practiced* (New York: Crossroad, 2003).

27. See William Paul, *et al.*, ed., *Homosexuality: Social, Psychological, and Biological Issues* (Beverly Hills: Sage, 1982); Pim Pronk, *Against Nature? Types of Moral Argumentation Regarding Homosexuality* (Grand Rapids, Mich.: Eerdmans, 1993); Richard C. Pillard and J. Michael Bailey, "A Biological Perspective on Sexual Orientation," *Clinical Sexuality* 18 (1995): 1–14; Lee Ellis and Linda Ebertz, *Sexual Orientation: Toward Biological Understanding* (Westport, CN: Praeger, 1997); Richard C. Friedman and Jennifer I. Downey, *Sexual Orientation and Psychoanalysis: Sexual Science and Clinical Practice* (New York: Columbia, 2002). For a contrary perspective see Robert L. Spitzer, "Can Some Gay Men and Lesbians Change Their Sexual Orientation? 200 Participants Reporting a Change from Homosexual to Heterosexual Orientation," *Archives of Sexual Behavior* 32 (2003): 403–17.

28. CDF, "Vatican List of Catechism Changes," *Origins* 27, no. 15 (September 25, 1997): 257.

29. See B. Bagemihl, *Biological Exuberance: Animal Homosexuality and Natural Diversity* (New York: St. Martin's Press, 1999).

30. James Allison, "The Fulcrum of Discovery Or How the 'Gay Thing' is Good News for the Catholic Church," unpublished essay, 8.

31. Joan Roughgarden, "Evolutionary Biology and Sexual Diversity," in *God, Science, Sex, and Gender: An Interdisciplinary Approach to Christian Ethics*, ed. Patricia Beattie Jung and Aana Vigen, with John Anderson (Chicago: University of Illinois Press, 2010), 153.

32. Lawrence A. Kurdek, "What Do We Know about Gay and Lesbian Couples?" *Current Directions in Psychological Science* 14 (2005): 251; "Differences between Partners from Heterosexual, Gay, and Lesbian Cohabiting Couples," *Journal of Marriage and Family* 68 (May 2006): 509–28; "Lesbian and Gay Couples," in *Lesbian, Gay and Bisexual Identities over the Lifespan*, ed. Anthony R. D'Augelli and Charlotte J. Patterson (New York: Oxford University, 1995), 243–61; "Are Gay and Lesbian Cohabiting Couples *Really* Different From Heterosexual Married Couples?" *Journal of Marriage and Family* 66 (2004): 880–900. See also, Ritch C. Savin-Williams and Kristin G. Esterberg, "Lesbian, Gay, and Bisexual Families," in *Handbook of Family Diversity*, ed. David H. Demo, Katherine R. Allen, and Mark A. Fine (New York: Oxford University, 2000), 207–12; and Philip Blumstein and Pepper Schwartz, *American Couples: Money, Work, Sex* (New York: Morrow, 1983).

33. John Paul II, *Veritatis splendor*, n. 112.

34. David M. McCarthy, "Relationship of Bodies," in *Theology and Sexuality: Classic and Contemporary Readings*, ed. Eugene F. Rogers, Jr. (Oxford: Blackwell, 2002), 201.

35. Ibid., 210.

36. Ibid., 212.

37. USCCB, *Always Our Children*, nn. 4–5; CDF, *Persona humana*, n. 8, http://www.vatican.va/roman_curia/congregations/cfaith/documents/rc_con_cfaith_doc_975129_persona-humana_en.html.

38. CDF, *Letter to the Bishops of the Catholic Church on the Pastoral Care of Homosexual Persons*, Origins 16, no. 22 (November 13, 1986): 379, emphasis added; CDF, "Vatican List of Catechism Changes," 257.

39. CCE, *EGHL*, n. 35.

40. McCarthy, "Relationship of Bodies," 212–13, emphasis added.

41. Ibid., 213.

42. We will address "orientation complementarity" in more detail below.

43. McCarthy, "Relationship of Bodies," 205.

44. Rogers, *Theology and Sexuality*, 309.

45. Rowan D. Williams, "The Body's Grace," in *Theology and Sexuality: Classic and Contemporary Readings*, ed. Eugene F. Rogers, Jr. (Oxford: Blackwell, 2002), 311–12.

46. Aquinas, *Summa Theologiae (ST)*, III (Suppl.), 41, 3.

47. Cited from Gareth Moore, *The Body in Context: Sex and Catholicism*, Contemporary Christian Insights (New York: Continuum, 2001), 43.

48. Cited from ibid., 47.

49. Augustine, *Contra Julianum Pelag.*, 3, 23, 53, *PL* 44, 729–30.

50. Aquinas, *ST*, III (Suppl.), 41, 4; 49, 5.

51. Ibid., II-II, 142, 1.

52. John Boswell, *Christianity, Social Tolerance, and Homosexuality* (Chicago: University of Chicago Press, 1980), chapter 5.

53. Ibid., 319.

54. Ibid., 317. For a more recent development of Trinitarian theology providing a hermeneutic for creation grounded in love and gift rather than nature, see John McCarthy, "Interpreting the Theology of Creation: Binary Gender in Catholic Thought," in *God, Science, Sex, and Gender*, 184–209.

55. See *Lumen gentium*, nn. 12, 34. See also Leo J. O'Donovan, *A World of Grace: An Introduction to the Themes and Foundations of Karl Rahner's Theology* (New York: Seabury, 1980), and Thomas F. O'Meara, *Loose in the World* (New York: Paulist, 1974).

56. For a detailed explanation of holistic complementarity, see Todd A. Salzman and Michael G. Lawler, *The Sexual Person: Toward a Renewed Catholic Anthropology* (Washington, DC: Georgetown University Press, 2008), chapter 4.

57. Though it is beyond the scope of this chapter, as in the magisterium's model, *how* these elements complement one another in a "truly human sexual act," heterosexual or homosexual, needs to be more fully developed.

58. While we recognize the reality of bisexual persons, for the sake of, first, unconfused focus and, then, allotted space, we do not address this orientation here.

59. *CCC*, n. 2337.

60. Keenan, "Virtue Ethics."

61. Jack Dominian, "Sexuality and Interpersonal Relationships," in *Embracing Sexuality: Authority and Experience in the Catholic Church*, ed. Joseph A. Selling (Burlington, VT: Ashgate, 2001), 13.

62. Mark D. Jordan, *The Silence of Sodom: Homosexuality in Modern Catholicism* (Chicago: University of Chicago Press, 2000), 74.

63. *CCC*, n. 2357.

64. James F. Keenan, "The Open Debate: Moral Theology and the Lives of Gay and Lesbian Persons," *Theological Studies* 64, no. 1 (2003): 146.

65. Thomas Aquinas, *ST*, II-II, 58, 1.

66. *Catechism*, n. 2358.

67. Aquinas, *ST*, I-II, 28, 1c.

68. *Gaudium et spes*, chapter 2.

69. Aquinas, *ST*, I-II, 57, 5; *Quaestiones Disputatae de Caritate*, 3.

70. *Catechism*, n. 1806.

71. Aquinas, *ST*, II-II, 47, 2.

72. Ibid., 53–55.

73. Jean Porter, "The Subversion of Virtue: Acquired and Infused Virtue in the *Summa Theologiae*," *Annual of the Society of Christian Ethics* (1992), 30.

74. A Catholic tradition, established in the controversy between Augustine and Pelagius and verified with constancy ever since, is that women and men are free persons and are graced, not against their will but only with their free cooperation. See H. Denzinger and A. Schönmetzer, *Enchiridion Symbolorum* (New York: Herder, 1964), nn. 373–97.

75. Keenan, "Virtue Ethics," 192.

Chapter Nine

Divorce and Remarriage
in the Catholic Church

In the previous two chapters, we discussed virtue ethics and its relationship to virtuous being and action. In this chapter, we discuss the virtuous Catholic in the context of civil divorce and remarriage without annulment. The Western world is now a culture in which divorce flourishes. Not only do some 40% of all marriages end in divorce (which means that some 60% achieve stability) but also divorce has become culturally acceptable. The earlier social stigma attached to it has been greatly reduced if it has not entirely disappeared. Catholics are as enculturated as any other Westerners, and there is no evidence to suggest that their rate of divorce is greatly different from the general population. Many civilly divorced[1] Catholics enter into second marriages while their first spouses are still alive, which makes their second marriage invalid in the eyes of their Church. These remarried Catholics are banned from full participation in the sacramental life of their Church, specifically they are banned from sharing in holy communion. Many are greatly pained by this ban and many Catholic theologians, canon lawyers, clerics, and lay people are asking what, if anything, can be done for them. In May, 1977, the United States Conference of Catholic Bishops (USCCB), the same body who imposed the penalty in the first place, dropped the automatic excommunication of Catholics who remarried while their first spouse was still alive. That removed one strand of pain for many divorced and remarried Catholics. We ask in this essay what more can be done.

Our response to that question is developed in ten cumulative theses of varying length. Since the argument is consciously intended to be cumulative, no one thesis by itself can resolve the disputes but, when taken together, they make a contribution for the communion-Church to consider.

211

THESIS 1: THE MARRIAGE BETWEEN BAPTIZED BELIEVERS IS A SACRAMENT, THAT IS, A PROPHETIC SYMBOL OF THE UNION BETWEEN THOSE BELIEVERS AND THE CHRIST.

Prophets were fond of symbolic actions. Jeremiah bought an earthen pot, dashed it to the ground, and proclaimed "Thus says the Lord of Hosts: so will I break this people and this city as one breaks a potter's vessel" (Jer 19:11). Ezekiel took a brick, drew a city on the brick, laid siege to the city, and proclaimed the city "even Jerusalem" and his action "a sign for the house of Israel" (Ezek 4:1–3; see also 5:5). Prophetic action-symbols reveal in representation the presence and action of God. Jeremiah's shattering of his pot is God's shattering of Jerusalem. The prophet Hosea cast marriage, the union of a man and a woman, as a prophetic symbol of the union between God and God's people. Marriage, he preached, is a reality not only of law but also of grace. On the one hand, it bespeaks the covenanted love of a man and a woman, of Hosea and his wife Gomer for instance; on the other hand, it also bespeaks the covenanted love of God and God's people. This Jewish view of marriage became the Christian view. The Letter to the Ephesians taught that marriage is a prophetic symbol of the new covenant between Christ and Christ's Church; later Christian history taught that it was sacrament.[2]

A sacrament, in the classical Roman Catholic definition, is "an outward sign of inward grace instituted by Christ," a prophetic symbol in which the Church reveals in representation the grace of God. To say that marriage is a sacrament is to say that it reveals, in outward reality, the intimate union of a man and a woman and, in inward reality, the intimate union of Christ and Christ's Church. A couple entering into any marriage say to one another "I love you and I give myself to and for you." A couple entering into a specifically sacramental marriage say that too, of course, but also more. They say "I love you as Christ loves his Church, steadfastly and faithfully." From its beginning, therefore, a sacramental marriage is intentionally more than only human covenant; it is also religious covenant. It is more than law; it is also grace. From its beginning, God and Christ are present in it, gracing it, modeling it, challenging it to become steadfast. This presence of the gracious God, grace in its most ancient Christian meaning, is not something extrinsic to Christian marriage but something intrinsic to it, something without which it would not be *Christian* marriage at all.

We note here, and will develop below in Thesis 6, an important sacramental fact. A truly *Christian* marriage is not simply a marriage between two people who *say* they are Christians.[3] It is a marriage between two Christian *believers*, for whom the steadfast love of God and of God's Christ is consciously present as model for their mutual love. The love of faith-filled spouses is, indeed, the very matrix of the sacrament of marriage, for it is in and through the spouses' love that God and Christ are prophetically represented as present. It is a matter for empirical verification, however, that not all Christian marriages become permanent. Some die, and when they die it makes no sense to claim they are still binding ontologically, for the death of a marriage is as definitive as the death of a spouse. When a marriage dies, the Church traditionally deals with it in one of its many canonical processes. Today it is challenged to nuance its response in the direction of gospel compassion and mercy as much as in the direction of canonical procedure. Its standard claim that it is precluded from doing so by "fidelity to the words of Jesus," as we shall show in the next Thesis, is not convincing under the honest light of its own ancient tradition. While holding fast to its belief that the gospel presents a demand for indissoluble marriage, the Catholic Church is invited also to acknowledge that marriages sometimes die and to deal with the former spouses from those marriages not only through canonical process but also in gospel compassion.

THESIS 2: NEITHER THE THEOLOGY NOR THE PRACTICE OF THE CATHOLIC CHURCH WITH RESPECT TO DIVORCE AND REMARRIAGE IS AS FAITHFUL TO THE NEW TESTAMENT WORDS OF JESUS AS THE CHURCH CLAIMS.

On October 14, 1994, the Congregation for the Doctrine of the Faith sent a letter to the Bishops of the Catholic world entitled "Concerning the Reception of Holy Communion by Divorced and Remarried Members of the Faithful."[4] That letter purported to articulate the doctrine of the Catholic Church concerning divorce and remarriage and claimed, citing Mark 10:11–12, it was in "fidelity to the words of Jesus Christ." The implication was that, since the doctrine in question is based on fidelity to the words of Jesus, it is irreformable. That argument might be true if the words of Jesus as cited from Mark were the only teaching in the New Testament on divorce and remarriage. That, of course, is well-known not to be the case.

In his First Letter to the Corinthians, Paul answers questions posed to him by the Corinthian community. One of those questions was a question about marriage and divorce, and Paul responds with a command from the Lord. "To the married I give this command—not I but the Lord—that the wife should not separate from her husband, but if she does separate let her remain unmarried or else be reconciled to her husband" (7:10–11). Having responded to the question of divorce and remarriage in the case of two believers, Paul proceeds to a case of conscience which must have been as prevalent in the earliest Christian communities as it is in mission territories today. The case asks about a marriage in which one of the spouses has been baptized as a Christian and the other remains a non-Christian, and asks specifically about divorce in such a marriage. Paul offers two pieces of advice, each of them hinging on the attitude of the non-baptized spouse.

The first advice relates to the case in which the non-Christian spouse is willing to continue to live with the Christian. In that case, "if any believer has a wife who is an unbeliever, and she consents to live with him, he should not divorce her. And if any woman has a husband who is an unbeliever and he consents to live with her, she should not divorce him" (7:12–13). Paul's advice is firm: when the unbelieving spouse is willing to continue to live in marriage with the believer, he or she is not to be divorced. The second advice relates to the case in which the non-believer is unwilling to continue to live with the believer. "But if the unbelieving partner separates, let it be so; in such a case the brother or sister is not bound. It is to peace that God has called you" (7:15). Note that it is the non-believing spouse who separates herself or himself; she or he is not to be dismissed by the believer. There is no suggestion that the marriage between a believer and non-believer is not valid; there is no suggestion that Jesus' command does not apply. There is only the clear suggestion that Paul is granting an exception: "*I say*, I and not the Lord" (7:12). For Paul, the preservation of peace, it would appear, is a greater value than an unpeaceful marriage which might threaten the faith of the believer. The Catholic Church sanctioned this approach to dissolving a valid marriage (that is, granting a divorce) in the twelfth century, continues to enshrine it today in its revised *Code of Canon Law,* and calls the process the Pauline Privilege.

Matthew also twice nuances the words of Jesus with his own Jewish exception (5:32; 19:9). Again there is Jesus' remembered saying: "What God has joined together let no one separate" (19:6). And again there is an interpretive nuance: "Whoever divorces his wife, *except for porneia,* and marries another commits adultery" (19:9). The meaning of the exceptive phrase, "except for *porneia,* " has been endlessly disputed. We will not enter into that debate here, since we agree with biblical scholar Raymond Collins that "its meaning is not self-evident to modern interpreters."[5] We raise here a different question: does the exceptive clause originate in the teaching of Jesus or of Matthew? We accept the majority scholarly judgment that the latter is the case, given both Matthew's acknowledged penchant for nuancing the words of Jesus in light of the needs of his Jewish-Christian community and the absence of the exceptive clause in Paul, Mark, and Luke, all of whom record Jesus' saying on divorce (1 Cor 7:10–11; Mark 10:11–12; Luke 16:19). We wish to underscore two conclusions from all this. First, Matthew did not hesitate to interpret the words of Jesus on the basis of the needs of his Jewish-Christian church, a church composed of Jews who had been converted to be followers of Jesus as the Christ but who still practiced Jewish law, including the law of divorce for *erwat dabar* or *porneia* (Deut 24:1–4). Second, there is not only one account of Jesus' saying about divorce, there are four divergent accounts that do not all derive from the words of Jesus. These divergent accounts, we now believe, exist because divergent Christian communities had divergent concerns about marriage and divorce that needed to be answered.

The nuancing of the words of Jesus on the basis of contextual need, begun by the early Church, was continued in the twelfth-century Church by Gratian of Bologna with respect to the question of the non-consummation of a marriage and its dissolubility and in the sixteenth-century by Popes Paul III, Pius V, and Gregory XIII with respect to questions arising out of polygamy and slavery. All the Church's nuances to the words of Jesus on divorce continue to be enshrined today in its revised *Code of Canon Law* under the headings of non-consummation (Can. 1142), Pauline Privilege (Can. 1143), and Petrine Privilege (Can. 1149).[6] This constant and well-known nuancing of the words of Jesus in the Church makes any argument based exclusively on the words of Jesus at best incomplete and at worst dishonest. Because divergent instructions on divorce and remarriage, including those deriving from Paul and Matthew, are part of the New Testament and of the word of God, any effort to single out one instruction to override all others as *the* word of God falsifies God's word and ought to be discontinued.

This brief consideration of the traditional Catholic data on divorce and remarriage leads to several important conclusions. First, it is incorrect to speak of one New Testament *teaching* on divorce and remarriage, as if there was only one. There are several *teachings* and they neither all agree nor all derive from Jesus. Second, diverging accounts of divorce and remarriage are an integral part of the New Testament and later Christian traditions because the diverse followers of Jesus continued to ask the meaning of his teachings for their concrete, cultural lives. Third, though popular unwisdom singled out one element in those diverging accounts, namely, Jesus' saying on divorce and remarriage, and allowed it to override all the others, that fact should not be permitted to obscure either the New Testament or ongoing diversity.

THESIS 3: THE SOLEMN TEACHING OF THE COUNCIL OF NICEA IS INTIMATELY RELATED TO THE CHURCH'S TEACHING ON DIVORCE AND REMARRIAGE, AND HAS MUCH TO CONTRIBUTE TO ITS PASTORAL PRACTICE TODAY.

There is a long tradition in the Church that venerates the solemn teaching of Ecumenical Councils, and that especially venerates the first four Councils above all others, and that most especially venerates the first of them, the Council of Nicea (325), whose Creed established the doctrinal basis of the Christian faith. Canon 8 of that Council goes to the very heart of the question of divorce and remarriage.

As regards those who define themselves as the "Pure" and who want to join the Catholic and Apostolic Church, the holy and great Council decrees that they may remain among the clergy once hands have been imposed upon them. But beforehand they will have to promise in writing to comply with the teachings of the Catholic and Apostolic Church and to make them the rule of their conduct. That is to say, they will have to communicate both with *those who married a second time* (*digamoi*) and with those who failed under persecution but whose time has been established and whose moment of reconciliation has arrived. They will, therefore, be bound to follow the teaching of the Catholic and Apostolic Church completely.[7]

According to this Canon, the "Pure," that is, those who belonged to the rigorous sect called Novatians,[8] had to promise in writing to accept the teaching of the Catholic Church before they could be reconciled with it. Specifically, they had to accept to live in communion with those who had been married twice (*digamoi*) and those who had apostatized during persecution but who had completed their period of penance and had been reconciled to the Catholic Church. We are concerned here only with those *digamoi* who have done penance and have been reconciled to the Church.

The Novatians excluded from the possibility of penance and reconciliation those who were guilty of certain sins "leading to death," among which was *digamia*. Now *digamia* refers to remarriage either after the death of a spouse or after a divorce or repudiation but, since remarriage after the death of a spouse was not considered a sin leading to death until long after the Council of Nicea, the Council's *digamoi* must be those who have remarried after a divorce or repudiation. According to the Council, that "sin" can be forgiven and reconciliation with the Church can be achieved after suitable penance. Acutely relevant is the fact that neither the Church before Nicea nor the Council itself required the repudiation of the new spouse as a pre-requisite for forgiveness and reconciliation. This was in keeping with the proscriptions of Deut 24:1–4, which were taken to be binding in the Church before Nicea and which forbade a husband to take back his repudiated wife after she had married another.[9] Basil explicitly reports the treatment of a man who had abandoned his wife and remarried, who had "done penance with tears," and who, after seven years, had been accepted back "among the faithful."[10] The man's second marriage is accepted and neither the repudiation of his second wife nor his taking back of the first is demanded as a pre-requisite for full communion. This teaching of Basil's is the foundation for the teaching and practice of the Orthodox Church known as *oikonomia*.

The Church in the twentieth century has much to learn from the first Ecumenical Council and from the *oikonomia* it practiced. It is past time for it to consider the applicability of *oikonomia* to its present pastoral practice requested by the Synod of Bishops in 1980.

THESIS 4: THE CATHOLIC CHURCH HAS NEVER PRACTICED WHAT IS ENSHRINED IN ITS LAW, NAMELY, THAT "THE ESSENTIAL PROPERTIES OF *MARRIAGE* ARE UNITY AND INDISSOLUBILITY" (CANON 1056). THE NUMBER OF MARRIAGES THE CHURCH HOLDS TO BE INDISSOLUBLE IS ACTUALLY VERY LIMITED.

If the Church truly believed that indissolubility was an essential property not just of Christian marriages but of all marriages (Can. 1056), and that by the will of God "from the beginning" (Mark 10:6; Matt 19:4), then it would treat all marriages as indissoluble. It does not and never has. The Church accepts the marriages of the non-baptized as valid when they have been performed according to the laws which govern them and yet, utilizing the Pauline Privilege, it regularly dissolves them "in favor of the faith of the party who received baptism" (Canon 1143). It has further extended the Pauline Privilege, as already noted, to embrace the dissolution of valid marriages utilizing the Petrine Privilege. In Christian marriages, indissolubility is said to acquire "a distinctive firmness by reason of the sacrament" (Can. 1056), and yet valid sacramental marriages which have not been consummated are dissolved "by the Roman Pontiff for a just reason, at the request of both parties or of either party" (Can. 1142). An official commentary from the Canon Law Society of America explains the discrepancy between Canon 1056 and Catholic practice by declaring that "the essential properties of marriage, unity and indissolubility, must be understood in the context of sacramental marriage defined as the intimate community of the whole of life."[11] Canon 1056, however, does not say that the essential properties of *sacramental marriage* are unity and indissolubility but that the properties of *marriage* without qualification are unity and indissolubility. If *marriage* without specification is indissoluble, then every marriage is indissoluble. As we have seen above, that is never what the Catholic Church has practiced and it is not what it practices today.

Long-standing Church practice with respect to the dissolution of valid marriages does everything but demonstrate a belief that an essential property of marriage is indissolubility. In Christian marriage, Canon 1056 adds, indissolubility is said to acquire "a distinctive firmness by reason of the sacrament." We can assume that it is on this statement that the Canon Law Society's statement cited above is based. Yet in practice this is no more true that the preceding statement. Valid sacramental marriages which have not been consummated are dissolved "by the Roman Pontiff for a just reason, at the request of both parties or of either party" (Can. 1142). Long-standing Church practice with respect to the dissolution of valid marriages does everything but demonstrate a belief that an essential property of marriage is indissolubility.

The full doctrine of the Church on the indissolubility of marriage is abundantly clear and demonstrates that fidelity to the words of Jesus is far from the only criterion for ecclesiastical judgments about divorce and remarriage. Only that marriage "which is ratified (as sacrament) *and* consummated cannot be dissolved by any human power other than death" (Can. 1141). The two conditions which make a marriage indissoluble in the eyes of the Church, that it be both sacramental *and* consummated, are not conditions ever mentioned or even insinuated by Jesus. They are both the result of historical Church nuancing long after Jesus, despite the patently false teaching of the recent *Catechism of the Catholic Church* that "the marriage bond has been established by God himself in such a way that a marriage concluded *and consummated* between baptized persons can never be dissolved."[12] That marriage was created by God no Catholic theologian would debate. That the marriage bond becomes indissoluble, even in a sacramental marriage, only when the marriage is consummated is, as historians well know, clearly a nuance added by Gratian and the Roman Church in the twelfth century to resolve the debate between the Roman and Northern European opinions about what makes marriage. For the sake of honesty and to avoid continuing confusion and alienation, the Church should cease teaching that indissolubility is an essential property of *marriage* and begin teaching ever more publicly what it really holds to be true, namely, that the only marriages which are indissoluble are those marriages which are both sacramental *and* consummated.

Jesus' saying about marriage in the Gospels declares "what God has joined together let no one separate" (Mark 10:9; Matt 19:6). For the first thousand years of Catholic history, the Church interpreted this saying as a moral demand: man *should not* put asunder. In the twelfth century, again under the influence of Gratian, the moral demand began to be spoken of as a legal demand. The *should not* gave way to *cannot,* as in "a ratified and consummated marriage *cannot* be dissolved by any human power or for any reason other than death" (Can. 1141). That progression from the words of Jesus, from the moral demand, to the canonical words of the Church, to the legal demand, is clearly another nuance the Church gave to the words of Jesus. Notice, however, that it is again not *marriage* but *sacramental and consummated marriage* that cannot be dissolved. We consider that question in the next thesis.

THESIS 5: THE CATHOLIC CHURCH, WHICH TEACHES THAT
THE ONLY MARRIAGE WHICH IS INDISSOLUBLE IS THE
SACRAMENTAL *AND* CONSUMMATED MARRIAGE, TODAY
HAS NO CRITERION FOR JUDGING WHEN CONSUMMATION,
AND THEREFORE INDISSOLUBILITY, HAS HAPPENED.

A theological question is consistently raised about the Catholic teaching on the effect of consummation: what is it that consummation adds to sacrament that makes the consummated sacramental marriage immune to dissolution? Pius XI suggested the answer is easily found "if we seek reverently" and that it lies in "the mystical meaning of Christian marriage," namely, its reference to that "most perfect union which exists between Christ and the church."[13] Though it does not specify as precisely as Pius that it is the consummated sacramental marriage that is indissoluble, the International Theological Commission offers the same reason for the indissolubility of Christian marriage. "The ultimate and deepest foundation for the indissolubility of Christian marriage lies in the fact that it is the image, the sacrament, the witness of the indissoluble union between Christ and the church."[14]

But questions remain. When Pius XI sought reverently in 1930, he took for granted the canonical tradition that dealt with marriage as a contract (1917 Can. 1012), that declared the object of the contract to be the exclusive and perpetual right to the body of the other for acts suitable for the generation of offspring (1917 Can. 1081,2), and that declared the ends of marriage to be primarily procreation and secondarily mutual help and the remedy of concupiscence (1917, Can. 1013). It is easy to see how, in such a legalistic and physicalistic context, a single act of sexual intercourse could be taken to be the definitive consummation of a marriage. It is not so easy to see in the changed theological and personalistic climate in which the Second Vatican Council rooted its doctrine on marriage.

The Council teaches that marriage "is rooted in the conjugal covenant of irrevocable personal consent."[15] Despite insistent demands to retain the legal word *contract* as a precise way to speak of marriage, the Council demurred and chose instead the biblical, theological and personal word *covenant*. This choice locates marriage as predominantly an *interpersonal* rather than a *legal* reality, and brings it into line with the rich biblical tradition of covenant between God and God's People and Christ and Christ's Church. The revised *Code* of 1983 also preferred *covenant* to *contract* (Can. 1055,1), though it relapses into contractual language some thirty times.

The Council made another crucial change to Catholic teaching about marriage, which is central to any modern theological discussion of consummation and which was later also incorporated into the revised Code. The traditional teaching on the ends of marriage was the primary end-secondary end hierarchy between procreation and spousal love as articulated in Canon

1013. Despite insistent demands to reaffirm this hierarchical terminology, the Council refused to do so. It taught explicitly that procreation "does not make the other ends of marriage of less account," and that marriage "is not instituted solely for procreation."[16] That this refusal to speak of a hierarchy of ends in marriage was not the result of oversight but a deliberate choice was confirmed when the Council's teaching on ends was incorporated into the revised Code (Can. 1055,1).

This change of root perspective raises questions about the claim that the spouses' first sexual intercourse is the definitive consummation of both their mutual self-gifting and their marriage. If the procreation of human life *and* the consortium-communion between the spouses are joint and equal ends of marriage, why should an act of sexual intercourse alone be the best symbol of the union of Christ and Christ's Church? Why should the extended marital *consortium*, itself symbolized in sexual communion, not be the symbol? These questions have been greatly exacerbated by the change in the way marital consummation is specified in both the Council and the *Code*. A marriage is now said to be "ratified and consummated if the spouses have in a human manner (*humano modo*) engaged together in a conjugal act in itself apt for the generation of offspring" (Can. 1061,1). The phrase we have underscored has placed Catholic teaching on conjugal sexuality, consummation, and indissolubility on hold theologically and canonically, for as yet a theology of sexuality that can elucidate what sexual intercourse in a human manner precisely means has not been elaborated. Since marital intercourse *humano modo* cannot be precisely defined, neither can the marital consummation it is said to effect, and that means that many more valid marriages than heretofore imagined are open to dissolution in the Catholic Church. A valid marriage may be dissolved by the Catholic Church when it has not been consummated *humano modo* (Can. 1142). Since the Church has no firm criterion on which to base a judgment that a marriage has been consummated *humano modo*, and has therefore become indissoluble, all marriages can be considered as dissoluble "in favor of the faith" (Can. 1143) or for some other "just cause" (Can. 1142).

THESIS 6: THE CODE'S CLAIM THAT "A VALID MARRIAGE CONTRACT CANNOT EXIST BETWEEN BAPTIZED PERSONS WITHOUT ITS BEING BY THAT VERY FACT A SACRAMENT" (CAN. 1055, 2) IS UNSOUND BY THE CHURCH'S OWN SACRAMENTAL THEOLOGY. THE SACRAMENTALITY OF MARRIAGE CANNOT BE PRESUMED SIMPLY FROM THE PHYSICAL FACT OF BAPTISM.

The Code presumes something that cannot be theologically presumed, namely, that all that is required for the *sacrament* of marriage is prior baptism and a valid marriage contract. That presumption stands in contradiction to the long tradition about the necessity of personal faith in Catholic teaching. The Gospels record that Jesus both complained about the absence of faith and praised its presence (Matthew 8:5–13; 8:23–27; 9:2; 9:20–22; 17:19–21; 21:18–22; Mark 5:25–34; 6:1–6). Paul vehemently defended the necessity of personal faith for salvation (Romans 1:16–17; 3:26–30; 5:1; Galatians 3:6–9). That tradition of the necessity of faith continued in the Church and flowered on both sides of the Reformation controversies.

Martin Luther made his stand on "faith alone" (*sola fides*). Though wishing to combat the Lutheran teaching that faith *alone* was necessary for salvation, the Council of Trent still left no doubt about the necessity of personal faith: "Faith is the beginning of man's salvation, the foundation and source of all justification, 'without which it is impossible to please God' (Hebrews 11:6)."[17] Baptism is "the sacrament of faith, without which no man has ever been justified."[18] The Latin text makes clear that "without which" (*sine qua*) qualifies faith and not sacrament or baptism, both of which would require *sine quo*. There is no doubt that the Fathers of Trent wished to affirm solemnly the primacy of active, personal faith for salvation. So also did both the First and Second Vatican Councils: faith is an act by which "a man gives *free* obedience to God by cooperating and agreeing with his grace, which can be resisted;"[19] faith is an act by which "man entrusts his whole self *freely* to God, offering 'the full submission of intellect and will to God who reveals,' and *freely* assenting to the truth revealed by him."[20] Since there is no doubt that a long and solemn Catholic tradition, fitting all the theological requirements for infallible teaching, establishes the necessity of free, personal faith for salvation, the Code should no longer be permitted to ignore that solemnly-defined theological tradition.

Convinced of the necessity of faith for the validity of baptism, Augustine sought to make good the evident lack of faith in infant baptism by arguing that *ecclesia fidem supplet* (the church makes good the faith required).[21] That argument cannot be applied in the case of marriage, a sacrament for adults who are required to have an active faith to participate in any sacrament. Aquinas never doubted that "every sacrament remains a sign and a proclamation of personal faith. Whoever receives it without believing in his heart places himself in a violent state of 'fiction' and deprives himself of sacramental grace."[22] Albert the Great is even more explicit: the sacrament of marriage derives its efficacy not only *ex opere operato*, the work of God in Christ, but also *ex opere operantis*, the faith-full work of the participant.[23] And Bonaventure agrees: the sacrament of marriage can be distinguished only by a modicum of personal faith.[24]

The 1980 Synod of Bishops gave quasi-unanimous support (201 *placet*, 3 non *placet*) to the following proposition: "We have to take into account the engaged couple's degree of faith maturity and their awareness of doing what the church does. *This intention is required for sacramental validity*. It is absent if there is not at least a minimal intention of believing with the church." Sacramental intention is critical in sacramental theology. To intend to receive a sacrament, the participant must intend by that action what the church intends by its sacrament. The question here is can a person have a real intention to participate in a sacrament without at least minimal personal faith?

Aquinas has no doubt: "Faith directs intention, and without [faith] intention cannot be right" (*fides intentionem dirigit, et sine ea non potest esse...intentio recta*).[25] The contemporary International Theological Commission stands in the same tradition: though intention and personal faith are not to be confused, they are not to be totally separated either. "The real intention is born from and feeds on living faith."[26] One cannot have a right sacramental intention without at least a minimum of personal faith. When personal faith is absent, so too is right sacramental intention; and when right intention is absent, as the tradition universally holds, the sacrament is not valid, but null. The theological judgment, no personal faith-no right intention, is a well-founded judgment. The further judgment that flows from it is equally well founded: without faith no one can enter into a valid sacramental marriage. The question of faith and its connection to sacrament is more acute today than ever before since contemporary Catholic theology distinguishes the baptized as *baptized believers*, those who have been baptized and also nurtured into active faith, and *baptized non-believers*, those who have been baptized and not nurtured into active faith.[27] The two should never be lumped together, neither in theology nor in law. Among the reasons for which a valid marriage may be dissolved by the Catholic Church is its non-sacramentality (Can. 1143). The non-sacramentality of marriages between the baptized, caused by their lack of the necessary faith for sacrament, should be added to the Pauline and Petrine Privileges to provide basis for dissolving a marriage, either "in favor of the faith" (Can. 1143) or for some other "just cause" (Can. 1142).

THESIS 7: THE CODE'S CLAIM THAT "A RATIFIED AND CONSUMMATED MARRIAGE CANNOT BE DISSOLVED BY ANY HUMAN POWER" (CAN. 1141) IS IRRELEVANT, FOR THERE IS IN THE CHURCH A REGULARLY-EXERCISED, MORE-THAN-HUMAN POWER CAPABLE OF CHANGING BREAD INTO THE BODY OF CHRIST, FORGIVING SIN, AND DISSOLVING THE RATIFIED AND CONSUMMATED MARRIAGE.

Though this question is now moot until the consummation of a marriage in a human manner can be securely verified, there is a more-than-human power in the Church to dissolve any ratified and consummated marriage. Two things are to be noted. First, the question asks about extrinsic indissolubility, the immunity of a marriage to dissolution by an agent other than the spouses. There is universal Western agreement that a marriage (not only a ratified and consummated marriage) is intrinsically indissoluble, that is, immune to dis-solution by the spouses. Secondly, the extrinsic indissolubility of a ratified and consummated marriage as prescribed in the Code is not a revealed truth. Billot's opinion that it is *de fide catholica* has never found support;[28] most theologians judge it to be *doctrina catholica*. Navarrette's claim that Pius XI implicitly and Pius XII explicitly affirm that the ratified and consummated marriage cannot be dissolved, not even by the vicarious power of the Roman Pontiff, is a canonical exaggeration.[29] Both Popes are doing nothing more than citing without comment the teaching then legislated in Canon 1118. They add nothing that would elevate the teaching to a theological level higher than *doctrina catholica*.

The history of the doctrine and law about ratified and consummated mar-riage in the Catholic tradition demonstrates three facts. First, it is a compro-mise introduced by twelfth-century Gratian (not first-century Jesus) between the Roman law in which consent makes marriage and the northern European custom in which sexual intercourse makes marriage. Secondly, the compro-mise emerges from a mixed cultural understanding of marriage, the southern culture of the Roman Empire and the northern culture of twelfth century Europe. Thirdly, it is not *de fide*; it is *doctrina catholica*. That is not to say that it is not true. It is to say only that it is not irreformable, and to suggest that the agent of reformation is the same agent that introduced the teaching in the first place, namely, the Church, whose power extends to the binding and loosing of sin, to the transformation of bread and wine, and certainly to the reformation of a reformable doctrine it itself inaugurated. If a non-consum-mated marriage between baptized believers, that is, a sacramental marriage which falls under God's law, "can be dissolved by the Roman Pontiff for a just reason" (Can. 1142) in the name of God, a ratified and consummated marriage which falls under the Church's law can also be dissolved by the Roman Pontiff for a similarly just reason. The bond of a ratified and consummated marriage is far from immune to the more-than-human power daily exercised in the Church. The Church, the Body of Christ in the world, should exercise and demonstrate its gospel *oikonomia* by applying its more-than-human power to the resolution of the pastoral problems that unnecessarily afflict those Catholics who are civilly divorced and remarried without annulment.

THESIS 8: THE ARGUMENT THAT CATHOLICS WHO ARE CIVILLY DIVORCED AND REMARRIED WITHOUT ANNULMENT ARE "IN A SITUATION THAT OBJECTIVELY CONTRAVENES GOD'S LAW (AND) CONSEQUENTLY THEY CANNOT RECEIVE HOLY COMMUNION AS LONG AS THIS SITUATION PERSISTS" [30] IS CONTRARY TO THE UNIVERSAL LAW OF THE CATHOLIC CHURCH, *OBEDIENCE TO WHICH TAKES PRECEDENCE OVER OBEDIENCE TO A ROMAN DICASTERY.*

Among the most serious and pervasive pastoral problems facing the Catholic Church today is the problem of Catholics who have divorced and remarried without first receiving an annulment. Their remarriage places them in an irregular situation in the Church and they are, consequently, banned from sharing in holy communion as long as their irregular situation continues. With respect to this situation, basing themselves on interviews with priests working with alienated Catholics in Boston, New York, Providence, and Wilmington (DE), Kenneth Himes and James Coriden comment that "the single biggest reason people cease active participation in the Church is that they have found themselves in irregular marital situations and felt themselves unwanted by the Church."[31] After a five-year study of divorced and remarried Catholics in England, Timothy Buckley reached a similar conclusion. He reports that the consensus of bishops, priests, and people is that "something is seriously wrong with the present teaching and that more than that it is a scandal."[32] The situation of civilly divorced and remarried Catholics is clearly a painful and pressing pastoral problem.

In July 1993, the three bishops of the Upper Rhine Province in Germany issued a joint statement of pastoral principles with respect to this situation. In their statement they outlined a differentiated pastoral approach by which *some* civilly divorced and remarried Catholics, whose subjective state has been judged not to be gravely sinful after serious discussion with a pastoral counselor, might be allowed to share holy communion. The approach suggested by the Bishops was not a blanket approach by which every civilly divorced and remarried Catholic could share in communion. It was a differentiated, case-by-case approach by which *some* Catholics, in certain situations, and under certain conditions, could be permitted to share communion.[33] In September 1994, the CDF issued a response to the German Bishops which strongly reaffirmed the exclusion of divorced and remarried Catholics from holy communion.

The CDF argued as follows.

> If the divorced are remarried civilly, they find themselves in a situation that *objectively contravenes* God's law. Consequently they cannot receive holy communion as long as this situation persists.... This norm is not at all a punishment or a discrimination against the divorced and remarried, but rather expresses an objective situation that of itself renders impossible the reception of holy communion.[34]

The argument is clear. The exclusion of civilly divorced and remarried Catholics from holy communion is based on the objective, presumed grave, sinfulness of their remarriage contrary to the laws of the Catholic Church. The CDF is an authoritative teaching voice of the Catholic Church and, therefore, should be listened to carefully. It is, however, neither the only nor even the primary Catholic authority pertaining to the reception of holy communion in the Church. The primary authority is the revised 1983 *Code of Canon Law,* and the matter is clear from Book IV, Title III, Chapter I, Article 2 of the current *Code,* "Participation in the Blessed Eucharist."

The relevant canons prescribe the following: "Any baptized person who is not forbidden by law may and *must* (*debet*) be admitted to holy communion" (Can. 912); "those upon whom the penalty of excommunication or interdict has been imposed or declared, and others who obstinately persist in manifest grave sin, are not to be admitted to holy communion" (Can. 915); "anyone who is conscious of grave sin may not celebrate mass or receive the Body of the Lord without previously having been to sacramental confession..." (Can. 916). Another canon also applies. "Ecclesiastical laws are to be understood according to the proper meaning of the words considered in their text and context. If the meaning remains doubtful or obscure, there must be recourse to parallel places, if there be any, to the purpose and circumstances of the law, and to the mind of the legislator" (Can. 17).

Since the first part of Canon 915 does not apply to Catholics who have been divorced and civilly remarried without annulment, because they are neither excommunicated nor placed under interdict, that leaves only the question of grave or mortal sin[35] in the terms of Canons 915 and 916. Our question can be put succinctly: does grave sin in the Catholic tradition, and therefore in the mind of the legislator, automatically follow from the fact that an action "objectively contravenes God's law" or constitutes gravely sinful matter? The answer can be put just as succinctly: in Catholic moral theology an objectively gravely sinful action does not *ipso facto* result in grave sin.

In addition to objectively grave matter, grave sin requires both full consciousness of the sinfulness of the action *and* free consent to the action. The

attempt of the divorced Catholic to remarry without annulment may constitute grave matter in the eyes of the Church; it may even constitute sin. But it
constitutes *grave* sin only where there is full awareness and free consent.
Those Catholics who have attempted remarriage after divorce without first
obtaining an annulment, or who have been unable to obtain an annulment for
some formal canonical reason, do not all necessarily have the required full
awareness and free consent required for grave sin. They are not, therefore, all
guilty of grave sin and are not all, therefore, prohibited by law from receiving
holy communion. Those who are not guilty of grave sin because the traditional conditions for grave sin, objectively grave matter, full consciousness,
and free consent, have not all been met, and whether or not the conditions
have been met will have to be decided on a case by case basis in discussion
with a pastoral counselor as the German bishops argued, *must* be admitted to
holy communion according to the universal law of the Catholic Church (Can.
912). No undifferentiated, blanket teaching of any Roman dicastery, or even
of the Bishop of Rome,[36] can bar them from the communion to which they
are entitled by faith and by law; and no Catholic minister should either be put
in or assume the invidious position of refusing them, at the risk of damaging
their good name and defaming them, the holy communion to which they are
entitled. Any sweeping prohibition from full communion on the basis of
"grave objective matter" without due consideration of specific circumstance,
consciousness, and consent has no foundation in the Roman Catholic moral
tradition and can safely be ignored.

    Any solution to the situation of Catholics civilly divorced and remarried
without an annulment, we have already stated, cannot be a blanket solution
but only an individual case-by-case solution. In those cases where a theological solution might be possible certain conditions will necessarily have to
apply. We suggest several to both spouses in second marriages and pastoral
counselors who help them discern their situation. First, no present canonical
solution can be applied in the case. Second, the first marriage must be irre-
trievably ended and reconciliation impossible; an uncontested divorce, refusal of one party to consider reconciliation, obligations to spouse and children
of the second marriage may be taken as signs of this. Third, obligations
arising from the first marriage must be fully accepted and discharged; reasonable alimony and child support, an equitable property settlement, acceptance
of any responsibility for the failure of the first marriage, and sorrow and
repentance for any personal sin in the failure of the first marriage are among
such obligations. Fourth, obligations arising from the second marriage must
be responsibly accepted and discharged, and the second-marriage spouses
must demonstrate that they intend to live in a stable marriage in a Church
community; the birth of children, the stability of the second marriage over a
period of years, the genuine desire to participate in the sacramental life of the
Church may be taken as signs of such responsibility. Fifth, the desire for the

sacraments must be motivated by genuine Catholic faith, the presence of which may be discerned in those who are sincerely pained by being banned from participation in the sacraments.

THESIS 9: THE SCANDAL THAT IS INSINUATED IN BOTH PAPAL AND CONGREGATION FOR THE DOCTRINE OF THE FAITH (CDF) STATEMENTS IF DIVORCED AND CIVILLY REMARRIED CATHOLICS ARE ADMITTED TO COMMUNION IS NO DIFFERENT FROM THE SCANDAL THAT COULD BE INSINUATED IN SOLUTIONS APPROVED BY THE CHURCH.

Pope John Paul II specifies the scandal that might ensue if the divorced and remarried were admitted to the Eucharist in this way, "the faithful would be led into error and confusion regarding the Church's teaching about the indissolubility of marriage,"[37] and the CDF letter repeats this judgment without comment.[38] The implication is that, if the civilly divorced and remarried are admitted to communion, people might come to believe that the Church no longer teaches that marriage is indissoluble or that fidelity is required in marriage. No one should ever underestimate the possibility and damage of scandal; nor, however, should anyone overestimate it. In fact, no one should ever be permitted to estimate it at all. Real scandal is not something to be estimated, or taken as a given; real scandal is a fact which can be empirically verified. Real scandal is in much the same category as real sin, it can be, and to be real must be, verified in reality on a case by case basis.

There are two cases in which the Church permits the civilly divorced and remarried to participate in communion. The first is the case in which the couple has received the necessary annulment(s) to be free to remarry; the second is the case in which the couple agrees to live as brother and sister. Neither case sufficiently removes the threat of scandal. The brother-sister solution, which involves abstention from all sexual intercourse, is wide open to the threat of the same scandal that is assigned to those not living as brother and sister, for no adult aware of the ways of men and women would ever presume such abstention in a couple living together publicly as husband and wife.[39] Kevin Kelly notes with some irony that, "unless a couple had a 'brother and sister' logo on their doorstep, neighbors and fellow parishioners would be none the wiser and so the alleged scandal would presumably still be given."[40] Given these obvious empirical considerations, it is astonishing to see Pope John Paul II[41] and the new *Catechism* (n. 1650) presenting the brother-sister solution as a genuine pastoral solution, completely ignoring the judgment of theologians and canon lawyers who teach that this option is full of danger and should be employed rarely and almost never.[42] The case of annulment runs the same peril. Unless a couple trumpeted their canonical annulment from the sanctuary, most fellow-parishioners would never know about its existence. Today, when annulment has become so commonplace, those fellow parishioners might be just as likely to assume that the couple had been granted annulment(s) and think no more of it. Most of them would take the same attitude to any divorced and remarried spouses approaching holy communion.

Any scandal given in the case of the civilly divorced and remarried Catholics may well be given not by the remarried spouses but by the Church that bars them from communion. Recall Himes' and Coriden's American report that "the single biggest reason people cease active participation in the Church is that they have found themselves in irregular marital situations and feel unwanted and rejected by the Church,"[43] and Buckley's English report that the consensus of bishops, priests, and people is that "something is seriously wrong with the present teaching and that more than that it is a scandal."[44] Cardinal Newman wrote of the general consensus of the faithful which senses error and at once "feels it as a scandal."[45] Sound empirical connection to Newman's sense of error and scandal among the faithful in the United States is provided in a 1992 survey which revealed that only 23% of Catholics agreed that the Magisterium alone should decide the morality of a civilly divorced Catholic remarrying without an annulment and that 72% agreed that civilly divorced and remarried Catholics should be able to receive communion.[46] Seven years later only 20% of Catholics agreed that the Magisterium alone should decide the morality of a civilly divorced Catholic remarrying without an annulment.[47] The faithful's sense of scandal and non-scandal could not be clearer.

THESIS 10: THE CATHOLIC CHURCH SHOULD EMBRACE THE ORTHODOX PRACTICE OF *OIKONOMIA*, DECLARED BY THE COUNCIL OF TRENT TO HAVE CERTAIN CLAIM TO THE GOSPEL AND TO THE NAME *CHRISTIAN*.

What is the solution to the Catholic Church's approach to the situation of civilly divorced and remarried Catholics? We suggest it should pay close attention to the Orthodox Church's practice of *oikonomia*. *Oikonomia* flourishes, not within a context of law but within a context of spirit and grace. It grows out of the powerful Orthodox belief in the continuing benevolent and merciful action in the Church of Christ and Christ's spirit. *Oikonomia* refers to the order of salvation in Christ. In that order of salvation, God the Father is the benevolent and merciful father of the household (*oikos*), Christ is the Good Shepherd who leaves ninety-nine good sheep to recover one that is lost (Luke 15:3–7), the Holy Spirit is the omnipresent comforter who makes possible every good in the household, and the Church is the householder, as benevolent and merciful as the Father of the household (Luke 6:36; Matt 5:44–48). *Oikonomia* heeds Paul's injunction that "the letter kills but the Spirit gives life" (2 Cor 3:6). *Oikonomia* cannot exist without great faith in the Father and the Spirit and the Christ they continue to send.

What does *oikonomia* have to do with the situation of Catholics who are civilly divorced and remarried? While holding firmly to the belief that the gospel presents to believers a demand for indissoluble marriage, the Orthodox Churches also believe that women and men sometimes do not measure up to the gospel. They acknowledge the human reality that marriages, even Christian marriages, die and that when they die it makes no sense to argue that they are still binding. When a marriage is dead, even when the former spouses live, *oikonomia* impels the Church to be not only sad, for the death of a marriage is always "the death of a small civilization,"[48] but also compassionate, for the Church represents the compassionate God. This compassion extends to permitting the remarriage of an innocent or repentant spouse. The marriage liturgy differentiates the second marriage from the first, highlighting that grace is always threatened by sin, that Christian ideal is always at the mercy of human frailty. It lacks the joy of the first-marriage liturgy; it ritually proclaims that no one in attendance, including the priest is without sin. It is in just such an economy that the household-Church is summoned to minister compassionately on behalf of the compassionate God.

A reasonable Christian objection arises at this point. Should not what the churches do about divorce and remarriage be based on the tradition of Jesus mediated to them in the New Testament? Yes, it should, and we considered that tradition briefly and found diverging accounts about divorce and remarriage in the New Testament as culturally diverse followers of Jesus sought to translate the meaning of his life, death, and resurrection into their diverse cultural lives. That early process of interpreting the Lord's saying about divorce and remarriage continued in the churches of both East and West. The East developed its doctrine of *oikonomia* related to marriage, divorce, and remarriage; the West developed its law related to marriage, divorce, and remarriage which continues in force today.

In the twelfth century, the Bologna canon lawyer, Gratian, developed two pieces of legislation that continue to be enshrined in Catholic law. The first was a continuation of Paul's exception, now called the Pauline Privilege, which remains today one of the bases on which the Catholic Church grants the dissolution (or divorce) of valid marriages (Can. 1143). The Pauline Privilege, as we noted earlier, was much extended by sixteenth-century Popes beyond what Paul ever envisioned by the misnamed and misleading Petrine Privilege which also remains today as a basis for dissolving (divorcing) a valid marriage (Can. 1149). The second piece of legislation was a compromise between the Roman and the northern European answers to the question of when a valid marriage comes into existence: The Roman practice was that consent makes valid marriage, the northern European practice was that sexual intercourse makes valid marriage. Gratian combined the two and decreed that "Marriage is initiated by betrothal (consent), perfected (consummated) by sexual intercourse."[49] The Catholic Church today holds as indissoluble *only* that marriage which is both sacramental *and* consummated by sexual intercourse (Can. 1141). It holds all other marriages to be dissoluble and it dissolves them on occasion "for a just reason" (Can. 1142) or "in favor of the faith" (Can. 1143).

Several things are clear. First, despite its claim to follow the Lord's command, the Catholic Church also follows Paul, Gratian, and medieval Popes in extending Jesus' saying in its ongoing contextual situations. Second, it is not true that the Catholic Church never grants divorces. It grants them regularly in marriages which are not sacramental or not consummated, though it disingenuously obscures that fact by naming the process dissolution rather than divorce. Third, though there is no warrant in the New Testament for these canonical processes other than the Pauline Privilege, there is ample warrant, as the Reformation Council of Trent attested, for *oikonomia*. Despite holding to a rigid line on the indissolubility of marriage, the Council steadfastly refused to condemn the practice of *oikonomia* or to declare that it did not have equal claim to the gospel tradition and to the name *Christian*.[50]

The 1980 Synod of Bishops presented to Pope John Paul II a request that the Orthodox practice of *oikonomia* be studied for any light it might shed on a pastoral approach for Catholics who are civilly divorced and remarried. Many of those second marriages have become so stable, and the families nurtured in them so Christian, that they cannot be abandoned without grave spiritual, emotional, and economic harm. The Catholic Church must discern whether its understanding of the gospel precludes the development of an *oikonomia* approach to the care of its members in second marriages. It is summoned to gospel *oikonomia* as a way to alleviate the sufferings of those thousands of Catholics civilly divorced and remarried without sin and as a way to attain the ecclesial peace and communion to which God has called all Christians (1 Cor 7:15).

There is strong support in every sector of the Church for reassessment of the pastoral practice with respect to divorce and remarriage, especially among women who know that women and their children suffer most from divorce.[51] The theological question for reassessment can be stated clearly. Can the Catholic Church continue to claim fidelity to the total economy revealed by the compassionate and merciful God and continue to permit its lone reading of Jesus' words on divorce and remarriage to override all else in that economy? The question, we admit, does not permit of an easy answer. But a Church faithful to the gospel, and to the Spirit who continues to reveal its meaning in contemporary contexts, can face the question secure in the belief that the Spirit of God will guide it into the truth of God as surely today as at any time in the past. The words of Pope Francis point to the future of this question. "The eucharist, although it is the fullness of sacramental life, is not a prize for the perfect but a powerful medicine and nourishment for the weak."[52] Among the contemporary Catholic "weak" are spouses who cannot conceive by the normal method of sexual intercourse and require the assistance of artificial reproductive technology. We conclude our analyses in the next chapter by examining their situation from the perspective of the virtuous person.

QUESTIONS FOR REFLECTION

1. What fidelity to the words of Jesus do Paul and Matthew practice? What fidelity to the words of Jesus does the Catholic Church practice when it dissolves valid marriages on the bases of the Pauline Privilege, the Petrine Privilege, and non-consummation?
2. The Catholic Church legislates that the only marriage that is indissoluble is the marriage that is both sacramental and consummated. When did Jesus teach this? If Jesus did not teach it, why does the Catholic Church, always claiming fidelity to the words of Jesus, follow this legislation in practice?
3. The Catholic Church teaches that Catholics who are civilly divorced and remarried without an annulment of their first marriage are in an objective situation that is contrary to God's law and, therefore, cannot receive holy communion. Thesis 8 argues that this practice is contrary to the Church's own law and moral practice. What do you think about this practice? What does this thesis have to say generally about conscience and morality?
4. Do you think that Catholics who are civilly divorced should be allowed to remarry in the Church and share in holy communion? What scandal would be given to ordinary Catholics if this practice was allowed?
5. What do you understand by the Orthodox practice of *oikonomia*? Do you believe it is or is not in accord with the gospel? What can the Catholic Church learn from it?

NOTES

This essay is a revised version of one that originally appeared in *New Theology Review* 12, no. 2 (1999): 48–63. It is reprinted here with permission.

  1. We shall use throughout this essay the term "civilly divorced Catholics" to distinguish those Catholics who have been granted a State divorce and may not remarry in the Church from those who have been granted a Church divorce (disingenuously called a "dissolution of a valid marriage") and may remarry without an annulment. We deal with the variety of Church divorces in Thesis 2.

2. See Michael G. Lawler, *Symbol and Sacrament: A Contemporary Sacramental Theology* (Omaha: Creighton University Press, 1995), 5–62.

3. 3 See Michael G. Lawler, "Faith, Contract, and Sacrament in Christian Marriage: A Theological Approach," *Theological Studies* 52, no. 4 (1991): 712–31.

4. We will cite it from *Origins* 24 (October 27, 1994), and will refer to it henceforth as "Concerning Reception."

5. Raymond F. Collins, *Divorce in the New Testament* (Collegeville: Liturgical Press, 1992), 205.

6. See Michael G. Lawler, *Marriage and Sacrament: A Theology of Christian Marriage* (Collegeville: Liturgical Press, 1993), 92–93.

7. J.D. Mansi, ed., *Sacrorum Conciliorum Nova et Amplissima Collectio* (Paris: Welter, 1903–1927), II, 672. Emphasis added.

8. See Charles J. Hefele, *History of the Christian Councils* (Edinburgh: Clark, 1883), I, 410.

9. See, for instance, Origen, *Comm in Matt. XIV,* 20, *Patrologia Graeca* 13, 1237 (henceforth *PG*); Cyril of Alexandria, *The Adoration and Worship of God in Spirit and Truth*, VIII, *PG* 68, 584; Jerome, *Epist.ad Amandum,* 4, *Patrologia Latina* 22, 563 (henceforth *PL*). A little earlier in the same epistle, Jerome makes what appears to be the very first request for the separation that now occupies such a prominent place in the discipline of the Western Church.

10. Basil, *PG* 32, 804–5.

11. James A. Coriden, Thomas J. Green, and Donald E. Heintschel, eds., *The Code of Canon Law: A Text and Commentary* (Mahwah, NJ: Paulist Press, 1985), 742.

12. *Catechism of the Catholic Church* (Mahwah: Paulist Press, 1994), n.1640, emphasis added.

13. Pius XI, *Casti Connubii, AAS* 22 (1930): 552.

14. "*Propositiones de quibusdam quaestionibus doctrinalibus ad matrimonium Christianum pertinentibus,*" *Gregorianum* 59 (1978): 462.

15. *Gaudium et spes*, n. 48.

16. Ibid., n. 50.

17. Denzinger-Schönmetzer (Hereafter DS), n. 1532.

18. DS, n. 1529. See also DS, n. 1532.

19. DS, n. 3010; see also DS, n. 3008.

20. *Dogmatic Constitution on Divine Revelation*, n. 5.

21. See *Epist.* 98, 5, *PL* 33, 362. See also *Summa Theologiae* 3, q. 68, a. 9; "Baptism for Children," in *The Rites of the Catholic Church* (New York: Pueblo, 1976), 188; Jean Charles Didier, *Faut-il baptiser les enfants?* (Paris: Cerf, 1967), *passim*.

22. Louis Villette, *Foi et sacrement: De Saint Thomas a Karl Barth* (Paris: Bloud et Gay, 1964), 40.

23. "*...in illo est actus personalis et moralis et civilis...et non trahit vim ab opere operato tantum sed etiam ab opere operantis*" (*In IV Sent.*, d.26, a. 14, q.1).

24. "*Sunt et alia (sacramenta), quae quodam modo ab instinctu naturae sunt, ut matrimonium in quo est maris et feminae coniunctio...partim etiam sunt a fide, scilicet quod illa coniunctio significet coniunctionem dei cum anima*" (*In IV Sent .*, d.26, a.2, q.1, conclusio).

25. *In IV Sent.*, d.6, q.1, a.3 ad 5.

26. Philippe Delhaye, "Propositions on the Doctrine of Christian Marriage," 2, 3, in *Contemporary Perspectives on Christian Marriage: Propositions and Papers from the International Theological Commission*, ed. Richard Malone and John Connery (Chicago: Loyola Press, 1984), 15.

27. See ibid., 14–21.

28. Louis Billot, *De Ecclesiae Sacramentis* (Rome: Pontificia Universitas Gregoriana, 1929), 440.

29. Urban Navarette, "*Indissolubilitas Matrimonii Rati et Consummati: Opiniones Recentiores et Observationes,*" *Periodica* 58 (1969): 449.

30. "Concerning Reception," *Origins* 24 (1994): 339.

31. Kenneth Himes and James Coriden, "Notes on Moral Theology 1995: Pastoral Care of the Divorced and Remarried," *Theological Studies* 57, no. 1 (1996): 118.

32. Timothy J. Buckley, *What Binds Marriage? Roman Catholic Theology in Practice* (London: Chapman, 1997), 178.

33. The Bishops' document, *"Respekt vor der Gewissensentscheidung,"* was first published in *Herder Korrespondenz* 47 (1993): 460–67. An English translation appeared later in *Origins* 23, no. 38 (March 10, 1994): 670–76.

34. CDF, *Epistola ad Catholicae Ecclesiae Episcopos de Receptione Communionis Eucharisticae a Fidelibus Qui Post Divortium Novas Inierunt Nuptias* (Roma: Libreria Editrice Vaticana, 1994), n. 4, our emphasis. An English translation appeared in *Origins* 24, no. 20 (October 27, 1994): 338–40.

35. See Canon 988 where *grave sin* (*peccata gravia*) is contrasted to the traditional *venial sin* (*peccata venialia*), in the same way as *mortal sin* traditionally is, indicating the synonymity of *grave* and *mortal* sin.

36. See Pope John Paul II, *Familiaris consortio*, n. 84.

37. Ibid.

38. "Concerning Reception," n. 4.

39. Given these obvious if "worldly" empirical considerations, it is astonishing to see *Familiaris consortio* (n. 84) and the *Catechism of the Catholic Church* (n. 1650) presenting the brother-sister solution as a genuine pastoral option. They ignore completely the tidal wave of Church theologians and canonists who teach that this pastoral option is *res plena periculis* (full of danger) and should be employed *raro* (rarely), *rarissime* (most rarely), *fere numquam* (almost never). See B. Sullivan, *Legislation and Requirement for Permissible Cohabitation as Invalid Marriages* (Washington: Catholic University, 1954), viii.

40. Kevin Kelly, "Divorce and Remarriage: Conflict in the Church," *Tablet* 248 (October 29, 1994): 1374.

41. See *Acta Apostolicae Sedis* 74 (1982): 186.

42. See B. Sullivan, *Legislation and Requirements for Permissible Cohabitation in Invalid Marriages* (Washington, DC: Catholic University of America Press, 1954), viii.

43. Himes and Coriden, "Notes on Moral Theology 1995," 118.

44. Buckley, *What Binds Marriage?*, 178.

45. John Henry Cardinal Newman, *On Consulting the Faithful in Matters of Doctrine* (London: Collins, 1986), 73.

46. William V. D'Antonio, *et al.*, *Laity American and Catholic: Transforming the Church* (Kansas City: Sheed and Ward, 1996), 53.

47. William V. D'Antonio, "The American Catholic Laity in 1999," *National Catholic Reporter* (October 29, 1999): 12.

48. Judith S. Wallerstein and Sandra Blakeslee, *Second Chances: Men, Women, and Children a Decade after Divorce* (New York: Ticknor and Fields, 1981), xxi.

49. Gratian, *Patrologia Latina* 187, 1429 and 1406.

50. See DS, n. 1807.

51. See the statistics reported in *Time* (June 22, 1992): 64–65 and in *National Catholic Reporter* (October 29, 1999): 12–20.

52. Pope Francis, *Evangelii gaudium*, Vatican.va/holy_father/Francesco/apost_exhortations/documents/papa-francesco_esortazione-apost_20131124_evangelii-gaudium_en.html.

Chapter Ten

Artificial Reproductive Technologies

Some ten percent of the married population is unable to conceive a child in the normal way by sexual intercourse because one or other or both of them are infertile. This chapter considers their situations and their ethical options under the umbrella of the virtuous person. In the 1950s, the marketing of effective oral contraceptives made it possible to have sexual intercourse without reproduction; in the present day, the marketing of artificial reproductive technologies (ARTs) makes it possible to reproduce without having sexual intercourse. The Catholic Church argues against the morality of both artificial contraceptives and ARTs on the basis of its principle of the inseparability of the unitive and procreative meanings of sexual intercourse. In this chapter, we deal with the teaching on ARTs. The CDF's Instruction, *Donum vitae*, enunciates the principle: "The Church's teaching on marriage and human procreation affirms the 'inseparable connection, willed by God and unable to be broken by man on his own initiative, between the two meanings of the conjugal act: the unitive meaning, the loving union and life of the spouses, and the procreative meaning,'"[1] the creation of a new human life. This inseparability principle prohibits *some* types of "artificial procreation" or "artificial fertilization," understood as "the different technical procedures directed towards obtaining a human conception in a manner other than the sexual union of man and woman."[2]

We have insisted earlier that traditional Catholic sexual morality is essentially marital morality; sexuality is confined within marriage and sexual intercourse between the spouses is moral only when open to procreation. There is a trinity that is intrinsically and inseparably interconnected: marriage, sexuality, and procreation. For the Church, artificial reproductive technologies (ARTs), defined as "non-coital methods of conception that involve manipulation of both eggs and sperm,"[3] interfere with this intrinsic connection by separating the unitive and procreative meanings of sexual intercourse. Revisionist theologians tend to think that, although ARTs often do not rely on sexual intercourse for reproduction, they may still fulfill on occasion both the unitive and procreative ends of *marriage* considered as an intimate interpersonal whole. When the marital relationship is seen, as it is seen since Vatican II in contemporary Catholic theology, as an interpersonal, procreative whole, and not just as a genital act, it seems reasonable to argue that, at least, some ARTs utilize modern science and technology to facilitate both the unitive and procreative meanings of the relationship. *Gaudium et spes* notes that "children really are the supreme gift of marriage"[4] and, if they are and ARTs can help infertile couples realize this supreme gift, we may legitimately ask about the credibility of the Magisterium's inseparability principle in condemning *all* ARTs that separate the two meanings of the conjugal act. This, then, concretely, is the debate in this chapter. First, we define various types of ARTs; second, we explain and critique Church teaching on ARTs, focusing primarily on the CDF's *Instruction*; third, we analyze and evaluate ARTs in light of our foundational principle for the morality of any sexual activity.

DEFINING ARTIFICIAL REPRODUCTIVE TECHNOLOGIES

ARTs are used when, at least, one spouse in a marriage is believed to be infertile. The American Society for Reproductive Medicine puts the level of infertility, "generally defined as the inability of a couple to conceive after 12 months of intercourse without contraception,"[5] at around 10%.[6] The causes of infertility are varied. They include hormonal imbalance, endometriosis, venereal infection (20 percent), contraceptive practices, abortions, incompatibility of gametes, cancer, and other causes,[7] but scientific developments in the last forty years have offered couples the ability to overcome infertility.[8] These developments include fertility drugs, which cause the woman to produce a number of ripe ova that can result in multiple pregnancies, and surgical operations, which can remove blockages in, for example, the fallopian tubes. The most popular of these modern developments is, however, the ART.[9]

One of the earliest ARTs to be used was artificial insemination. In this procedure male sperm is collected, from either masturbation or a condom used in sexual intercourse, and is inserted into the woman's cervical canal at or near the time of ovulation in order to fertilize the released ovum. The collected sperm may be used within a few hours of collection or frozen for later use. When fertilization takes place within the woman's body, the procedure is known as *in vivo* (in the body) artificial insemination. When the sperm is collected from the woman's husband, the entire procedure is known as *homologous fertilization*; when it is collected from a donor not the woman's husband, it is *heterologous fertilization*.

Another ART, one that differs from *in vivo* in terms of where fertilization takes place, is *in vitro fertilization with embryo transfer* (IVF-ET). In this procedure, used in over 70% of all ART procedures,[10] both sperm and ova are collected, and fertilization takes place outside the woman's body in a laboratory. There are various ways to collect the ova. Hormonal treatments with human menopausal gonadotropin (HMG) cause ova to mature in the woman's body, and these ripe eggs or oocytes are harvested via laparoscopic surgery or transportation by ultrasound guidance to the vagina. Once sperm and ova are collected, the sperm is washed or *capacitated* to enhance penetration and fertilization of several oocytes, creating several zygotes in a lab container. Since fertilization in this case takes place outside the woman's body in a laboratory container, the procedure is known as *in vitro* (in glass) fertilization. After fertilization and about forty hours of development, during which time the zygote is scientifically in the *pre-embryo* stage,[11] one to six healthy embryos are selected and transferred through the woman's cervix to her uterus anticipating implantation and development. Excess healthy embryos can be frozen, a process known as *cryopreservation*, and used later if the embryo transfer is unsuccessful or if the couple desires another pregnancy. They may also be used for research. Unhealthy embryos are typically destroyed. The processes of destruction, use in research, and the cryopreservation of fertilized embryos raise their own moral issues with regard to respect for human life. The Catholic principle on these issues is firm: "The human being must be respected—as a person—from the very first instant of his existence."[12]

Moral theologians who argue against the morality of ARTs in general do so on the basis that "fertilization is not directly the result of the marital act, since the semen used is not deposited by that act in the vagina, but by a technician's manipulation which substitutes for the marital act."[13] We argue that it is the intention of the couple, in conjunction with their sexual intercourse, to *maintain the unitive and procreative meanings of their overall marital, interpersonal relationship* that defines the moral meaning of any artificial technique. Since the integrity of marital intercourse and its direct relationship with reproduction is at the heart of the Church's moral analysis of ARTs, we next explore this analysis as it is articulated in the CDF's *Instruction*.

THE CDF'S INSTRUCTION AND ARTS

The *Instruction* was issued by the CDF in 1987 in response to questions posed by bishops, theologians, doctors, and scientists about the scientific and biomedical ability to intervene in the process of procreation. [14] It draws some clear lines on the morality of fertility-related interventions. These technologies "must be given a moral evaluation in reference to the dignity of the human person, who is called to realize his vocation from God to the gift of love and the gift of life." [15]

As its full title indicates, the *Instruction* addresses two main issues. The first is the fundamental respect due to human life and the long-standing Catholic principle that "human life must be absolutely respected and protected from the moment of conception." [16] This principle rules out by definition any destruction of, experimentation with, and cryopreservation of embryos. The second issue, "Interventions upon Human Procreation," [17] specifically addresses artificial insemination and IVF-ET. Interventions are to be assessed morally on the basis of "the respect, defense and promotion of man, his dignity as a person who is endowed with a spiritual soul and with moral responsibility," [18] but no definition is offered for the dignity of the human person in relation to either natural law or the meaning and nature of marriage, human sexuality, procreation, and parenthood. All these dimensions of the question will be considered next.

Natural Law: Biologist and Personalist Interpretations

In general, the CDF's Instruction "argues its case in terms of the traditional natural-law teaching of the Catholic Church, amplified by revelation and mediated though papal and magisterial teaching." [19] The American Fertility Society, which met in 1987 to reconsider its statement about the morality of ARTs in light of the CDF's *Instruction*, questioned the procedure used by the CDF to derive its conclusions from the stated premises. "While stating that 'the individual integrally and adequately considered' is to be the basis of the moral judgment, the fact is that most conclusions are based on and referred to past Catholic statements." [20] We question the teaching of the *Instruction* largely because of its biological and physicalist approach to natural law.

Like *Gaudium et spes* and *Humanae vitae*, the *Instruction* evinces a tension between biologist, i.e., the physiological process of reproduction, and personalist, i.e., the relational meaning of reproduction, approaches to natural law. Thomas Shannon articulates this tension in relation to *Gaudium et Spes* and Vatican II. The Second Vatican Council "vacillated between a less biological and more personalistic understanding of natural law, suggesting that, while physical reality is important, one also needs to look at the good of humanity and one's vocation in that context." [21] It is never a question of either/or, either the biological or the personal in natural law, but a question of both/and, both biological and personal. The personalist account of natural law in *Gaudium et spes*, however, has yet to be fully integrated into Church teachings on both human sexuality and reproduction.

Though it does offer intimately personalist reflections on the unitive meaning of marital sexual intercourse, *Humanae vitae*'s absolute prohibition of artificial means of regulating conception demonstrates a clear prioritization of the biologist over the personalist approach to natural law. This prioritization allows for "therapeutic means necessary to cure bodily diseases, even if a foreseeable impediment to procreation should result there from,"[22] but does not allow such means to facilitate the unitive meaning of the marital relationship. For example, if for "serious reasons" a couple chooses not to reproduce, or for the sake of responsible parenthood chooses not to have more children, and practicing natural family planning (NFP) proves to be detrimental to the unitive meaning of the marital relationship, artificial contraceptives are not permitted. In this situation, treating a biological pathology justifies using artificial contraceptives, but addressing relational complications that may arise from practicing NFP does not.

The *Instruction* also demonstrates a clear prioritization of the biologist over the personalist emphasis in natural law, but it vacillates between these two interpretations in assessing different types of reproductive technologies. This vacillation is clearly evident in its different analysis of *heterologous artificial fertilization* (AFD), in which the semen comes from a third party male beyond the couple, and *homologous artificial fertilization* (AFH),[23] in which the semen comes from the male in the coupled relationship. While the *Instruction* draws on personalist interpretations in its reflections on marriage, marital union, and parenthood, it is unwilling to follow through with the logical and normative implications of that interpretation in the case of certain ARTs. We explore how it vacillates in its use of natural law when addressing AFD and AFH.

Heterologous Artificial Fertilization (AFD) and the Personalist Principle

While the *Instruction* utilizes personalist language to explain marriage and human sexuality, the tension between the personalist and biologist interpretations of natural law is evident in its treatment of heterologous (AFD) and homologous (AFH) artificial fertilization. The *Instruction* begins its treatment of AFD by answering the question: "Why must human procreation take place in marriage?" Procreation "must be the fruit and the sign of the mutual self-giving of the spouses, of their love and of their fidelity."[24] Notice that the emphasis is not on the biological act of intercourse, but on the interpersonal marital *relationship*, its mutual self-giving, love, and fidelity. Fidelity pertains to the marital relationship where there is "reciprocal respect of their right to become a father and a mother only through each other."[25] The *Instruction* grounds its moral assessment of AFD in the personalist dimension of natural law. Procreation must take place in marriage because of the personal and relational implications for the spouses with one another, "mutual self-giving," and with the child, "the child is the living image of their love," the "permanent sign of their conjugal union."[26] The clear focus of the *Instruction*'s treatment of AFD is on the personal and relational dimensions of the spouses, their union, and their relationship with the child.

In light of these relational criteria, the *Instruction* then asks whether AFD conforms to the "Dignity of the Couple and to the Truth of Marriage?" and illustrates its negative answer by highlighting several ways in which AFD violates marital and familial relationships. First, AFD violates the marital relationship. "Heterologous artificial fertilization is contrary to the unity of marriage, to the dignity of the spouses, to the vocation proper to parents, and to the child's right to be conceived and brought into the world in marriage and from marriage."[27] Second, the introduction of a third party into reproduction through the use of donor gametes "constitutes a violation of the reciprocal commitment of the spouses and a grave lack in regard to that essential property of marriage which is its unity." Third, AFD "violates the rights of the child; it deprives him of his filial relationship with his parental origins and can hinder the maturing of his personal identity."

Fourth, AFD threatens the vocation to parenthood since "it offends the common vocation of the spouses who are called to fatherhood and motherhood...it brings about and manifests a rupture between genetic parenthood, gestational parenthood and responsibility for upbringing." Finally, AFD negatively impacts broader social relationships. "Such damage to the personal relationships within the family has repercussions on civil society: what threatens the unity and stability of the family is a source of dissension, disorder and injustice in the whole of social life." The fundamental violation of all of these relationships leads "to a negative moral judgment concerning heterologous artificial fertilization."[28]

This entire section of the *Instruction* focuses on the various relationships the spouses have to one another, to their child, and to their society, and argues to the immorality of AFD on the basis that it fundamentally violates those relationships. If the *Instruction* were consistent in its ethical reasoning, it would continue with this personalist, relational principle in morally evaluating homologous artificial insemination (AFH). It does not. When it addresses AFH, it shifts emphasis to a different foundational principle.

Homologous Artificial Fertilization (AFH) and the Biologist Principle

The CDF's treatment of AFH opens with the question: "What connection is required from the moral point of view between procreation and the conjugal act?"[29] The shift in the question from "Dignity of the Couple and the Truth of Marriage" to "Procreation and the Conjugal Act" reflects a methodological shift from the primacy of a relational, personalist emphasis to the primacy of an act-centered, biologist emphasis. Three questions emerge regarding the

Instruction's shift. First, why does the *Instruction* make this methodological shift from a focus on *relationship* when morally evaluating AFD to a focus on the *act* of intercourse when morally evaluating AFH? Second, what are the weaknesses of this inseparability principle with regard to AFH? Third, what would be the moral implications for AFH if the *Instruction* was methodologically consistent?

First, while the arguments against AFD seem reasonable to us given the relational complications of donor gametes and their potential impact on the marital relationship, the relationship of the parents with the child, the donor's relationship with both the parents and the child, and the social implications with regard to the nature of the family, the same relational complications do not apply in AFH. Where the gametes belong to the spouses, and a surrogate is not used to carry the embryo, the relational complications do not exist. All that can be claimed with certainty in the case of AFH is that the act of sexual intercourse is not *immediately* responsible for procreation. This point, however, while it gives us insight into the *procedure* facilitating reproduction, gives us no insight into the *moral meaning* of that procedure. As was indicated earlier, moral meaning is discerned not through the *givenness* of reality, in this case the givenness of the use of technology and science to assist reproduction, but in the *meaning* of those facts for human relationships. If the same personalist principle were to be applied to AFH as is applied to AFD, one could come to a different conclusion about the morality of AFH.

Second, by focusing on the act of intercourse and the inseparability principle in its discussion of AFH, the *Instruction* clearly recognizes that there is a shift in the foundational moral principle in analyzing and morally evaluating AFH and AFD. The *Instruction*'s condemnation of AFH is strictly dependent on the inseparability principle, i.e., the inseparability of the unitive and procreative meanings of sexual intercourse. It follows from the *Instruction*'s strict dependence on this principle to justify its moral argument against AFH that the argument is only as strong as the principle; if the principle is weak, so too is any moral conclusion drawn from the principle.

We believe the "inseparability principle" used to prohibit AFH (and contraception) is a weak principle on several counts. First, there is no essentially procreative meaning to each and every sexual act. Sexual acts in an infertile or post-menopausal relationship, or sexual acts during the lengthy periods when the woman is known to be infertile, do not have an essentially procreative meaning.

Second, the basis for the inseparability principle is a product of the biologism and physicalism that has controlled the Catholic natural law tradition, grounded in both a flawed biology and a flawed theology of marriage. In the Catholic tradition up until the Second Vatican Council, the *primary end* of marriage was always said to be procreation. This teaching reflected a long history that recognized procreation as the only legitimate meaning and purpose for sexual intercourse.[30] Our modern understanding of biology and human sexuality, however, teaches us that procreation is not even possible in the vast majority of sexual acts. A couple can morally justify having sexual intercourse without the procreative meaning, but they can never justify having sexual intercourse without the unitive meaning. It is logical, therefore, to argue that not only are the unitive and material procreative meanings of the sexual act separable, and on occasion in fact legitimately separated, but also that the unitive meaning is now primary and the procreative meaning secondary.

Third, while the *Instruction* correctly notes that "the one conceived must be the fruit of the parents' love," it has not adequately explained how the one conceived in AFH is not the fruit of the parents' love. It is not enough simply to state that AFH separates the unitive and procreative meanings of the sexual act and to conclude, therefore, that the child conceived in AFH is not the fruit of the parents' love, for that conclusion is a *non sequitur*; it does not follow from the premise. The forty-year experience with artificial insemination appears to show that the desperation of infertile couples and the inconvenience they are willing to undergo, emotional, physical, economic, is frequently a very powerful sign of their mutual love and their desire to offer to one another "the supreme gift of marriage,"[31] namely, a child. The meaning of ARTs and the intentions for choosing them are determined concretely case by case within the context of particular human relationships; meaning and intention are determined by the motives, desires, hopes, dreams, and reasons of the particular couple choosing ARTs.

Fourth, the tension between the personalist principle used to morally evaluate AFD and the inseparability principle used to morally evaluate AFH is highlighted all the more when the *Instruction* claims that "homologous IVF and ET fertilization is not marked by all that ethical negativity found in extra-conjugal procreation; the family and marriage continue to constitute the setting for the birth and upbringing of the children."[32] The relational considerations of AFD make it more morally objectionable than the violation of the inseparability principle in AFH. By its own admission, then, the inseparability principle on the basis of which the *Instruction* condemns AFH does not carry the same moral weight as the relational principle condemning AFD. The *Instruction* focuses on the marital act to argue against AFH; it focuses on relational dimensions to argue to the "ethical negativity" of AFD. It is relational considerations that make AFH less morally reprehensible than AFD. Since there may be no conjugal act in AFH, however, why would the *Instruction* base its moral condemnation of AFH on the conjugal act and the inseparability principle? It must do so because the relational considerations do not warrant an absolute prohibition of AFH, though the inseparability principle may so warrant if one accepts the principle as morally compelling. We do not find it morally compelling.

The Morality of AFH

Based on the foregoing analysis, we draw what we believe is a logical conclusion about the morality of homologous artificial insemination (AFH). As we noted at the beginning of this section, if the premise, in this case the inseparability principle, is weak, then any conclusion drawn from that premise will also be weak. We believe the inseparability principle cannot bear the weight of the *Instruction*'s conclusions absolutely prohibiting AFH. Given the desperation of an infertile couple to have a child and their intention, grounded in justice, mutual love, respect, responsibility, and human dignity, to have their marital relationship "crowned"[33] by their child, we believe the use of AFH can be moral and facilitate both the unitive and procreative meanings of marriage.

We are in agreement here with Lisa Cahill. Many Catholics, she notes, "perceive a difference larger than the Vatican allows between therapies used in marriage, even if they do temporarily circumvent sexual intercourse, and methods which bring donors into the marital procreative venture." She believes, and we agree, that "donor methods are more morally objectionable because they do not appreciate the unity as *relationships* of sexual expression, committed partnership, and parenthood."[34] While procreation in AFH would not be the result of one act of *physical coitus*, it would be the fruit of an overall *marital relational act* that expresses and facilitates the just love, commitment, care, concern, and dignity of the couple shared with a new human being, their child. Our argument defending the moral acceptability of AFH is grounded not in the inseparability of the unitive and procreative meanings of a *sexual act*, but in the meaning and nature of *marital relationship*, *marital sexuality*, and parenthood that is its crown. It is in the overall marital relationship, not in each and every sexual act, that the unitive and procreative meanings are legitimately inseparable.[35] With the *Instruction*, we affirm the intrinsic connection of marriage, sexual love, and parenthood. We judge, however, that its claim that genuine marital love is absolutely incompatible with the occasional use of artificial means to bring about conception without an immediate sexual act is unsupported and meaningless apart from consideration of the context of particular marital relationships.

The Meaning and Nature of Parenthood

While the *Instruction* uses the inseparability principle to condemn AFH, it indicates a parallel consideration between this principle and the relational emphasis it uses to condemn AFD. This parallel consideration revolves, first, around the relationship between the conjugal act and parenthood and, second, around the meaning and nature of parenthood in itself. After positing the inseparability principle as the foundational principle prohibiting AFH, the

Instruction quotes *Humanae vitae*. "By safeguarding both these essential aspects, the unitive and the procreative, the conjugal act preserves in its fullness the sense of true mutual love and its ordination towards man's exalted vocation to parenthood."[36] In addressing AFD, the *Instruction* notes that "it offends the common vocation of the spouses who are called to fatherhood and motherhood: it objectively deprives conjugal fruitfulness of its unity and integrity; it brings about and manifests a rupture between genetic parenthood, gestational parenthood, and responsibility for upbringing."[37] Two points need to be addressed when parenthood is offered as a parallel consideration in the condemnation of AFD and AFH. First, we must investigate the *Instruction*'s assertion that the conjugal act is ordained towards parenthood. Second, we must investigate parenthood in its genetic, gestational, and social dimensions.[38]

Interrelationship between Parenthood and the Conjugal Act

Gaudium et spes teaches that "children are really the supreme gift of marriage."[39] In the abstract and in general, one can say there is an essential relationship between the conjugal act and parenthood in its three dimensions, genetic, gestational, and social. Approximately one out of ten couples in the United States, however, is infertile,[40] and for these infertile couples it is impossible that any conjugal act will lead to genetic, gestational, or social parenthood. The CDF's teaching on ARTs that replace the marital act prescribes that the only morally acceptable path to parenthood for these infertile couples is through adoption or fostering.

The magisterium applauds the moral validity and nobility of post-natal adoption,[41] which incarnates the fundamental Christian imperative to care "for the least of these" (Matt 25:40). In the case of an adopted child, however, the nature of the relationship between the conjugal act and parenthood is fundamentally transformed. The sexual acts of infertile couples can never result in genetic or gestational parenthood, but they do express and promote the union of the spouses, thereby strengthening their ordination to social parenthood, that is, the nurturing of a child into functional adulthood. In and through just and loving sexual intercourse, a couple promotes shared life in their relationship, and that shared life permeates all their relationships, including a possible relationship with an adopted child in social parenthood. It also, of course, makes possible a sacramental relationship with God, a fact deeply important for Catholics. While adoption may not preserve "in its fullness" the relationship between sexual intercourse and genetic and gestational parenthood, it certainly preserves the unitive, relational dimension of the marriage and, therefore, the social dimension of parenthood.

Technology has complicated the definition of parenthood. Couples who utilize IVF-ET or its technological equivalents[42] generally produce excess embryos that are frozen. If a couple decides not to have more children, these embryos remain frozen to be eventually destroyed, used for stem cell research, or adopted. The *Instruction*, as we have seen, clearly condemns destroying embryos or any experimentation that will damage or destroy them. The first successful birth of an adopted frozen embryo occurred in Australia in 1984. Even though the publication of the *Instruction* followed that first case of frozen embryo adoption by three years, it did not address embryo adoption. The question of adopting frozen embryos has been discussed by theologians,[43] but the Church's silence on the question continues. The reality of the possible adoption of frozen embryos, however, challenges us to rethink the meaning and nature of parenthood.

The *Instruction* notes that AFD "brings about and manifests a rupture between genetic parenthood, gestational parenthood and responsibility for upbringing,"[44] but it does not explain the moral meaning of that rupture. Nor does it explain the interrelationship between the three dimensions of parenthood or suggest any hierarchy among them. We offer two comments. First, as is indicated in both pre- and post-natal adoption, there is no intrinsic relationship between the various dimensions of parenthood. A couple can experience one, two, or all three dimensions. Second, in the case of AFD, the *Instruction* makes no moral distinction between the three dimensions of parenthood. It would seem that these dimensions are of equal value and constitute various dimensions of the vocation of parenthood. In both pre- and postnatal adoption, no genetic parenthood is involved; in pre-natal adoption there is both gestational and social parenthood; in post-natal adoption, there is neither genetic nor gestational but only social parenthood. Social parenthood is common to all three scenarios and, in fact, is the most important dimension of parenthood. On this we agree with Paul Lauritzen, who writes that the core of parenthood is "the commitment to, and the activities of, caring for a child in a way that promotes human flourishing,"[45] and with Germain Grisez, who writes that "parenthood is far more a moral than a biological relationship: its essence is not so much in begetting and giving birth as in readiness to accept the gift of life, commitment to nurture it, and faithful fulfillment of that commitment through many years."[46]

The primacy of social parenthood has moral implications for the definition of the rupture between the three types of parenthood the *Instruction* notes and for the relationship between parenthood and the conjugal act. The rupture *may* have moral implications for AFD, but its deliberate rupture in the case of embryo adoption leads to an untenable position in the case of AFH. John Berkman highlights this position. "Catholic teaching seems to allow [adoptive embryo transfer] which separates genetic parenthood from gestational and 'raising' parenthood, but prohibits [AFH embryo transfer] that would maintain the bond between genetic, gestational, and 'raising' parenthood."[47] While AFH does not rely on the act of sexual intercourse for

its realization, it does realize parenthood "in its fullness." The rupture between the three types of parenthood may be *descriptively* relevant, but it is
not necessarily *morally* relevant in evaluating ARTs.

The Church's apparent approval of embryo adoption, and undoubted approval of post-natal adoption, also recognizes the moral legitimacy of separating the conjugal act from genetic parenthood. In the case of AFH, like pre-
and post-natal adoption, there is not a conjugal act of the parents immediately
responsible for procreation. The conjugal act between the spouses, however,
is unitive in that it sustains and nurtures both the marital relationship between
the spouses and the parental relationship between the parents and the child.

PARENTAL COMPLEMENTARITY,
RELATIONAL CONSIDERATIONS, AND SOCIAL ETHICS

Since the Church's principle of the inseparability of the procreative and
unitive meanings of the marital act, used to prohibit AFH, is subject to
fundamental critiques, a credible moral analysis of ARTs needs to focus
more on the relational dimensions and implications of these procedures. We
agree with the *Instruction*'s prioritization of the relational considerations of
ARTs over the inseparability principle in its moral assessment of AFD and,
for the sake of internal consistency and credibility, we use the relational
principle to analyze and evaluate all ARTs. Since there is not an act of
spousal sexual intercourse immediately responsible for reproduction in most
ARTs, since the genetic link is severed from the act of intercourse and
parenthood in pre-natal adoption, and since the genetic and gestational link is
severed from the conjugal act in post-natal adoption, our option for this
principle, we believe, is compelling. Focus on personal relationships is at the
heart of the foundational, sexual, moral principle we espouse in this book.
Since reproduction is fundamentally about parenthood, we focus on the
meaning of parenthood in morally assessing ARTs. Parenthood includes the
relationship between the spouses, the relationship between the parents and
their child, and the broader social relationships in which the family exists,
functions, finds support, and contributes to society.

Since the relationship between husband and wife, the "coupled-we" in
marriage, is the foundational relationship in which children are procreated,
nurtured, and educated, this relationship requires special focus and attention
in the case of ARTs. We share with many theologians and the CDF concerns
about the potential relational complications associated with AFD. While it is
not necessarily the case that the use of donor gametes is destructive of the
marital, parental, or child-parent relationship, there are legitimate relational
concerns that warrant a *presumption against* the use of donor gametes. At the
root of these concerns is the notion that "conjugal exclusivity should include

the genetic, gestational and rearing dimensions of parenthood. Separating these dimensions (except through rescue, as in adoption) too easily contains a subtle diminishment of some aspect of the human person"[48] and the spousal relationship. The diminishment of the human person could take many different forms: feelings of reproductive inadequacy, loss of the self-esteem so necessary for a healthy sexual life, and resentment toward the other spouse who may have been demonstrated to be infertile. These personal issues may affect the marital relationship and create disharmony between the spouses. Where donor gametes are the only means for a couple to reproduce, the couple must discern the impact of gamete donation on their relationship and their mutual relationship with any child that might be born. This discernment process requires open and honest reflection, dialogue, and prayer. A realistic assessment of the issues and their potential impact on human relationships must be made and, in light of this assessment, a responsible decision can be reached.

The great challenge in speculating about the relational implications and consequences of reproductive choices is, of course, that we are finite human beings, and our vision, knowledge, and understanding is limited. This is especially true of any reality that lies in the future. We cannot fully understand or accurately assess all the complications or blessings that may arise from our decisions on reproductive, or any other, issues. Though certitude is not an absolute requirement for moral judgment, prudence always is. We believe an infertile couple could make, in good conscience, a prudential moral judgment to use AFD. The couple would, however, bear the burden of proof that the concerns voiced by the *Instruction* about the use of donor gametes would not endanger their various relationships.

If, after reflection, an infertile couple comes to the conclusion that AFD would entail a disproportional risk to their human relationships, there are alternatives for reproduction. Rather than using AFD and creating new embryos or practicing artificial insemination, a couple could adopt existing, cryopreserved embryos. While, technically, the woman is carrying the embryo of another couple, there is a fundamental difference between embryo adoption and surrogacy. In the former, the gestational mother will give birth to and nurture a wanted child; in the latter the gestational mother will "surrender the child once it is born to the party who commissioned or made the agreement for the pregnancy."[49] Surrogacy is a means to an end, in which the gestational mother's obligations to the child end shortly after the child's birth and the responsibility of nurturing the child is taken over by another person or persons. Embryo adoption, on the other hand, includes both the gestational and social dimensions of parenthood.

The distinction between surrogacy and embryo adoption is helpful for addressing the issue of ARTs and same-sex parenthood. Some argue that, if AFD is permitted as a moral option, then there is nothing to prevent lesbian or gay couples (through surrogacy) from reproducing children. The same relational concerns we highlighted in the case of heterosexual couples and their marital relationship, with the exception of reproductive inadequacy, apply to homosexual couples and their union. While these concerns do not rule out, *ipso facto*, AFD for homosexual couples, there is a presumption against such procedures. Embryo adoption, however, is another matter and would provide, for lesbian couples, an opportunity to participate in both the gestational and nurturing dimensions of parenthood. There is no credible social-scientific evidence to support the claim that homosexual parenting has a negative impact on the children.[50]

There is no doubt that genes are biological material, but there is a more profound relational consideration that defines the moral meaning of the genetic, biological consideration. If biological, genetic material were the only morally determinative reason that AFD is morally acceptable or unacceptable, then spousal rape that results in pregnancy could be morally justified, since parenthood is respected genetically, gestationally, and socially. No one, however, would ever condone spousal rape, even if it does fulfill all three dimensions of parenthood. Spousal rape is absolutely wrong because of the unjust violence and relational implications of the act. Similarly, in the case of AFD where the biological genes are not from one or both of the partners, the moral assessment of the procedure rests, not in the presence or absence of the requisite genes but in the relational implications of the genetic connection for the partners individually, for the couple, and for their relation to a possible child. The genetic dimension of parenthood is morally relevant only in light of these relational considerations. If it could be demonstrated that the genetic dimension does not have a negative influence on these relationships, then, in theory, AFD could be morally acceptable. We hold, however, a *presumption against* AFD. The burden of proof, as we have already argued, rests with the couple to demonstrate that there would not be negative relational complications due to AFD and that there would be positive relational implications for the couple in relation to one another, the child, and the common good. While these concerns would apply to AFD, they would not apply to embryo adoption.

ARTs and Health Complications among Children

While the relational implications of AFH and adoptive surrogacy for the spouses as individuals, as a couple, and as parents do not establish an *absolute* moral prohibition against ARTs, either AFH or AFD, other considerations would seem to indicate caution in the use of such procedures. The first important consideration is the multiple pregnancies that result from the use of an ART and the medical complications for the mother and child that accompany those pregnancies. In the United States in 2002, 35.4% of all fresh embryo, non-donor cycles utilizing ARTs were multiple births and 3.8% involved triplets or more.[51] This statistic contrasts with 3% of multiple birth rates in natural reproduction. For the mother, the medical complications include anemia, increased risks of hypertensive disorders, premature labor and delivery, the possibility of cesarean section with the accompanying risks, and death. For infants the major risks include low birth weight, prematurity, congenital anomalies, and death.[52]

The second important consideration, which expands on medical risks to the child, is scientific studies that seem to indicate a direct correlation between ARTs and the heightened risk of birth defects among children. A systematic meta-review of the literature investigating the prevalence of birth defects in infants conceived through the use of IVF suggests "that infants born following ART treatment are at increased risk [30–40%] of birth defects, compared to spontaneously conceived infants."[53] While the increase in the likelihood of birth defects would not influence the moral assessment of embryo adoption for either heterosexual or homosexual couples, it would certainly have moral implications for those who choose to use ARTs for reproductive purposes. Using ARTs knowing that such procedures have a higher incidence of birth defects may demonstrate a lack of care and concern for a child's human dignity. Studies that demonstrate this correlation recommend that couples seeking ARTs should be informed of this possibility.[54] We would expand this recommendation to require reproductive clinics to inform potential parents about the increased likelihood of birth defects from using ARTs. Informed parental ethical choice demands knowledge that is accurate, complete, and readily understood. This provides a strong argument for more legislation and moral guidelines in an industry that remains largely unlegislated.[55]

In addition to consideration of a couple's emotional, psychological, and relational capabilities to care for a child with a birth defect, whether that child is the result of ART or natural procreation, there is also an economic consideration. The ethical challenge of factoring the financial consideration into the discernment process is that those who can afford to use ARTs can have access to the technology and those who cannot afford to do so are usually denied access. In addition, those who can afford to use ARTs may or may not be able to afford to pay for the short and long-term health complications that may result from those technologies. The social justice issues become more prevalent the more we explore the issues surrounding ARTs.

Family and Society: ARTs and the Common Good

Another consideration related to the moral acceptability of ARTs is the relationship between the procedures and the Catholic tradition of the common good. A recent estimate puts the cost of *in vitro* fertilization with a woman's own eggs at $12,500 to $25,000 and the cost with donor eggs up to $35,000,[56] and "less than 25% of cycles involving fresh, non-donor eggs result in a live birth."[57] Some insurance companies cover part of the initial costs. By far the greatest costs of ARTs, however, are associated with multiple births and post-natal care for those infants. In 2000, multiple births from ARTs accounted for more than $640 million dollars in additional hospital costs,[58] an amount that does not include the cost of caring for a child with a lifelong disability that may result from the use of an ART.

This is where an important Catholic ethical question arises. The biblical prophets consistently proclaim that to know and love God requires action against the injustice perpetrated against God's people.[59] The reciprocation between God and the poor "underside"[60] reaches its high point in Jesus of Nazareth who, in Guttierez' pregnant words, is "precisely God become poor."[61] In the Catholic ethical tradition, this reciprocation is framed in the language of distributive justice, the common good, a preferential option for the poor, and solidarity.[62] Given the equal dignity of every human being before God, distributive justice demands that each and every person be accorded equal right to have their minimum human needs satisfied. Ambrose of Milan articulates the root principle. "The earth belongs to all, not to the rich."[63] His disciple, Augustine of Hippo, agreed. "God commands sharing, not as being from the property of those he commands but as being from his own property, so that those who offer something to the poor should not think they are doing so from what is their own."[64] Strange language in the contemporary highly individualistic world, but thoroughly consonant with the biblical action and teaching of Jesus.

Two items of statistical information frame the present question. First, besides the financial costs of ARTs and post-natal care to families, insurance companies, and hospitals, there are also major costs in medical resources, professional talent, and research and development. According to the Center for Disease Control, there were 428 fertility clinics in the United States in 2002, an exponential increase from the thirty or so in 1995. Second, a serious question is whether or not fertility treatment for well-off individuals, almost exclusively in the first world, is the wisest and most efficient use of limited medical resources and personnel? Are ARTs a luxury that should be offered only after we have provided necessary minimum health care for everyone, in the third as well as in the first world?

If we grant that ARTs are a luxury, second to basic health care for all on a medical hierarchy, does this national hierarchy have international implications as well? What about basic health-care resources in third world countries? Should financial and medical aid to third world countries come before infertility treatments on our medical hierarchy? While these considerations may seem to be blowing the moral question surrounding

ART out of proportion, we believe that, just as the sexual relationship between a couple has both personal and social implications, so too the reproductive choices a couple makes have both personal and social implications. A holistic moral evaluation of ARTs requires that we take the common-good implications of their use into consideration when rendering a moral judgment on a couple's reproductive decisions. "[T]he procreative interests of infertile persons have to be evaluated in light of the obligation of society to provide universal access to a decent minimum level of care. From our reading of Catholic social teaching…guaranteeing basic primary and emergency care takes precedence over curative therapies that benefit a small number of individuals."[65]

The approach we recommend to this hierarchical question and to the questions surrounding the Catholic debate about ARTs is to shift the focus from sexual ethics and a biologist understanding of natural law to social ethics, and a personalist, relational understanding of natural law. When the focus shifts, so also the questions and the answers found acceptable shift. We submit that discussions about the moral acceptability of ARTs should not revolve exclusively around individual sexual acts. Reproduction is never simply a private, individual matter; the birth of a child, whether by natural intercourse or ART, is always a social reality. It establishes inescapable social relations, between the parent and the child, between the child and society, and between individuals and the social or common good. Maura Ryan frames the question. "How should we understand the relationship between individual wants, needs, and desires, and the social or 'common' good? How do we weigh the importance of 'saving' lives versus 'creating' lives?"[66] We agree with Lisa Cahill. "Low success rates, disproportionate expense, the priority of other medical needs, and the availability of other solutions should be part of public deliberation about the ethics and practice of assisted reproduction."[67] We suggest that the approach to questions about ARTs from a Christian perspective in which distributive justice, preferential option for the poor, and agapaic love of neighbor hold priority is a more fruitful approach than the approach from the meaning of individual sexual acts and would help to restore much-needed credibility in the public forum to the Catholic voice on reproductive issues.

CONCLUSION

In this chapter, we explained Artificial Reproductive Technologies (ARTs), considered and critiqued the CDF's judgment on their morality, and examined their morality in light of our foundational principle guiding human sexual morality. We considered also the relational considerations between parents and between parents and their children that might impact judgments about the morality of ARTs. Although we judge the use of the Church's inseparability principle to condemn Homologous Artificial Fertilization (AFH) lacks credibility, we also judge that the personalist and relational considerations of the CDF's *Instruction* are in line with our foundational principle guiding human sexuality.

According to this principle, we argued that AFH is morally acceptable *in se*, though warning that the issues of multiple embryos and their human right to life, birth defects, and social justice must be factored into a couple's discernment process. These latter considerations, however, do not *ipso facto* prohibit the moral use of AFH. We further argued that, though there is a *presumption against* Heterologous Artificial Fertilization (AFD) because of the potential relational complications between the spouses, the spouses and child, and the family and society, these considerations do not lead to an *absolute* norm prohibiting the use of AFD. A couple is required to discern the relational implications of their reproductive choices on these various relationships and to make a conscientious, socially just, prudent, and responsible moral decision. These considerations apply to both heterosexual and homosexual couples, though we warn there are further complications with gay couples and surrogacy. Embryonic adoption may be morally acceptable for all couples, though again, the surrogacy issue would arise for gay couples. We believe that, again, the strength of our argument rests in the consistency of a holistic, interpersonal approach to human anthropology rather than in a physiological understanding of human sexuality grounded in exclusive heterogenital or organic complementarity.

QUESTIONS FOR REFLECTION

1. What do you understand by the term *artificial reproductive technologies* (ART)? One ART, *in vitro fertilization with embryo transfer* (IVF-ET), is predominantly used more than any other. What is the process of IVF-ET?
2. Artificial fertilization may be either heterologous (AFD) or homologous (AFH). In AFD, the male semen or female ovum comes from a third party extraneous to the couples' relationship, and the Catholic Church condemns AFD on the basis of this third party intrusion into the couples' relationship. What possible relationship problems do you foresee for the couple and for any child that may be conceived from AFD? Are such problems sufficient, in your judgment, to condemn AFD as immoral? Why?
3. The Church also condemns AFH, not on the personal basis of possible relationship problems but on the biological basis that it destroys the supposed inseparable connection between the procreative and unitive meanings of the marital act. Do you know any couples that have

conceived via AFH? Do you believe it is true that, as traditionalists sometimes argue, their child is a "product of technology" rather than of their love? Do you think their relationship is any more or less loving and their child any less loved if conceived by AFH? Does your answer to the previous question have any moral implications?

4. There are three kinds of parenthood: genetic, gestational, and social. AFD ruptures the connection between genetic and gestational parenthood but does AFH? It is generally agreed that the most important parenthood is social parenthood, "the commitment to, and the activities of, caring for a child in a way that promotes human flourishing." Does this judgment have any moral implications for AFH, and for pre- and post-natal adoption?

5. Scientific studies appear to indicate a direct correlation between the use of ARTs and heightened risks of birth defects among children. These risks, the high costs of dealing with birth defects for a lifetime, and the initial cost of IVF in the first instance cause us to raise moral questions about the common good related to the use of ARTs. Do you believe these related costs raise any moral questions about justice and the common good in the United States and even internationally? Or do you believe, rather, that the risks and the costs are questions only for the couple seeking IVF? If you believe the latter to be the case, how then do you deal with the biblical calls for action on behalf of the poor?

6. What other questions arise for you from the reading of this chapter?

NOTES

An earlier version of this chapter appeared in Todd A. Salzman and Michael G. Lawler, *Sexual Ethics: A Theological Introduction* (Georgetown: Georgetown University Press, 2012). It is reprinted here with permission.

1. CDF, *Instruction on Respect for Human Life in its Origin and on the Dignity of Procreation: Replies to Certain Questions of the Day* (Washington, DC: Office of Publishing and Promotion Services, United States Catholic Conference, 1987), II, B, 4, a. Cited henceforth as *Instruction.*

2. Ibid., II.

3. Linda J. Beckman and S. Marie Harvey, "Current Reproductive Technologies: Increased Access and Choice?" *Journal of Social Issues* 61 (2005): 2.

4. *Gaudium et spes*, n. 50.

5. Office of Technology Assessment, *Infertility, Medical and Social Choices* (Washington, DC: OTA, 1988), 3; Mary B. Mahowald, "Ethical Considerations in Infertility," in *Infertility: A Comprehensive Text, Second Edition*, ed. Machelle M. Seibel (Stamford: Appleton and Lange, 1997), 823.

6. American Society for Reproductive Medicine, "Frequently Asked Questions about Infertility," http://www.asrm.org/Patients/faqs.html. See also Seibel, *Infertility*, 4.

7. Benedict Ashley and Kevin O'Rourke, *Health Care Ethics: A Theological Analysis*, 4th edition (Washington, DC: Georgetown University Press, 1997), 241.

8. For an historical overview of ARTs, see Don P. Wolf and Martin M. Quigley, "Histori-cal Background and Essentials for a Program in *In Vitro* Fertilization and Embryo Transfer," in *Human in Vitro Fertilization and Embryo Transfer*, ed. Don P. Wolf and Martin M. Quigley (New York: Plenum Press, 1984), 1–11; and Annette Burfoot, ed., *Encyclopedia of Reproductive Technologies* (Boulder, CO: Westview Press, 1999).

9. For more detailed descriptions of ARTs, see Burfoot, ed., *Encyclopedia of Reproductive Technologies*; Ashley and O'Rourke, *Health Care Ethics*, 240–48; and Peter J. Cataldo, "Reproductive Technologies," *Ethics & Medics* 21/1 (January, 1996): 1–3.

10. Resolve of Minnesota, "Assisted Reproductive Technologies," http://www.resolvemn.org/index.php?option=com_content&task=view&id=17&Itemid=2.

11. The pre-embryo stage lasts from the completion of fertilization to the development of the primitive streak, which occurs "on about the fourteenth day of development" (Howard W. Jones and Susan L. Crockin, "On Assisted Reproduction, Religion and Civil Law," *Fertility and Sterility* 73 [2000]: 450).

12. *Instruction*, I, 1.

13. Ashley and O'Rourke, *Health Care Ethics*, 247. See, also, Germain Grisez, *Difficult Moral Questions: The Way of the Lord Jesus, Volume Three* (Quincy IL: Franciscan Press, 1997), 244–49 (hereinafter, *DMQ*); Donald T. DeMarco, "Catholic Moral Teaching and TOT/GIFT," *Reproductive Technologies*, 122–39; and John M. Haas, "GIFT? No!" *Ethics & Medics* 18/9 (September 1993): 1–2.

14. *Instruction*, Foreword.

15. Ibid., Introduction, 3.

16. Ibid., I, 1.

17. Ibid., II.

18. Ibid., Introduction, 1.

19. Thomas A. Shannon and Lisa Sowle Cahill, *Religion and Artificial Reproduction: An Inquiry into the Vatican "Instruction on Respect for Human Life in its Origin and on the Dignity of Human Reproduction"* (New York: Crossroad, 1988), 55.

20. Cited in Jones and Crockin, "On Assisted Reproduction," 449.

21. Thomas A. Shannon, "Reproductive Technologies: Ethical and Religious Issues," in *Reproductive Technologies: A Reader*, ed. Thomas A. Shannon (New York: Sheed and Ward, 2004), 47.

22. *Humanae vitae*, n. 15.

23. The *Instruction* distinguishes between heterologous artificial fertilization or procreation and homologous artificial fertilization or procreation. Within each classification, it addresses two types of reproductive technology: artificial insemination (AI) and in vitro fertilization and embryo transfer (IVF-ET). In this chapter, we use AFD to designate both types of heterologous artificial fertilization, and AFH to designate both types of homologous artificial fertilization. We specifically distinguish between AI or IVF-ET when it is necessary for a point of clarification.

24. Ibid., II, A, 1.

25. Ibid.

26. Ibid.

27. Ibid., II, A, 2.

28. Ibid.

29. Ibid., II, B, 4.

30. See Michael G. Lawler, *Marriage in the Catholic Church: Disputed Questions* (Collegeville: Liturgical Press, 2002), 27–42.

31. *Gaudium et spes*, n. 50.

32. *Instruction*, II, B, 5.

33. See *Gaudium et spes*, n. 48.

34. Lisa Sowle Cahill, *Women and Sexuality* (New York: Paulist, 1992), 75; emphasis in original. See also Shannon and Cahill, *Religion and Artificial Reproduction*, 103–32.

35. The Ethics Committee of the American Fertility Society accuses the CDF of "barnyard physiology." "This means that the concept that intercourse is intended entirely for reproduction derives from observation of those animals who exhibit 'heat' and give an external sign of

ovulation during which period the female will accept the male and at no other time." Cited in Jones and Crockin, "On Assisted Reproduction," 449.

36. *Instruction*, II, B, 4, a.

37. Ibid., II, A, 2.

38. The classic legal case that demonstrates the *Instruction*'s legitimate concern for the relational complications of surrogacy is the case of "Baby M" and the contractual and custodial dispute between Elizabeth and William Stern who contracted with Mrs. Whitehead to both donate her egg and her womb to bear a child for the Sterns. The bond that Mrs. Whitehead developed over the nine month gestational period as well as through the genetic link with "Baby M" led her to deny her contractual obligations to the Sterns. In turn, this denial lead to a complex legal custody battle that illustrates well the relational complications of AFD in which the *Instruction* is legitimately concerned. In the end, the New Jersey Supreme Court nullified the surrogacy contract, arguing that commercial surrogacy was tantamount to selling babies and unethical. The basis for deciding the case was on the parental considerations of genetic, gestational, and social parenthood. While Mrs. Whitehead fulfilled the first two criteria of parenthood, social parenthood seems to be morally decisive. We agree with Glannon: "the social mother (or father) is arguably more important than genetic or gestational mothers, because the social mother is responsible for the welfare of the child from birth onward" (*Biomedical Ethics* [New York: Oxford University Press, 2005], 84). In the end, the Supreme Court granted full custody to Mr. Stern and Mrs. Whitehead was granted visitation rights. For our purposes, the important points in this case are twofold: first, the importance of the distinction the New Jersey Supreme Court made between different types of parenthood, genetic, gestational, and social, a distinction that the *Instruction* highlights as well; second, the primacy of social parenthood over genetic and gestational parenthood.

39. *Gaudium et spes*, n. 50.

40. Cataldo, "Reproductive Technologies," 1.

41. Pope John Paul II, *Familiaris consortio*, n. 14.

42. For a full listing of these equivalents, see Todd A. Salzman and Michael G. Lawler, *The Sexual Person: Toward a Renewed Catholic Anthropology* (Georgetown: Georgetown University Press, 2008), 237–40.

43. See John Berkman, "The Morality of Adopting Frozen Embryos," *Studia Moralia* 40, no. 1 (2002): 115–41; Grisez, *DMQ*, 239–44; Mary Geach, "Are there any Circumstances in Which it Would be Morally Admirable for a Woman to Seek to Have an Orphan Embryo Implanted in Her Womb? – 1," in *Issues for a Catholic Bioethic*, ed. Luke Gormally (London: The Linacre Centre, 1999), 341–46; William B. Smith, "Rescue the Frozen?" *Homiletic and Pastoral Review* 96 (October 1995): 72–74; Smith, "Response," *Homiletic and Pastoral Review* 96 (August-September, 1995): 16–17; and Geoffrey Surtees, "Adoption of a Frozen Embryo," *Homiletic and Pastoral Review* 96 (August-September, 1995): 7–16.

44. *Instruction*, II, A, 2.

45. Paul Lauritzen, *Pursuing Parenthood: Ethical Issues in Assisted Reproduction* (Bloomington: Indiana University Press, 1993), 76–84.

46. Grisez, *LCL*, 689.

47. Berkman, "Morality of Adopting," 132.

48. Richard A. McCormick, *The Critical Calling: Reflections on Moral Dilemmas Since Vatican II* (Washington, DC: Georgetown University Press, 1989), 341.

49. *Instruction*, II, A, 3.

50. See Charlotte J. Patterson, "Lesbian and Gay Parenting," (APA, 1995), 9; Joan Laird, "Lesbian and Gay Families," in *Normal Family Processes*, ed. Froma Walsh (New York: Guilford Press, 1993), 316–17; APA, "Resolution on Sexual Orientation and Marriage," (2004), 7; Ann Sullivan, ed., *Issues in Gay and Lesbian Adoption: Proceedings of the Fourth Annual Peirce-Warwick Adoption Symposium* (Washington, DC: Child Welfare League of America, 1995), 24–28. See also E. D. Gibbs, "Psychosocial Development of Children Raised by Lesbian Mothers: A Review of Research," *Women and Therapy* 8 (1988): 65–68; P. J. Falk, "Lesbian Mothers: Psychosocial Assumptions in Family Law," 44 (1989): 941–47; Fiona Tasker and Susan Golombok, "Children Raised by Lesbian Mothers: The Empirical Evidence," *Family Law* (1991): 184–87; Tasker and Golombok, *Growing Up in a Lesbian Family: Effects*

on Child Development (New York: Guilford, 1997); Golombok and Tasker, "Children in Lesbian and Gay Families: Theories and Evidence," *Annual Review of Sex Research* 5 (1994): 73–100; Jeffrey Weeks, Brian Heaphy, Catherine Donovan, *Same-Sex Intimacies: Families of Choice and Other Life Experiments* (London: Routledge, 2001); Stephen Hicks, "The Christian Right and Homophobic Discourse: A Response to 'Evidence' that Lesbian and Gay Parenting Damages Children," *Sociological Research Online* 8, 4 (2003), http://www.socresonline.org.uk/8/4/kicks.html; Lawrence A. Kurdek, "Are Gay and Lesbian Cohabiting Couples Really Different from Heterosexual Married Couples?," *Journal of Marriage and Family* 66 (2004): 880–900.

51. CDC, American Society for Reproductive Medicine, Society for Reproductive Technology, "2002 Assisted Reproductive Technology Success Rates: National Summary and Fertility Clinic Reports," http://www.cdc.gov/reproductivehealth/ART02/sect5_fig40-46.htm.

52. Robert W. Rebar, M. D., and Alan H. De Cherney, M.D., "Assisted Reproductive Technology in the United States," *New England Journal of Medicine* 350, no. 16 (April 15, 2004): 1603.

53. Michèle Hansen, *et al.*, "Assisted Reproductive Technologies and the Risk of Birth Defects—A Systematic Review," *Human Reproduction* 20 (2005): 335; and Z. Kozinsky, "Obstetric and Neonatal Risk of Pregnancies after Assisted Reproductive Technology: A Matched Control Study," *Acta Obstet Gynecol Scand.* 82, no. 9 (September 2003): 850–56. These studies contradict earlier studies that indicate there is minimal, if any, risk to IVF-ET embryos. See Thomas A. Shannon and Lisa Sowle Cahill, *Religion and Artificial Reproduction* (New York: Crossroad, 1988), 7–9, and their references including John D. Biggers, "Risks of In Vitro Fertilization and Embryo Transfer in Humans," in *In Vitro Fertilization and Embryo Transfer*, ed. R. F. Harrison (London: The Academic Press Inc., 1983), 393–409; and Ian L. Pike, "Biological Risks of In Vitro Fertilization and Embryo Transfer," in *Clinical In Vitro Fertilization*, ed. Carl Wood and Alan Trounson (Berlin: Springer-Verlag, 1984), 137–46.

54. Hansen, *et al.*, "Assisted Reproductive Technologies."

55. Rebar and De Cherney, "Assisted Reproductive Technology in the United States," 1603–4, note that while assisted reproduction in the United States "is not legislated…it is highly regulated" (1604). One source of this regulation passed by congress in 1992 to curb misleading advertising on success rates by fertility clinics as well as ethical, financial, and scientific scandals, is the Fertility Clinic Success Rate and Certification Act (also known as the "Wyden Law," which is a misnomer since reporting is voluntary). This act "promotes uniformity in data reporting and requires the listing of clinics that do not report their data" (1604) but it does not require clinics to participate. See also, W.Y. Chang, A.H. DeCherney, "History of Regulation of Assisted Reproductive Technology (ART) in the USA: A Work in Progress," *Human Fertility* 6 (2003): 64–70; Andrea D. Gurmankin, Arthur L. Caplan, and Andrea M. Braverman, "Screening Practices and Beliefs of Assisted Reproductive Technology Programs," *Fertility and Sterility* 83 (2005): 61–67.

56. Gina Kolata, "The Heart's Desire," *New York Times* (May 11, 2004): D1; see also Maura A. Ryan, *Ethics and Economics of Assisted Reproduction: The Cost of Longing* (Washington, DC: Georgetown University Press, 2001), 2.

57. Linda J. Beckman and S. Marie Harvey, "Current Reproductive Technologies: Increased Access and Choice?" *Journal of Social Issues* 61 (2005): 2.

58. Carol J. Rowland Hogue, "Successful Assisted Reproductive Technology: The Beauty of One," *Obstetrics and Gynecology* 100, no. 5 (November 2002): 1017. See also, John A. Collins, "Reproductive Technology: The Price of Progress," *New England Journal of Medicine* 331, no. 4 (July 28, 1994): 270–71.

59. See Deut 24:18–22; Jer 7:2–7; Is 61:1–8; Matt 25:31–46.

60. We borrow this metaphor from Jorg Rieder, *Remember the Poor: The Challenge to Theology in the Twenty-First Century* (Harrisburg: Trinity Press International, 1998), 1–5.

61. Gustavo Guttierez, *The Power of the Poor in History* (New York: Orbis, 1983), 13.

62. See John Paul II, *Sollicitudo rei socialis*, nn. 39–42; Christina Traina, *Feminist Ethics and Natural Law* (Washington, DC: Georgetown University Press, 1999); David Hollenbach, *The Common Good and Christian Ethics* (Cambridge: Cambridge University Press, 2002).

63. Ambrose, *De Nabuthe Jezraelita*, 1, *PL*, 14, 747.

64. Augustine, *Sermo L*, 1, *PL* 38, 326.

65. Ryan, *Ethics and Economics of Assisted Reproduction*, 134.

66. Ibid., 8

67. Lisa Sowle Cahill, *Theological Bioethics: Participation, Justice, Change* (Washington, DC: Georgetown University Press, 2005), 210.